In this
Japan,
repress
opened
never
works
instead ...., mentalities, economics, and specific groups. .
analyzing them, the chapters of the book help to provide a more complete
and balanced view of the phenomenon of terror as a whole.

STALINIST TERROR: NEW PERSPECTIVES

STALINIST TERROR
NEW PERSPECTIVES

Edited by
J. ARCH GETTY *and* ROBERTA T. MANNING

CAMBRIDGE
UNIVERSITY PRESS

Published by the Press Syndicate of the University of Cambridge
The Pitt Building, Trumpington Street, Cambridge CB2 1RP
40 West 20th Street, New York, NY 10011-4211, USA
10 Stamford Road, Oakleigh, Melbourne 3166, Australia

© Cambridge University Press 1993

First published 1993
Reprinted 1994

Printed in the United States of America

Library of Congress Cataloging-in-Publication Data is available.

A catalogue record for this book is available from the British Library.

ISBN 0-521-44125-0 hardback
ISBN 0-521-44670-8 paperback

Contents

Contents

Part III: *Case Studies*

Part IV: *Impact and Incidence*

Acknowledgments

We are grateful to a number of friends and colleagues who encouraged our efforts in this work. First of all, we are thankful to our contributors for providing us with such fine work and for meeting deadlines with efficiency and general good grace.

In particular, Arch Getty is indebted to Viktor G. Bortnevskii, Nikolai P. Iakovlev, and Andrei K. Sokolov for their logistical help and moral support, and to Oleg V. Naumov for his special assistance. Roberta Manning is grateful to Joseph Berliner, Franklin Holtzman, and Holland Hunter for their help and comments on economic matters. We also offer our thanks to the several Moscow archivists and administrators at the former TsGAOR SSSR, TsGANKh, and the former Central Party Archive who have recently opened up new vistas to us all. Finally, our respective spouses Nancy and Jerry were understanding and patient with bothersome telephone calls, ever more frequent research trips to the former USSR, and occasional eccentric behavior.

Most of this work has been supported at various times by the good offices of the International Research and Exchanges Board (IREX), with funds provided by the American Council of Learned Societies, the Andrew W. Mellon Foundation, the National Endowment for the Humanities, and the US Department of State.

Of course, none of these individuals or organizations is responsible for the views expressed in this volume.

Gábor Rittersporn's "The Omnipresent Conspiracy: on Soviet Imagery of Politics and Social Relations in the 1930s" was first published in Nick Lampert and Gábor Tamás Rittersporn (eds.), *Stalinism: Its Nature and Aftermath* (Armonk, NY and London, 1992). Reprinted here in a revised form by permission of M. E. Sharpe, Inc., Armonk, New York, and The Macmillian Press, Ltd., London.

Roberta T. Manning's "The Great Purges in a Rural District: Belyi Raion Revisited" was first published in *Russian History/Histoire Russe,* vol. 16, nos. 2–4, 1989, and appears here in a slightly amended form.

Hiroaki Kuromiya's "Stalinist Terror in the Donbas: A Note" was previously published in *Slavic Review*, no. 1, 1991, 157–162. It is copyrighted by, and reprinted here in a revised form with the permission of, the American Association for the Advancement of Slavic Studies.

Stephen Wheatcroft's "More Light on the Scale of Repression and Excess Mortality in the Soviet Union in the 1930s" was first published in *Soviet Studies*, no. 2, vol. 42, 1990, 355–367, and is reprinted here by permission.

Introduction

J. Arch Getty and Roberta Manning

Serious academic study of the Stalin period began in the 1950s. Carried
out mostly by political scientists and supported by the "know your enemy"
mandate of the Cold War, research on the USSR fairly quickly led to a
"shared paradigm" of Soviet history.[1] That view, which was loosely labeled
totalitarian, reflected scholarly consensus in a scientific manner and seemed
to explain Soviet reality in a satisfactory way. Of course, like all scientific
paradigms, it did not spring from nothing. Writings and testimonies of
active anti-Soviet or anti-Stalin politicians (Trotskyists, Mensheviks, and
former Whites) combined with memoirs of victims and with our limited
external view of a closed society to produce a vision of a monolithic and
unitary dictatorship whose existence and survival were based on terror.
Research evidence available at the time confirmed totalitarianism as logical,
honest, and scientific.

In a nutshell, and necessarily at the expense of nuance, the totalitarian
paradigm went as follows. The Soviet system under Stalin consisted of a
nonpluralist, hierarchical dictatorship in which command authority existed
only at the top of the pyramid of political power. Ideology and violence
were monopolies of the ruling elite, which passed its orders down a
pseudo-military chain of command whose discipline was the product of
Leninist prescriptions on party organization and Stalinist enforcement of
these norms. At the top of the ruling elite stood an autocratic Stalin whose
personal control was virtually unlimited in all areas of life and culture,
from art to zoology. Major policy articulation and implementation involved
the actualization of Stalin's ideas, whims, and plans, which in turn flowed
from his psychological condition. By definition, autonomous spheres of
social and political activity did not exist at all in Soviet society, although
the more sophisticated advocates of totalitarianism, like Merle Fainsod,
allowed for the input of bureaucratic interest groups, like the party and

---

[1] The term "shared paradigm" comes from Thomas Kuhn, a historian of science. Thomas A.
Kuhn, *The Structure of Scientific Revolutions* (2d ed.) (Chicago, 1970).

1

state apparatuses, the armed forces, and the NKVD (*Narodnyi Komissariat Vnutrennykh Del*, Peoples' Commissariat of Internal Affairs), which intervened periodically in politics to promote and defend their own institutional concerns. In any case, the Soviet populace and rank-and-file party members remained outside the political process, objects acted upon or manipulated from above but never historical actors in their own right.[2]

For some scholars, the totalitarian system had its origins in Communist ideology and was thus the inevitable product of the Russian Revolutions of 1917 or of socialism in general. For others, the nondemocratic traditions of prerevolutionary Russian autocracy accounted for the intolerant and unified political dictatorship of Stalin's time. But for all, terror was an indispensable part of the political essence of Stalinism; it spread downward in a planned, systemic fashion to enhance the dictator's power and envelop every corner of society in an irrational but functional way.

With the death of Stalin, ever larger numbers of his victims began to record their experiences in memoirs, and literary accounts of the terror proliferated. Based largely on such sources, interviews with terror victims, and Soviet revelations of the Khrushchev era, Robert Conquest, Roy Medvedev, and Aleksandr Solzhenitsyn published the first major empirical studies of Stalin's terror in the late 1960s and early 1970s, when Soviet archives on the subject remained closed and seemed likely to stay that way.[3] These works focused on the well-known show trials of the Old Bolsheviks and the arrest, interrogation, and prison experiences of countless other victims. Conquest and Medvedev followed Stalin's successor Nikita Khrushchev in attributing the terror to Stalin's personality and political needs,[4] whereas Solzhenitsyn blamed the Communist system, as did much of the earlier, largely nonempirical body of Western scholarly writings on totalitarianism.[5] Despite their differing emphases, these studies adhered

---

[2] Most Western studies of Stalinist Russia published after Hannah Arendt's classical study of totalitarianism in 1951 described the Soviet system under Stalin as *totalitarian*. Major examples of such works include Hannah Arendt, *The Origins of Totalitarianism* (New York, 1951); Merle Fainsod, *How Russia is Ruled* (Cambridge, MA, 1963); Carl Friedrich and Zbigniew Brzezinski, *Totalitarian Dictatorship and Autocracy* (Cambridge, MA, 1956); Alex Inkeles and Raymond Bauer, *The Soviet Citizen* (Cambridge, MA, 1959). Only recently have scholars abandoned such terms and begun to suggest that Stalin's enforcement of Leninist norms developed gradually and later than we hitherto thought. For this latter point of view, see Graeme Gill, *The Origins of the Stalinist Political System* (Cambridge/ New York, 1990).

[3] Robert Conquest, *The Great Terror: Stalin's Purge of the Thirties* (New York, 1968); Roy A. Medvedev, *Let History Judge: The Origins and Consequences of Stalinism* (New York, 1971); Aleksandr I. Solzhenitsyn, *The Gulag Archipelago 1918–1956: An Experiment in Literary Investigation* (New York, 1973). Recently a new, somewhat updated edition of the Conquest study has been released: Robert Conquest, *The Great Terror: A Reassessment* (New York/Oxford, 1990).

[4] Nikita S. Khrushchev, *The Crimes of the Stalin Era: Special Report to the 20th Congress of the Communist Party of the Soviet Union* (New York, 1956).

[5] Of the large body of works on totalitarianism, only the studies of Brzezinski and Fainsod dealt with the terror in an empirical manner. Brzezinski drew on the materials of the Harvard Emigre Interview Project and the press, whereas Fainsod used the Smolensk

to the totalitarian paradigm and agreed on the monolithic and strictly hierarchical nature of political power in the Soviet system of Stalin's time.

This view of the Stalinist system, like all coherent scientific paradigms, was, in its time, capable both of satisfactorily interpreting reality and of encompassing counter examples. Totalitarian theory was never dogmatic and was able to withstand what might appear to be powerful critiques. Thus, the theory had always posited mass participation (by labeling it elite mobilization of the masses and a tool for rational control at the top). Struggles among courtiers were integrated into the interpretation, as was evidence of confusion, chaos, and disobedience. Similarly, apparently challenging points of view, like conflict and interest group theory, which appeared even in the infancy of totalitarianism, could be accommodated by the reigning consensus without threatening its supremacy. These alternative views did, after all, follow the theoretical prescriptive rules of the totalitarian school by focusing attention on politics at the top. Moreover, a pervasive and widespread terror, evident to all, provided both a powerful defence for the theory and a unifying theoretical mechanism to explain away or minimize discrepancies.

Totalitarianism posed the questions, provided the tools, and set the agenda for research. For decades, research was oriented toward the entirely valid goal of filling in the blanks and probing the unknown corners that a broad theory necessarily leaves unfilled. As Thomas Kuhn, a historian of science, has pointed out, the work of filling in the gaps left by a major theory fall entirely within the bounds of "normal science" and is the proper work of researchers in the field. The result in the case of Soviet studies was a significant body of research disseminated in important books and articles.

Researchers continued to seek new material and subjects to which ever more sophisticated research tools could be applied. But naturally in the process of this work within a shared paradigm, "anomalies" arose, as Kuhn argues inevitably happens in the development of any science. These anomalies multiplied after historians began to join political scientists in the study of the Stalin era and focused their attention more on society and its relationship to politics and less on structural models of power. Beginning in the 1970s, a generation of trained historians, educated in the social history of prerevolutionary Russia and that of other lands, applied the methodologies of their discipline, along with the tools of the reigning paradigm, to investigate Stalin-period history as *history*.[6] This book

Archive. Fainsod, however, qualified his use of the term "totalitarianism" considerably, describing the political system that existed in Smolensk in the 1930s as "inefficient totalitarianism," although totalitarianism was supposed to be efficient by definition. Zbigniew K. Brzezinski, *The Permanent Purge: Politics in Soviet Totalitarianism* (Cambridge, MA: 1958), pp. 49–115, and Merle Fainsod, *Smolensk Under Soviet Rule* (Cambridge, MA, 1958), pp. 132–137 and 210–237.

[6] For a description and debate on this new work, see *Russian Review*, vol. 45, no. 4 (October, 1986), pp. 357–400 and vol. 46, no. 4 (October, 1987), pp. 382–431.

consists of part of their research. The essays in this volume thus build on
the pioneering studies of Stalinist terror, even as they pose anomolous
conclusions.

This collection of writings by scholars from six nations – the United States,
Great Britain, Canada, Australia, France, and Russia – makes several
major contributions to our knowledge of Stalinist terror in the 1930s.
They explore in greater depth than before the background of the terror
and patterns of persecution, while providing more empirically founded and
substantiated estimates of the numbers of Stalin's victims. Some contributors tap unexplored or underutilized source materials long available
in the West. Others have taken advantage of *glasnost'* and the recent
opening of Soviet archives and libraries for the years of the terror to draw
on newly available archival and secondary materials. Many do both. All
the authors try to handle their sources systematically and critically and
concentrate on a particular period or aspect of the terror. The contributors
to this volume, with the exception of Alec Nove and David Hoffman, the
oldest and youngest of our authors, began their research on Stalinist terror
in the late 1970s and 1980s. They were stimulated, in part by the works of
Conquest, Medvedev, and Solzhenitsyn, to want to learn more about the
terror and the society that spawned it.

The main emphasis in much of this new work, some of which has been
labeled *revisionist*, was the inclusion of society into the Stalinist equation.
Indeed, this was not new. The totalitarian view had always encompassed
society; researchers in the traditional mode had shown that totalitarian
regimes depended on a mobilized (if atomized) society. But borrowing
from the long-established state–society dichotomy in Russian history,
scholars working within the totalitarian paradigm had ultimately seen
society as a completely passive participant in the relationship. Society
was something used and molded by the totalitarian leadership; social
support for the regime was created by propaganda and enforced with
terror. Social support for the regime was therefore artificially induced and
coerced.

Initially making no assumptions about the society part of the state–
society relationship (their first violation of the paradigm's rules), historians
have recently described a group of historical situations and relationships
that seem anomalous within the shared concept of totalitarianism. Signs of
chaotic administration, indecision and lack of planning, a wide disparity
between central pronouncements and local outcomes, the relative autonomy
of some social processes, and more ambiguous multicausal origins of
terror all seemed increasingly inconsistent with the tenets of the ruling
paradigm. A monolithic and efficient state/party regime now seems an
exaggeration. As Moshe Lewin, the pioneer social historian of the Stalin
era, wrote,

For no matter how stern or cruel a regime, in the laboratory of history only rarely can state coercion be so powerful as to control fully the course of events. The depth and scope of spontaneous events that counter the wishes and expectations of a dictatorial government are not a lesser part of history than the deeds and misdeeds of the government and the state.[7]

Although it would be perfectly appropriate to concentrate entirely on social history and case studies, no collection on Stalinist terror would seem complete without dealing with politics and the role of personality. Our collection therefore begins with two contributions, by Boris A. Starkov and J. Arch Getty, on Stalin's role and that of his leading henchman at the time of the Great Purges of 1936–8, Nikolai Ezhov, the head of the Soviet secret police, the NKVD.

Boris Starkov uses previously closed party archives to present the first serious survey of the life and activities of the notorious Nikolai I. Ezhov, Stalin's secret police chief at the height of the terror in the late thirties. Starkov shows conclusively that Stalin supported Ezhov's activity and personally directed key events of the terror. Stalin knew full well when he appointed Ezhov to head the NKVD in September 1936 that Ezhov believed the nation was riddled with a vast conspiracy of former Party Oppositionists, directed by Trotsky from abroad, committed to the assassination of Soviet leaders and the sabotaging of the economy. Stalin also knew that Ezhov was prepared to act on these convictions by extending the terror to industrial leaders and the Right Opposition.

But Starkov's work also raises intriguing questions about police politics in the 1930s and confirms some previous speculation about the importance of factional conflicts within the Stalinist leadership. Writing in *glasnost'*-era Moscow, far from any "revisionist" influences, Starkov shows, for example, that there was a center–periphery conflict in the early 1930s. Moreover, opposition to Ezhov arose from within his own NKVD apparatus *during the terror* and this opposition was the beginning of the end of Ezhov's career. In showing that Ezhov was attacked by other Politburo members despite Stalin's support of him and that Ezhov's replacement, Beria, was forced upon Stalin (whose candidate was Malenkov), Starkov confirms revisionist arguments about the alternative, anti-Ezhov position of A. A. Zhdanov (who began the final assault on Ezhov) and about Stalin's ambiguous power at the end of the terror.[8] Finally, Starkov's intriguing observation that at the time of his fall "Ezhov's primary crime consisted in

---

[7] Moshe Lewin, *The Gorbachev Phenomenon: A Historical Interpretation* (Berkeley, 1991), p. 25.

[8] See J. Arch Getty, *Origins of the Great Purges: The Soviet Communist Party Reconsidered, 1933–1938* (New York), chaps. 4, 6, 7 for Zhdanov's role; and Gábor T. Rittersporn, *Stalinist Simplifications and Soviet Complications: Social Tensions and Political Conflicts in the USSR, 1933–1953* (London, 1991), especially chap. 4: "Stalin in 1938: Rhetorical Apotheosis, Political Defeat."

the fact that he had not informed Stalin of his actions" invites further research.

Getty's article, "The Politics of Repression Revisited," uses recent *glasnost'* revelations published in the former USSR to raise some nagging questions about Stalin's ability to plan the terror in advance. Although it is clear that Stalin perpetrated much of the terror, his input and activites in *organizing* it remain obscure: We still do not know what he decided and when. Using newly available materials, Getty discusses the strange zigs, zags, and periodic indecision displayed by Stalin and his clique and shows that the newly available evidence is consistent with several possible explanations. The problem of Stalin's exact role is not likely to be resolved until the stenographic proceedings of the Politburo and Central Committee meetings of 1928–53 have been published and assimilated by scholars and Stalin's personal archives and NKVD archives have been made freely available. Happily, as of this writing, this possibility may soon materialize.

Having briefly looked at the role of leaders in the terror, we then move on to survey the social and economic context in which the Soviet leadership, including Stalin and Ezhov, functioned in the 1930s in four articles on the background and preconditions to the terror. In the first of these articles, "The Second Coming: Class Enemies in the Soviet Countryside, 1927–1935," Lynne Viola finds consistency among chaos in the rural repression of the collectivization period. Utilizing Soviet legal journals to study the kinds of persons persecuted as kulaks or expelled from collective farms in the 1927–35 period, Viola concludes that traditional village culture shaped the patterns of persecution, especially before 1930 and in 1932–4, when outside agents and actors, dispatched by Moscow to oversee the collectivization process, were absent from the countryside. Although the victims of rural repression between 1927 and 1935 range far beyond the much publicized kulak, as previous scholars have long indicated, persecutions were far from random. Indeed, one finds "certain clearly identifiable victims of repression," not unlike those found in Russia and other peasant societies under stress in earlier times–traditional elites, outsiders to the village, marginal types, economically weak households, and women of ill repute. Such persecutions often proceeded against explicit strictures from Moscow to the contrary and were apparently fueled by the suffering engendered by "the economy of scarcity," created by onerous export-oriented government procurements and low harvests of this period. Viola attributes the prevalence of such traditional forms of victimization in rural Russia of the 1930s to the exodus of the more modern village elements – the young, the skilled, and the educated – under the impetus of industrialization and collectivization.

"The Omnipresent Conspiracy: On Soviet Imagery of Politics and Social Relations in the 1930s," by Gábor Tamás Rittersporn, discusses the widespread belief in the existence of conspiracies on the part of elites and ordinary people alike in the Soviet Union in the 1930s. Such beliefs surfaced repeatedly in the interrogations of Soviet POWs during World War II and in citizen complaints found in the Smolensk Archive.[9] According to the transcript of the interrogation of General G. S. Liushkov (a provincial NKVD chief who defected at the end of 1938 to avoid arrest), Stalin, national NKVD chief Ezhov, and highly placed NKVD operatives sincerely believed that the nation was riddled with plots and conspiracies.[10] Rittersporn maintains that such theories were used by both the populace and those in power to explain the hardships of daily life and the chronic disfunctioning of the system, which were attributed to various conspiracies and sabotage. He intimates that this response was rooted in traditional rural beliefs that the machinations of evil spirits accounted for commonplace misfortunes.[11] Like Viola's, Rittersporn's work suggests that elements of prerevolutionary rural culture helped fuel Stalinist persecutions, under the impact of the omnipresent economy of scarcity, the widespread misery of these years, and leaders who shared, politicized, and used such traditional beliefs.

The role of the economy of scarcity in the repression also looms large in the contribution by Roberta T. Manning, "The Soviet Economic Crisis of 1936–1940 and the Great Purges." Earlier scholars have attributed the sharp drop in Soviet economic growth rates after 1936 to the impact of the repressions on economic administrators and planners. Manning instead argues that an unexpected slowdown and, in some areas of the economy, even a slump in growth rates that set in midway through 1936 was as much a cause as a consequence of the terror, although the purges exacerbated existing economic difficulties considerably. She attributes the upsurge in repression in the second half of 1936 to a series of economic problems, like stagnating production of key fuels and construction materials, which in turn checked the growth of much of the remainder of the economy, and the 1936 crop failure (the worst harvest

---

[9] The Smolensk Archive consists of Soviet Communist Party archives from the Smolensk region (Western Oblast), which were seized by the Germans during World War II and subsequently fell into American hands at the end of the war. The archive was used by Merle Fainsod to write his classic study *Smolensk Under Soviet Rule*. The archive is now kept in the U.S. National Archives and is available for sale on microfilm from the U.S. Government Printing Office. A not entirely accurate guide to the archive also exists: *Guide to the Records of the Smolensk Oblast of the All-Union Communist Party of the Soviet Union, 1917–1941* (Washington, DC, 1980) and J. Arch Getty, "Guide to the Smolensk Archive," in Sheila Fitzpatrick and Lynne Viola (eds.), *A Researcher's Guide to Sources on Soviet Social History in the 1930s* (Armonk, NY/London, 1990), pp. 84–96. The archive is not complete and appears to consist of files saved at random from a fire by German occupation authorities. Many documents are charred and difficult to decipher, which has limited use of the archive by American scholars until recently.

[10] *British Foreign Office Russia Correspondence*, 1939, Reel 10, vol. 23698, pp. 318–339. A copy of Liushkov's interrogation by the Japanese made its way into British hands.

[11] For a discussion of such beliefs, see Moshe Lewin, *The Making of the Soviet System: Essays in the Social History of Interwar Russia* (New York, 1985), pp. 57–71.

since the 1932–3 famine), which strained food supplies throughout the nation. These problems manifested themselves at a point when the terror of the collectivization and famine period had abated and the urge to seek scapegoats had apparently died down. The new economic difficulties were attributed to enemy sabotage or "wrecking," the prime charge against the victims of the terror from the fall of 1936 to the fall of 1938.[12]

Robert Thurston in "The Stakhanovite Movement: The Background to the Great Terror in the Factories, 1935–1938" uses newly available Soviet archives to examine the impact of the Stakhanovite movement on the shop floor in an attempt to discern whether the rise of this movement in the fall of 1935 could have contributed to the wave of terror that swept over industrial managers and administrators a year later. Stakhanovism arose in the fall of 1935 after the widespread publicity given Aleksei Stakhanov's increasing of his coal hewing by a factor of fourteen in a single shift resulted in numerous workers the nation over seeking to emulate and exceed Stakhanov's achievements.[13] According to Thurston, Stakhanovism from its inception encouraged conflicts and exacerbated existing tensions in the factories, because workers, prompted by the high material rewards and publicity accorded Stakhanovites, sought to reorganize their work methods in ways that could only be detrimental to productivity of the enterprise as a whole. Managers in turn, hardpressed by the high targets of the Five-Year Plan, had little choice but to resist such efforts.[14] Consequently the rise of Stakhanovism was immediately accompanied by the proliferation of accusations of wrecking leveled against managers by workers, along with repeated efforts in many areas of the country to prosecute managers for sabotage.

The next section of the collection presents a series of case studies of the Great Purges of 1936–8 in a variety of different settings, including Moscow factories, a rural raion, the Red Army, and the Donbas coal-mining region. By presenting these case studies, we hope to assess how the terror affected different regions and social strata. We need far more specific, detailed studies like these for *all* phases of Stalin's Terror, not just the Great Purges of 1936–8. Only then can we discern the mechanisms, motives, incidence, and scope of the repression over space and time and make the comparisons that need to be made among different geographic regions and the various periods and phases of the terror, which may well have differed markedly in terms of the kinds of victims affected,[15] the means by which the terror

[12] Lewis H. Siegelbaum, *Stakhanovitism and the Politics of Productivity in the USSR, 1935–1941* (Cambridge, 1988), pp. 248–259.

[13] Siegelbaum, 66–98.

[14] For a manager's attitude toward Stakhanovism, see Viktor Kravchenko, *I Chose Freedom: The Personal and Political Life of a Soviet Official* (New York, 1946), pp. 187–197.

[15] Brzezinski was the first to suggest on the basis of the Harvard Project interviews with Soviets displaced by World War II that the victims of Stalinist terror in the first half of the thirties (the period of the First Five-Year Plan and the cultural revolution) differed

spread, and the relative involvement of government and society in the process.

David L. Hoffman in "The Great Terror on the Local Level: Purges in Moscow Factories, 1936–1938" examines the ensuing purge activities of the Moscow Party committees and factory party organizations, found in the Moscow Party Archive. He suggests that the repressions in the factories were directed almost exclusively against managers and technical specialists and "often echoed the antimanagerial tone of Stakhanovitism." In the process, "few rank and file workers were victimized" and Stakhanovites appeared oddly immune, although the purge victims were frequently charged with "sabotaging the Stakhanovite movement or ignoring it."[16] Moreover, Stakhanovites along with newly educated specialists of working class origins actually benefited from the terror by being promoted en masse to the many empty managerial positions, vacated by the purge victims.[17]

The second of our case studies, "The Great Purges in a Rural District: Belyi Raion Revisited" by Roberta T. Manning, moves from city to countryside to explore popular input and the process by which the repression unfolded among local Communist Party members in the heavily agricultural Smolensk region in 1937. Manning argues that documents from Belyi Raion indicate that a groundswell of sentiment and resentment among local Communists, brewing for months, played an important role in purging the local political establishment by expelling them from the Communist Party and sometimes recommending their arrest by the NKVD. Like some of our other authors, Manning maintains that within the party the prime victims of the terror were leaders or "bosses," including the heads of most local institutions of any importance.

Roger Reese in "The Red Army and the Great Purges" follows Manning in extending the concept of the Great Purges and "purge victim" to include those expelled from the Communist Party and dismissed from their official positions as well as those arrested, imprisoned, or executed. Drawing upon recently published Soviet data in *Voenno-istoricheskii zhurnal* and *Izvestiia TsK KPSS*, Reese maintains that primary party organizations in the armed forces, which included both officers and enlisted men among their membership, engaged in mass expulsions of officer Communists that raged "out of Moscow's control" after the arrest of Marshal Tukhachevskii and other military leaders in June 1937 and that "with rare exception, it was only officers who were expelled." Reese also shows that newly released statistics on the military purges indicate that at most 9.7% the officers at the height

---

significantly from those of the second half of the thirties (the Great Purges), a conclusion upheld by the works of Sheila Fitzpatrick (including her contribution to this volume) and the contribution to this volume by Chase and Getty. Brzezinski, 98–115.

[16] Siegelbaum earlier, without access to the archives, made these same points on the basis of published sources. Siegelbaum, 255–257, 267–276.

[17] Siegelbaum, 255, 266–277.

of the terror in 1937 were "repressed," in contrast to earlier estimates by Robert Conquest and John Erickson that 25–50% of the officer corps fell victim to arrest in 1937 and 1938.[18]

In the last of our case studies, Hiroaki Kuromiya explores the repression in one of the nation's leading industrial regions, the Donbas coal mines in "Stalinist Terror in the Donbas: A Note." On the basis of Commissariat of Heavy Industry archives and the local press, Kuromiya concludes that terror reverberated through the Donbas from the summer of 1936 to the autumn of 1938, usually erupting in full force in the wake of visits to that region by Politburo member Lazar Kaganovich, who also played a key role in unleashing terror against local elites in the Western, Ivanovo, and Iaroslavl oblasts and in Bessarabia.[19] Kuromiya points out that the Great Purges in the Donbas as elsewhere fell heavily but not exclusively on higher administrative levels and the party apparatus.

At this point our collection passes to more general overviews of the quantitative impact of the terror on the Soviet elite and Soviet society as a whole. The first of these articles, "Patterns of Repression Among the Soviet Elite in the Late 1930s: A Biographical Approach" by J. Arch Getty and William Chase, suggests that one way to approach the causes of the terror is to examine the biographies of the repressed. They conclude that elite members with higher official positions in the armed forces, party work, and the direction of the economy were most likely to have fallen victim to the repressions, with the Soviet intelligentsia significantly less impacted. Although certain biographical variables were important in determining purge vulnerability, the authors' quantitative analysis of their data leads them to conclude overall that statistical analysis of strictly biographical factors is not the best approach to studying vulnerability. They call on us to examine more closely the problems that beset the Communist Party, economic administrators, and the Soviet armed forces on the eve of the terror and to avoid monocausal explanations of Stalinist repression.

In the next article, Sheila Fitzpatrick attempts to gauge the impact of the repression on Soviet elites in a manner quite different from Getty and Chase. Fitzpatrick studies the "dropout rates" of random samples taken

[18] Conquest *The Great Terror: Stalin's Purge*, 228, 485, and John Erickson, *The Soviet High Command* (New York, 1962), 449, 451–452.

[19] Getty, *Origins of the Great Purges*, 168–71 and *Moscow News*, no. 48 (Dec. 4–11, 1988), p. 9. The article in *Moscow News* is an excerpt from the memoirs of an Ivanovo NKVD man, Mikhail Shreider, that discusses Kaganovich's visit to Ivanovo in August 1937 as an emissary of the Central Committee. Although Shreider blames Kaganovich (and Stalin with whom Kaganovich was in frequent telephone contact) with greatly expanding the terror in Ivanovo, he also mentions casually that when Kaganovich arrived in Ivanovo, the local prisons were already filled to capacity with "leading Party functionaries and local government officials," leaving no room for bandits or other common criminals. Hopefully when Shreider's memoirs are published in full, they will reveal what was happening in Ivanovo *before* the arrival of Kaganovich.

from Moscow and Leningrad telephone directories of the 1930s and a list of the top officials in the Commissariat of Heavy Industry on the assumption that the impact of terror would be reflected in increased dropout rates from the telephone books. Fitzpatrick's study indicates that the impact of the events of 1936–8 on the broader Soviet elite who enjoyed telephone service was far more modest than we have hitherto realized and that high office holding (like a senior position in the Commissariat of Heavy Industry) seems to have influenced one's vulnerability to the purges significantly, a finding she shares with our other authors.

More surprisingly, Fitzpatrick points out that the dropout rate for individual telephone subscribers was higher in Moscow between 1928 and 1935 and in Leningrad in 1934–5, during the Cultural Revolution, passportization, and the expulsions of large numbers of members of the prerevolutionary privileged classes from Leningrad in the wake of the Kirov assassination. She concludes that although the period of the Great Purges (1937–8) was "an unparalleled episode of terror as far as the top political and bureaucratic elite was concerned, this was not so for a more broadly defined social elite (or, it might be inferred, for the urban population as a whole)."

Alec Nove in "Victims of Stalinism: How Many?" analyzes the great volume of statistical data released in the former USSR in the last two years on "abnormal" deaths, executions for "counterrevolutionary" crimes, and the numbers imprisoned and exiled during the Stalin era. In the process, Nove points out consistencies and inconsistencies among various kinds of data and indicates clearly the limitations of different sets of statistics, which are not always easy to discern. He concludes on the basis of long suppressed 1937 census figures and the studies of S. G. Wheatcroft and S. Maksudov that 10 to 11 million abnormal deaths occurred in the USSR between 1927 and the start of 1937[20] but that no major demographic abnormalities of any great magnitude occurred between the 1937 and 1939 censuses, during the period of the Great Purges. Although this does not mean that large numbers of executions did not take place in this period, the Nove article suggests that the numbers executed were not so high as to be reflected in census data.

In "More Light on the Scale of Repression and Excess Mortality in the Soviet Union in the 1930s," S. G. Wheatcroft agrees with Nove on the number of prisoners of various categories in Stalin's time. (Both based their conclusions on this subject on recently published archival research by Soviet scholars.) Wheatcroft, however, departs from Nove in his estimates of the abnormal deaths that occurred in the interval between the 1926 and

---

[20] S. G. Wheatcroft, "More Light on the Scale of Repression and Excess Mortality in the Soviet Union in the 1930s," *Soviet Studies*, vol. 42, no. 2 (April 1990), 355–367, and S. Maksudov, *Poteri naseleniia SSSR* (Benson, VT, 1989).

1937 censuses. Here, Wheatcroft based his calculations on his own research in recently declassified Soviet archives, especially the records of the 1939 census and those of local government registry offices (ZAGs) that recorded births and deaths in the USSR. On the basis of such data, Wheatcroft concludes that 4 to 5 million persons perished as the result of the 1932 famine,[21] fewer than Nove's estimate of abnormal deaths in this period, not to mention the many more millions of excess deaths claimed by Robert Conquest.

This collection makes several major points about the Stalinist terror in the 1930s. The articles published here (especially those by Viola, Manning, Thurston) would suggest that economic problems, and a widespread belief in conspiracies on the part of both leaders and the led (Viola, Rittersporn) fueled the terror of both the First Five-Year Plan and famine period (1928–33) and the Great Purges of 1936–8.

Several contributors (Viola, Rittersporn, Thurston, Manning) also indicate that input from "below," as well as interventions from the NKVD and agents of the Center, played an important role in the spread of the repressions of 1936–8. It would be interesting to see if such input from below also figured in all major periods of Stalin's terror. For political repression (as measured by the volume of arrests and executions for political crimes) did not remain at a constant level throughout the Stalin period but tended to ebb and flow over time, reaching a crescendo during the First Five-Year Plan and ensuing famine (1928–32), the Great Purges of 1936–8, and the upsurge of repression toward the end of and immediately after World War II. The presence or absence of popular input in various periods and phases of the terror could reveal major changes in the Stalinist polity and its evolution over time.

Fitzpatrick, Getty and Chase, Hoffman, Manning, and Reese also demonstrate in a variety of settings and with a variety of methods and source materials that the terror of 1936–8 fell heavily on Soviet political, economic, and military leaders, especially those in high offices and in positions managing the economy; other groups were less exposed. (The coincidence of Fitzpatrick's and Getty and Chase's statistical findings, reached by separate research paths, is striking.) Did such patterns of persecution prevail in the other major periods of Stalin's terror or throughout the Stalin era in general? The articles by Lynne Viola and Sheila Fitzpatrick suggest the prime victims of repression during the Cultural Revolution (1928–32) period came from quite different social strata, in the main old regime elites and the intelligentsia. We need to begin to

---

[21] Actually Wheatcroft's estimates of the numbers of excessive deaths in areas, like Kazakstan, not covered by his ZAGs data, is 1 to 2 million, amazingly close to the estimates of 1.75 million such deaths in Kazakstan, advanced recently by three Kazakh historians and cited in the article by Nove in this volume. Wheatcroft, 357–358, 360.

identify clearly just who comprised Stalin's victims and what social strata were predominantly affected at different times.

The contributions of Fitzpatrick, Getty and Chase, Nove, Reese, and Wheatcroft to this collection also present new statistics on the number of Stalin's victims, based on recently declassified Soviet archival data, that are considerably lower than earlier estimates. Thus, the number of "excess" deaths in the 1927–37 period in the estimates of both Nove and Wheatcroft range between 4 and 11 million, much lower than those of Robert Conquest, who maintains that abnormal deaths ran as high as 20 million, not to mention those of Roy Medvedev and the new Soviet high school textbooks that claim that 40 million victims perished under Stalin.[22] Nove and Wheatcroft also indicate that the population of the camps, prisons, special settlements and colonies peaked not in the 1930s, but in 1953, when 5.5 million persons were incarcerated. These figures, too, are significantly less than S. Rosefielde's estimates of 10 million in the Gulag system in the late thirties and Robert Conquest's estimates of 7 to 8 million for the camps alone in late 1938 and 12 million in 1952.[23]

Writings on the Stalin era by some of the authors represented in this volume have been promiscuously and unfortunately labeled *revisionist*, often by those who did not read their work carefully or who discussed it without reading it at all. The essays in this volume should demonstrate, however, that our contributors adhere to no single approach in studying the Stalin period. They present us with different interpretations, perspectives, and points of view and disagree with one another on many points. Certainly most would vigorously deny being a revisionist altogether. It is a sign of the continued strength of the totalitarian thesis that they should even feel compelled to do so. All too often, scholars who come to conclusions anomalous to the reigning totalitarian school have been grouped as dissidents and denounced as perverse or even of seeking to absolve Stalin of his crimes.[24]

[22] Conquest, *The Great Terror: A Reassessment*, 486, and *The Boston Globe*, Feb. 5, 1989.
[23] Conquest, *The Great Terror: A Reassessment*, 486, and S. Rosefielde, "An Assessment of the Sources and Uses of Gulag Forced Labour, 1929–56," *Soviet Studies*, vol. 33, no. 1 (Jan. 1981). The archives thus show that Wheatcroft's previously published estimates of 4 to 5 million prisoners maximum were amazingly accurate. To be sure, his earlier estimate of abnormal deaths in the 1930s was approximately a million too low, as he himself admits (i.e., 3–4 million compared to 4–5 million). Still, the figure of 3–4 million was closer to the truth than Conquest's estimate of 20 million. S. G. Wheatcroft, "On Assessing the Size of Forced Concentration Camp Labour in the Soviet Union, 1929–56," *Soviet Studies*, vol. 33, no. 2 (April 1981), and S. G. Wheatcroft, "Towards a Thorough Analysis of Soviet Forced Labour Statistics," *Soviet Studies*, vol. 35, no. 2 (April 1983).
[24] Sheila Fitzpatrick, "New Perspectives on Stalinism," *Russian Review*, vol. 45, no. 4 (Oct. 1986), 357–373; Stephen F. Cohen, "Stalin's Terror as Social History," ibid., 375–384; Peter Kenez, "Stalinism as Humdrum Politics," ibid., 395–400. For the "revisionists" replies and more criticism of their views, see *Russian Review*, vol. 46, no. 4 (Oct. 1987), 382.–431.

Although many of our contributors share common ground in recognizing the importance of such factors as social psychology, economic scarcity, tensions from below, antielitist aspects of the repression, and the need for precision in calculating the number of victims, they neither agree among themselves on all issues, nor do they seek to write Stalin out of the equation. For example, Nove and Wheatcroft substantially disagree on the numbers of abnormal deaths under Stalin and on the conclusions one should draw from available statistical data. The stress Kuromiya and Hoffman place on the importance of intervention "from above" needs to be reconciled with seemingly spontaneous pressures "from below" described by Manning and others. Hoffman, Reese, and Manning see a role for the primary party organizations in the terror, whereas Kuromiya's case study emphasizes the input of Soviet leaders, like Kaganovich. Starkov and Getty differ notably on whether Stalin's actions during the Great Purges of 1936–8 display any consistency or evidence of prior planning; and the contributions of Starkov, Thurston, and Rittersporn present different views of what may have motivated N. I. Ezhov, Stalin's secret police chief at the height of the terror in the late thirties. Starkov portrays Ezhov as a disciplined and diligent agent of Joseph Stalin pure and simple, who cynically and knowingly forced confessions from innocent people to please his superior. Thurston's Ezhov was above all else a former worker in the mammoth Putilov Works at the height of labor militancy in pre-revolutionary times and 1917, predisposed by his early work experiences to sympathize with, encourage, and accept worker complaints (or denunciations) against their bosses. Rittersporn's article suggests that Ezhov could very likely have shared the widespread belief in conspiracies characteristic of significant segments of Soviet society in Stalin's time. There is no "party line" running through these works.

Similarly, our contributors have neither desired individually nor conspired collectively to minimize the role of Stalin. Their published work without exception has posited his participation in and responsibility for the terror. But even while admitting his enormous role in the terror, the scholars represented here risk stepping on numerous toes simply by raising questions about how much the terror was fueled from above or from below, the efficiency or inefficiency of the state in this process, and the relative influence of state and society. To deal with issues other than Stalin's personality and to reduce the personal factor to something less than one hundred percent of the cause has seemed to some like apologeia. For many, an omniscient and omnipotent Stalin has long provided simple, convenient, and useful interpretations. For Trotskyists, it explained their political defeat at the hands of the incredibly cunning dictator. For neo-Leninists, the totality of the personal factor allowed them to save Leninism from its subsequent perversion. For Western leftists, this "cult of personality" permitted one to save socialism from a not inevitable Stalinist outcome. For many others, it provided a gigantic evil personal figure, akin to Jengiz Khan or Hitler, whose deeds sufficed to explain everything without the necessity for detailed historical analysis.

As far as they go, all of these views of Stalin are true. He was, of course, responsible for the terror as the topmost Soviet leader, and the Great Purges would not have unfolded as they did without him. None of our authors have ever argued for a completely spontaneous terror that originated from below over opposition from higher up, or even for the autonomy of social processes in the USSR of Stalin's time. All of them, for all the stress on spontaneity and local input into the terror, recognize the importance of developments in the center for the course of the purges in the localities. At the same time, though, the research and the very subjects that many of our contributors tackle show that they believe that an understanding of the personal factor is necessary, but not sufficient, to explain the phenomenon of repression completely. Although Stalin lit the match, the cataclysm also required dry tinder and favorable winds to become what it did. There are at least two halves to this story, which interacted with one another constantly to feed the repressions: the personal and the contextual; the input from above and that from below. Because so much has been written about Stalin's role, it seemed useful to many contributors to this volume to begin to flesh out the other half of the walnut, to study why so much dry timber was available and why the prevailing winds blew in the direction that they did. Scholars will have to decide for themselves the relative weights of personal, social, economic, and status factors as phenomena that fueled the terror.

This book, of course, leaves many important questions and issues unanswered. We need to examine the "democracy campaign" of 1936 and 1937, launched in the wake of the introduction of the new Stalin Constitution of 1936, more closely and fully than we have done thus far. Three of our contributions (by Hoffman, Reese, and Manning), based on empirical research in three different sources – the Smolensk Archive, the Moscow Party Archive, and Soviet scholarly studies that draw on military archives – indicate that this short-lived populist campaign to encourage citizen complaints and involve rank-and-file party members more actively in the operations of the Communist Party definitely did play a role in the spread of the repressions, as J. Arch Getty and Gábor Rittersporn suggested some time ago.[25] The establishment by the February–March 1937 Central Committee Plenum of secret ballot elections within the Communist Party, a key component of the democracy campaign, facilitated involvement of the primary party organizations in the purges, as discussed by Hoffman, Reese, and Manning, by encouraging "self-criticism," which, according to the British ambassador of the time to the USSR, Lord Chilton, tended to take the form of criticism of one's superiors rather than one's self.[26] The

[25] Getty, *Origins of the Great Purges*, 92–112, 137–171, and Rittersporn, 1–253.
[26] *British Foreign Office Russia Correspondance*, 1937, reel 4, vol. 21104, pp. 269–77.

plenum also created a variety of forums, in which such criticism could be vented, in the form of quarterly meetings of raion and oblast party organizations and monthly meetings of party members (or *aktiv*) in all Soviet government institutions, including the armed forces, from the national Peoples' Commissariats and their subdepartments to these agencies' local affiliates, including economic enterprises. At these meetings, held regularly throughout 1937 and into 1938, long suppressed scandals and incidents of mismanagement were aired against responsible officials and often resulted in the dismissal of such officials, their expulsions from the Communist Party, and sometimes their arrest by the NKVD.[27]

Scholars need to study from whence and why did the democracy campaign originate? Who were its original authors and what was its original motivation and goals? Was the democracy campaign a clever ploy of a devious dictator out to terrorize his subordinates and to pass the buck for the ensuing repression to others? Was it a strategy to coopt and undermine the appeal of the defunct and persecuted Party Oppositionists by stealing a key plank of their political program? Or was the democracy campaign originally designed to appeal to public opinion in the Western democracies, with which the USSR in the mid-thirties desperately sought to ally itself against German and Japanese expansionism? The fact that this campaign was originally announced in an interview of Stalin by the American newspaper mogul Roy Howard of the giant Scripps-Howard newspaper chain might strongly suggest the latter.[28] But then, how did this campaign get so out of control as to contribute to the Great Purges, which inexorably alienated Western, especially American, opinion from the USSR? Stalin surely wasn't stupid or crazy enough to woo American opinion and promote terror at one and the same time? Or was he?

Besides the origins and purposes of the democracy campaign, a number of other factors and issues related to the Great Purges are not covered in the articles in this volume. Center–periphery conflicts, which figured prominently in earlier works by some of our contributors, are not mentioned here except in passing.[29] Nor does this volume discuss conflicts over military policies and procurements, which no doubt preceded the terror in the armed forces. Yet these were surely sensitive issues in an overstrained economy like that of the USSR, plagued by an external threat

---

[27] For the establishment of such meetings, see the resolution of the February-March 1937 Central Committee Plenum. *Pravda*, Mar. 6, 1937. For examples of what transpired at such meetings, see *British Foreign Office Russia Correspondance* 1937, reel 6, vol. 21104; *Sotsialisticheskoe zemledelie*, Mar. 9, 1937; D. Gurevich, "Za bol'shevitskuiu organizatsiiu aktiva v narkomatakh," *Partiinoe stroitel'stvo* no. 9 (May 1, 1937), pp. 19–24, and Siegelbaum, 150–154. These meetings, the transcripts of which can no doubt be found in party archives or in the archives of the institutions in which these meetings were held, need to be studied in depth by scholars of the terror.

[28] *Pravda*, March 8, 1936.

[29] Getty, 10–37, 163–171.

from two Great Powers – Germany and Japan – and a military establishment growing at a record pace. This collection tends to leave the victims of Stalin's terror at the prison gates, without exploring the process of arrest, interrogation, and imprisonment, which have dominated earlier studies of the terror by Conquest, Medvedev, and Solzhenitsyn. Moreover, only Nove's and Wheatcroft's contributions touch on the third major wave of Stalinist terror that developed at the end of World War II and in the immediate postwar period (1944–8), although available statistics indicate that the prison populaion – as opposed to the number of executions – peaked *after*, not before, the war. Space and the state of current research preclude us from touching every base.

Scholars need to address the issues that we neglect and to explore the terror of the late twenties and early thirties, the war, and postwar periods in as much detail as the repressions of the mid- to late 1930s have been studied in recent years. Terror could very well have sought completely different victims at different times and proceeded in a different manner, by different means, with different causes in different periods, although the consequences would have seemed quite similar for its victims. Similarities and differences between the various phases and periods of Stalinist terror, once established, could tell us a good deal about the causes of the terror and the workings of the Soviet political system and its development over time. The investigation of such questions is easier today than it has ever been, thanks to *glasnost'*.

Those who judge historical works by what they fail to do, rather than what they have actually done, should be warned at the onset that this volume makes no effort to provide a comprehensive or definitive study of the Great Terror. For no such study can be written at present until all the archives recently made available to scholars in the former USSR have been thoroughly explored, a process that could well take decades. Instead, we seek to facilitate the process of mastering these archives by presenting recent research on the repression by some of the leading scholars of the Stalin era, including many of the first professional historians to take up the study of this period. These articles should give our readers new insights into the terror, its scope, the processes by which it unfolded, and the political and social context in which it transpired. In the process, we hope to facilitate future research by indicating gaps in our knowledge of the terror and demonstrating different approaches and methods of studying these political persecutions, which can be utilized by other scholars.

The works represented in the present volume do not claim to supplant the totalitarian model. For that to happen, one would have to offer a workable new paradigm, with equivalent explanatory power and scope, capable of replacing the old one. But most of the contributors to this volume, being historians rather than political scientists, are uncomfortable with any synthetic paradigm that might define their research and impose limits to their inquiries, especially at a time when Soviet archives still need to be explored with an open mind. It is not certain whether the exploration of the archives will, or necessarily should, generate a replacement para-digm. But the nature and growing volume of anomalous conclusions drawn already, along with the violent defensive attacks on the new scholarship from the adherents of the totalitarian thesis, do suggest that the development of Soviet historical studies is following a recognizable process of scholarly evolution and change, similar to that which normally occurs in any field of study.

Part I: Persons and politics

1

Narkom Ezhov

Boris A. Starkov

So who was he anyway, this executor of the leader's schemes and designs? Really, there was nothing particularly unusual about him. He was a fairly colorless, mediocre individual who was raised up to the heights of party and state leadership by the will of Stalin, an ordinary product of the creation and establishment of a totalitarian, coercive, and bureaucratic system. He was truly a servant of the regime of personal power who compensated for his low moral and political qualities by exhibiting selfless love for, faith in, and devotion to the leader.

Nikolai Ivanovich Ezhov was born into a working class family in 1895 in Petersburg. At the age of fourteen, he took his first job in the Putilov Works. During the First World War, he was drafted. After the February Revolution, he ran for a position on the regimental committee but was not elected. He deserted from the army with a group of soldiers soon afterwards and turned up in Petrograd in the spring of 1917.

The turbulent political life of the capital at that time literally overwhelmed all layers of society. Demonstrations and meetings at which representatives of various political parties and tendencies appeared were going on constantly. N. I. Ezhov took part in them very actively and, in May of 1917, joined the Bolshevik party. He participated in the October Revolution and enlisted in the Red Army in the beginning of 1918. As a military commissar, he took part in battles with parts of General Yudenich's Northwestern army near Petrograd. Then he was sent to Kazan on the Eastern front to work as a military commissar in a radio-telegraphic school. On May 13, 1921, he was appointed "to the post of military commissar for the second base of the radio-telegraphic unit."[1]

N. I. Ezhov's work evaluations from this period contain references to his discipline and his diligence in fulfilling orders, qualities that he later developed to the uttermost extreme. At the beginning of the 1920s, he

---

[1] Prikaz RVSR chastiam 2-i bazy Radiotekhicheskikh formirovanii, no. 54.

switched over into party work. He was first named secretary of the Semi-palatinsk obkom of the party and then of the Kazakhstan kraikom of the All-Russia Communist Party. In particular, he took part in the struggle against the basmachis (anti-Bolshevik guerrillas in Central Asia) as an active participant in the Enver detachment, according to the testimony of G. S. Agabekov.[2] His acquaintance with I. F. Moskvin and L. M. Kaganovich dates from this period. In 1927, he was transferred to Moscow, to the offices of the Central Committee of the party, where he worked as the assistant to the head of the records and assignment (*uchraspred*) department.[3]

In 1929–30, he filled important state posts, having been appointed the Assistant to the Peoples' Commissar of Agriculture of the USSR. During this period, processes took place that consolidated Stalin's regime of personal power in the party, and the government, and the distinctive peak in the excesses of the collectivization movement occurred. It was at this time that Ezhov's discipline, his diligence in fulfilling orders, and even his servantlike demeanor were noted by Stalin and judged to be virtues.

In 1930, Ezhov was again transferred to party work. At this time he was named the head of the assignment department and, later, of the cadres department of the Central Committee of the All-Russia Communist Party (Bolsheviks). Personnel decisions, including appointments, transfers, and the dismissal of leading personnel in the party, government, and the economy, were concentrated in his hands. His position was an important tool for consolidating Stalin's absolute rule. With Ezhov's direct participation and his single-minded pressure on the Party Central Committee, a campaign was launched to politically discredit all of the representatives of the old guard of the party who were trying to oppose Stalinism.[4] During this period, Ezhov was governed only by the personal orders of the leader, which had acquired for him the force of law. Cruelty and refusal to compromise in carrying out the general line, the unreasoning implementation of the orders of the leader, comprised his workstyle.

In accordance with a decision of the January (1933) Central Committee Plenum, an immediate purge of party organizations was carried out, Stalin and his henchmen using it to further consolidate their power. N. I. Ezhov became a member of the Central Committee after the purge and ensured its connection to the organs of the OGPU (*Ob'edinennaia Gosudarstvennaia Politicheskaia Administratsiia*, United State Political Administration), as the NKVD's predecessor was known. As a rule, information about all expulsions from the party went to the secret-political department of the OGPU for consideration and political elaboration. From this time

[2] See O. S. Agabekov, *Zapiski Chekista*. Paris, 1939.
[3] *Tsentral'nyi partiinyi arkhiv* (hereafter TsPA), fond 17, opis 67, delo 368, list 82.
[4] *Tsentral'nyi gosudarstvennyi arkhiv okt'iabrskoi revoliutsii* (hereafter *TsGAOR SSSR*), "Materialy TsK VKP(b)."

on, Ezhov would work more closely with OGPU chief Iagoda's staff, including Ia. S. Agranov, G. A. Molchanov, and others. It was during this period, in particular, that the resistance of the old party guard was broken, and Stalin's authoritarian regime of personal power was firmly consolidated. Changes in the political structure of Soviet society were anchored in the structure of the party bureaucracy.

N. I. Ezhov worked out a plan for the Seventeenth Congress of the party and put forward his proposals for the reorganization of the party bureaucracy. We should note that the idea itself belonged to L. M. Kaganovich and that Ezhov only carried it through. He was a member of the committee that prepared for and conducted the congress and adopted what was at that time the height of organizational technology for it. For the first time in the history of the party, the organs of the OGPU were brought in and used to safeguard the work of the congress. They not only answered for its work but also kept track of the voting procedure and the behavior and speeches of the former leaders of the opposition at the congress. This group of people, including N. I. Bukharin, L. B. Kamenev, G. E. Zinoviev, V. V. Lominadze, A. I. Rykov, and others, was kept under constant surveillance by employees of the Secret Political and Special departments of the OGPU.[5]

At the congress, N. I. Ezhov was elected to the Party Central Committee and to the Party Central Control Commission, the control organs of the party at that time that investigated complaints against party members and reviewed the cases of members who were censured or expelled. Ezhov was also elected to the Orgbureau and simultaneously was confirmed as the head of the Industrial Department of the Party Central Committee.

During the summer of 1934, the conflict between central and local party and state organizations became very serious. This was also reflected in the activities of punitive and administrative organs like the OGPU. More and more frequently, representatives of the local, regional, and republic organs of Soviet power informed the center of illegalities and arbitrary rule. Facts revealed the falsification of a number of closed judicial trials. A number of people who had been arrested were freed and turned to the Central Committee and the Party Control Commission with well-founded complaints. A special commission was created by decision of the Politburo to look into the question of the activities of the OGPU. N. I. Ezhov was not a member of this commission, but documents allow us to confirm that his role in its work was significant. A draft resolution that the OGPU be reorganized into the NKVD was prepared and the question was supposed to be considered on December 10, 1934. N. I. Ezhov's name appeared on the list of possible candidates under consideration for posts in the OGPU's

---

[5] This was also L. M. Kaganovich's idea. N. I. Ezhov was responsible for it during the course of the congress.

successor organ. Ezhov was suggested for the post of Assistant People's Commissar of Internal Affairs (the *Narodnyi Komissariat Vnutrennykh Del*, or NKVD).[6]

On December 1, 1934, however, S. M. Kirov was killed at Smolny. N. I. Ezhov arrived in Leningrad along with Stalin as part of a government commission. He took control of the course of the investigation at Stalin's personal request, which was made in the name of the Politburo. This was, in essence, an extremely flagrant violation of Soviet legislation. Ezhov participated directly in fabricating and releasing the story about the special moral responsibility of former members of the opposition, including Zinoviev, Kamenev, and others, for Kirov's murder. This action eventually lead to their arrest and conviction.

At the Seventh Congress of the Comintern (1935), N. I. Ezhov was elected to the Executive Committee of the Comintern. Friction and difference of opinion between him and the secretary of the Executive Committee, I. A. Piatnitskii, immediately appeared.[7] In the end, Piatnitskii was transferred to the post of head to the political-administrative department of the Central Committee of the party. That same year, Ezhov was elected secretary of the Central Committee and simultaneously named Chairman of the Party Control Commission. A great deal of power was thus concentrated in his hands, and he also enjoyed the complete trust of I. V. Stalin. At his order, N. I. Ezhov conducted a complicated investigation of the work of the organs of the NKVD in both the center and in the provinces during the summer of 1936. During this period, preparations were being made for the trial of Zinoviev, Kamenev, and the other oppositionists.

Stalin and his closest henchmen demanded that Peoples' Commissar of Internal Affairs G. G. Iagoda take the most active measures possible to liquidate the "counterrevolutionary," "anti-Soviet," and "anti-party" activities of the former members of opposition groups. N. I. Ezhov was particularly zealous about this. Already in 1935, not long after the conclusion of the investigation of the Kirov murder, he began to work on a large "theoretical work" under the title of "From Factionalism to Open Counterrevolution." In it he formulated basic theses/accusations about the likes and terrorist inclinations of the leaders of the right and Trotskyist-Zinovievist oppositions. At Ezhov's request, Stalin personally edited this work and gave appropriate instructions and recommendations that were incorporated by the author during further work on the manuscript. It was the author's intention that this work become a program for the liquidation of all former oppositionists and dissidents in the country.

Ezhov sent the first chapter of this work to Stalin on May 17, 1935,

---

[6] *TsPA*, f. 77, op. 1, d. 269, l. 8.
[7] This conflict was deliberately aggravated by Comintern official D. Z. Manuil'skii. See *TsPA*, f. 589, op. 31, d. 2615, ll. 72–74 and *Tsentral'nyi arkhiv KGB SSSR*, "Arkhivno sledstvennoe delo Pyatnitskogto, I.", volumes 1 and 2.

accompanied by the following note: "I am asking you to please look over the work I have sent you. It is the first chapter of a book on 'Zinovievshchina' about which you and I have already spoken. Please send me your suggestions."[8] Stalin read through the contents of the work thoroughly. The many marks in the margins and underlinings in the text testify to this. For instance, he singled out the phrase, "The Zinovievist counter-revolutionary band definitively chooses terror as its weapon in this battle against the party and the working class."[9] The assertions that "the Zinovievist-Kamenevist Mensheviks tried to behead the revolution, to wipe out Comrade Stalin," and that "the terrorists prepared parallel attacks on Comrades Kirov and Stalin," are particularly clearly marked in the margins.[10]

Without any particular proof, Comrade N. I. Ezhov wrote that

a strong link has existed between the Zinovievists and the Trotskyists throughout this entire period. The Trotskyists and Zinovievists regularly inform each other about their activities. There is no doubt that the Trotskyists were aware of the terrorist side of the activities of the Zinovievist organization as well, the testimony of individual Zinovievists during the investigation of the Kirov murder and during the consequent arrests of Zinovievists and Trotskyists establish that the latter have also taken the path to terrorism.[11]

So, in the middle of 1935, a story about the Trotskyists' and Zinovievists' entry into terrorist activity was worked out. Practical actions began to be implemented on the basis of it. N. I. Ezhov gave instructions to the Assistant Peoples' Commissar of Internal Affairs, the boss of the Main Directorate of State Security, Ia. S. Agranov, to pursue Trotskyists and other dissidents actively. Later, Ia. S. Agranov said this about his instructions:

Comrade Ezhov announced that, according to his own information and in the opinion of the Central Committee of the party, an undiscovered Trotskyist center existed which had to be found and liquidated. Comrade Ezhov gave me sanction to produce a massive operation against the Trotskyists in Moscow.[12]

In February of 1936, the Deputy Peoples' Commissar of Internal Affairs, G. E. Prokofiev, issued a directive to the local organs of the NKVD concerning the complete liquidation of the entire Trotskyist-Zinovievist underground:

Having directed the investigation towards the discovery of underground counter-revolutionary formations, of all of the organizational links of the Trotskyists and the Zinovievists and to the discovery of terrorist groups, quickly move to liquidate all of these Trotskyist and Zinovievist affairs, not limiting yourselves by making exceptions for the most active members of the party.[13]

[8] *Arkhiv TsK, KPSS*, rukopis' Ezhova "Ot fraktsionnosti k otkrytoi kontrrevoliutsii."
[9] Ibid.
[10] Ibid.
[11] Ibid.
[12] Cited from *Reabilitatsiia politicheskie protsessy 30–50 godov.* Moscow, 1991, 6.
[13] *Izvestiia TsK KPSS*, 1989, no. 8, p. 83.

The purges increased and in April of 1936, 508 former oppositionists were arrested.

In 1936, during the arrest of the nonparty literary employee of the Communist Academy, I. M. Trusov, a personal archive of L. D. Trotsky was found and confiscated. At Stalin's suggestion, which was formulated as a decision of the Politburo, the archive was turned over to N. I. Ezhov. Simultaneously, this same decision ordered the NKVD to conduct all interrogations together with Ezhov.[14]

During the spring and summer of 1936, the NKVD sent a number of directives to local offices concerning the intensified battle against the Trotskyists. At the same time, their activity in terms of "rooting out Trotskyist nests" was under the constant control of the party organs and, most importantly, of the Politburo, which is to say, under Stalin and Ezhov's personal control. In April of 1936, by the order of the Politburo, all of those whose guilt in the terror had been established were to "be turned over to the court of the military collegia of the Supreme Court of the USSR with execution by firing squad as the ultimate penalty."[15] On May 20, 1936, a directive of the Politburo instructed that "all Trotskyists should be sent to a concentration camp for 3–5 years. This primarily concerned those who had shown some signs of hostile activity and who lived in Moscow, Leningrad, Kiev, and other cities in the Soviet Union."[16] The intensification of the preparations for the first Moscow show trial began. Zinoviev, Kamenev, and others found themselves in the dock.

The investigation wasn't even finished when, on July 26, 1935, a closed letter entitled "About The Terrorist Activities of the Trotskyist-Zinovievist, Counterrevolutionary Bloc" was sent out to local party organs in the name of the Central Committee. In the letter, it was asserted that Kamenev and Zinoviev were not just responsible for ideologically inspiring terrorist activities against other party and state leaders, but that more importantly they had prepared an attempt on Stalin's life, and that a united bloc of Trotskyists and Zinovievists had directed all of the terrorist activity. This terrorist activity began in 1932 as a result of talks between the leaders of the counterrevolutionary groups. The main condition for "the unification of the two groups was the acceptance of terror directed at party and state leaders as the only and decisive means of gaining power."[17] The author of the letter was N. I. Ezhov. On the eve of the Kamenev-Zinoviev trial, local party and government organs were given a directive to organize mass demonstrations and meetings of workers who would demand the conviction of all of the accused according to the highest category.

However, very few people in the country and in the party believed that

[14] Ibid.
[15] *Izvestiia TsK KPSS*, 1989, no. 9, pp. 35–36.
[16] Ibid.
[17] *Reabilitatsiia*, pp. 196–210.

these old, honored revolutionaries had become terrorists. Stalin considered this a sign that the organs of the NKVD and, most of all, its head, G. G. Iagoda, had not done enough preparatory work. In September of 1936 it was decided to change the leadership of the NKVD. On September 25, 1936, Stalin sent a telegram from Sochi with the following contents:

We consider it absolutely necessary and urgent to appoint Comrade Ezhov to the post of Peoples' Commissar of Internal Affairs. Iagoda clearly was not up to the task of bringing to light the Trotskyist-Zinovievist bloc. The OGPU was four years late in this affair. All of the party workers and most of the regional representatives of the NKVD are talking about this. We can leave Agranov as Ezhov's assistant in the Commissariat of Internal Affairs.[18]

Stalin and Zhdanov signed the telegram. A little later Ezhov acquired the lofty title of General Commissar of State Security of the USSR.

Documentary sources allow us to piece together the picture of G. G. Iagoda's dismissal. It happened at a meeting of the Sovnarkom (Council of Peoples' Commissars) of the USSR, which was under the chairmanship of V. M. Molotov. The Commissar of Defense, K. E. Voroshilov, reported the results of the investigation of the NKVD and read Stalin's telegram. Iagoda immediately left for the Lubianka, the Moscow headquarters of the NKVD, in the company of the commander and officers of the Moscow Military District in order to turn over his affairs. Simultaneously, at a conference of local NKVD commanders and commissars, the change in leadership was announced. Then they set off for the Lubianka with the commanders of the front line units of the Moscow Military District "in order to be presented to the new Peoples' Commissar."[19]

As the new Commissar of Internal Affairs, Ezhov was faced with having to fulfill a number of Stalin's crucial missions. First of all, he had to destroy "the government within a government": to end the growing independence of the organs of state security in which there still remained more than a few companions-in-arms of F. E. Dzerzhinskii and V. P. Menzhinskii. He had to conduct a purge of the structure and composition of the cadres that the NKVD inherited from its predecessor, the OGPU. It was proposed that the reorganized NKVD be used to end not only all real opposition but also all potential opposition to the party and the government.

At that time, the Red Army began to frighten Stalin. Its best representatives were raising the question of the replacement of the Peoples' Commissar of Defense, Stalin's long-time political associate Vorshilov. Stalin could not risk entrusting a purge of the army to Voroshilov, knowing his capabilities. Only Ezhov could handle this assignment. Finally, the new Commissar of Internal Affairs had to safeguard the elections to the Supreme

---

[18] N. S. Krushchev, *The Secret Speech Delivered to the Closed Session of the 20th Congress of the CPSU*, with an introduction by Zhores and Roy Medvedev, London, 1956, 35–36.
[19] *TsGAOR SSSR*, "Materialy sekretariata NKVD SSSR za 1936g."

Soviet and the local soviets according to the new system that agreed with the 1936 Soviet constitution.

On September 29, 1936, the new Peoples' Commissar moved into his office in the Lubianka. On the first of October, he signed order no. 411: "As of this date, the Peoples' Commissar of Internal Affairs of the Soviet Union has begun to fulfill his duties. Transmit this order to the local organs of the NKVD by telegram. Peoples' Commissar of Internal Affairs, USSR. N. Ezhov."[20]

N. I. Ezhov's appointment as Peoples' Commissar of Internal Affairs was accompanied by a new intensification of repression against former oppositionists. The following directive for party organizations and the organs of the NKVD was prepared by L. M. Kaganovich and approved at a meeting of the Politburo on September 20, 1936. "Concerning treatment of counter-revolutionary Trotskyist-Zinovievite elements," it was stated, in part, that

a. up until the present time, the Party Central Committee has viewed the Trotskyist/ Zinovievist scoundrels as the advanced detachments of the international bourgeoisie. The latest facts indicate that these gentlemen have slid even further, and it is now necessary to view them as secret service men, as spies, saboteurs, and fascist bourgeoisie wreckers in Europe.
b. In connection with this, it is essential to deal with the Trotskyist-Zinovievist scoundrels, including not only those who have been arrested, whose cases we have already finished investigating, and not only those already under investigation like Muralov, Pyatakov, Beloborodov, and others, whose cases have not yet been completed, but also those who were exiled earlier.
Secretary of the Central Committee I. Stalin[21]

Zealously fulfilling Stalin's instructions, Ezhov assisted in much of this not only by formulating the story about the existence in the country of a deeply secret conspiracy, but also by undertaking practical measures to bring the conspiracy to light and to liquidate it. He personally participated in the interrogations, confrontations, arrests, and searches of the oppositionists. For instance, his participation, along with L. M. Kaganovich and A. Ia. Vyshinskii, in the September 8, 1936 confrontation between N. I. Bukharin, A. I. Rykov, and G. Ia Sokolnikov was noted in the record of the proceedings. At this confrontation the rightists Bukharin and Rykov were accused of being in league with the Trotskyist-Zinovievist opposition.

The Central Committee Secretary, Chairman of the Commission of Party Control – "the embodiment of the conscience of the party" – N. I. Ezhov, having become Peoples' Commissar of Internal Affairs, carried on "the glorious chekist tradition of F. E. Dzerzhinskii." He successfully compensated for his lack of high moral and political qualities by being personally devoted to Stalin. Exactly ten days after taking up his new post, Ezhov sent Stalin the following letter:

[20] *TsGAOR SSSR*, "Prikazy po lichnomu sostavu NKVD SSSR za 1936g."
[21] *Izvestiia TsK KPSS*, 1989, no. 9, p. 39.

In the light of the latest testimony of those arrested, the role of the rightists appears quite different. Having become familiar with the materials of previous investigations into the case of the rightists, Uglanov, Riutin, Eismont, Slepkov, and others, I have come to think that we did not dig down far enough at that time. In the light of this, I have instructed that some of the rights arrested in the last year be called back. We called back Kulikov who was convicted in the Nevskii case and Lugov. Their preliminary interrogation has yielded extraordinarily intriguing material about the activities of the rightists. We will send you the examination records in a few days. In any case, there is every reason to suppose that we will be able to discover a lot of new things and that the rightists will look different to us, including, Rykov, Bukharin, Uglanov, Schmidt, et al.[22]

In the light of the documents that we possess, we can claim with complete assurance that every step of the organs of state security toward the realization of the "great terror" thoroughly conformed with Stalin's intentions. His instructions were incorporated into the methodology of investigators, prosecutors, and judges. N. I. Ezhov acted the part of most zealous executor. So, in May of 1937, he sent Stalin a copy of A. G. Beloborodov's statement about persons sharing the views of the Trotskyists. Stalin was dissatisfied with the contents of this document and sent Ezhov the following note:

To Ezhov.
One might think that prison for Beloborodov is a podium for reading speeches, statements which refer to the activities of all sorts of people but not to himself. Isn't it time to squeeze this gentleman and make him tell about his dirty deeds? Where is he, in prison or in a hotel?
I. St.[23]

Ezhov bears great personal responsibility for the destruction of legality, for the falsification of investigative cases. According to his own instructions, the responsible workers of the NKVD personally prepared those who had been arrested for confrontations, considering with them the possible questions and various answers to them. This preparation consisted of reading previous testimony given about persons with whom the confrontation was planned. After this, as a rule, Ezhov sent for the prisoner, went to the investigator's room himself, asked the person being interrogated if he would confirm his testimony, and, as if in passing, announced that members of the government might be present at the confrontation. If the arrested person retracted his testimony, Ezhov left, and let the investigator "rehabilitate" the prisoner, which meant obtaining from the accused his previous testimony. Before confrontations with the participation of members of the Politburo, Ezhov sent for investigators and prepared the case again. According to evidence given by people who worked for the NKVD, he was not very concerned with the substance of the case, but was only worried about ending up face down in the mud in front of members of the Politburo and that the prisoners would retract their testimony.

---

[22] *Dialog*, Leningrad, 1990, no. 4, p. 21.
[23] Ibid., p. 22.

Having become Peoples' Commissar, Ezhov carried out a complete
purge of the organs of state security during the end of 1936 and the
beginning of 1937. His speech to party activists in the national NKVD
headquarters became a unique program of action for the purge. This
meeting of activists was dedicated to the results of the February–March
Plenum (1937) of the Central Committee. To the surprise of many chekists,
the meeting resounded with accusations of espionage and counterrevolutionary wrecking. During Ezhov's speech, a shadow of suspicion fell on F.
Dzerzhinskii. "What is there to say about you who are sitting in this hall if
even Dzerzhinskii wavered during 1925 and 1926 about whether he should
support the opposition or not." Making reference to a personal assignment
from Stalin, Ezhov announced that he would "get rid of all of that scum
which the revolution and the Civil War had sent sloshing into the organs
of state security. People who have come from the Central Committee
Orgbureau will sweep out all of that grime with an iron broom."[24]

This announcement was not just idle talk. Virtually all of the departmental heads, all of the bosses of the regional and republic divisions of the
NKVD, were arrested and repressed, primarily those who had worked
with F. Dzerzhinskii and V. P. Menzhinskii. Ia. Kh. Peters was among
those arrested and accused of spying for England. The only basis for the
accusation was that his first wife had been English. A letter from Dzerzhinskii
dated 1912 was used to compromise I. S. Unshlikht. (A party court had
vindicated Unshlikht, it is true, and Dzerzhinskii apologized to him and
even went on to work with him again.) However, in May of 1937, M. F.
Frinovskii used this document to make political accusations. On May 13,
1937, A. Kh. Artuzov, a second-rank commissar of state security and the
head of the central division of the NKVD USSR, was arrested on the basis
of personal instructions from Ezhov. In the records of the interrogation
that were made by investigator Alentsov, Artusov confessed that in 1913 he
was recruited into "the (tsarist) intelligence service." In 1914, he became a
French intelligence agent, in 1925, a German agent, and in 1933, a Polish
agent. Moreover, he admitted belonging to an anti-Soviet organization of
rightists that was active within the NKVD and was headed by G. G.
Iagoda.[25]

A number of departmental heads were freed only to be purged later "for
not having satisfactorily completed the work as chekists," or "for not
wanting to struggle against the enemies of the people." Veteran chekists
like T. D. Deribas and P. A. Piliar can be numbered among this group. T.
D. Deribas headed the organs of state security in the Far East for a long
time. In 1936, he was recalled to the central office of the NKVD, and, on
June 19, 1937, he was reappointed to a post in the Far East. On the

[24] *TsGAOR SSSR*, "Stenogramma partiinogo aktiva NKVD SSSR." March 1937.
[25] *Arkhiv Glavnoi Voennoi Prokuratury SSSR* (hereafter *AGVP SSSR*), "Reabilitatsionnye
dela A. Kh. Artuzova, T. D. Deribasa, I. S. Unshlikhta and R. A. Pilyar von Pilkhau."

instructions of N. I. Ezhov, a large group of chekists under the leaders
of M. P. Frinovskii, the head of the main department of state security of
the NKVD USSR, arrived in the Far East in early June with the aim of
"striking a crushing blow at rightist-Trotskyist, military-fascist, white
guardist-insurgent, SR-ist, Menshevik, and nationalist organizations, in the
secret service of Japan and other foreign countries, and also to purge
the Far East of all elements hostile to Soviet power."[26] Having become
acquainted with the state of affairs in the NKVD administration of the Far
Eastern area and with several regional offices, Frinovskii came to the
conclusion that the battle against "enemies of the people" was not moving
along satisfactorily. A directive was quickly sent out to all of the heads of
the organs of the NKVD that instructed them to conduct a massive, seven-
day operation to capture the anti-Soviet elements listed above. Prominent
party and state workers of the Far Eastern region were among those
arrested. The records of the interrogation of the Chairman of the Far
Eastern Kraispolkom, G. N. Krutov, were taken down by investigator A.
A. Arnoldov. Having become familiar with these records, T. D. Deribas
announced that "they appeared to be the testimony of investigator Arnoldov,
not Krutov," and refused to carry out any further arrests. This information
was reported to N. I. Ezhov. On July 31, 1937, Deribas was fired from his
post and subsequently purged.

Roman Alexandrovich Piliar von Pilkhau had been working in the
investigatory organs since 1920. In 1937, he was working as head of the
Saratov regional division of the NKVD. In the spring of 1937, N. I. Ezhov
sent for him, and they had the following conversation:

EZHOV: Why are you acting so indecisively in the arrests of the enemies of the
    people?
PILIAR: We have arrested whoever needed to be arrested.
EZHOV: Yes but these are isolated individuals, and they aren't the kind of people
    that constitute a real danger. Here, read through this list.
PILIAR: As far as I know, there is no proof that these people are engaged in hostile
    activities. How can you arrest people, and, moreover, communists who hold
    important posts in the party, the government, or in the Red Army without
    any legal basis?
EZHOV: Without what kind of basis?
PILIAR: A legal basis.
EZHOV: Take this list. In three days, I will check your work.[27]

According to his wife, T. A. Baranova, Piliar was arrested three days
after this conversation with Ezhov.[28]

G. I. Boky, the main custodian of party and state secrets was arrested in
May of 1937 and later shot. He had headed the Special Department of the

[26] *TsGAOR SSSR*, "Materialy sekretariata NKVD SSSR za 1937g."
[27] Ibid.
[28] *AGVP SSSR*, "Pis'mo T. A. Baranovoi."

NKVD and its predecessor organs, the Cheka and OGPU, for a long time. The reason for his arrest was that he had refused to prepare falsified accusations against old members of the Bolshevik party, charging them with working as agent provocateurs. He was accused of malfeasance in office and leading an amoral lifestyle, "with engaging in amoral putrefaction along with his closest co-workers." However, a completely different charge ran throughout the materials of the investigation: "He was in contact with and a participant in a secret Masonic organization which he joined in 1918."[29]

G. E. Prokofiev (Deputy Peoples' Commissar of Internal Affairs), M. I. Gai (the former head of the Special Department of the All-Union NKVD, who up until the moment of his arrest had been filling the post of head of the Eastern-Siberian regional division of the NKVD), and G. A. Molchanov (former head of the Secret-Political Department and, at the time of his arrest, Belorussian Peoples' Commissar of Internal Affairs), were all arrested in March and April of 1937. All of them held the high rank of Commissar of State Security Second Rank. The testimony about the conspiracy in the Red Army was received from them specifically as well as from Z. I. Volovich, K. I. Pauker, and N. I. Gorb, who were arrested later. All of this testimony was obtained with the help of deception, provocation, and physical force. The cadres of Soviet espionage agents and counterespionage agents by whose strength, to a large extent, the subversive activities of White emigrant intelligence services and secret organizations had been paralyzed were repressed. Thirty agents of the Soviet intelligence service leading secret espionage work in Europe, America, and the Far East were recalled to the Soviet Union and eliminated.[30]

While he was in the process of carrying out the purge, Ezhov was simultaneously reorganizing the organs of the NKVD. Personnel increased by almost four times. Between October 1936 and October 1937, the central offices and the local organs of the NKVD were continuously restaffed with Communists and Komsomol members who had to be "turned into model chekists in the space of 3–4 months." These cadres frequently did not have the slightest idea of the character and methods of the work they would engage in. Frequently, far from the best representatives of the cadres of chekists served as their instructors, which could not help but have an effect on the quality of the new reinforcements. This took a particularly heavy toll on the effectiveness of the investigative apparatus. In 1937 and 1938, almost the entire staff of the NKVD was engaged in investigative work, including operational and office workers.[31]

M. P. Frinovskii, who later landed in the dock himself, gave the following testimony:

---

[29] AGVP SSSR, "Nadzorno-sledstvennoe delo Bokiia G. I."
[30] TsGAOR SSSR, "Prikazy po lichnomu sostavu GUGB NKVD SSSR za 1937g."
[31] Ibid., "Prikazy po lichnormu sostavu NKVD SSSR za 1938g."

Ezhov demanded that I select investigators who would be completely bound to him, who had some kind of sins in their pasts and who would know that they had these sins in their pasts, and then that I, on the basis of these sins, kept them completely in line. In my opinion, I would be telling the truth, if, generalizing, I said that often the investigators themselves gave the testimony and not those under investigation. Did the leadership of the Peoples' Commissariat, that is, Ezhov and I, know about this? They knew and they encouraged it. How did we react to it? I, honestly, didn't react at all, and Ezhov even encouraged it.[32]

Shneidman, a former investigator in the central offices of the NKVD who was called to account in the 1950s, gave the same kind of testimony:

Ezhov's authority in the organs of the NKVD was so high that I, like the other employees, did not doubt the guilt of individuals who were arrested on his direct orders even when the investigator did not have any materials which compromised the given individual. I was convinced of the guilt of such an individual even before the interrogation and then, during the interrogation, tried to obtain a confession from that individual using all possible means.[33]

N. I. Ezhov, to a great extent, facilitated the creation of his own cult in the organs of state security. The best apartments, special rations and consumer goods, the privilege of transportation, housing, and public utilities according to one's pay – these were just a few of the luxuries that were connected with his name. "We must train chekists now," he announced during an appearance before the students of the Dzerzhinskii Academy, "so that this becomes a closely-welded, closed caste which will unconditionally fulfill my orders and be faithful to me, just as I am faithful to Comrade Stalin."[34]

With the strength of the reorganized organs of the NKVD, Ezhov and his closest aides, Frinovskii, Zakovskii, Leplevskii, et al., launched a broad compaign to root out "enemies of the people." Thousands of honest workers in the party, the government, and the economy, the leading cadres of the Soviet army, and representatives of the creative and academic intelligentsia were subjected to unfounded punitive measures. In June of 1937, M. P. Frinovskii said, while giving instructions to investigators, "We need to expand the picture of the great and deep conspiracy in the Red Army, the discovery of which would expose Ezhov's enormous role and service to the Central Committee."[35]

During Ezhov's tenure, the use of convictions by list came into practice. Before this, lists were prepared by the OGPU after an investigation was completed and after the actual pronouncement of sentence. Now, the sentence was decided in the Party Central Committee. According to information given by N. S. Khrushchev, N. I. Ezhov prepared 383 such lists. Current research, however, allows us to assert that there were many more

---

[32] *Arkhiv KGB SSSR*, "Sledstvennoe delo Frinovskogo M. P."
[33] *TsPA*, "Lichnoe delo Ezhova N. I."
[34] Ibid.
[35] *Arkhiv KGB SSSR*, "Sledstvennoe delo Frinovskogo M. P."

of them. In November of 1937, Stalin was sent a list naming 292 people as "the Moscow center." In July of 1938, Ezhov sent a list of 138 names. The accompanying note stated the following: "Secret. To Comrade Stalin. I am sending a list of the people who have been arrested and are subject to the verdict of the military tribunal according to the first category. Ezhov. 26 July 1938." The following resolution can be found on the sheet: "Shoot all 138. I. St., V. Molotov."[36]

As a result of the monstrous accusations and the groundless repression, the authority of central and local, party and government organizations was shaken. On average, party and state leaders in the provinces changed five to six times between 1937 and 1938. Existing legality was overthrown in favor of a rule of arbitrariness and illegality. Things reached a state of utter absurdity. Norms for convictions with the ultimate penalty were established everywhere. The NKVD of the Kirgizian SSR, with the aim of successfully completing the task of routing the rightist-Trotskyist and other anti-Soviet organizations, announced a socialist competition. In an NKVD order concerning the results of the competition between departments, it was stated that

the fourth department surpassed the third department by $1\frac{1}{2}$ times in terms of the number of arrests, having exposed 13 more spies and counter-revolutionaries. The same fourth department also surpassed the third department in terms of the number of cases reviewed by the three man tribunals at the center by 100.[37]

All of this was accordingly encouraged by various forms of material and moral stimuli.

B. D. Berman, the Peoples' Commissar of Internal Affairs of Belorussia, created a terrifying reputation for himself. Every week, on Saturday, he organized a review of the work that had been carried out. At these times, the investigators who had brought in the largest number of death verdicts could expect encouragement, whereas those who had completed fewer investigative cases could expect disciplinary penalties and, not infrequently, arrest and repression.[38] Ezhov encouraged all of this. "Progressive experiments" were studied and reported in special instructions and directions. In the fall of 1937, Ezhov's activity reached its apogee. On the first anniversary of his appointment to the post of Commissar, he was awarded the Order of Lenin, and at the October 1937 Central Committee Plenum, he was made a member of the Politburo.

Ezhov led a modest everyday life. Questionnaires from the All-Union census of 1937 have survived, and from them, it is clear that Ezhov lived in a modest apartment in the Kremlin. His mother, Anna Anatolievna, who turned seventy in 1937, and his six-year-old daughter, Natalya

---

[36] See *Dialog*, Leningrad, 1990, no. 4, p. 22.
[37] *TsGAOR SSSR*, "Perepiska NKVD SSSR."
[38] *Arkhiv KGB SSSR*, "Sledstvennoe delo Bermana, B. D."

Nikolaena, lived with him. Ezhov's wife was an actress in the Od(theater. She killed herself in 1938.[39]

In the spring of 1938, the last of the big Moscow show trials was prepared. Representatives of the "Rightist-Trotskyist bloc," including N. I. Bukharin, A. I. Rykov, N. N. Krestinskii, and others, now found themselves in the dock. Undoubtedly, the third most important figure in the trial was G. G. Iagoda, the former Peoples' Commissar of Internal Affairs. He had been arrested in 1937 for official malfeasance and amoral conduct. This was a standard formula. However, during the course of the trial, he was charged with entirely different crimes: espionage, acting as an agent provocateur, counterrevolutionary wrecking, and anti-Soviet and terrorist activities.

The trial was entirely the offspring of Stalin and Ezhov, and had been in the works since 1936. At the Central Committee plenums of December 1936 and February–March 1937, Ezhov, appearing as a speaker, asserted that the accused had deceived the party and had been carrying out a clandestine counterrevolutionary struggle against the party since 1929. (At the latter meeting, A. I. Mikoyan spoke in support of Ezhov, and chaired the subcommission that condemned the rightists.)[40] The main aim of the rightist-Trotskyist conspirators consisted of acting in league with the Trotskyists, Mensheviks, and also the anti-Soviet emigré political parties and organizations to seize power in the party and the government by means of a "palace coup."

Already on June 2, 1937, Bukharin wrote to Ezhov and began to confess.[41] The political discrediting and then conviction of Bukharin and Rykov, prominent figures in the Communist Party and the Soviet government, was something of a high point of "the great terror" that Ezhov had organized. A. S. Bubnov, Ia. E. Rudzutak, and S. V. Kosior were compromised and then repressed on the basis of Ezhov's personal orders. The organs of state security had turned into a means for settling personal scores. The repression of state and party leaders, the leading cadres of the Red Army, the rout of the USSR's diplomatic representatives abroad, seriously undermined the international prestige of the Soviet government. By the spring of 1938, Ezhov's name already inspired fear. The magazine *Krokodil* and others published cartoons on the topic of the day that showed "enemies of the people" convulsing in "Ezhov's steel gauntlets."[42]

During this period, did anyone attempt to speak out against Ezhov and

---

[39] *TsGAOR SSSR*, "Oprosnyi list Ezhova, N. I.," f. 9430, op. 1, d. 160, l. 6.

[40] *Stenograficheskii otchet fevral'sko-martovskogo plenuma TsK VKP(b) 1937 g.* See also *Voprosi istorii*, no. 2, 1992.

[41] *Tsentral'nyi arkhiv KGB*, "Zaiavlenie Bukharina N. I. na imia narkoma vnutrennikh del SSSR Ezhova N. I., 1 iiulia 1937g.

[42] An untranslatable pun. The expression "derzhat' v yezhovykh rukavisakh" means to rule with an iron rod.

try to limit the absolute power of the organs of state security? Until recently, this topic was off limits for Soviet historians. Now that the situation has changed, we can say that there was resistance. In the summer of 1937, while the June Central Committee Plenum was in session, the Commissar of Public Health, G. N. Kaminskii, spoke out against the groundless repression. In his speech, he took note of the illegalities and the arbitrariness that were going on in party organizations in the Caucasus and spoke out categorically against the proposed extraordinary powers and rights of the NKVD. On June 25, during the work of the plenum, Kaminskii was arrested by M. N. Frinovskii. He was accused of creating a rightist-Troskyist terrorist organization in the Commissariat of Public Health.[43]

I. A. Pyatnitskii, the head of the Central Committee's Political-Administrative Department spoke out against the implementation of repressive policies particularly sharply. He suggested that a special commission be created to check up on the work of the NKVD as a means of beginning to limit its power. Stalin interrupted the work of the plenum and, during the break, Molotov, Kaganovich, and Voroshilov tried to convince Pyatnitskii to retract his statement. All of these attempts, however, turned out to be unsuccessful. Then, during the next session, Ezhov suddenly accused Pyatnitskii of having been an agent provacateur since before the revolution and having installed Trotskyist-Bukharinist agents in the Comintern and the Communist parties of capitalist countries for a long time. At Stalin's suggestion, Pyatnitskii was given two weeks to defend himself against the substance of the accusations before the party. During this period of time, a political denunciation about Pyatnitskii was received from secretaries of the Moscow party raikoms, and also the necessary testimony was dragged out of Comintern officials who had been arrested previously. Ezhov personally arrested Pyatnitskii on June 7, and, within a year, Pyatnitskii was shot in accordance with his conviction for attempting to assassinate L. M. Kaganovich and for conducting espionage for Japan.

Other opposition to Ezhov manifested itself at the beginning of 1938. At that time, a large group of NKVD employees complained to the Central Committee about Ezhov. They accused him of illegal use of government funds and also of the secret execution of a number of prominent party members without investigation or a court examination. In January 1938, the Central Committee Plenum produced a resolution criticizing excessive vigilance. Prominent in the movement to criticize Ezhov's actions was A. A. Zhdanov, who played an important role in drafting the January 1938 resolution.

Although they had taken part in the repression, A. A. Zhdanov and A. A. Andreev began in spring and summer of 1938 to take an active role in criticizing its effects. In the Politburo, they complained about the low

[43] *TsGAOR SSSR*, "Materialy VTsIK o Kaminskom G. N."

quality and poor education of the new party leaders promoted as a result of the repression, pointing out that they were now forced to assign leading party workers to the oblasts and krais who had only secondary educations. They, along with K. E. Voroshilov, said that the repression had seriously begun to undermine the economic, cultural, and defence potential of the country.[44] Even Ezhov had been forced to promote "nonparty Bolsheviks" to leading posts in the NKVD bacause of the shortage of cadres.[45]

In order to increase his own authority, Ezhov initiated and organized his own assassination attempt. The terrorist act (mercury poisoning) was inspired by Ezhov personally and N. G. Zhurid-Nikolaev, the head of the counterespionage department of the NKVD. Having received a consultation on mercury poisoning, Nikolaev wiped the upholstery of the soft furniture in Ezhov's office with mercury, and then ordered an analysis. An NKVD employee, Sivolaynen, was accused of the assassination attempt. At the moment of his arrest in the entryway to his apartment building, he was tossed a jar of mercury. With the aid of torture, a "sincere confession" was dragged out of him.[46]

With the same aim of protecting himself, Ezhov initiated the plan to rename Moscow "Stalinodar" in the beginning of 1938. This aim inspired an appeal by all categories of workers to change Moscow's name. The question was raised at a session of the Presidium of the Supreme Soviet of the USSR. Stalin, however, reacted entirely negatively to this idea, and, for this reason, the city remained Moscow.[47]

Ezhov's position was weakened significantly in the summer of 1938. At that time, the poor preparation of postrepression cadres was again posed sharply by A. A. Zhdanov and A. A. Andreev in Politburo meetings in August 1938.[48] The defection of G. Liushkov, NKVD chief in the Far East, to Japan that month served to discredit Ezhov further. Liushkov was a trusted intimate of Ezhov's who had played an active part in organizing the Great Terror. His betrayal struck at the authority of Ezhov and served as the occasion for mass repression of the leadership group in the Far Eastern Krai. By August and September of 1938, L. M. Kaganovich and A. I. Mikoyan had joined A. A. Zhdanov and A. A. Andreev against Ezhov.

Relying on Stalin's support, Ezhov went too far and stopped taking the opinions of the other members of the Politburo and the Soviet government into account. In the summer of 1938, he had a run-in with the Chairman of the Sovnarkom (SNK), V. M. Molotov. In the course of a meeting of the SNK USSR, in answer to a question from Molotov, Ezhov suddenly announced:

[44] *TsPA*, f. 79, op. 1, d. 536, ll. 4–5, 5 oborot.
[45] *TsGAOR*, f. 9401, "Prikazy po lichnomu sostavu NKVD SSSR za 1937–1938gg."
[46] *TsPA*, "Lichnoe delo Ezhova, N. I."
[47] B. A. Starkov, "Kak Moskva chut'ne ne staia Stalinodarom," *Izvestiia Tsk KPSS*, 1990, no. 12.
[48] *TsPA*, f. 79, op. 1, d. 536, ll. 4–5, 5 oborot.

If I were in your place, Viacheslav Mikhailovich, I would not ask competent organs those kinds of questions. Do not forget that one previous Chairman of the Sovnarkom, A. I. Rykov, has already been in my office. The road to me is not off limits even for you.

V. M. Molotov interpreted this as a personal insult, and, at Stalin's suggestion, Ezhov submitted a personal apology.[49] Ezhov's authority was seriously shaken.

In August 1938, Ezhov was named Commissar of Water Transport while remaining Commissar of Internal Affairs. V. G. Filaretov and L. P. Beria were appointed Ezhov's new assistants without his preliminary agreement. At that time, the Sovnarkom took a series of decisions limiting the rights of the NKVD. The NKVD Special Boards were transferred to Sovnarkom and their composition increased by representatives of party organizations and the procuracy. The NKVD was forbidden to interfere in party personnel matters without the preliminary agreement of the relevant party committee. At that time, G. M. Malenkov, the chief of the Central Committee Department of Leading Party Organs made an active attack on Ezhov.

Ezhov's primary crime, however, consisted in the fact that he had not informed Stalin of his actions. Stalin ordered a commission headed by L. Z. Mekhlis, the chief of the Soviet Control Commission, to check into the work of the NKVD. During the brief period between September 13 and December 1, five resolutions about the work of the NKVD were passed by the Party Central Committee: on September 1, "Changes in the Structure of the NKVD;" on September 23, "About the Structure of the NKVD;" on October 14, "On the Examination and Confirmation of the Workers of the NKVD;" on November 17, "About the Arrests, the Supervision of the Prosecutor, and the Conduct of Investigations;" and on December 1, "About the Procedure for Conducting Arrests." The last two resolutions were passed together with the Sovnarkom of the USSR.[50]

In the fall of 1938, when the question arose of removing Ezhov from his position at NKVD, Stalin proposed the candidacy of G. M. Malenkov as the new Commissar of Internal Affairs. But a majority of the Politburo recommended L. P. Beria for the post.[51] Finally, Ezhov was fired from his post of Peoples' Commissar of Internal Affairs. On November 26, the new Peoples' Commissar of Internal Affairs, L. P. Beria, signed an order that brought the resolutions that had been passed by the Central Committee since November 17, 1938, into effect.[52]

[49] *TsGAOR SSSR*, "Materialy NKVD SSSR za 1938g."
[50] *Arkhiv TsK KPSS*, "Postanovleniia Politbiuro TsK VKP(b) 1938g."
[51] *Arkhiv Obshchego otdela TsK KPSS*, "Materialy Sekretariata TsK VKP(b) noyabr'–dekabr' 1938g." See also the speech of M. I. Kalinin to the party activists of the NKVD in December, 1938: *TsGAOR SSSR*, f. 9491, "Materialy partiinogo aktiva NKVD SSSR dekabr' 1938g–ianvar' 1939g."
[52] *TsGAOR*, "Prikazy po NKVD SSSR za 1938g."

The star of the all-powerful Ezhov had fallen. During his last months, he stayed away from his office and, claiming illness, accepted reports at home. He bowed out of participating in the sessions of the Politburo and the Sovnarkom unless Stalin was present. Certain sources assert that he began to drink too much. Ezhov was seen for the last time in February 1939 on the Presidium of a meeting commemorating the death of V. I. Lenin. Soon he was arrested and charged with "leftist overreaction." The next purge of the NKVD began at the same time. His assistants, the heads of departments, and his closest henchmen were arrested. There is evidence that Ezhov was held in the Sukhanov prison, and that Beria personally interrogated him. On February 4, 1940, Ezhov was finally convicted and shot. According to one story, Ezhov died saying, "Long live Stalin." His daughter was sent to a special orphanage for children of "enemies of the people" and was exiled to Magadan when she reached adulthood. Thus ended the career of one of the most terrible figures in Soviet history.

Ezhov's fall and Beria's assumption of the leadership of the NKVD did not, however, bring an end to the Great Terror. Despite expectations, rehabilitations did not take place, and only a partial amnesty was granted in connection with a number of cases that were dropped. L. P. Beria was the first professional policeman to serve as the head of the organs of State Security. In 1939 and 1940 the repression continued. Now headquarters concentrated upon work with agents and informers. The totalitarian regime could not exist without relying on the terror of illegal, mass repression. Beria eventually became the same kind of executor of Stalin's orders that Ezhov had been. He was just smarter, more devious, and more lacking in principle, when pursuing his mercenary aims.

2

The politics of repression revisited

J. Arch Getty

Every national history has its oral tradition. Like folklore, such traditions relate popularly accessible histories without reference to documentary analysis or other tools of the trade of professionally trained historians. Sometimes they are based on self-attesting personal accounts and memoirs, on logical constructs of "what must have happened," or on simple repetition of seemingly authoritative stories of unknown origin. The ideas that Franklin Roosevelt wanted the Japanese to attack Pearl Harbor, that Adolf Hitler did not know about the Holocaust, or that modern history is manipulated by huge but secret conspiracies (organized by Elders of Zion, Masons, or other secret fraternities) are examples of such traditions. Oral historical traditions are persistent, often surviving in the face of contradictory sources and evidence, because they are simple, comfortable, or tantalizing. Sometimes, of course, they can be true.

Russian history has always provided fertile soil for such folkloric history. The last thousand years are filled with tsars secretly living out their final years as monks, heirs to the throne spirited away from death at the last minute by loyal nannies, and a perhaps inordinate number of secret conspiracies. The obsessive secrecy of the Soviet regime further stimulated the oral tradition. Stories about Stalin have circulated at least since the 1920s and include aspects of his genealogy (he was said to be descended from Georgian or Ossetian princes), personal life (secret wives, amorous ballerinas, and illegitimate children in the Kremlin), and the circumstances of his youth and death. Even at this writing, characterizations of Bolshevism as a Jewish conspiracy are routinely heard even in educated circles in Moscow.[1]

Given Russian cultural traditions, there is nothing particularly unusual about such folklore. What should be surprising is that so much of the oral tradition has found its way into the corpus of scholarly literature. Second-

---

[1] In late 1991, the author was told in Moscow that Stalin's father was really Alexander Prlszewski, the Siberian biologist after whom the famous diminutive horse is named.

hand personal memoirs, gossip, novels, and lurid accounts by defecting spies eager to earn a living in the West are soberly reviewed in scholarly journals, cited in footnotes, and recommended to graduate students. Fictionalized "letters of old bolsheviks," political histories with invented Stalin soliloquies, and even dramatic plays are routinely incorporated into academic treatments in ways that would be laughable in other national historical studies.[2]

Glasnost' and the collapse of the Communist Party have put the secretive history of Stalinism on a more evidentially sound footing. Archives began to open; official and unofficial document collections were published. After some years, detailed empirical studies of important aspects of the phenomenon have begun to appear.[3] Doors and windows are now opening in the former Soviet Union. This essay reevaluates the oral tradition in light of new documentation on two points that have sparked considerable controversy: the assassination of Kirov and the presumed planned origins of the Great Purges. It is too early in our source investigation conclusively to solve these problems; our purpose is rather to compare the traditional views with currently available documentation.

Especially since 1987, new information about political events in the 1930s has been surfacing in the former Soviet Union, and various historians in the West have been claiming vindication for their interpretations. What do we know that we did not know before? First, we have an abundance of gruesome new details. We know that there is human blood splattered on Marshal Tukhachevskii's "confession." We know that Zinoviev denounced Kamenev, that Ezhov would not permit Piatakov to execute his own wife, and that M. Riutin never capitulated to his interrogators. In addition, we now have confirmation on several details of Stalin's participation in the repression. We know, for example, that he personally edited the lists of defendants and their statements for the 1936 and 1937 show trials, adding some and removing others. He attended "confrontations" staged by Ezhov between arrested officials and their accusers. He helped draft the indictments of Marshall Tukhachevskii and his fellow military defendants, chose the composition of their court, and personally ordered death sentences for them. (Indeed he signed numerous death sentences, including a record 3,167 on December 12, 1938.) We also know that Stalin personally

---

[2] I have discussed this problem in connection with older "sources" in *Origins of the Great Purges: The Soviet Communist Party Reconsidered, 1933–1938*, New York, 1985, 211–220. For more recent examples of invented dialog, see Anatoli Rybakov, *Children of the Arbat*, trans. by Harold Shukman, Boston, 1988; Anton Antonov-Ovseyenko, *The Time of Stalin: Portrait of Tyranny*, New York, 1980; Mikhail Shatrov, "Dal'she, dal'she, dal'she", *Znamia*, no. 1, 1988. A compilation of folklore about Stalin is presented in Iurii Borev, *Staliniada*, Moscow, 1990.

[3] See A. V. Afanas'ev, ed., *Oni ne molchali*, Moscow, 1991; and A. N. Mertsalov, ed., *Istoriia i stalinizm*, Moscow, 1991; O. V. Khlevniuk, *1937-i: Stalin, NKVD i sovetskoe obshchestvo*, Moscow, 1992; B. A. Starkov, ed., *Na koleni ne vstanu*, Moscow, 1992, for examples of serious, evidence-based historical monographs.

ɔcked attempts to lighten the prison regimen or to allow exiles to return home after completing their sentences, and he sponsored the persecution of his enemies' innocent family members.[4] In the fall of 1937, he approved a plan to summarily shoot tens of thousands of "anti-Soviet elements" and to establish target figures for the shootings by province.[5] As Stalin privately told Georgi Dmitrov, head of the Comintern, in 1937,

Whoever tries to break the unity of the socialist state, whoever hopes to separate from it specific parts or nationalities, is a sworn enemy of the state, of the peoples of the USSR. And we will destroy any such enemy, even if he is an old Bolshevik, we will destroy his kin, his family. [We will destroy] anyone who by his actions or thoughts, yes even thoughts, encroaches on the unity of the socialist state.[6]

Russians are still struggling with the myth that Stalin somehow did not know what was happening. For decades, this was part of an oral tradition that was rationalization and consolation for millions who otherwise found it difficult to reconcile their own fates with their admiration of him as a strong leader. Most of the new material seems presented to make two points long accepted in the West: that the terror was widespread and that Stalin had a personal role in it. Virtually all of the latest historical revelations are aimed at illustrating these points and the documents presented seem chosen with this in mind. For us in the West, this is knocking at an open door; there has never been any question about his responsibility for the terror or participation in it from 1937. Nevertheless, the factual material that is coming to light on the preceding period, the "origins" of the terror, is quite interesting and raises as many questions as it answers.

The Kirov affair

The standard view of Stalinist prepurge politics in the thirties, derived from an oral tradition, runs roughly as follows. At the end of the first Five-Year Plan (1932), a majority of the Politburo favored relaxation and reconciliation with political opponents. Led by Leningrad party chief Serge

---

[4] See the accounts in *Izvestiia TsK KPSS*, no. 4, 1989, 42–73; no. 8, 1989, 78–94; no. 9, 1989, 30–50; and Dmitri Volkogonov, *Triumf i tragediia*, Moscow, 1989, vol. 1, part 2, 301 and passim. The present essay does not use the vast corpus of writings from *publitsisty* (journalists) that has appeared since 1985 in *Moscow News, Ogonek, Novyi mir*, and other journals. This material is almost always presented without footnotes, documents, or citations and it is impossible to verify the sources of information. Other opinions exist on the question; for works that incorporate such material see Robert C. Tucker, *Stalin in Power: The Revolution from Above, 1928–1941*, New York, 1990, and Robert Conquest, *The Great Terror: Stalin's Purge of the Thirties* (revised edition), Oxford, 1990.

[5] "Rasstrel po raznariadke," *Trud*, June 4, 1992, 1. See also "Iosif Stalin: 'Vinovnykh sudit' uskorenno. PRIGOVOR–rasstrel,'" *Izvestiia*, June 10, 1992, 7.

[6] From the personal archive of Comintern specialist F. I. Firsov, based on his archival notes from Dmitrov's diary. The author is deeply grateful to Professor Firsov for sharing his encyclopedic knowledge of repression in the Comintern.

Kirov, this group of Stalinist "moderates" opposed Stalin's plans to apply the death penalty to dissident party members. Stalin is believed to have argued in the Politburo for imposition of the death penalty on adherents of the "Riutin Platform," a document conceived and circulated by rightist Bolshevik M. Riutin. The Kirov faction is said to have blocked this bloody suggestion.[7] Stalin became fearful as the moderates gained strength and as Kirov established a reputation for a softer line. At the Seventeenth Party Congress in 1934, Kirov's optimistic and liberal speech evoked huge ovations. More threatening to Stalin, the delegates to the Congress apparently gave Kirov more votes than Stalin in the pro forma elections to the Central Committee. A large number of anti-Stalin ballots had to be destroyed and the voting results falsified to avoid embarrassment.[8]

After that, Stalin planned to eliminate the popular Kirov, whose standing made him a direct rival. Stalin ordered the secret police (NKVD) to arrange Kirov's assassination. Leningrad Deputy NKVD Chief Ivan Zaporozhets chose one Leonid Nikolaev, a frustrated and bitter party member, to kill Kirov. Zaporozhets won Nikolaev's trust, gave him a revolver, and helped him stalk his victim by informing him of Kirov's habits. He even secured Nikolaev's release on three occasions when watchful policemen stopped the armed assassin for suspicious behavior. Finally, on December 1, 1934, Zaporozhets arranged for Kirov's bodyguard to be away from his charge in the corridor of Leningrad party head-quarters, and Nikolaev fatally shot Kirov outside the latter's office. Stalin, ready for the assassination, quickly traveled to Leningrad with most of the Politburo to supervise the investigation. Knowing in advance of the crime, Stalin had a list of conspirators to hand, consisting of former Leningrad supporters of Zinoviev. Kirov's bodyguard, who probably knew too much, died in a mysterious traffic accident on his way to talk to Stalin. At a personal interview with Stalin, Nikolaev cried out that the Leningrad NKVD had put him up to it. Stalin, angry at this lapse and at Zaporozhets's weak control over Nikolaev, then struck Zaporozhets in the presence of the other politburo members.[9]

Recent revelations, intended to show Stalin's personal participation in the repression, have paradoxically produced documents and factual evidence that disprove or contradict key elements of this story. The traditional understanding of Stalin's motive, means, and opportunity to

---

[7] See Tucker, *Stalin in Power*, 212, 238–242; Roy Medvedev, *Let History Judge: The Origins and Consequences of Stalinism* (revised edition), New York, 1989, 329–330.

[8] For example, Medvedev, *Let History Judge*, 331–332.

[9] This scenario of the Kirov affair comes to us almost entirely from two sources: the 1936 "Letter of an Old Bolshevik" (Boris I. Nicolaevsky, *Power and the Soviet Elite: "The Letter of an Old Bolshevik" and Other Essays*, New York, 1965), and NKVD defector Alexander Orlov's *Secret History of Stalin's Crimes*, New York, 1953. Virtually all versions of the story inside and outside the USSR can be traced to one of these two original presentations.

arrange Kirov's assassination, or indeed his supposed grand plan for terror, can no longer be comfortably reconciled with the sources now available. Indeed, professional historians in Russia writing the latest textbooks on Soviet history now consider that although Stalin certainly made use of the assassination, the question of his complicity is now open. The leading Russian specialists on opposition to Stalin similarly now make no judgment on the matter.[10]

The most important source for much of our speculation about politics in the 1930s was always the "Letter of an Old Bolshevik." Purporting to be Bukharin's 1936 reporting of Soviet events to Boris Nicolaevsky in Paris, this document is the origin and first evidence for the belief that Kirov represented some kind of liberal alternative to a hard-line Stalin in the early 1930s. This idea has been used to illustrate Stalin's long-term plan to destroy party opponents and to explain why Stalin found it necessary to organize the assassination of an obstructionist and "soft" Kirov. Every subsequent account that describes this scenario originates with the "Letter," which is an oft-cited foundation of the oral tradition.[11]

Some scholars have long questioned the validity of the "Letter" as a source.[12] With the *glasnost*'-era publication of the memoirs of Bukharin's widow, we find that his conversations with Nicolaevsky were purely official and took place in connection with unsuccessful negotiations to purchase some of Marx's manuscripts.[13] Anna Larina disputes Western misuse of the "Letter," and concludes that Nicolaevsky must have invented the document for political purposes. With her discrediting of the "Letter," the original source for an anti-Stalinist, moderate Kirov and for a Stalin opposing him is seriously weakened.

The idea of a soft Kirov was always problematic. Trotsky and the remnants of the Leningrad oppositionists certainly did not regard him as a liberal. Kirov had been Stalin's Leningrad point man during the savagery of collectivization and industrialization; he had supervised the rout of the left and right oppositions in his city. Under his leadership, the Leningrad party destroyed more churches than under either Zinoviev or Zhdanov. The Politburo Commission's examination of the Riutin group did not find

---

[10] S. V. Kulashov, O. V. Volobuev, E. I. Pivovar, et al., *Nashe otechestvo. chast' II*, Moscow, 1991, 310; Boris A. Starkov, "Ar'ergardnye boi staroi partiinoi gvardii," in Afanas'ev, ed., *Oni ne molchali*, 215; Khlevniuk, 1937, 46.

[11] For a recent example of Moscow-based historians quoting such Western stories, see B. A. Starkov, "Delo Riutina," in Afanas'ev, ed., *Oni ne molchali*, 170.

[12] Roy A. Medvedev, *Nikolay Bukharin*, New York, 1980, 115–118; Robert H. McNeal, *Stalin: Man and Ruler*, New York, 1988, 355; Jerry Hough and Merle Fainsod, *How the Soviet Union Is Governed*, Cambridge, MA, 1979, 159–160; Getty, *Origins*, 214–216.

[13] Anna Larina, *Nezabyvaemoe*, Moscow, 1989, 272–289. Of course, Larina's account, written fifty years after the event, should not be uncritically accepted as gospel on the matter. Still, her evidence supports the mounting criticisms of the "Letter" made by Western historians.

any evidence that Stalin demanded their execution in 1932, or that Kirov opposed it.[14]

Kirov's speech to the 1934 Party Congress, often taken as a sign of his liberalism, actually praised the secret police's use of forced labor and ridiculed the opposition.[15] The thunderous applause Kirov received is sometimes used to show that he was more popular than Stalin. But Kirov was identified with Stalin, and the parts of his speech producing general ovations were the parts in which he praised Stalin and abused the opposition. Applause for him and his accomplishments in Leningrad was rare and only polite.[16] Careful scrutiny of Kirov's speeches and writings reveals little difference between them and Stalin's utterances, and Soviet scholars familiar with closed party archives scoff at the notion that Kirov was a moderate, an opponent of Stalin, or the leader of any bloc.[17]

Even if he were not a liberal, perhaps Kirov's popularity worried or threatened Stalin, who feared a rival. But V. M. Molotov, when asked by an interviewer whether Kirov posed a threat or alternative to Stalin, replied contemptuously, "Kirov? A mere agitator."[18] It has become part of sovietological lore, nevertheless, that 300 delegates voted against Stalin at the Seventeenth Party Congress in 1934, and that Kirov received many more votes than Stalin.[19] This story originated with the testimony of ballot counting official V. M. Verkhovykh, who said in 1960 that "125 or 123" ("I do not remember exactly") delegates voted against Stalin. He said that the embarrassing ballots were destroyed, and that the other members of the ballot commission knew of the destruction and falsification of the results. (Stalin was then officially reported to have received only three negative votes, of a total of 1,059.) In recently published sections of his

[14] *Izvestiia TsK*, no. 6, 1989, 103–115; no. 3, 1990, 150–178.
[15] *XVII s"ezd Vsesoiuznoi Kommunisticheskoi Partii (b) 27 ianvaria–10 fevralia 1934g: stenograficheskii otchet*, Moscow, 1934, 252, 253–259. Leon Trotsky, *The Revolution Betrayed*, New York, 1937, 286; Grigori Tokaev, *Betrayal of an Ideal*, Bloomington, 1955, 241, *Sotsialisticheskii vestnik*, no. 8, April 1934, 19.
[16] "Vokrug ubiistva Kirova," *Pravda*, Nov. 4, 1991, 4; and *XVII s"ezd*, 251–259.
[17] Personal communications to the author from Boris A. Starkov and Oleg Khlevniuk. See also Francesco Benvenuti, "Kirov in Soviet Politics, 1933–1934," Discussion Paper no. 8, Soviet Industrialization Project Series, University of Birmingham, 1977. The memoir of one of Kirov's Leningrad co-workers can remember nothing from his experience with Kirov that suggests "liberal" opposition to Stalin: See Mikhail Rosliakov, "Kak eto bylo," *Zvezda*, no. 7, 1989, 79–113.
[18] D. Volkogonov, "Triumf i tragediia," *Oktiabr'*, no. 12, Dec. 1988, 81, probably taken from F. Chuev's purported interviews with Molotov (*Sto sorok besed s Molotovym*, Moscow, 1991, 308, 322, 353). Molotov used the word *massovik* to describe Kirov. The authenticity of Chuev's book rests on a series of recorded tapes he made with Molotov. The tapes have not been scientifically authenticated, and Molotov's general veracity is of course questionable.
[19] Various versions of the story give 282, 123, 125, 2–4, 5–6, or 3, as the number voting against Stalin. See L. S. Shaumian's "Na rubezhe pervykh piatiletok. K 30-letiiu XVII s"ezda partii," *Pravda*, Feb. 7, 1964, where the number 300 is given.

memoirs, Anastas Mikoian repeated the rumor that he heard only in the 1950s, although he had been a leader at the 1934 Congress.

Although one of the 1960 special commissions charged with investigating the Kirov assassination looked into the archives, it concluded that 166 delegates simply "did not take part in the voting." In 1989, there was *another* investigation into the 1934 voting that found that other surviving members of the ballot counting commission had contradicted Verkhovykh's story even back in 1960. They would have known of such a ballot discrepancy, and it was presumably safe for them to reveal the story in the first heyday of anti-Stalinism, but none of the other participants would confirm it. The 1989 investigation concluded that 166 ballots were indeed missing, but because the number of original paper ballots is unknown, "it is impossible definitely to confirm" how many may have voted against Stalin.[20] The evidence is still inconclusive; Stalin may indeed have regarded Kirov as a dangerous rival.

Olga Shatunovskaia has recently written that the Kirov investigation in the 1960s had uncovered convincing evidence that Stalin was behind the assassination.[21] She also revived the story that hundreds voted against Stalin at the Seventeenth Congress, and claimed that materials from the 1960 investigation have since been removed by Party Control Commission (KPK) personnel in order to change that investigation's conclusion. Yet in 1989, investigators checked the earlier commission's documents against KPK and KGB files and concluded that nothing is missing from the earlier collection. They also found that as a Khrushchev-backed KPK investigator back in 1960, Shatunovskaia had not concluded that anyone had voted against Stalin and at that time agreed with the conclusion that Stalin had not organized the killing; she agreed that Leonid Nikolaev was a lone assassin.[22]

The latest attempt to come to grips with the Kirov assassination was the work of A. Iakovlev's Politburo Commission, which in 1989 appointed an interagency investigative team consisting of personnel from the USSR Procurator's Office, the Military Procuracy, the KGB, and various archival administrations. For two years, this team conducted interviews, reviewed thousands of documents, and attempted to check all possible scenarios; their work has added another fifteen volumes to the thirty-year-old efforts.[23] Like all of the other research efforts organized by the Politburo Commission to probe aspects of the repression for publication in *Izvestiia*

[20] *Izvestiia TsK*, no. 7, 1989, 114–121.
[21] O. Shatunovskaia, "Fal'sifikatsiia," *Argumenty i fakty*, no. 22, 1990.
[22] *Izvestiia TsK*, no. 7, 1989, 120; "Vokrug ubiistva Kirova," 4. Shatunovskaia claims to have been in close contact with Khrushchev at the time and thus presumably could not easily have been pressured to vote against her conscience.
[23] We now know that there were at least two investigations in the 1960s: the Pel'she Commission and the Shvernik Commission. A. Iakovlev, "O dekabr'skoi tragedii 1934 goda," *Pravda*, Jan. 28, 1991, p. 3.

TsK, the team's charter was to show Stalin's complicity in the repression. It had little political incentive to let him off the hook; quite the contrary. Nevertheless, members of the working team concluded that "in this affair, no materials objectively support Stalin's participation or NKVD participation in the organization and carrying out of Kirov's murder."[24]

The team's report opened some rather large holes in the popular version. According to the oral tradition, Leningrad NKVD Deputy Chief Zaporozhets had approached assassin Nikolaev, put him up to the crime, and provided the weapon and bullets. It now seems that Zaporozhets had not been in Leningrad for months before the killing and that he never met Nikolaev.[25] Nikolaev had owned the revolver in question since 1918 and had registered it legally in 1924 and again in 1930. He had purchased the bullets used in the crime legally, with his registration, back in 1930. Contrary to the popular version, Nikolaev was not detained three times while carrying a gun and following Kirov, and then mysteriously released by the Leningrad NKVD. Actually, he had been stopped only once, on October 15, 1934, and the circumstances at that time were not suspicious. A frustrated apparatchik with delusions of grandeur and lifelong chronic medical problems, Nikolaev wrote in his diary that he wanted to be a great revolutionary terrorist.[26]

The Politburo Commission's team also checked the origins of the rumors that Stalin was behind the crime. Most of them come from NKVD defector Alexander Orlov, whose celebrated *Secret History of Stalin's Crimes* has now been published in the former USSR. Contrary to the oral tradition (and published claims[27]) Orlov turns out not to be a highly placed NKVD general, but rather an ordinary investigator (with the rank of major) serving under an assistant chief of department. Orlov's story that assassin Nikolaev told Stalin the day after the killing that Zaporozhets had recruited him (and that Stalin then struck Zaporozhets) "does not correspond to reality," according to the team's report. Nikolaev had said no such thing; Zaporozhets did not return to Leningrad until days later. The team concludes that only "one-sided, superficial, unverified facts, rumors and conjectures" support Stalin complicity.[28] With the collapse of Orlov's always improbable version, much of the folklore of the Kirov murder falls apart.

The new point most incriminating to Stalin is that he was prepared to blame the opposition in the immediate aftermath of the assassination. In the very first days after the crime, Stalin eagerly told several people that

---

[24] "Vokrug ubiistva Kirova," 4.
[25] This would also explain why Zaporozhets received light punishment for negligence in the Kirov killing.
[26] "Vokrug ubiistva Kirova," 4.
[27] See A. Rybakov's introduction in *Ogonek*, no. 46, 1989.
[28] "Vokrug ubiistva Kirova," 4.

the assassin was a Zinovievist, even before arrests of them began.[29] The implication is that he anticipated the crime and was ready with a useful version of a conspiracy. This raises an old problem. Without doubt, Stalin used the Kirov assassination to move against the opposition. But the fact that he was immediately prepared to blame the Zinovievists does not show that he arranged Kirov's death. Indeed, if Stalin arranged the murder (and was as clever as we think he was) would he have been so foolish as to raise suspicion by pushing a prepared list so quickly?

We know that for more than a year before the Kirov assassination, the secret police (OGPU, then NKVD) had infiltrated Leningrad discussion circles, and their reports had convinced Ezhov and others that there was credible OGPU evidence of dangerous underground activity.[30] We also now know that the Leningrad NKVD handed Stalin such anti-Zinoviev agent reports (having to do with the alleged "Green Lamp" and "Svoiaki" operations) on December 2, the day after the assassination and the same day that he began telling people that Zinovievists were to blame.[31] Casting about for scapegoats in the wake of the assassination, it did not take Stalin long to fasten onto the former Zinovievists. Even then, the matter was not settled. Although their former followers were being rounded up, *Pravda* announced on December 23, 1934, that there was "insufficient evidence" to try Zinoviev and Kamenev for the crime.[32]

The 1991 results of the investigating team's work on the Kirov matter were not well received by the Politburo Commission's leadership, which suppressed their publication.[33] Stating that such results do not serve a useful political-historical purpose today, Politburo Commission chairman Iakovlev has accused the working group of following a "mainly juridical" approach.[34] Iakovlev notes that although the investigating team may be right, questions remain. He raises several points, some of which are indeed still unclear: What was the nature of Kirov's relation to Stalin? How did

---

[29] *Izvestiia TsK*, no. 7, 1989, 69; ibid., no. 1, 1990, 39. He told this to Ezhov, Kosarev (head of the Komsomol), Bukharin (editor of *Izvestiia*), and Mekhlis (editor of *Pravda*). See ibid., 65–93 for arrests of Zinovievists, which began on December 8 and which coincided with random shootings of former White Guards, already in prison.

[30] See the handling of the case of Ia. S. Tseitlin, former Leningrad Komsomol leader, related in *Izvestiia TsK*, no. 1, 1990, 50.

[31] Iakovlev, "O dekabr'skoi tragedii 1934 goda," 3. Of course, Stalin may have ordered preparation of such reports.

[32] *Pravda*, Dec. 23, 1934. A few days later, the regime changed its mind again, and Zinoviev and Kamenev were brought to trial the next month.

[33] "Vokrug ubiistva Kirova," 4. Iakovlev angrily charged that the investigating team had improperly leaked a memo he wrote to them: Iakovlev, "O dekabr'skoi tragedii 1934 goda," 1.

[34] Iakovlev wrote that a verdict on the Kirov matter is *mainly* important as an indicator of whether Stalin or socialism was to blame for the terror. "That is why knowing the truth means much more to us than merely satisfying our intellectual curiosity. That is why the question continues to retain political relevance." Iakovlev, "O dekabr'skoi tragedii 1934 goda," 4.

the assassin know Kirov's route? How did he reach the third floor of the Smolny? Was not Kirov's bodyguard with him at the time of the shooting, and why was the bodyguard killed before Stalin could question him?

Actually, some of these questions have been answered in the former Soviet Union. Anyone with a party card could be admitted to the third floor (Nikolaev had one). Neither the bodyguard nor his closest collaborators expected Kirov to come to Smolny that day; he had telephoned and said he was staying at home. Kirov arrived unexpectedly and ran into the unbalanced, gun-toting assassin, who was in Smolny that day not to ambush Kirov, but to secure a pass to the upcoming city party meeting. The assassin and his victim met by accident in Smolny; Nikolaev was not stalking Kirov.[35]

So the question remains, did Stalin organize the murder of Kirov? We still do not know. Since the beginning of *glasnost'*, the press has contained articles both pro and con. Some view Stalin's guilt as an established fact.[36] Others are more doubtful.[37] The well-known Khrushchev-era secret reports on the Kirov assassination have not been released. It would seem to be an easy thing to release or summarize their findings officially if they contained proof one way or the other.

According to the persistent oral tradition, Stalin had organized the assassination; only a few anomalies remained. Now, at least in the former Soviet Union, this assumption is not officially supported. The politburo's team has flatly contradicted it and both textbooks and scholarly articles have retreated from it. Of course, it may be that Stalin really instigated the murder. But the two main written accounts of his supposed machinations, from which all other texts derive, have now been shown to be spurious: Their secondhand stories are inconsistent with known facts about the circumstances of the crime. There was always reasonable doubt about Stalin's participation, and now there is more than before.

A planned terror?

According to the oral tradition, Stalin planned his terror and beginning in late 1934 carried it out in measured but sequential steps. The killing of Kirov led to the 1935 party purges (*chistki*), which in turn led to the condemnation of Zinoviev and Kamenev in 1936. Their show trial led in turn to that of Piatakov and Radek in January, the purge of the Red Army in mid-1937, and finally to the trial of Bukharin and Radek in 1938.

[35] Ibid. See Rosliakov ("Kak eto bylo"), who was a Kirov intimate present that day in Smolny. See also Kirilina, "Vystrely v Smolnom."
[36] See, for example, Rosliakov, "Kak eto bylo," 111–113.
[37] Anna Kirilina, "Vystrely v Smolnom," *Rodina*, no. 1, 1989, 33–78.

According to this view, Stalin knew where he was going from the beginning
and proceeded to orchestrate a crescendo of terror.

Of course, it is impossible for us to know conclusively what Stalin
thought and when. We must be guided by our inferences from known
events. If we look at the political history of the early 1930s, we find that
the Stalinist leadership frequently pursued initiatives that seemed to run
counter to a repressive policy. Beginning with Stalin's 1931 speech reha-
bilitating the old intelligentsia, a "moderate line" extended into 1933 with
a Stalin/Molotov telegram releasing large numbers of prisoners and with a
decision to reduce planned industrial targets in the Second Five-Year
Plan.[38] It continued in 1934 with the readmission and rehabilitation of
former oppositionists at the Seventeenth Party Congress and the abolition
of bread rationing at the end of that year. Indeed, at Stalin's initiative a
special commission of the Politburo was formed in 1934 to look into
excessive arrests and other misdeeds of the secret police. Among other
things, the commission, of which Stalin and Ezhov were members, drafted
a policy statement limiting the punitive rights of the dreaded Special
Conferences of the NKVD.[39] The commission's work was abruptly
terminated by the assassination of Kirov at the end of the year.[40]

But even after the assassination, the policy endured with the anti-Fascist
Popular Fronts, the announcement of the new constitution and a campaign
to expand party participation and political education as an alternative to
"administrative measures" or repression. A. A. Zhdanov's name is persistently associated with such "party revival" moves. His Leningrad
organization produced numerous resolutions calling for increased political
education and popular participation in party committees. He participated
in the 1934 Politburo Commission on excessive arrests and took the lead
in calling for the restoration to party membership of those expelled in the
1933–6 party purges; his idea was that errant party members should
be trained and nurtured, rather than expelled.[41] In June 1936, Stalin

---

[38] Within the Russian Federation the number of criminal sentences in 1934 was more than
    25% lower than the previous year. Verdicts against "counterrevolutionaries" numbered
    some 4,300 in 1934, a drop of over 50% from the previous year. Estimates based on P. H.
    Juviler, *Revolutionary Law and Order*, New York/London, 1976, 50, 52.

[39] *Rossiiskii tsentr khraneniia i izucheniia dokumentov noveishei istorii*, fond 17, opis 3
    (Politburo), delo 943, list 10 (for Stalin and Ezhov's participation), and f. 17, op. 3, d.
    954, l. 38 for the resulting "polozhenie" dated October 28, 1934. Compare its limited
    provisions to the more severe statement adopted in April of 1937: f. 17, op. 3, d. 986,
    l. 24. *RTsKhIDNI* is the recently renamed Central Party Archive (TsPA), Institut
    Marksizma-Leninizma. Because at this writing it is not clear which archival collections
    will ultimately be included in *RTsKhIDNI*, and because the following fond, opis, and delo
    numbers refer to the former *TsPA*, I shall hereafter cite this collection as *RTsKhIDNI*
    (TsPA).

[40] Kulashov et al., *Nashe otechestvo*, 309–310.

[41] One of the most famous of these was "Zadachakh partiino-organizatsionnoi i politiko-
    vospitatel'noi raboty," *Partiinoe stroitel'stvo*, no. 8, April 1935, 7–16. Its call for
    nurturing and promoting new cadres, collective leadership of party cells, and increased

interrupted Ezhov at a Central Committee Plenum to complain about so many party members being expelled:

EZHOV: Comrades, as a result of the verification of party documents, we expelled more than 200,000 members of the party.
STALIN: [interrupts] Very many.
EZHOV: Yes, very many. I will speak about this . . .
STALIN: [interrupts] If we expelled 30,000 . . . [inaudible remark], and 600 former Trotskyists and Zinovievists, it would be a bigger victory.
EZHOV: More than 200,000 members were expelled. Part of this number of party members, as you know, have been arrested.[42]

At about this time, Stalin wrote a letter to regional party secretaries complaining about their excessive "repression" of the rank and file.[43] This led to a national movement to reinstate expelled party members, on the eve of the Great Terror.

A campaign against bureaucratic practices in regional party organizations also attracted national visibility in 1935, when in a highly publicized attack, Zhdanov accused the Saratov kraikom of "dictatorship" and "repression." In 1936, the all-union discussion of the draft Constitution and even a decline in the population of the labor camps occurred.[44] At the February 1937 Central Committee Plenum, Zhdanov gave the keynote speech on democratizing party organizations, ending bureaucratic repression of "little people," and replacing the cooption of party leaders with grass-roots elections.[45] Indeed, under pressure of this line, contested secret-ballot *party* elections were held in 1937.

Terror and antiterror seem to have proceeded simultaneously. A good

participation were picked up and discussed around the country. See Smolensk Archive files WKP 322, p. 81, and WKP 89, p. 3. See also David Seibert, "Andrei Zhdanov and the Politics of Moderation," unpublished Ph.D. dissertation, University of California, Riverside, 1992.

[42] *RTsKhIDNI (TsPA)*, f. 17, op. 2, d. 568, ll. 135–136. Later in this plenum, Stalin spoke specifically on this question. Circumstantial evidence suggests that he was genuinely concerned that too many of the rank and file had been expelled because such large numbers of disaffected former members could become an embittered opposition. See *TsGAOR SSSR*, f. 3316, op. 40, d. 22, for a secondhand TsIK report on Stalin's speech. Perhaps because his soft remarks in 1936 were hard to reconcile with his hard sentiments of the following year, they were removed from the archive. According to the pagination, they once were in *RTsKhIDNI (TsPA)*, f. 17, op. 2, d. 568, ll. 460–472.

[43] *RTsKhIDNI (TsPA)*, f. 17, op. 21, d. 4091, l. 171.

[44] Getty, *Origins*, ch. 4. See J. Arch Getty, "State and Society Under Stalin: Constitutions and Elections in the 1930s," *Slavic Review*, 50:1, Spring 1991, 18–35 for a discussion of the importance of the new constitution to these developments. For the decrease in GULAG population, see V. Zemskov, "Arkhipelag GULAG: glazami pisatelia i statistika," *Argumenty i fakty*, no. 45, 1989.

[45] *RTsKhIDNI (TsPA)*, f. 17, op. 2, d. 612, ll. 3–10, and Pravda, June 12, 1935. See also Zhdanov's mass-circulation pamphlet, *Uroki politicheskikh oshibok Saratovskogo kraikoma*, Moscow, 1935. See also "The preparation of party organizations for elections to the USSR Supreme Soviet under the new electoral system and the corresponding reorganization of party political work," *Pravda*, Mar. 6, 1937.

example of this ambiguity is the strange story of the fall, rise, and fall of Avel' Enukidze, Secretary of the Central Executive Committee of Soviets. As is known, Enukidze was attacked at the June 1935 Plenum of the Central Committee, when he was denounced by Ezhov for laxity and for protecting "enemies" within the service apparatus of the Kremlin. Often seen as a landmark in the escalation of the terror, the Enukidze Affair seemed to represent the first political attack on an "Old Bolshevik" with no oppositionist past.

Actually, the affair was more complicated. Ezhov did indeed deliver a blistering attack on Enukidze, complete with "testimony" from the latter's arrested subordinates. Ezhov argued that these Kremlin conspirators had planned to assassinate Stalin as part of a Trotskyist-Zinovievist conspiracy (said to have been an outgrowth of the recent Kirov assassination), and that Enukidze's lax attitude toward them made him at least negligent. Secondarily, he accused Enukidze of having used official funds to provide support to the families of certain Old Bolsheviks exiled by the Stalin regime. Enukidze defended himself by noting that although there were of course enemies in his apparatus, the same could be said of all Soviet agencies, including the NKVD itself. He noted that his personal control over his employees was neither better nor worse than that of other top leaders.[46]

More interesting is the plenum's reaction to Ezhov's charges. Ezhov had concluded his remarks by formally proposing Enukidze's expulsion from the party Central Committee. But several of the speakers who followed Ezhov called for sterner penalties. Beria, Shkiriatov, and Akulov, for example, said that the officially proposed and approved expulsion from the Central Committee was not enough; Enukidze should be expelled from the party.[47] NKVD chief Iagoda, who is sometimes seen as being soft on persecution of party officials, called not only for Enukidze's expulsion from the party, but for his arrest and conviction: "It is necessary to say that Enukidze not only facilitated the enemy, but that objectively he was also a sympathizer with counterrevolutionary terrorists."[48]

Although it is possible that this was all part of a Stalin game to use others as stalking horses of repression, Stalin and his team seem rather to have been unprepared for this escalation of the attack on Enukidze. For his part, Stalin's comments on the speeches were limited to criticizing Enukidze's use of state funds to aid exiles, noting that Enukidze could have innocently used his own money for this without censure. His interjections never touched on the political side of the accusations, never supported Ezhov's terrorist characterization (or Iagoda's strong remedies),

---

[46] *RTsKhIDNI (TsPA)*, f. 17, op. 2, d. 542, ll. 55–86 for Ezhov's report; and ll. 125–141 for Enukidze's defense.

[47] Ibid., 87, 107, 120.

[48] Ibid., 175.

and were, in general, not particularly hostile.[49] L. M. Kaganovich then recounted to the plenum the Politburo's deliberations on proper punishment for Enukidze. He noted that at first Stalin had suggested only removing him from the national TsIK (*Tsentral'nyĭ Ispolnitel'nyĭ Komitet*, Central Executive Committee) and sending him to run the TsIK of the Transcaucasus. Then, when the matter seemed more serious (possibly after another Ezhov report to the Politburo), Stalin had agreed to remove Enukidze from the TsIK system altogether and to send him to run a resort in Kislovodsk, concluding that expulsion from the Central Committee was in fact warranted "to make an example." Kaganovich took no position on the newly proposed harsher punishments, but his remarks suggested that Ezhov's softer proposal had been thought out ahead of time.[50]

Finally, at the end of the plenum, the matter came to a vote. Ezhov's original, officially approved proposal (to expel Enukidze only from the Central Committee) passed unanimously. Then they voted on "a second suggestion by a series of speakers, as a supplement," to expel Enukidze from the party. This proposal passed, "by a majority" in show of hands.[51]

But, oddly enough, Enukidze's surprise expulsion from the party was not the end of the story. Exactly one year later, at the June 1936 Plenum of the Central Committee, the Enukidze affair resurfaced. Molotov, who was chairing the meeting, said that at the beginning of 1936, Enukidze had applied for readmission to the party. That had been too soon for consideration (Stalin interjected: "That would have been to expel him at one plenum and accept him at the next."). After Molotov observed that readmitting him would make Enukidze very happy, and after Stalin spoke in favor, the plenum voted to approve his readmission.[52]

In a final contradictory twist, though, Enukidze was never readmitted to the party. Shortly after the June 1936 approval, Enukidze applied for a party card to a primary party organization in Kharkov and was accepted. But two months later, his acceptance was overturned by the Kharkov City Party Organization.[53] The main event between approval of his readmission and rejection of it was Ezhov's ascension to leadership of the secret police. Apparently, Stalin changed his mind once again about Enukidze, and it is possible that Ezhov's new power in the fall of 1936 gave him the possibility to make his original attack stick once and for all. Enukidze was arrested and shot in 1937.

[49] Ibid., 165, 170, for example.
[50] *RTsKhIDNI (TsPA)*, f. 17, op. 2, d. 547, l. 66.
[51] Ibid., 70. Unfortunately, the actual vote was not recorded.
[52] *RTsKhIDNI (TsPA)*, f. 17, op. 2, d. 568, ll. 165–168. Again, Stalin's 1936 remarks may have seemed incompatible with his hard line of the following year; his remarks were removed from the archive. Formerly, they were ibid., l. 167.
[53] *RTsKhIDNI (TsPA)*, f. 17, op. 21, d. 5258. For a Gorbachev-era account of the Enukidze affair, which manages not to mention the strange twists of Enukidze's fate, see *Izvestiia TsK*, no. 7, 1989, 86–93.

In this atmosphere of contradictory initiatives, consider as well the strange story of the fall of Iu. Piatakov at about the same time.[54] In mid-1936, Stalin decided to bring Zinoviev, Kamenev, and others to trial on capital charges. Even though the defendants included other ex-Trotskyists, Piatakov was appointed to be one of the state's prosecution witnesses (*obvinitel'*). But on August 10, in connection with ongoing searches and interrogations, Iagoda and Ezhov uncovered "evidence" of Piatakov's connection to "enemies" and immediately sent it to Stalin. Ezhov then confronted Piatakov on August 11, telling him that because of this compromising material, Stalin had decided to remove him as one of the prosecution's helpers; on the same day, Ezhov drafted an order for Stalin to sign appointing Piatakov chief of the Chirchikstroi construction project.[55] Nevertheless, in the course of the Zinoviev-Kamenev trial, Piatakov was indeed mentioned as a possible conspirator by one of the defendants. But by the time the court transcript was published, Piatakov's name had again disappeared as a culprit.[56] Thus, in the course of one month, Piatakov had gone from trial accuser to construction director to potential trial defendant to a mysterious limbo. Someone had changed his mind more than once.

During this time, a confused and desperate Piatakov hardly displayed moderation or humanism; he told Ezhov that he was willing personally to execute Zinoviev, Kamenev, and even his (Piatakov's) former wife, should they turn out to be guilty! He wrote to Stalin on the same date, pledging his loyalty and repeating his dramatic offer, which Ezhov characterized as "absurd."[57]

Stalin did not finally decide on Piatakov's arrest until September 12, when he sanctioned his expulsion from the party and arrest. Even then, as Ezhov was arresting economic managers and grilling Piatakov, Stalin's Central Committee secretariat was ordering Ezhov to release several high-ranking industrial leaders.[58] One hand seemed not to know what the other was doing.

There can be several possible explanations for such zigging and zagging. First, Stalin may simply have been trying to project an image of liberalism

---

[54] A Trotskyist in the 1920s, Piatakov had broken with the left opposition and in the 1930s had been working in industry. In mid-1936, he was Ordzhonikidze's Deputy Commissar of Heavy Industry.

[55] *Izvestiia TsK*, no. 9, 1989, 36–37. This was another strange appointment if Stalin *planned* to later accuse Piatakov of industrial wrecking, which ultimately he would do two months later. Technically, of course, the appointment of the "industrial wrecker" Piatakov to head a construction project made Stalin guilty of wrecking, according to the mores of the time.

[56] Conquest, *Great Terror*, 102.

[57] *Izvestiia TsK*, no. 9, 1989, 36–37.

[58] See O. V. Khlevniuk, "1937 god: protivodeistvie repressiiam," in Afanas'ev, ed., *Oni ne molchali*, 26–27. Khlevniuk believes that this liberalism took place when Stalin was out of town, but it is difficult to believe that Central Committee Secretariat orders to Ezhov could have been issued without Stalin's initiative or approval.

to cover his administration of terror. That would certainly have been a wise policy for him, and it is difficult to believe that it is not at least part of the explanation. But several facts mitigate against it as the complete answer.

First, Stalin clearly and publicly associated himself with the hunt for enemies after the February 1937 Plenum of the Central Committee, thus destroying any reputation he might have been building as a liberal. We now know that there was resistance to the growing terror on the parts of some low-level functionaries.[59] Stalin's liberal 1934–7 measures zigging and zagging away from terror would have sent the "wrong signals" and would have supported those trying to *block* repression. That would seem to be counterproductive to a careful Stalin plan for terror.

Another explanation might be based on the existence of a high-level, antirepression Stalinist faction, variously said to consist of Kirov, Ordzhonikidze, Kuibyshev, Postyshev, and others, that attempted to block the designs of Stalin, Ezhov, Kaganovich, and Molotov. The contradictory twists and turns are thus explained by Stalin probing and retreating in the face of antipolice sentiment in the politburo.[60]

The trouble here is that anti-Ezhov liberals in high places are hard to find before the main onslaught of the terror in mid-1937.[61] As we have seen, Kirov is a poor candidate for moderation. Ordzhonikidze, for his part, tried to defend his own subordinates (particularly industrial managers) against Ezhov's depredations and there are persistent but dubious stories that he tried to intercede for Piatakov.[62] Although his lieutenants invoked his name posthumously with the claim that he had opposed the hunt for enemies in industry,[63] Ordzhonikidze does not seem to have objected to terror in general, including that directed against Zinoviev, Kamenev, and Bukharin, and was in fact asked by Stalin to give the main speech on wrecking in industry to the February 1937 Plenum of the Central Committee.[64]

[59] See Afanas'ev, ed., *Oni ne molchali*, for cases of resistance and reluctance by some mid- and junior-level procurators, army, and even police officers.

[60] Robert Conquest, *The Great Terror: A Reassessment*, New York, 1990, is the best presentation of this view. See especially Chapters 4–6.

[61] Later, in June 1937, Central Committee members Piatnitskii and Kaminskii spoke against Ezhov, but by then the terror was in full swing and they were swept away in short order. See B. A. Starkov's "Narkom Ezhov" in this volume.

[62] See Khlevniuk, *1937*, 115–144, although Khlevniuk notes that there is no documentary evidence that Ordzhonikidze tried to save Piatakov. See also *RTsKhIDNI (TsPA)*, f. 17, op. 2, d. 573, l. 33, for Ordzhonikidze's telegram "completely approving and voting yes" on the question of Piatakov's expulsion from the party in September 1936. Similarly, shortly after Piatakov's execution, Ordzhonkidze told a meeting of his department heads that "damned Piatakov" had been a real enemy and that they must be continually vigilant: *RTsKhIDNI (TsPA)*, f. 85, op. 29, d. 156, ll. 56–63.

[63] *RTsKhIDNI (TsPA)*, f. 17, op. 2, d. 612, tom. 2, l. 39 (Gurevich's speech to the February 1937 Plenum); and Khlevniuk, "1937 god: protivodeistvie repressiiam."

[64] The draft of the speech Ordzhonkidze was preparing to give to the February 1937 Plenum, as chief reporter on wrecking in industry, was approved by Stalin and was in

P. P. Postyshev, who according to the oral tradition stood up at the February Plenum in protest against Ezhov, actually interrupted the latter's February 1937 remarks several times with cries of "Right!"[65] In fact, he would be expelled from the party a year later for being too fierce in his hunt for enemies in the Ukraine.[66] Similarly, rumors that S. V. Kosior, who would be shot the following year, was some kind of closet Bukharinist turn out to be false: At the February 1937 Plenum, he was one of the most vociferous supporters of the Ezhov line.[67] As of this writing, no evidence has been found for a moderate bloc, the influence of which might explain Stalin's strange zigs and zags on the eve of the *Ezhovshchina*. Evidence from the December 1936 and February 1937 Central Committee plenums suggests that no speaker defended the victims of Ezhov and his NVKD.

We must therefore at least entertain a third possible explanation, that the confused and contradictory evolution of the repression before mid-1937 was the product of indecision and chaos. For example, the decision to destroy N. I. Bukharin also followed strange and contradictory twists and turns. Although Ordzhonikidze may have slowed down the attack on industrial leaders, nobody seems to have opposed the crushing of Bukharin and it is difficult to credit the delays to anyone but Stalin.

Bukharin had come under official suspicion until August 1936, when Ezhov initiated the process in a letter to Stalin suggesting that former rightists were implicated in the Zinovievist-Trotskyist "plot." Ezhov asked Stalin's permission to reinterrogate Uglanov, Riutin, and other rightists already sentenced on other charges. Stalin agreed.[68] During August and September, Ezhov worked diligently to assemble "evidence" against Bukharin by pressuring former rightists Uglanov, Riutin, Rovinskii, and Kotov. The culmination of his effort was a dramatic confrontation between Bukharin and the already arrested G. Sokol'nikov on September 8 in the presence of Kaganovich, Vyshinskii, and Ezhov. The attempt failed, because at the meeting Sokol'nikov denied personal knowledge of Bukharin's participation in the treasonous opposition "bloc." The record of the confrontation was sent to Stalin and two days later Vyshinskii

character with the hard line of the times: *RTsKhIDNI (TsPA)*, f. 558, op. 1, d. 3350, ll. 1–16.

[65] *RTsKhIDNI (TsPA)*, f. 17, op. 2, d. 612, tom. 2, l. 57. The supposed liberal Postyshev also suggested burning down churches to quell religion (ibid., tom. 1, l. 27), and complained that leaders were trying to protect their own against Ezhov's rightful cause. Postyshev did, in fact, say that it was "strange" that one of his subordinates had "suddenly" become a Trotskyist in 1934, but concluded that of course the man had always been an enemy. He was not interrupted by Stalin, as the folklore has it. (Ibid., tom. 2, l. 26).

[66] *RTsKhIDNI (TsPA)*, f. 17, op. 2, d. 639, ll. 13–33.

[67] See his attacks on Gurevich in *RTsKhIDNI (TsPA)*, f. 17, op. 2, d. 612, tom. 2, l. 39; and on Postyshev (ibid., tom. 2, ll. 10–12, 15). His speech to the February Plenum called for a virtual witchhunt against Trotskyists in the Ukraine.

[68] It was in connection with this embryonic inquiry that prosecutor Vyshinskii mentioned Bukharin and Rykov at the August show trial.

announced that there was insufficient evidence to proceed legally against Bukharin. Only Stalin could have decided this, and we have no evidence that anyone was defending Bukharin.[69]

Ezhov continued to smear the former leader of the rightists. Articles appeared in the press questioning the loyalties and records of both Bukharin and Rykov, and on October 7, 1936, Ezhov sent Stalin the protocol of the interrogation of former rightist M. Tomskii's secretary, who accused Bukharin of being part of a "counterrevolutionary organization." In November, several of Bukharin's former editorial colleagues were arrested and interrogated, and on November 23, V. I. Nevskii, former head of the Lenin Library, directly accused Bukharin of leading a "terrorist center." Altogether in the last quarter of 1936 and the first month of 1937, Ezhov sent his boss more than sixty anti-Bukharin protocols of interrogations and personal confrontations.[70]

December 4–7, 1936, saw a Central Committee Plenum that approved the upcoming (second) show trial of Piatakov et al., and discussed the question of Bukharin's possible guilt. Ezhov gave a report summarizing the mounting "evidence" against Bukharin as leader of the "terrorist plot" along with the Trotskyists.[71] Stalin's role and position at the December Plenum are unclear. During the four days of the plenum, Ezhov arranged several "confrontations" between Bukharin and his already broken accusers, and continued to send Stalin protocols of damning interrogations every day. Before, during, and after the December 1936 Plenum, Bukharin denied his guilt.[72] Stalin debated Bukharin at the plenum, demanded explanations and recantations from him, and even told the Central Committee members, "You can shoot [him] if you want, it's up to you."[73] None of the other speakers questioned the case against Bukharin, and every single speaker accused him. Nevertheless, *Stalin* ended the meeting by "abruptly" suggesting only to continue "verification" and to postpone any decision on Bukharin.[74]

Between this plenum and the next, in February–March 1937, Ezhov had forced K. Radek and Piatakov to testify directly against Bukharin, and perhaps it was the cooperation of such big fish that finally tipped the scales against Bukharin. In any case, we know that Stalin directly attacked Bukharin at the February 1937 Plenum. We are told that Stalin "pressured" the February Plenum's participants, although given the apparent lack of

[69] *Izvestiia TsK*, no. 5, 1989, 70–71. The writers of the account in *Izvestiia TsK* call this only a "maneuver" (p. 72), but do not say why or against whom. That Stalin knew of and approved of the decision not to bring Bukharin and Rykov to trial (although he later claimed to have had doubts) is shown in *RTsKhIDNI (TsPA)*, f. 17, op. 2, d. 575, l. 98.
[70] *Izvestiia TsK*, no. 5, 1989, 73–74, no. 2, 1990, 48, no. 5, 1989, 84.
[71] *RTsKhIDNI (TsPA)*, f. 17, op. 2, d. 575, ll. 6–68.
[72] *RTsKhIDNI (TsPA)*, f. 17, op. 2, d. 575, ll. 69–93.
[73] *RTsKhIDNI (TsPA)*, f. 17, op. 2, d. 576, l. 67.
[74] *Izvestiia TsK*, no. 5, 1989, 72–77.

opposition to Ezhov the previous December, it is not clear why he should need to do so. Again, it seems that nobody at the plenum defended Bukharin and Rykov.[75]

A subcommission, chaired by Anastas Mikoian, was formed at the February Plenum to decide the fate of Bukharin. According to folklore, all the committee's participants voted to "arrest, try, and shoot" Bukharin and Rykov.[76] Again, the lore is wrong; documents show that the event went quite differently and showed continued indecision and confusion, even on Stalin's part. The final protocol of the committee meeting shows that everyone indeed voted to expel Bukharin and Rykov from the party. Ezhov, Budennyi, Manuilskii, Shvernik, Kosarev, and Iakir were for shooting them outright. Postyshev, Shkiriatov, Kosior, Petrovskii, and Litvinov were for sending them to trial but forbidding a death sentence. The rest voted "for the suggestion of Comrade Stalin," which in the final text is given as: "to expel from the party, not to send them to trial, and to refer the matter to the NKVD for further investigation."

But what exactly was "the suggestion of Comrade Stalin"? A careful comparison of the first and final drafts shows that Stalin's suggestion was originally quite different. He had at first suggested that Bukharin and Rykov be expelled from the party, *not* sent to trial, and merely exiled [*vyslat'*]. This was the "suggestion of Comrade Stalin" that committee members supported at the meeting when, after Stalin's remarks, they voted "tozhe" or "za predlozhenie Tovarishcha Stalina." Later, apparently in Mikoian's hand, the draft was corrected to read "refer the matter to the NKVD," instead of simple exile. When was the change made and why? What did Stalin really say? We still do not know.[77]

Finally, even in the printed final version of the resolution, personally drafted by Stalin, we find the strange formulation, "The Central Committee Plenum considers that comrades [!] Bukharin and Rykov deserve to be immediately expelled from the party and sent to trial. But because, in contrast to the Trotskyists and Zinovievists, they had not received a serious party reprimand," they should simply be expelled and referred to the NKVD.[78]

---

[75] *Izvestiia TsK*, no. 5, 1989, 77–79. The materials of the February Plenum, including Bukharin's defence, are being published in *Voprosi istorii*, beginning with no. 2–3, 1992, 3–44.

[76] See, for example, Roy Medvedev, *Let History Judge*, 367.

[77] *Izvestiia TsK*, no. 5, 1989, 81–83. For the originals, see *RTsKhIDNI (TsPA)*, f. 17, op. 2, d. 577, ll. 30–33. It is of course possible that the discrepancy was only a clerical or stenographic error, although this would require confusing "vyslat" with "napravit' delo Bukharina-Rykova v NKVD." And why did the researchers *Izvestiia TsK* include the contradictory photostat without comment? Could it be that they found their political mandate (to show a straight-line Stalin plan of terror) was inconsistent with the evidence?

[78] Indeed, the oral tradition got the entire February Plenum wrong. Although many accounts deal with the plenum only in connection with the terror issue (see, for example, Medvedev, *Let History Judge*, 364–368), the real – and only – argument at the meeting was about

Of course, Piatakov and Bukharin were eventually shot, and the decision to transfer Bukharin and Rykov to the NKVD in March 1937 was an accusation, if not a final condemnation.[79] There has never been any doubt that once Stalin decided someone was an enemy, he showed no mercy or vacillation. The only question is what he decided and when. He was assuredly cruel, vindictive, and sadistic. At the same time, the evidence actually suggests rather the opposite of any careful plan for terror. There was certainly repression, but there is no evidence of a planned straight line to it. There was, on the other hand, considerable indecision, ad hoc campaigns, false starts, and retreats.

The current state of our knowledge provides few details about the roles of Stalin and others in the mounting repression. In particular, the new information presented permits more than one view of the role of N. I. Ezhov. The first, and easiest, is the traditional one in which Ezhov is merely Stalin's tool with no independent position or initiative. He would receive his deadly instructions orally from Stalin and thereby become (for Stalin) a conveniently visible administrator of repression. Any criticism of repression could be deflected toward Ezhov by Stalin, who could pose as a reluctant follower of the NKVD chief at party meetings and other venues. In the end, Stalin could dispose of his tool quietly when the need had passed. Stalin's devious cruelty and our knowledge of his personal participation in the repression makes this version attractive and plausible.

But the sequence of events presented in the written evidence is also consistent with a second scenario (not mutually exclusive with the first) in which Ezhov pursued initiatives, prepared dossiers, and pushed certain investigations in order to promote his own agenda. Although that agenda was often the same as Stalin's, it may not have been identical. We know, for example, that although Stalin agreed to review a (no doubt grisly) manuscript Ezhov was writing on how opposition inevitably becomes terrorism, he never allowed publication.[80] We also know that in his struggle to undermine Iagoda and take over the NKVD, Ezhov did not get Stalin's final nod until after nearly two years of bickering.[81] Events seem to show that in the cases of Piatakov and Bukharin, Ezhov and others were possibly ahead of Stalin in pushing the need for severity. Maybe Stalin was

---

Zhdanov's and Kalinin's calls to subject regional party secretaries to secret ballot elections. See the uproar that greeted this suggestion in *RTsKhIDNI (TsPA)*, f. 17, op. 2, d. 612, tom. 1, ll. 10–42. This substantially confirms the earlier speculation in Getty, *Origins*, 137–149.

[79] Stalin and Ezhov did not put the question of Bukharin and Rykov's trial and "physical liquidation" before the Central Committee until June 1937, in the hysteria and savage retribution that followed the fall of the military leaders.

[80] *Izvestiia TsK*, no. 5, 1989, 73.

[81] For this struggle, see *Izvestiia TsK*, no. 9, 1989, 30–50. Although Stalin sometimes supported Ezhov against Iagoda in 1935 and 1936 (at one point even calling up Iagoda and threatening to "smash his snout" [*mordu nab'em*]), Stalin did not replace him until the fall of 1936.

only playing at being reluctant, making Ezhov "prove" his (or their) case for a doubting audience of Central Committee "liberals." But we have seen that, sadly, no such audience seems to have existed. Especially in the internal secret documents we now know about, Stalin had no need to be coy. Certainly he supported Ezhov at key points in the latter's struggle with Iagoda, at the February 1937 Plenum and afterwards. But at specific points along the way it is not always clear whether Ezhov was actively promoting or simply administering repression.[82]

No one has ever doubted or questioned Stalin's participation in organizing the repression. Even from his published writings, not to mention myriad other sources, we have always known that he was an active organizer of the violence and was the person most responsible for the repression.[83] But much of the new information seems to support revisionist doubts about older interpretations and their source bases. The confirmation is necessarily oblique, because new documents and accompanying commentary have to date been chosen and published to illustrate a different interpretation: the innocence of prominent party victims and Stalin's direct organization of their repression. It may well be that Stalin killed Kirov as part of a bloody long-term plan. On the other hand, the documents we have today do not prove it and unavoidably provide details that support alternative or revisionist views of events.

Given the one-sided nature of discourse in the field, it may perhaps not be gratuitous to point out some of the minor, more technical aspects of the revisionist view of the origins of the terror that are being confirmed by new archival evidence. First, when Stalin said in the fall of 1936 that the NKVD was "four years behind" in uncovering oppositionist plots, he was indeed referring to the 1932 united oppositionist bloc brokered by Trotsky and I. N. Smirnov, and not to the Riutin platform. The 1932 bloc was, then, the catalytic event in the escalation of Stalinist terror.[84] Second, we also now have confirmation of the fact that party expulsions in the 1935–7 period (that is, after the Kirov assassination and before the onslaught of the terror) were steadily *decreasing* in number, even after the first show trial of summer 1936 and were not especially directed against oppositionists, "wreckers," or "spies."[85] Third, the January 1938

---

[82] B. A. Starkov writes in this volume that at the time of his fall, "[Ezhov's] primary crime, however, consisted in the fact that he had not informed Stalin of his actions." Stalin's relationship to Ezhov's predecessor Iagoda was equally complex. In March 1936, Iagoda proposed to Stalin that all Trotskyists everywhere – even those convicted already – should be resentenced to five additional years out of hand and that any of them involved in "terror" should quickly be shot. Stalin referred Iagoda's plan to Vyshinskii for a legal opinion, which came back positive in six days. Although Iagoda was ready to move immediately, it was nearly two months before Stalin issued an order to this effect. See *Izvestiia TsK*, no. 9, 1989, 35–36.

[83] Getty, *Origins*, 8–9, 206.

[84] Getty, *Origins*, 119–122; RTsKhIDNI (TsPA), f. 17, op. 2, d. 577, l. 9a.

[85] Roughly 264,000 were expelled in 1935, 51,500 in 1936. In both years of "chistka," only 5.5% of those expelled were accused of opposition and 0.9% for being "spies" or having

Central Committee resolution criticizing excessive vigilance and unjust persecutions was directed against regional party machines and their leaders who, like Postyshev, expelled rank-and-file members to divert attention from their own people. It had nothing to do with the NKVD.[86] Finally, it now seems clear that regional (oblast) party "family circles" were able to protect their own from arrest until 1937,[87] because of their power and ability to direct the fire toward the rank and file.

Certainly confirmation of no such technical point "proves" the revisionist case. But the growing fund of archival evidence does show that the period preceding the great terror was complicated and contradictory and the questions raised or confirmed by the new materials are persistent.

In all these matters, we must constantly question our sources. The evidence presented is based on sensitive documents long suppressed. It might be objected that documents and archives should not be our main sources for the repression. Indeed, we must consider the possibility that they have been altered or falsified. Fearful, culpable, and powerful officials over the years since 1937 certainly would have reason to take an interest in the paper trail of these crimes, and such people were capable of far more than adjusting the documentary record. Certainly, the record is incomplete and we must maintain a healthy suspicion of all official sources from the 1930s.[88] But simply on the basis of suspicion and without any evidence, it would be rash to decide a priori that the archival record is false. Until and unless independent historians and documentary experts are able to examine all the sensitive documents in their physical form and contexts, the scholarly community is not in a position finally to establish their veracity – or lack of credibility for that matter.[89]

Undoubtedly, many will not be convinced by the appearance of anomalies in the traditional paradigmatic folklore of the Kirov assassination and Stalin's plan for repression. In other areas ranging from agriculture to industry to institutional administration, scholars have noted the patchwork, reactive nature of Stalinist decisions, which often seemed to follow events rather than make them. Although we can recognize his hesitation and bungling on all other issues, we seem to have difficulty

"connections to spies." Class-alien origins and personal corruption comprised the overwhelming majority. *RTsKhIDNI (TsPA)*, f. 17, op. 120, d. 278, ll. 2–3.

[86] Getty, *Origins*, 185–189; *RTsKhIDNI (TsPA)*, f. 17, op. 2, d. 639.

[87] Getty, *Origins*, ch. 6; *RTsKhIDNI (TsPA)*, f. 17, op. 71, d. 34 lists party leaders expelled and arrested in the provinces. Although a few raion secretaries were expelled before 1937, it is difficult to find a single obkom official who fell before that year. But in 1937, the oblast party organizations were suddenly decimated.

[88] Getty, *Origins*, 8.

[89] We do know, however, that those who have seen, used, and publicized such documents both in the 1960s and 1980s have done so under an official and quite proper mandate to show Stalin's connection with the repression, and would presumably have alerted us to any possibility of documentary fakery. Yet no such claims or suspicions have been voiced by those working with the documents.

accepting them when it comes to terror, even though information on politics in the 1930s seems to permit the parallel thesis that there were strange moments of indecision. It is easier to reject contradictory evidence with the deus ex machina of Stalin's supposed cleverness: All twists and turns, hesitations and contradictions are thus the result of his incredible deviousness, sadism, or calculating shrewdness. There is really no counter to such ahistorical assertions, except that they are based on faith: the a priori presumption of a plan and the belief that anomalies were intentionally part of it. Such elaborate constructs are unnecessary to explain events; the simplest explanation with the fewest assumptions and consistent with the evidence is usually the best.

We need not turn Stalin into an omniscient and omnipotent demon in order to comprehend his evil. Indeed, making him into a superman diminishes the real horror of the period. Stalin was a cruel but ordinary mortal unable to see the future and with a limited ability to create and control it. He was not a master planner, and studies of all of his other policies before and after the 1930s have shown that he stumbled into everything from collectivization to foreign policy. Stalin's colossal felonies, like most violent crimes everywhere, were of the unplanned erratic kind. His evil, like Eichmann's, was ordinary and of this world; it was banally human and is more horrifying for being so.

Part II: Backgrounds

3

The second coming: Class enemies in the Soviet countryside, 1927–1935

Lynne Viola

In 1930, a Red Army soldier returned to his native village to discover that a number of his neighbors – people whose socioeconomic status was similar to his own – had been dekulakized. The soldier went to the local soviet to lodge a protest. He told the soviet officials that if they considered his neighbors to be kulaks, then he, too, must be a kulak and should be dekulakized. Complying with the soldier's demands, the soviet issued a resolution calling for the dekulakization of the soldier "according to his personal wish."[1] At about the same time that the soldier found himself subject to voluntary dekulakization, a village teacher in the Central Black Earth Region faced a similar fate. Local authorities accused the teacher of being the daughter of a priest and therefore decided to dekulakize her. The teacher gathered together documentation to prove that she in fact was not the daughter of a priest, but was unable to convince the local authorities, who claimed, "If her mother visited the priest, then it is possible that the priest is her father."[2] During this time and after, for a glass of vodka or a bottle of *samogon* (moonshine), a kulak could be transformed into a poor peasant or, in the absence of a glass of vodka or a bottle of *samogon*, a poor peasant could be transformed into a kulak.[3] These were years of widespread repression in the Soviet countryside, as officials foraged through the villages in search of class enemies and proclaimed a "second coming"

I would like to acknowledge the commentary and criticism of Stephen Frank, William Husband, Tracy McDonald, Timothy Mixter, and especially Roberta Manning, who encouraged me to take *byvshie liudi* seriously and who provided invaluable editorial aid. I would also like to thank the SSRC for support for research on this project.

[1] S. Syrtsov, *Nakanune partiinogo s"ezda* (M-L, 1930): 40–41.
[2] *Sovetskaia iustitsiia*, no. 11 (20 April 1930): 8–9. (Hereafter *SIu*)
[3] On the use of bribery in altering official social status, see *SIu*, no. 10 (10 April 1930): 4–5; no. 7 (15 April 1937): 34–35; *Krest'ianskii iurist* (*KIu* hereafter), no. 2 (Jan. 1931): 11; *Derevenskii iurist* (*DIu*, hereafter), no. 18 (Sept. 1931): 8; no. 3 (Feb. 1933): 13; no. 2 (Jan. 1934): 12; no. 17 (Sept. 1934): 13–14. On local officials giving false papers to so-called kulaks, see *DIu*, no. 7 (April 1934): 11; and no. 13 (July 1935): 10–11.

(to borrow a phrase from Platonov's *Chevengur*)[4] for real and perceived enemies of the state. The kulak seemed to be largely in the eye of the beholder.

The vagaries and subjectivity of the definition of the kulak (or capitalist farmer) are well known and were the subject of intense debate prior to collectivization.[5] During the years of collectivization and after, however, the definition of a kulak ceased to be merely a theoretical issue and became one of practical politics. The failure of the center to equip its cadres with a workable definition of the kulak, as Moshe Lewin has noted,[6] meant that cadres in the field were given a great deal of latitude in defining and identifying kulaks. Consequently, the kulak label served as a political sledgehammer applied readily and arbitrarily to peasants for opposition to state policies. Poor peasants, middle peasants, and better-off peasants (*zazhitochnye*), as well as actual kulaks, often found themselves subject to dekulakization (i.e., repressive measures ranging from expropriation to deportation and incarceration) by way of taxation assessment, civil or criminal prosecution, or administrative fiat. Repression was wholesale and struck many innocent victims. The question arises, however, as to whether there was any consistency, any rationale in the identification of kulaks on the local level within this whirlwind of repression. Were there patterns of repression at work in the Soviet countryside in the late 1920s and the first half of the 1930s?

The campaign against the kulak began in the second half of 1929. The use of "extraordinary measures" in grain procurements was legalized in a VTsIK-SNK RSFSR (All-Russian Central Executive Committee–Council of People's Commissariats) decree of June 1929, widening the rights of local soviets and empowering local officials to apply article 61 of the penal code to peasants who failed to fulfill their taxes and other obligations to the government, including grain deliveries. At the same time, VTsIK-SNK revised article 61 to allow officials to assess a fine of one-fifth of the value of grain or other taxes due for first-time violators, to imprison repeat offenders, and to imprison with confiscation of property those whose actions were considered to be either premeditated or based on group resistance.[7] These decrees granted local officials wide powers to fine, expropriate, or arrest peasants who failed to fulfill grain delivery quotas or to pay their taxes. Peasants who were categorized as kulaks were taxed

---

[4] Andrei Platonov, *Chevengur* (Ann Arbor, 1978): 182–184.
[5] See Moshe Lewin, "Who Was the Soviet Kulak?" in idem., *The Making of the Soviet System* (New York, 1985): 121–141. Also see M. Lewin, *Russian Peasants and Soviet Power* (New York, 1975).
[6] Lewin, "Who Was the Soviet Kulak?"
[7] *Sobranie uzakonenii i rasporiazhenii raboche-krest'ianskogo pravitel'stva RSFSR*, no. 60 (5 Sept. 1929): 846–847.

heavily at this time and large grain delivery quotas were levied on their farms. It was impossible for many of them to fulfill their obligations to the state. Consequently, by the end of 1929, dekulakization had become a reality, as district and local officials made use of the penal code to arrest, exile, or expropriate peasants for nonpayment of taxes, failure to fulfull grain deliveries, and the destruction or sale of livestock and agricultural inventory as peasants sought to avoid the kulak label through self-dekulakization.[8]

Although the center equipped local officials with the legislative powers necessary for de facto dekulakization, many regional party organizations, particularly those in grain-producing regions, went one step further and issued orders for the expropriation or exile of kulaks on a relatively large scale from the fall of 1929.[9] In the Lower Volga, Middle Volga, Siberia, and Ukraine, thousands of peasants were expropriated and/or exiled on the basis of regional party decisions made prior to the adoption of the central decree on dekulakization on January 5, 1930.[10] By the time of the central decree, the center was recognizing and endorsing what had already become a reality in many parts of the countryside.

Implementation of dekulakization following the central decree spread far beyond the grain-producing regions into grain-deficit and national minority regions in spite of the center's directives not to implement dekulakization outside of regions of wholesale collectivization, which was then limited mainly to grain-producing regions.[11] The result was massive violations that soon led the center to issue more precise directives in late January and early February, in hope of establishing control over the campaign and standardizing and regulating procedures.[12]

The new national legislation stipulated that a differential approach be taken in the application of repression. Kulaks were divided into three categories and officials were ordered to impose penalties on kulaks (ranging from execution and imprisonment to exile and expropriation) according to these categories. The new directives also warned officials not to allow middle peasants or the families of Red Army soldiers to be affected by repressive policies, and the (kulak) families of industrial workers of long tenure were to be approached with "caution." Finally, the center issued a

---

[8] These actions occurred under article 79 ("willful" destruction of livestock and inventory), art. 107 (speculation), and art. 169 (illegal property sales). See N. Ia. Gushchin, "Likvidatsiia kulachestva kak klassa v Sibirskoi derevne," *Sotsial'naia struktura naseleniia Sibiri* (Novosibirsk, 1970): 125–126; *Penal Code of the RSFSR* (London, 1934): 30–32, 36–38, 46, 61.

[9] Lynne Viola, "The Campaign to Eliminate the Kulak as a Class, Winter 1929–1930: A Reevaluation of the Legislation," *Slavic Review*, vol. 45, no. 3 (Fall 1986): 508–511.

[10] Ibid., 509–510; *KPSS v rezoliutsiiakh i resheniiakh s"ezdov, konferentsii i plenumov TsK*, 7th ed. (M, 1953), pt. 2, 544–547.

[11] Viola, "Campaign," 518–519.

[12] Ibid., 507 (n. 12–14), 511–515.

strict warning that dekulakization was to occur only in regions of wholesale collectivization and that dekulakization should not be considered an end in itself.[13] These directives represented the center's belated attempt to regain the initiative in policy implementation. The directives, however, failed to stem the tide of violence and anarchy unleashed in the countryside, and the center was finally forced in early March to signal a retreat with the publication of Stalin's famous article, "Dizziness with Success," and a Central Committee decree of March 14, 1930.[14]

This first phase of dekulakization led to repressive mayhem and massive peasant discontent. The center had unleashed its cadres in the field from the time it adopted extraordinary measures to deal with the grain procurement crisis and quickly discovered that it was no easy task to bring them back under control. The center was not prepared to deal with either the army of recently dekulakized or the peasant unrest thus generated. The first consequence of this lack of preparation was the March retreat. The second consequence was the formation of commissions to review complaints from dekulakized peasants seeking redress. According to Soviet data, in the Central Black Earth Region alone, some 32,583 peasants were rehabilitated in 1930; an additional 5,000 in the Middle Volga and 5,500 in the Lower Volga were also said to have been rehabilitated in 1930.[15]

Dekulakization resumed in late 1930 and the first half of 1931. Although policy implementation in this period was no less repressive and no less destructive in consequence than the first phase of dekulakization, it appears to have been less anarchic and more subject to central control. In certain parts of the country, deportations of already dekulakized peasants began somewhat earlier, in the late summer and early fall of 1930. Elsewhere, dekulakization resumed in late 1930 and extended into the early summer of 1931. After this second phase of dekulakization, the state claimed that dekulakization was basically accomplished in the major grain-producing regions. According to Soviet estimates, as many as 600,000 farms may have been dekulakized in 1930 and 1931 alone, over 240,000 of whose owners were deported.[16]

The final phase of dekulakization extended from 1932 to 1934. Soviet scholars are divided as to whether this time period should be properly

[13] Ibid., 513.

[14] I. Stalin, "Golovokruzhenie ot uspekhov," *Sochineniia* (M, 1952), vol. 12, 191–199; *KPSS v rezoliutsiiakh*, 548–551.

[15] M. L. Bogdenko, "Kolkhoznoe stroitel'stvo vesnoi i letom 1930 g.," *Istoricheskie zapiski*, vol. 76 (1965): 35.

[16] Estimates are from Ivnitskii, in "Kollektivizatsiia: istoki, sushchnost', posledstviia. Beseda za 'kruglym stolom,'" *Istoriia SSSR*, no. 3 (1989): 44. Danilov provides a higher figure of 381,000 exiled families for 1930 and 1931 (of which 115,231 were exiled in 1930 and 265,795 in 1931). His figure for dekulakized farms in the years from 1929 to 1933 is approximately 1,100,000. This figure includes farms that were exiled as well as those left in place and those who self-dekulakized. See *Pravda*, 16 Sept. 1988, 3.

counted as a phase of dekulakization at all.[17] In May 1932, TsK-SNK SSSR (Central Committee–Council of People's Commissars) issued a decree ordering the end of mass deportations of kulaks.[18] From this point on, wholesale dekulakization was restricted to national minority areas and backward regions. The primary mechanism for dekulakization elsewhere seems to have been heavy taxation of kulak households and, in cases of failure to pay taxes or to fulfill other state obligations, civil or criminal prosecution. Another form of dekulakization, perhaps better called simple repression, occurred in conjunction with the notorious *tikhaia sapa* (on the sly) activities of the kulak and included civil and criminal penalties for a large range of offenses, such as infiltration of collective or state farms and MTS (Machine-Tractor Stations) units, theft of socialist property (under the law of August 7, 1932), and so on. In reference to kulak work on the sly, Soviet sources generally stress the frequency of such activities in Ukraine and North Caucasus, in particular, and the Volga regions as well – the prime areas hit by the 1932 famine.[19] Repression accelerated further with the establishment of the MTS political sections in 1933 and the massive purge of officialdom. These measures resulted in the unearthing of more kulaks and a diverse galaxy of class enemies. The final phase of dekulakization tapered off after 1934 and was followed by several amnesties for an undetermined part of the repressed.[20]

The offensive against the kulak was an enormous exercise in state repression. Repression, however, should not be mistaken for central control. Although the center was responsible for setting policy, the cadres in the field were responsible for interpreting and implementing policy. The vague and frequently contradictory directives of the center, as well as the very broad official definition of the kulak,[21] allowed local cadres great latitude in labeling peasants kulaks, resulting in an explosion of local *proizvol* or arbitrariness. To be sure, central policy was repressive and inevitably led to excess. Moreover, local cadres often faced the threat of being labeled right deviationists if they did not fulfill central directives. But beyond that, rural cadres operated within the general political culture of the early 1930s, a culture that was based on a mixture of traditional Russian radical

[17] N. M. Volkov et al., "Sovremennaia istoriografiia agrarnoi istorii Sovetskogo obshchestva," *Sel'skoe khoziaistvo i krest'ianstvo SSSR v sovremennoi Sovetskoi istoriografii* (Kishinev, 1977): 46–48.

[18] I. Ia. Trifonov, *Likvidatsiia ekspluatatorskikh klassov v SSSR* (M, 1975): 344. Also see *Istoriia krest'ianstva SSSR*, vol. 2 (M, 1986): 225.

[19] On the repression of peasants in these years, see N. Ia. Gushchin, *Sibirskaia derevnia na puti k sotsializmu* (Novosibirsk, 1973): 441–455; and Trifonov, *Ocherki istorii klassovoi bor'by v SSSR v gody NEPa* (M, 1960): 250–263.

[20] Gushchin, 441–455; Trifonov, 250–263. Amnesty decrees are in *Sobranie zakonov i rasporiazhenii raboche-krest'ianskogo pravitel'stva SSSR*, no. 40 (11 Aug. 1935): 613–614; and no. 44 (4 Sept. 1935): 674–675.

[21] See *Sobranie zakonov*, no. 34 (13 June 1929): 641–642, for an official statement on the identification of kulak households.

fanaticism and voluntarism, a siegelike paranoid mentality, and the force of unleashing years of pent-up class rage and retribution. These factors go a long way to explain why repressive policies so often turned into *proizvol*. Yet rural cadres also functioned within the context of a traditional culture shaped by political and social interactions dating from both before and after the 1917 Revolution. Within this context, some (but certainly not all) of the cadres' actions that were perceived by the center (and by Western scholars) as *proizvol* may in fact have been logical, demonstrating a pattern of consistency amid the chaos. Random repression may have been less random than apparent and there may have been certain clearly identifiable victims of repression. It will be argued here that the kulak was something more and something less than a kulak. He was joined by other intended and unintended victims of repression, most notably *byvshie liudi*, outsiders, and marginal people within the village. This is not to suggest either that "real kulaks" did not exist or that all rural repression had an inner logic to it, but that certain patterns may have prevailed amid the seemingly irrational mechanism of repression at work in the countryside.

The most easily identifiable victims of rural repression fell under the general rubric of *byvshie liudi*. *Byvshie liudi* were social elements closely tied in the popular mind to the political, social, or economic system of the ancien regime. The cast of characters subsumed under this category was large and included noble landowners, clergy, church elders, members of religious sects (especially Baptists and Evangelists), large landholders, genuine "kulaks" (in the sense of very wealthy farmers), Stolypin *otrubniki* (peasants who split from the commune during the Stolypin land reform and owned their land privately), factory or rural enterprise owners, merchants, traders, certain categories of rural homeowners, tsarist officers, cossack atamans, prerevolutionary policemen, estate stewards, and village and *volost'* elders. The term was elastic enough to include not only ancien regime *byvshie liudi*, but post-1917 groupings that, loosely defined, had opposed the Bolsheviks in the Revolution or Civil War, like White Army officers and sometimes rank-and-file soldiers, repatriated cossacks, and members of other political parties (Socialist Revolutionaries, SRs, in particular).

After the Civil War, the state partially accommodated a sizable proportion of the *byvshie liudi* within Soviet society and within Soviet institutions. Landlords, who managed to survive the Revolution and Civil War intact, were left in relative peace at least until 1925 (and probably longer given the difficulties of enforcement), when the state issued a decree ordering the exile of noble landowners and certain additional categories of large landowners.[22] Many monasteries, sometimes camouflaged as

[22] *Ezhenedel'nik Sovetskoi iustitsii*, no. 50 (17 Dec. 1926): 1398–1401; Trifonov, *Likvidatsiia*, 267–272. See also John Channon, "Tsarist Landowners After the Revolution: Former

agricultural collectives, continued to exist right up until wholesale collectivization.[23] The Soviet government authorized the repatriation of several thousand White cossacks (as well as other emigres of the Revolution and Civil War) in an amnesty of the mid-1920s.[24] Most important, the Soviet government employed large numbers of *byvshie liudi* within its commissariats and the soviet apparatus, particularly in the countryside, given the dearth of qualified, literate personnel to staff state agencies.[25] The accommodation of the *byvshie liudi*, however, was limited and conditional. Problems in state agencies and all types of crimes generally assumed a much more sinister character (with a correspondingly sinister punishment) if *byvshie liudi* were involved or present. Local *proizvol* (on the part of rural party and soviet cadres) and local enthusiasm (on the part of village Komsomol members and other activists) often found great ideological inspiration in interactions with local *byvshie liudi*, to the detriment of the latter.[26] And after the mid-1920s, the center became increasingly apprehensive about the existence (especially within the state apparatus) of *byvshie liudi* who, it should be noted, were also increasingly familiar to Soviet audiences as officially designated class aliens and counterrevolutionaries.

On the eve of wholesale collectivization, the state launched its first campaign against *byvshie liudi*. The campaign began as an exercise in administrative purging. Coming in the aftermath of the Shakhty Affair and the grain crisis, this campaign was both an attempt to socially cleanse rural institutions and an attempt to find convenient scapegoats for the country's grain difficulties. The state conducted a series of investigations into the social composition of the rural party, soviets, cooperatives, and collective farms. The investigations generally concluded that *byvshie liudi* had infiltrated the rural networks of Soviet power.[27] The Communist Party underwent a purge from 1929 to 1930. According to incomplete data,

Pomeshchiki in Rural Russia During NEP," *Soviet Studies*, vol. 39, no. 4 (Oct. 1987): 580, 583, who estimates that some 10,756 *pomeshchiki* remained in rural Russia in 1925 and that, of these, approximately 40% were subject to internal exile in 1927.

[23] V. F. Zybkovets, "Likvidatsiia monastyrskogo zemlevladeniia v Sovetskoi Rossii," *Problemy agrarnoi istorii Sovetskogo obshchestva* (M, 1971): 31–32.

[24] P. G. Chernopitskii, *Na velikom perelome* (Rostov-na-Donu, 1965): 8. Also see Trifonov, *Likvidatsiia*, 178.

[25] Lynne Viola, "Notes on the Background of Soviet Collectivisation," *Soviet Studies*, vol. 36, no. 2 (April 1984): 207. On former tsarist officials in the Soviet apparatus, see *Gosudarstvennyi apparat SSSR* (M, 1929): 59–62; and Channon, "Tsarist Landowners," 580, who notes the presence of former landowners among administrative-technical personnel in state farms.

[26] On the nature of rural party activities, see Stalin, "Ob ocherednykh zadachakh partii v derevne," *Sochineniia*, vol. 6: 302–312; "O zadachakh partii v derevne," vol. 6: 313–320; "K voprosu o proletariate i krest'ianstve," vol. 7: 25–34; and "Politicheskii otchet TsK 18 dekabria 1925," vol. 7: 333–337.

[27] Lynne Viola, "The Case of Krasnyi Meliorator or 'How the Kulak Grows into Socialism,'" *Soviet Studies*, vol. 38, no. 4 (Oct. 1984): 512–513; and Idem., *The Best Sons of the Fatherland. Workers in the Vanguard of Soviet Collectivization* (New York, 1987): 29–30.

12.7% of rural party members purged were classified as aliens and an additional 6.4% were said to have "ties" to aliens.[28] Investigations and purges of the soviet apparatus in the countryside led to similar findings,[29] and in 1927 the state began to probe the social composition of the collective farm system, which culminated in the exposure of the model collective farm Krasnyi Meliorator and the November 1929 decision to purge the collective farms of kulaks and *lishentsy* (disenfranchised people – mostly *byvshie liudi*).[30]

Political and social geneology appears to have become a national pastime in the countryside in the witch-hunt atmosphere of the late 1920s. While the center pursued its investigations, local cadres undertook their own studies of village history. The local soviet generally proved to be the key target. Reports poured into the press – from journalists, *sel'kory* (village correspondents, usually peasants), and cadres – concerning the presence of class aliens in the lower soviet apparatus.[31] One worker was told that there were no kulaks in the village he visited. He then went on to uncover in the local soviet what he considered to be the equivalent: six old regime *volost'* elders, six former village policemen, one kulak, and two drunks.[32] Local soviets in the Penzenskii district were declared to be full of class aliens, including traders, criminals, and one Stolypin *otrubnik*.[33] The investigation of local soviets continued into 1930 – partly in response to central directives and partly in response to the increasing conflict between collective farm boards and local soviets.[34]

In the collectivization drive, the campaign against *byvshie liudi* often merged with and became indistinguishable from dekulakization and was (with some important exceptions) centered in the village and collective farm. *Byvshie liudi*, who were also generally *lishentsy*, were not eligible for collective farm membership and subject to be purged if already members

[28] *Derevenskii kommunist*, no. 11–12 (21 June 1930): 46.
[29] For data on purges of the soviet administration in the North Caucasus and Smolensk, see *Sovetskoe stroitel'stvo*, no. 5 (May 1929): 115; and *Litsom k derevne*, no. 17 (Sept. 1929): 4.
[30] Viola, "Krasnyi Meliorator," 512–514; *Kollektivist*, no. 20 (Oct. 1929): 24–25, no. 23 (Dec. 1929): 5; *KPSS v rezoliutsiiakh*, 523–540. On the purge of rural cooperatives and collective farms at this time, see *Kollektivizatsiia sel'skogo khoziaistva. Vazhneishie postanovleniia Kommunisticheskoi partii i Sovetskogo pravitel'stva* (M, 1957): 75–77; V. A. Sidorov, *Klassovaia bor'ba v dokolkhoznoi derevne* (M, 1978): 209–210; *Kollektivizatsiia sel'skogo khoziaistva v Zapadnom raione RSFSR* (Smolensk, 1968): 253; *Saratovskaia partiinaia organizatsiia v period nastupleniia sotsializma po vsemu frontu* (Saratov, 1961): 177; *Sploshnaia kollektivizatsiia sel'skogo khoziaistva Uzbekistan* (Tashkent, 1980): 251.
[31] E.g., see Viola, "Notes," 215–216; *Litsom k derevne*, no. 2 (Oct. 1928): 23; no. 17 (Sept. 1929): 4; no. 6 (Mar. 1930): 20; *Sputnik agitatora (dlia derevni)*, no. 9–10 (May 1929): 73–75; *Put' sovetov* (Middle Volga), no. 4 (Feb. 1929): 20; *Derevenskii kommunist*, no. 12 (26 June 1929): 1–3.
[32] *Metallist*, no. 11 (21 Mar. 1929): 5.
[33] *Put' sovetov* (M. Volga), no. 19 (Oct. 1929): 15.
[34] *Izvestiia*, 20 Jan. 1930, p. 1; *Pravda*, 22 Jan. 1930, pp. 1, 3; 26 Jan. 1930, p. 1.

of a collective farm. Despite their noneligibility for membership, *lishentsy* (except kulaks and priests) were not officially subject to dekulakization.[35] This superlative example of legislative legerdemain often led in practice to the dekulakization of *byvshie liudi* as *lishentsy* either during purges of collective farms or during dekulakization. In fact, in the Central Black Earth Region, on January 21, 1930 (*before* the central legislation on dekulakization), authorities decided to exile kulaks, *pomeshchiki*, former tsarist army officers, and gendarmes who were deemed dangerous beyond their native counties (*okrugs*). Less dangerous kulaks, traders, mill owners, and large renters were to be resettled within their native counties.[36] Elsewhere local cadres on their own authority enlarged the definition of a kulak to encompass a broad variety of aliens. As a consequence, dekulakization struck not only genuine kulaks and regime critics, but villagers who were still perceived as having a connection to the old regime. For many cadres, bitter memories of the tsarist regime and its representatives remained real and potentially lethal.

In some areas of the country, kulaks were identified on the basis of both pre- and postrevolutionary social status. The People's Commissariat of Justice condemned the dekulakization of middle peasants in the Central Black Earth Region. Here middle peasants who were kulaks before 1917 found themselves subject to dekulakization.[37] The Commissariat was disturbed in general about the genealogy mania. It complained in 1931 that the lower courts too often tried people on the basis of their social status of ten to twenty years earlier and spent needless time researching village history of fifty to one hundred years earlier in search of what happened in 1905, what happened before Emancipation, and so on.[38]

In one village, a peasant brought suit against local authorities, claiming that he had been unjustly dekulakized and that, moreover, his son was a party member and a soldier in the Red Army. The village party cell countered by reminding the court that this peasant owned a mill before the Revolution and continued to be a better-off peasant after the Revolution.[39] A *sel'kor* called for the purge of a collective farm in the Moscow Region, which, he claimed, had slowed down the pace of collectivization due to its unsavory social composition. Among the farm's members were a former trader, a tavern owner ("from the old days" and presently collective farm treasurer), and a "*bol'shaia shishka* [big shot]" who was once renown for owning the biggest brick works in the village (and who now served as the

---

[35] *Kollektivist*, no. 20 (Oct. 1929): 24–25; no. 23 (Dec. 1929): 5; *SIu*, no. 7–8 (20 Mar. 1930): 9; and see N. A. Ivnitskii, *Klassovaia bor'ba v derevne i likvidatsiia kulachestva kak klassa* (M, 1972): 232–33, for a Northern Region decree to this effect.
[36] Ivnitskii, *Klassovaia bor'ba*, 214–215.
[37] *SIu*, no. 2 (20 Jan. 1931): 20–21.
[38] Ibid., no. 18 (25–30 June 1931): 32–33.
[39] *KIu*, no. 2 (Jan. 1931): 12.

farm bookkeeper).[40] In many areas, repression was extended to the children and relatives of *byvshie liudi*.[41]

Repression also struck people associated with the anti-Bolshevik cause in the Civil War. In all probability, this hostility was most intense in cossack villages and especially in those villages with large numbers of repatriated cossacks or a record of inadequate postrevolutionary land reform.[42] Justice officials warned cadres to be cautious in concluding anti-Soviet status on the basis of an individual's Civil War activities, noting that eight to ten years had passed since the Civil War and that the situation may very well have changed.[43] Nevertheless, SRs, White officers, even some rank-and-file White Army soldiers, and other formerly anti-Bolshevik activists often appeared among the roster of the repressed and dekulakized.[44] Former White Army officers and sometimes soldiers had also been a target of the state in the administrative purges of the late 1920s.[45] Civil War animosities remained alive into the 1930s (not surprising when compared to the longevity of American Civil War hostilities in the United States) and appear to have become a very lively and potentially deadly issue during collectivization.

The state also claimed that the *byvshie liudi* (of course, with the kulak in its ranks) were among the leading actors in *tikhaia sapa* (on the sly) activities. The two major and, for our purposes, most significant forms of repression in 1932–4 were purges of and expulsions from the Communist

---

[40] Ibid., no. 13 (July 1931): 14.

[41] E.g., *Put' sovetov* (Middle Volga), no. 21 (Nov. 1929): 4; *Bednota*, 15 Aug. 1930, pp. 2–3; *Litsom k derevne*, no. 2 (Oct. 1928): 23. Also see Viola, "Krasnyi Meliorator," for examples of the "children of" as a category of alien; as well as *SIu*, no. 11 (20 April 1930): 4; and *KIu*, no. 11 (June 1931): 14.

[42] See Chernopitskii, *Na velikom perelome*, 8; E. N. Oskolkov, "Bor'ba za ovladenie zemel'nymi obshchestvami v kazach'ikh raionakh Severo-kavkazskogo kraia nakanune sploshnoi kollektivizatsii," *Ezhegodnik po agrarnoi istorii* (Vologda, 1976): 146–159; and Ia. A. Perekhov, "Ob agrarnykh preobrazovaniiakh na Donu i Kubani v pervye gody sotsialisticheskogo stroitel'stva (1920–1925 gg.)," *Problemy agrarnoi istorii Sovetskogo obshchestva*, 45–48. Soviet sources point to considerable tensions in cossack villages and divisions between cossacks and *inogorodnye* peasants. See *Kollektivizatsiia sel'skogo khoziaistva na Severnom Kavkaze* (Krasnodar, 1972): 6–7; and *Kollektivizatsiia sel'skogo khoziaistva na Kubani* (Krasnodar, 1959, 1981), vol. 1: 120–121; vol. 2: 113–115.

[43] *Sudebnaia praktika*, no. 5 (10 April 1930): 4–6. In April 1930, the North Caucasus regional party committee issued a decree condemning hostility to cossacks and refusal to admit them into collective farms based simply on old Civil War hostilities. See *Kollektivizatsiia... na Severnom Kavkaze*, 295–297.

[44] E.g., K. M. Shuvaev, *Staraia i novaia derevnia* (M, 1937): 44–45. For other cases of repression of peasants who fought with the Whites, see *KIu*, no. 11 (June 1931): 15; and *Kollektivizatsiia sel'skogo khoziaistva Bashkirskoi ASSR* (Ufa, 1980): 125.

[45] E.g., *Sel'sko-khoziaistvennaia zhizn'*, no. 46 (18 Nov. 1929): 17; *Derevenskii kommunist*, no. 14 (27 July 1929): 9; *XIV vserossiiskii s"ezd sovetov. Sten. otchet* (M, 1929), Biulleten' No. 15: 9; N. Ia. Gushchin and M. I. Kornienko, "Rol' zemleustroitel'noi politiki v regulirovanii sotsial'no-ekonomicheskikh protsessov v Sibirskoi derevne nakanune massovoi kollektivizatsii," *Bakhrushinskie chtenie*, no. 1 (1973): 84–85; Sidorov, *Klassovaia bor'ba*, 209–210.

Party and the state and collective farms, and court cases tried under the law of August 7, 1932, for theft of socialist property. The state claimed that class aliens and kulaks had infiltrated soviet offices and were trying to subvert Soviet power. This "subversion," in fact, derived from the absolute chaos within the countryside and collective farm system – a natural result of collectivization – leading to a breakdown in discipline and the poverty and starvation in large parts of the countryside that, in turn, precipitated further chaos and theft, fueled by desperation. The state needed to reassert control and, in the midst of famine, it also needed scapegoats. Therefore, the state launched a new wave of repression and claimed to direct it at class enemies. This wave of repression hit *byvshie liudi* en masse.

Although many of the purges were led by outsiders (e.g., the employees of the MTS political sections), many of the collective farm expulsions and the indictments under the law of August 7, 1932, appear to have originated more locally. As may be expected, the dangers of the class enemy in these years were perceived to be the most acute in the famine-stricken areas of the North Caucasus and the Ukraine, thereby indicating the extent to which this wave of repression was an exercise in scapegoating.[46] It should be noted, however, that other key problem areas appear to have been regions to which kulaks had been deported, like Siberia and the Urals.[47] Each of these areas, in addition, had served as key theaters for White or Green activities during the Civil War. Finally, it should be mentioned that *byvshie liudi* most often turned up on state farms and in trade establishments – possibly their last refuge of employment – and in key collective farm positions, like those of accountant, bookkeeper, warehouse-man, storeman, and stablemen – perhaps another refuge (especially in cases of the more literate) or perhaps just sensitive posts highly vulnerable to accusations (false or otherwise) of theft and wrongdoing during hard times.[48]

During the party and soviet purges of 1932–3, there were constant accusations that officials had merged with or fallen under the influence of

---

[46] On the North Caucasus, see *DIu*, no. 3–4 (Feb. 1932): 30; *SIu*, no. 32 (30 Nov. 1932): 2; no. 2–3 (Jan. 1933): 28–29; no. 6 (Mar. 1933): 11; and Nobuo Shimotomai, "A Note on the Kuban Affair (1932–1933)," *Acta Slavica Iaponica*, tomus I (1983).

[47] *SIu*, no. 6 (Mar. 1933): 15–16; no. 21 (Nov. 1933): 9; *DIu*, no. 1 (Jan. 1935): 12; no. 11 (Sept. 1933): 16–17. According to Soviet sources, these were also areas where White officers and tsarist officials settled after the Civil War. See *Istoriia kollektivizatsii sel'skogo khoziaistva v Vostochnoi Sibiri* (Irkutsk, 1979), 6–7.

[48] *KIu*, no. 10 (May 1931): 13; *DIu*, no. 1 (Jan. 1933): 10; no. 2 (Jan. 1933): 1–2; no. 15 (Aug. 1934): 12; no. 14 (July 1935): 9; *SIu*, no. 5 (1934): 4–5. These posts were clearly targeted by the state in the purge of rural institutions. See Ivnitskii, *Klassovaia bor'ba*, 278–279; and Iu. S. Borisov and D. M. Ezerskii, eds., "Dokumenty o politicheskoi i organizatsionno-khoziaistvennoi deiatel'nosti politotdelov sovkhozov v 1933–1935 gg.," *Materialy po istorii SSSR* (M, 1959), vol. 7: 353. However, it also seems clear that the Machine-Tractor Stations (MTS) and state farms served as refuges for many *byvshie liudi* into the mid-1930s. See Merle Fainsod, *Smolensk Under Soviet Rule* (Cambridge, MA, 1958): 302–303.

the kulak and other enemies if they were not themselves aliens.[49] Quite often, "merging" was simply a matter of officials casting their lot with the starving villlagers in an effort to survive or to help others to survive. At other times, mergers were based on alliances of profitable convenience for corrupt or drunken officials. In the Western Region in 1932, for example, 29% of all soviet chairmen were fired for "ties" to aliens.[50]

The *byvshie liudi*, in addition to their infiltration of the organs of Soviet power, it was claimed, had made their presence felt in the state farms and trade establishments. Rudzutak noted the presence of *byvshie liudi* in the trade and cooperative centers in his speech at the Seventeenth Party Congress in 1934.[51] The state farm Serp i Molot was purged due to the alleged presence of former clergy and dekulakized kulaks.[52] The director of one state farm was said to be a former White guard officer.[53] A report on Surgutskii district in the Urals indicated that *byvshie liudi*, counter-revolutionaries, and common criminals were flowing into the north, many with fake documents. These elements, according to the report, sought and gained employment in the soviets, collective farm administrative boards, and especially in the trade apparatus.[54]

Most of the available information on *byvshie liudi* comes from cases of *byvshie liudi* who were collective farm members and/or who engaged in theft as collective farmers. This is natural, since the center of repression, where the state sought its scapegoats, was the collective farm. The members of the MTS political sections, who were to be the party's eye in the countryside, were instructed that the "sabotage" in the collective and state farms was comparable to the Shakhty Affair in terms of its political and social implications. The rural enemies to beware of included kulaks, White officers, clergy, former estate stewards, village policemen, and SR and Petlura intelligentsia – along with their offspring.[55] The establishment of the MTS political sections in 1933 initiated a new witch-hunt in the villages, although it should be emphasized that the political sections were not necessarily the most important actors in this witch-hunt. Among the leading cadres in this wave of repression were *sel'kory*, village officials, court officials, and ordinary, but disgruntled, peasants. During this time, there were mass expulsions from the collective farms, which appear even-

[49] See Shimotomai, "A Note on the Kuban Affair," 45, 47–51; and *SIu*, no. 17–18 (30 June 1932): 30–31; no. 1 (Jan. 1933): 2.
[50] *SIu*, no. 32 (30 Nov. 1932): 22–23.
[51] *XVII s"ezd vsesoiuznoi kommunisticheskoi partii (b). 26 ianvaria–10 fevralia 1934 g. Sten. otchet* (M, 1934): 276.
[52] *DIu*, no. 1 (Jan. 1933): 10.
[53] *SIu*, no 5 (1934): 4–5.
[54] Ibid., no. 1 (1934): 23–24.
[55] *DIu*, no. 2 (Jan. 1933): 2–5; no. 8 (June 1933): 11–12; no. 9 (July 1933): 14–15; no. 12 (Oct. 1933): 15–16; no. 1 (Jan. 1934): 12; no. 15 (Aug. 1934): 2; no. 1 (Jan. 1935): 12; *SIu*, no. 12 (30 April 1932): 13–14; no. 32 (30 Nov. 1932): 2; to cite just a few examples.

tually to have gotten out of hand. Once again, the alien was often defined according to prerevolutionary social status. Reports of "kulaks" present in collective farms often provided information on their prerevolutionary social and economic status.[56] In Zaraiskii district, Moscow Region, it was reported that a number of collective farm administrations were in the hands of village church councils.[57] The chairman of a collective farm in another area was reported to be a "close relative" of a former monastery steward.[58] In another collective farm, a church elder, earlier opposed to collectivization, became the chairman of the farm and a party candidate to the great dismay of a local activist who reported the case.[59] Former village and *volost'* elders (sometimes described as kulaks) were also victims of repression in the collective farm purges. A peasant woman who complained that she was illegally expelled from a collective farm was later "unmasked" as the wife of a former *volost'* elder.[60] The son of a village elder was unmasked by a *sel'kor* when the latter discovered his presence in the collective farm.[61] Other collective farms were reportedly dominated entirely by class aliens.[62] In most of these cases, the "unmasking" of aliens was connected to accusations of theft and/or wrecking within the collective farm or else took place on economically troubled farms.

Sel'kory and activists appear to have been in the forefront of those who unmasked *byvshie liudi* on the collective farms in these years.[63] The *sel'kory* were often able to report on the prerevolutionary past of *byvshie liudi* on the basis of personal recollection. One *sel'kor* wrote of the presence of "aliens" (*chuzhoi*) in his collective farm: the son of a disenfranchised trader and a criminal who had been in prison for twelve years before the Revolution.[64] Another activist reported that the chairman of his farm was a kulak, for he had had a two-story house, three cows and two horses, and hired labor before collectivization.[65] Once again, in many of these reports,

---

[56] E.g., *DIu*, no. 9 (July 1933): 15; no. 11 (Sept. 1933): 2–3; *SIu*, no. 23 (20 Aug. 1932): 18–19; no. 1 (1934): 21–22.

[57] *DIu*, no. 6 (April 1933): 14.

[58] Ibid., no. 1 (Jan. 1934): 12.

[59] Ibid., no. 3 (Feb. 1933): 13.

[60] Ibid., no. 16 (Aug. 1934): 14.

[61] Ibid., no. 20 (Oct. 1934): 13–14. Also see the case of the daughter of a White ataman in no. 4 (Feb. 1933): 11.

[62] E.g., ibid., no. 1 (Jan. 1933): 11. For further data on the collective farm purges, see *DIu*, no. 2 (Jan. 1933): 2–5; no. 5 (Mar. 1933): 14; no. 12 (Oct. 1933): 15–16; no. 1 (Jan. 1934): 12; no. 15 (Aug. 1934): 2; no. 16 (Aug. 1934): 13–14; *SIu*, no. 12 (30 April 1932): 13–14; *Kollektivizatsiia sel'skogo khoziaistva Tsentral'nogo promyshlennog. raiona* (Riazan', 1971): 594–596; and *Kollektivizatsiia sel'skogo khoziaistva v Zapadnom raione,* 589 (for data from 1935).

[63] See the regular column in *DIu*, variously entitled, "nam pishut" or "signaly aktiva," with letters or excerpts of letters from activists and *sel'kory*. (Specific cases cited below.)

[64] *DIu*, no. 1 (Jan. 1934): 12.

[65] Ibid., no. 10 (Aug. 1933): 26. For further denunciations from *Sel'kory* and other activists, see ibid., no. 6 (March 1934): 4; no. 7 (April 1934): 14; and no. 12 (June 1934): 11.

the presence of *byvshie liudi* was linked to theft or other problems in the collective farm.

In addition to the unmasking of enemies on the basis of their pre-revolutionary status, enemies were once again defined according to their Civil War activities. Prominant among this type of enemy were veterans of the White Army.[66] The North Caucasus was described in one report as a "hotbed" of White guard activity.[67] The administrative board of the collective farm Krasnoarmeets in a Kuban cossack village was said to be made up of former White Army soldiers and "kulak relatives."[68] In the Lower Volga, the warehouseman of a collective farm plagued by theft was unmasked as a former White guard.[69] In Western Siberia, Kolchak White guards were reported to be on many collective farm boards.[70] The *sel'kory* were also active in reporting the presence of White guards in the collective farms. One *sel'kor* wrote that the chairman of his collective farm was a former White guard, and another *sel'kor* reported armed bands of former Antonovites (and two brothers who had owned a mill before the Revolution) attacking the collective farm's stables.[71]

The final scourge of the collective farms were dekulakized kulaks, who had fled from exile and were hiding out with false documents in the collective farms or stealing from the collective farms. Escapes from exile on the part of kulaks were apparently not uncommon given the relatively large number of escapes reported in legal journals.[72] Along with escaped kulaks, there were also reports that dekulakized (but not necessarily exiled) kulaks had caused all manner of problems. Much of the collective farm theft that was reported in 1932–4 was linked to organized gangs of

[66] *SIu*, no. 12 (30 April 1932): 13–14; *DIu*, no. 9 (May 1934): 10–11; no. 12 (June 1934): 11; no. 14 (July 1935): 9.
[67] *SIu*, no. 2–3 (Jan. 1933): 28–29.
[68] Ibid., no. 32 (30 Nov. 1932): 2.
[69] *DIu*, no. 4 (Feb. 1933): 11.
[70] *SIu*, no. 6 (Mar. 1933): 15–16.
[71] *DIu*, no. 9 (May 1934): 10–11.
[72] See, for example, *Kollektivizatsiia sel'skogo khoziaistva v Severnom raione (1927–1937 gg.)* (Vologda, 1964): 601. A July 1930 report from Siberia (in *Istoriia kollektivizatsii... Vostochnoi Sibiri*, 163–164) tells of kulaks running away from exile back to their villages. Also see *Vestnik krest'ianskoi Rossii* (izdanie TsK Trudovoi krest'ianskoi partii/Prague), no. 9–10 (Feb.–Mar. 1931): 15–16, for a report indicating that escapes from the concentration camp "Artem" (consisting largely of peasant inmates) occurred almost on a daily basis. For other cases of escaped kulaks, see *DIu*, no. 11 (Sept. 1933): 16–17; no. 6 (Mar. 1933): 4; no. 17 (Sept. 1934): 12; *SIu*, no. 27 (30 Sept. 1932): 23; no. 30 (30 Oct. 1932): 8; no. 2–3 (Jan. 1933): 28–29; no. 14 (July 1933): 4–5; no. 15 (Aug. 1933): 4–6; no. 16 (Aug. 1933): 6; no. 1 (1934): 23–24; no. 20 (1934): 2–3. For information on "kulak bands," see also the documents collected in *Vnutrennie voiska v gody mirnogo sotsialisticheskogo stroitel'stva. Dokumenty i materialy* (M, 1977). For a first-hand account of life on the run by a "kulak" escapee, see the poignant memoir by Ivan Tvardovskii (brother of Alexander, former editor of *Novyi mir*), "Stranitsy perezhitogo," *Iunost'*, no. 3 (1988).

dekulakized peasants.[73] This kind of accusation, needless to say, may simply have been a convenient ruse for leaders of farms who were engaged in theft and sought to transfer the blame to others. In the Ivanovo Industrial Region, there were rumors that many kulaks had entered the region's collective farms from another district, that of Cherepovetskii.[74] One *sel'kor* reported the presence of dekulakized kulaks in his collective farm, and another *sel'kor* reported that the son of an exiled kulak was the chair of a collective farm with serious problems.[75] The chairman of the collective farm Krasnaia Borozda in Ivanovo Industrial Region was reported to be the son of a kulak miller and to have personally served two months of forced labor for speculation.[76]

The search for *byvshie liudi* took on a central impetus as the center sought scapegoats and the social cleansing of its institutions. Local cadres and activists, however, carried the manhunt further than the center wished in their zeal for genealogical purity. Central authorities and legal officials, in particular, often inveighed against the extremes that the genealogical craze assumed. The problem with these protests was that they were seldom consistent and often contradicted one another. There were some genuine concerns, however, that some of the activities of local cadres, the collective farm expulsions in particular, were getting out of hand. For example, in one district in the Ivanovo Industrial Region, collective farm expulsions were condemned because they were implemented "formally" on the basis of prerevolutionary social and economic status, including information on the property holdings of parents and even grandparents.[77] In Ordinskii district in the Sverdlov Region, local authorities suggested purging from the collective farms all those with even the most distant kulak relatives and all those who served in the White Army; as a consequence, there were massive illegal expulsions in this district, later condemned by the center.[78] The legal journal *Sovetskaia iustitsiia* criticized the massive expulsions, claiming that expulsions were often decided according to the following indicators: Was the father or grandfather a kulak; did the farm use hired labor before 1917 or during NEP; was there any cottage industry in the household?[79] Perhaps the extremes to which local cadres took the offensive against the *byvshie liudi* dwell somewhere in the background of an

[73] *DIu*, no. 9 (May 1934): 11; no. 15 (Aug. 1934): 2; *SIu*, no. 6–7 (10 Mar. 1932): 2–6; no. 1 (Jan. 1933): 2; no. 16 (Aug. 1933): 6–7.
[74] *DIu*, no. 9 (July 1933): 14–15.
[75] Ibid., no. 6 (Mar. 1934): 13–14; no. 3 (Feb. 1934): 12.
[76] *DIu*, no. 5 (Mar. 1933): 6–7. Also see ibid., no. 8 (June 1933): 11–12. Also see *DIu*, no. 24 (Dec. 1934): 4; and no. 15 (Aug. 1934): 12.
[77] Ibid., no. 11 (Sept. 1933): 2–3.
[78] Ibid., no. 1 (Jan. 1935): 12. Also see *DIu*, no. 11 (Sept. 1933): 6–7; and no. 3–4 (Feb. 1932): 28.
[79] *SIu*, no. 1 (1934): 21–22.

apparent decision in 1935 to attempt to halt in part the genealogical witch-hunt with Stalin's announcement that sons were no longer responsible for the sins of their fathers.[80]

Not all activists were genealogists and not all victims of the genealogical witch-hunt were "authentic" *byvshie liudi*. Surely the label was politically convenient for many local officials. And lest too much reason or too simplistic an explanation be offered here, it is necessary to note once again that there remained much that was arbitrary and senseless in the rural repression of these years. Repression was massive and as the state experienced economic crisis, it sought scapegoats. Yet despite this caveat, *byvshie liudi* were indeed victims of repression.

It is clear that a person's past was meaningful to Soviet officials, and perhaps it was more meaningful the lower down the official was on the regional hierarchy of command. Soviet society in the 1930s was far from a classless society. It remained a society acutely – and pathologically – conscious of prerevolutionary and NEP social categories and the personal political histories of its members. The campaign against the *byvshie liudi* sheds light on the pervasiveness and persistence of antipathy toward the old enemies. The hatreds, unleashed by the Revolution and Civil War, were perhaps now more narrowly channeled and far less spontaneous than the passionate outburst of 1917. Nevertheless, the roots of such hatred were the same. The hatred manifested in the search for *byvshie liudi* was directed toward representatives of the old regime and the Bolshevik opposition in the Civil War, resulting in wave upon wave of denunciation, fanaticism, and brutality that helped acclimatize the country for the next round of repression in the late 1930s.

The genealogical craze in the countryside, especially in its more extreme forms, also reveals a good deal about rural politics. The key victims of the genealogical craze included certain important categories of rural inhabitants who were traditionally the object of peasant antipathy. Landlords, estate stewards, tsarist officials, tsarist army officers, policemen, and unpopular elders represented an alien social and political order against which the Revolution had been made. (The same could be said about members of the clergy in certain localities.) Many peasants could easily remember who among their fellow villagers stood on which side of the barricades in 1905, in 1917, and during the Civil War. Traders, merchants, tavern owners, and mill owners often were outsiders who, it was believed, engaged in economic exploitation. The Stolypin *otrubniki*, who had suffered the wrath of the commune during the Civil War, apparently continued to be viewed as outsiders. Although "kulaks" in the form of the wealthier

---

[80] The decision has been attributed to Stalin, although there is no such statement in his works. See Sheila Fitzpatrick, *Education and Social Mobility in the Soviet Union, 1921–1934* (Cambridge, 1979): 235, 323–324/note 1.

peasants of the postrevolutionary epoch appear among the *byvshie liudi*, perhaps the "kulak" was not the main "enemy" and gradations of wealth were not the most important cleavages in the village. It may well be that the repression of the early 1930s was shaped in part by a rural political culture that identified the enemy as the prerevolutionary elite. Elsewhere, lines of division may have been Red versus White.[81]

These conclusions, of course, are highly speculative. What is interesting to note, however, is that the *byvshie liudi* figure much more prominently in the sources before and after the most intensive years of wholesale collectivization. During the heyday of collectivization, the countryside was subjected to a veritable invasion from the towns as all manner of plenipotentiaries and more permanent cadres were dispatched to rural localities. Before and after this period, peasant cadres administered the collective farms and held most other rural offices. Villagers, such as *sel'kory*, rural party members, Komsomols, and rank-and-file peasants figure largely among those who wrote letters to the press to unmask *byvshie liudi*. And there is little doubt that local definitions of *byvshie liudi* were far more extensive than central definitions and that certain categories of the repressed could only have been counted as *byvshie liudi* according to local definitions. Perhaps the withdrawal of outside forces allowed the emergence of otherwise hidden cleavages, much more likely to remain under the surface in the face of an onslaught from the outside. If this suggestion is correct, it may well be that with the withdrawal of the collectivization forces old – and in normal times, mundane – village tensions reemerged to shape the actions of peasant officials and activists. But instead of working themselves out in the old ways, these tensions assumed a violent and politicized form in the aftermath of collectivization and in the midst of the devastating famine.

There was a degree of method to the madness of dekulakization writ large. Kulaks, variously defined, *byvshie liudi*, and critics of various persuasions were all victims of repression in the Soviet countryside. In the context of the times, these categories of rural inhabitants were logical targets. Each category (with some exceptions among the extremes) represented a perceived political threat to Soviet power and, in the deterministic order of things, a socioeconomic threat as well. But other victims were neither centrally designated targets nor deterministically ordered enemies. An important category of victim that emerges from the sources could be

[81] Several Western works have illuminated the social and estate cleavages dividing the countryside before the Revolution. Roberta T. Manning discusses village divisions and notes attacks on "kulaks, merchants, and larger renters" in 1905 in *The Crisis of the Old Order in Russia* (Princeton, 1982): 156–157. In *The Roots of Otherness: Russia's Turn of Century* (New Haven, 1985), 2 vols., Teodor Shanin writes, "As for the *kulaks* of the Russian countryside, at least in the peasant meaning of this term, these were neither the richer farmers nor the employers, but the 'not quite peasants' who stood apart or against the commune" (vol. 2: 172).

labeled as "outsiders" within the village or collective farm. Outsiders, for our purposes, included members of the rural intelligentsia and rural inhabitants who did not earn their subsistence solely on the basis of agriculture, like *otkhodniki* (seasonal workers, especially those working in industry) and *kustari* (artisans). The repression of victims in this category was generally condemned by authorities above the village and district levels.

The rural intelligentsia figured among the victims of repression throughout the years of wholesale collectivization and beyond. Members of the rural intelligentsia subject to repression included doctors, *fel'dshers* (doctor's assistants), veterinarians, agronomists, and especially teachers, who accounted for the largest proportion of the rural intelligentsia.[82]

The government consistently noted and condemned the repression of rural school teachers.[83] The dekulakization of teachers (along with other rural specialists) was expressly forbidden.[84] Also forbidden was the expulsion of teachers from collective farms in the collective farm purges of the famine years.[85] According to the central authorities, teachers could not be subject to repression regardless of their social origin.[86]

The government's directives to stem the tide of repressive measures aimed at teachers and other rural specialists were prompted by an unanticipated rash of attacks on teachers. Yet the directives and the constant appeals of the center appear to have had little effect on alleviating the victims' plight. As early as spring 1930, the dekulakization of teachers was reported.[87] Their repression in the Central Black Earth Region was described in one source as "massive."[88] In the Western Region, sixty-three teachers were reportedly subject to incorrect dekulakization.[89] Teachers continued to be subject to dekulakization in later years and in other areas. In one district in the Leningrad Region, ten teachers were designated as

---

[82] For statistical information on the rural intelligentsia from the 1926 census, see V. P. Danilov, *Sovetskaia dokolkhoznaia derevnia: naselenie, zemlepol'zovanie, khoziaistvo* (M, 1977): 66. On the status of rural teachers, see Ben Eklof, *Russian Peasant Schools* (Berkeley, 1986), chap. 7–8, who notes (p. 244) that teachers were subject to violence as outsiders in 1905, 1917, and the Civil War.

[83] *SIu*, no. 7–8 (20 Mar. 1930): 3; no. 11 (20 April 1930): 4; no. 13 (10 May 1930): 9–11; no. 32 (Nov. 1931): 7; no. 15 (Aug. 1933): 19–20.

[84] Ibid., no. 10 (10 April 1930): 31. See also the Leningrad regional soviet executive committee letter of 24 Mar. 1930 forbidding the dekulakization of the rural intelligentsia in *Kollektivizatsiia sel'skogo khoziaistva v Severo-Zapadnom raione* (L, 1970): 170–171.

[85] *SIu*, no. 1 (1934): 21–22.

[86] Ibid., no. 10 (10 April 1930): 31.

[87] Ibid., no. 7–8 (20 Mar. 1930): 3; no. 11 (20 April 1930): 4; no. 13 (10 May 1930): 9–11.

[88] See the information in ibid., no. 11 (20 April 1930): 4, 6–7. Also see no. 32 (30 Nov. 1932): 7, for similar court cases in 1931.

[89] Fitzpatrick, *Education and Social Mobility*, 165. Fitzpatrick notes that these cases represented one-tenth of all cases of "incorrect" dekulakization noted in the Western Region.

kulaks and taxed accordingly. When they could not pay their taxes, their property was confiscated and they were exiled.[90] In Shablykinskii district in the Western Region, twelve teachers were taxed as kulaks in 1933.[91]

The rural intelligentsia in many cases were outsiders to the village. Although many specialists, and especially many teachers, were peasant in social origins, they often came from outside the area where they worked. In addition, they were frequently viewed as outsiders of undesirable social origins, for the status of intellectual, in and of itself, could be perceived as socially alien by rural cadres and ordinary peasants. Similarly, the family connections of some specialists to members of the old village elite could mark them as aliens. For example, one teacher was dekulakized because she had been married to a priest, who had died twenty-five years earlier.[92]

In other cases, teachers and specialists who were activists figured among the repressed. The official reasons for their repression were based on contrived charges of alien social origin. This was the case of the teacher activist, whose mother, it was claimed, may have visited the priest.[93] This was also the case of the teacher Zhiliakov, a collective farm board member and local activist, who was dekulakized in 1930. Zhiliakov was accused of being a former White officer by a better-off peasant who was opposed to the collective farm.[94] In the Tambov area, the teacher Slepushkin was responsible for the disenfranchisement of a peasant named Struchkov. According to a report, Struchkov was in thick with officials at the district soviet (supposedly his drinking companions). With their aid, he managed to have Slepushkin arrested and charged with exploitation (of a woman who cooked his food and washed his clothes) and arson.[95] In these cases, political conflict emerges alongside real or perceived problematic social

[90] SIu, no. 23 (20 Aug. 1932): 15.
[91] Ibid., no. 4 (Feb. 1933): 12–14. See also the 1934 report noting the large number of teachers and medical workers purged from collective farms in 1933–4 in Kollektivizatsiia... Bashkirskoi ASSR, 226. Reports about the expulsion of teachers' families from collective farms continued to be heard throughout the 1930s. E.g., see SIu, no. 17 (15 June 1936): 8–9.
[92] SIu, no. 11 (20 April 1930): 4. Also see DIu, no. 18 (Sept. 1934): 2. See Eklof, Russian Peasant Schools, 188–189, 214, 221, 229, on teachers as outsiders. Eklof also discusses social origins of teachers, noting a relatively high percentage (32.6% of female teachers) of teachers who were from the clergy estate. Scott J. Seregny, in Russian Teachers and Peasant Revolution (Bloomington, IN, 1989): 197–213, concludes that the post-1905 repression against teachers led to more passive teachers, who would play little role in politics in 1917 and who would be viewed by peasants even more as outsiders due to the increased polarization of society after 1905.
[93] SIu, no. 11 (20 April 1930): 8–9. (See her case on the first page of this article.)
[94] In fact, Zhiliakov had been a junker during World War I, but left the army before the Civil War. KIu, no. 1 (Jan. 1931): 16.
[95] He was held in prison for thirty-three days until higher authorities cleared him of all charges. SIu, no. 11 (20 April 1930): 6–7. See also the 21 December 1930 reference to "kulak" attacks on two female teachers (activists) and other collective farm activists in the collective farm "Progress" in Demianskii district, cited in Kollektivizatsiia... Severo-Zapadnom raione, 206–207.

igins as the cause of repression. Revenge for political activism by the targets of such activism may account for some of the repression aimed at the rural intelligentsia. In fact, as early as 1929, it was reported that teachers were subject to persecution from "kulaks and clergy" for political activism. This report noted 150 cases of persecution against teachers between August 1928 and May 1929.[96]

Other, more mundane reasons for the persecution of the rural intelligentsia suggest themselves. Rural specialists, teachers first and foremost, were often supported financially by the village community through the local soviet, which was required to provide them with salaries and/or food rations. In the 1920s, cases were reported of villages and lower level officials resisting the payment of teachers' salaries.[97] With the advent of the collective farm, teachers continued to be a financial burden on the village and local soviet. In addition, teachers were entitled to a plot of land (the *usad'ba*) even though they did not participate in collective agriculture. The expense of maintaining an intellectually productive, but agriculturally unproductive teacher may have been a factor in the expulsion of teachers from collective farms and their designation as kulaks.[98] As late as 1937, collective farms complained about the right of their white-collar members to have an *usad'ba*.[99] Additionally, the fact that many village teachers were women in positions of relative authority in what was still a very patriarchal rural society may have conditioned the wave of persecution directed against teachers.[100]

Other outsiders were subject to persecution during these years, like the *otkhodniki* and *kustari*, both of which were subject, at varying times, to dekulakization, expulsion from the collective farm, and taxation as kulaks. The term *outsider* in this context, however, is much more problematic because the outsiders were generally peasants, but peasants who earned their living either wholly or in part through nonagricultural pursuits. Neither the *otkhodniki* nor the *kustari* were officially designated targets

---

[96] *Ezhenedel'nik Sovetskoi iustitsiia*, no. 34 (3 Sept. 1929): 785. See *XIV Vserossiiskii s"ezd sovetov. Sten. otchet* (M, 1929), Biulleten' No. 14: 42, for a report of thirty cases of "terrorist attacks" against teachers during the same period. Despite Soviet claims that many teachers were activists before and after 1917, it is likely that most teachers were apolitical and simply attempted to do the best they could under difficult circumstances.

[97] *SIu*, no. 2 (20 Jan. 1930): 30; no. 9 (31 Mar. 1930): 32; Fitzpatrick, *Education and Social Mobility*, 30–33; and A. M. Bol'shakov, *Derevnia 1917–1927* (M, 1927): 232, 239–241.

[98] On the teacher's position in the collective farm, see Fitzpatrick, *Education and Social Mobility*, 165; and Roberta T. Manning, "Government in the Soviet Countryside in the Stalinist Thirties: The Case of Belyi Raion in 1937," *Carl Beck Papers in Russian and East European Studies*, no. 301: 54, n. 56. For cases of expulsions, see *SIu*, no. 15 (Aug. 1933): 19–20; no. 1 (1934): 21–22. See Eklof, *Russian Peasant Schools*, 226–227, 229, 232, for information on teachers' economic dependency on the commune.

[99] *SIu*, no. 17 (5 Sept. 1937): 13–14.

[100] See Eklof, *Russian Peasant Schools*, 181, 188–189, on the difficulties of female teachers in the prerevolutionary village.

of repression. On the contrary, the government had warned officials to be cautious in approaching kulak households who had family members working in industry.[101] Furthermore, cases of repression aimed at *otkhodniki* or *kustari* were often overturned by higher authorities.[102] However, there was a lack of clarity in regard to the status of these groups in certain instances. For example, the official definition of a kulak household defined as kulak certain categories of *kustar'* households that made use of hired labor.[103] Likewise, a TsIK-SNK (Central Executive Committee–Council of People's Commissariats) decree of March 17, 1933, permitted the "deprivation of the collective farm rights" of *otkhodniki* who entered the industrial labor force "spontaneously" – that is, not through the official labor recruitment channels (*orgnabor*).[104] These directives served to undermine the center's attempts to prevent *kustari* and *otkhodniki* who did not fall into these categories from escaping the repression. As a result, it was noted that certain types of "unusual farms," those of *otkhodniki* among others, were often subject, incorrectly, to dekulakization.[105]

During collectivization, *otkhodniki* were often among the dekulakized.[106] In the Central Black Earth Region, workers who earned over one hundred rubles were subject to dekulakization in some areas.[107] From 1932, the families of *otkhodniki* also found themselves subject to expulsion from the collective farm on occasion. Such cases were reported in the Middle Volga and Ivanovo Region in 1932 and elsewhere as late as 1935 and 1936.[108]

Otkhodnichestvo occurred among all social strata of the peasantry in the 1920s, but the numbers of middle peasants and kulaks involved in *otkhod* appear to have increased on the eve of collectivization with the intensification of repression.[109] It may be then that many farms with

---

[101] See the regional decrees on dekulakization in *Kollektivizatsiia ... Zapadnom raione*, 246–250; *Kollektivizatsiia ... Severnom Kavkaze*, 248–250; *Kollektivizatsiia sel'skogo khoziaistva v Srednem Povolzh'e* (Kuibyshev, 1970): 156–158; *Kollektivizatsiia sel'skogo khoziaistva Zapadnoi Sibiri* (Tomsk, 1972): 135–138.

[102] E.g., *KIu*, no. 6 (Mar. 1931): 13; *DIu*, no. 11 (June 1934): 13; no. 16 (Aug. 1935): 10–11; *SIu*, no. 21 (30 July 1932): 14.

[103] *Sobranie zakonov*, no. 34 (13 June 1929): 641–642.

[104] *Pravda*, 18 Mar. 1933. See A. M. Panfilova, *Formirovanie rabochego klassa SSSR v gody pervoi piatiletki* (M, 1964): 118; and *Kollektivizatsiia ... Zapadnom raione*, 663, n. 65.

[105] *SIu*, no. 2 (20 Jan. 1931): 21.

[106] *Za kollektivizatsiiu*, 12 Feb. 1930, p. 2; *SIu*, no. 13 (10 May 1930): 9–11; no. 17 (20 June 1930): 8. Also see Panfilova, *Formirovanie*, 26; and L. S. Rogachevskaia, *Likvidatsiia bezrabotitsy v SSSR* (M, 1973): 203–204.

[107] *SIu*, no. 11 (20 April 1930): 4; no. 17 (20 June 1930): 8.

[108] *DIu*, no. 5–6 (Mar. 1932): 26–27; *SIu*, no. 17 (15 June 1936): 8–9; *Kollektivizatsiia ... Srednem Povolzh'e*, 509–510; *Kollektivizatsiia ... Severnom raione*, 617. Also see Iu. V. Arutiunian, "Kollektivizatsiia sel'skogo khoziaistva i vysvobozhdenie rabochei sily dlia promyshlennosti," in *Formirovanie i razvitie Sovetskogo rabochego klassa* (M, 1964): 107–108, on expulsions of *otkhodniki* families from collective farms.

[109] V. P. Danilov, "Krest'ianskii otkhod na promysly v 1920-kh godakh," *Istoricheskie zapiski*, vol. 94 (1974): 55–122. Danilov notes that *otkhod* was more a function of family size and seasonal underemployment than poverty.

otkhodniki were subject to repression as a function of economic wealth. It may also be that the number of kulaks and *lishentsy* who were *otkhodniki* increased further during the years of wholesale collectivization in response to their exclusion from the collective farms, the taxes levied on their individual farms, and the increasingly desperate economic plight of their families, and this then could account for the persecution of *otkhodniki*.

Political activism or, alternately, political opposition to collectivization may have also served as factors in the repression of *otkhodniki*. For example, the former *otkhodnik* Priakhin returned to his native village sometime before 1932. He became an activist and disclosed what was defined as "waste" in the local soviet. Following this disclosure, the soviet chairman made false accusations about Priakin's prerevolutionary past, which led to Priakin's disenfranchisement and expulsion from the collective farm. The district authorities ignored Priakin's complaints and only the intervention of the newspaper *Krest'ianskaia gazeta* saved him from his fate at the hands of the local and district authorities.[110] Conventional wisdom on the progressive nature of the *otkhodniki* within the village context might even support a hypothesis that some *otkhodniki* were activists and, in the course of their work, may have come into conflict with corrupt local officials, who sought to repress them.[111] However, it is not clear that the supposed political and cultural superiority of the *otkhodniki* was necessarily manifested in support for the collective farm. In fact, archival sources point to a different kind of activism. In the Ukraine in 1929, working-class grain requisitioning brigades noted that *otkhodniki* and peasants who commuted to nearby factories were the most vocal opponents of grain requisitioning and other official policies.[112] It may well be that exposure to the city granted some *otkhodniki* the independence of mind and broader cultural experience necessary to step forward and protest. Certainly *otkhodniki* had figured prominently as leaders of earlier peasant protests.[113]

Some *otkhodniki* may also have been subjected to repression simply because they were *otkhodniki* and, within the village context, were relative outsiders or perceived representatives of a sometimes resented working class. In Bronnitskii District, Kolomenskii County, peasants hated workers, according to one report, largely because of the excesses of collectivization. Here peasant-workers were told either to stay in the village permanently

[110] *SIu*, no. 21 (30 July 1932): 14.
[111] Conventional wisdom was that *otkhodniki* brought back to the village more advanced views adopted while working in the cities.
[112] TsGAOR, f. 5469, op. 13, d. 122, ll. 162–169; d. 23, ll. 78–91.
[113] Manning, *Crisis of the Old Order*, 165–166. See also Sheila Fitzpatrick, "New Perspectives on the Civil War," in Diane Koenker et al., eds., *Party, State, and Society in the Russian Civil War* (Bloomington, IN, 1989): 10, for role of returning workers in Civil War village conflicts.

or to leave forever. According to the report, local officials encouraged *otkhodniki* to leave and many in fact did leave with their families.[114] Additionally, the *otkhodniki* may have been resented for their ability to escape the countryside and to earn supplemental wages in industry. An August 1934 Western Region Communist Party report noted that many workers and railroad employees with large agricultural plots did not want to join the collective farms. Because they were not members of a collective farm, these individuals were exempt from meat and milk requisitioning. Their exemption and survival outside of the collective farm system, according to the report, had a "negative influence" on the neighboring collective farmers, who viewed the private farmers as "privileged."[115]

Other *otkhodniki* suffered within the context of the new collective farm system. In the early period of collectivization, many collective farms attempted to prevent villagers from going to work in the cities and some actually recalled workers from factories.[116] In some cases, collective farms were hurt by the loss of labor, particularly the loss of skilled labor.[117] In other cases, the collective farms may have resented their responsibility to provide the families of *otkhodniki* with certain rights and privileges, including the *usad'ba*, because the *otkhodnik's* household was sometimes economically weak within the collective farm and may not have been able to contribute its "fair share" of collective farm labor due to the loss of its able-bodied workers.[118] This resentment may explain why many families of *otkhodniki*, who remained behind, were subject to expulsion from the collective farms or were, as one report noted, in desperate economic straits because the collective farm boards would not give them food.[119] In other cases, the collective farms deducted a portion of the *otkhodnik's* salary to compensate for the loss of his labor.[120] Even before collectivization, villagers sometimes resented the *otkhodniki's* right to land within the village. According to one 1929 report, peasants in the Vladimir Region complained about workers with farms, claiming that the workers did not

---

[114] *Moskovskaia derevnia*, 7 Feb. 1930, p. 2. See also *KIu*, no. 6 (Mar. 1931): 13.

[115] *Kollektivizatsiia ... Zapadnom raione*, 523–526.

[116] Arutiunian, "Kollektivizatsiia," 107–108; Panfilova, *Formirovanie*, 26–30; Rogachevskaia, *Likvidatsiia*, 203–204.

[117] Arutiunian, "Kollektivizatsiia," 111.

[118] Ibid., 109. Arutiunian mentions the responsibility of the collective farms to provide privileges to *otkhodniki* families.

[119] *Sotsialisticheskaia rekonstruktsiia sel'skogo khoziaistva*, no. 11 (Nov. 1931): 19. Also see Arutiunian, "Kollektivizatsiia," 107–108; and Panfilova, *Formirovanie*, 26.

[120] At first, collective farms were told not to take more than 20% of an *otkhodniki's* salary. This percentage was soon lowered to 10%, and then, in June 1931, collective farms were forbidden to take any part of the salary. From 1931, with the introduction of orgnabor, the enterprises, which recruited collective farm labor, were supposed to compensate the farms for loss of labor. The enterprises rarely lived up to their side of the bargain. See Panfilova, *Formirovanie*, 114–116.

take care of their farms and that their continued title to land interfered with *zemleustroistvo* (land reform).[121]

There are several other factors that may explain the repression of *otkhodniki*. The return of *otkhodniki* in some areas may have placed an undue economic burden on the villages, particularly in traditional areas of *otkhod* that tended to suffer from overpopulation in the first place.[122] In other cases, *otkhodniki* may have chosen to remain outside of the collective farms, taking advantage of their official exemption from dekulakization that made them less vulnerable to pressures to join a collective farm.[123] Local officials may have had no other resort but to dekulakize illegally or tax as kulaks the households of *otkhodniki* in order to raise the collectivization rates or increase the landholding of the collective farms. Finally, it is possible that some *otkhodniki* were expelled from collective farms after 1933 because they left the farms and went to industry outside the official channels of *orgnabor*. In such cases, local authorities acted according to central directives.[124]

The *otkhodniki's* fate was sometimes shared by the *kustari*, who were often dekulakized during collectivization. Many of them were "liquidated" as NEPmen (private traders, small manufacturers, or artisans who arose as a result of the New Economic Policy), particularly in early 1930, when the liquidation of NEPmen was at its zenith. Some were returning to the village from the city as a result of the repression and, in all probability, their status as "returnees" complicated their situation.[125] Even in 1931, the journal *Sovetskaia iustitsiia* noted that authorities in the Central Black Earth Region tended to dekulakize "unusual farms," like those of the *kustari* and *otkhodniki*.[126] The *kustari*, like the teacher and the *otkhodnik*, may have been resented by their fellow collective farmers or the collective

---

[121] *Litsom k derevne*, no. 9 (May 1929): 28. Also see the case in *KIu*, no. 8 (30 April 1928): 15.

[122] Rogachevskaia, *Likvidatsiia*, 201–203.

[123] See references to regional legislation on dekulakization in n. 101 above. In the Northwest, the lowest percentages of collectivization in 1934 were in districts where *kustari* and workers lived (as well as areas with large numbers of khutory and otruby). Here, the collective farmers were forced to do the bulk of work outside the collective farm (e.g., timbering, school repairs, etc.) while private farmers were incorrectly exempted from this work. This inequality may very well have created tensions between collective farm labor and private farmers. See *Kollektivizatsiia ... Severo-Zapadnom raione*, 338. Also see *Kollektivizatsiia ... Zapadnom raione*, 523–524, which tells of workers and railroad workers with farms who did not want to join the collective farm (report of 1934).

[124] Panfilova, *Formirovanie*, 118.

[125] See Alec Nove, *An Economic History of the USSR* (New York, 1984): 193–194, for information on the liquidation of cottage industry. Also see Sheila Fitzpatrick, "After NEP: The Fate of NEP Entrepreneurs, Small Traders, and Artisans in the 'Socialist Russia' of the 1930s," *Russian History*, vol. 13, nos. 2–3 (1986): 206, who discusses the new occupations of "liquidated" NEPmen and notes that one-third of her sample of 34,242 returned to the village.

[126] *SIu*, no. 2 (20 Jan. 1931): 21. Also see the case of the middle peasant tailor, whose sewing machine was confiscated after he could not pay the tverdoe zadanie, in *SIu*, no. 1

farm board for not doing their fair share of farm work, while continuing to enjoy the benefits of collective farm membership in the form of the *usad'ba*. The return of *kustari* (as well as *otkhodniki*) may have placed an added burden on the already hard-pressed village. In addition, many *kustari* used hired labor, sometimes apprentices, in their work. Although the 1929 law defining kulak households included certain vaguely defined categories of *kustari* with hired labor, the central authorities exempted blacksmiths with hired hands from kulak status (during the campaign to uncover all kulak households for taxation) in 1931.[127] Whereas the center claimed, perhaps disingenuously, that not all who hired labor were kulaks, the local authorities may have continued to view the presence of hired labor as a most convenient indicator for defining kulak status. Local authorities may also have resorted to repression as a way to force the *kustari* to join the collective farms or, at least, to confiscate their lands when they remained outside of the collective farm system. By the end of 1935, some 3.5 million farms remained outside of the collective farms and some proportion of them were involved in cottage industry.[128]

These categories of outsiders, unlike the kulak and most but not all of the *byvshie liudi*, were not centrally designated targets of repression, despite a lack of legal clarity in some instances. Their victimization may have been based, in large part, on motivations that, however irrational or brutal to the outside observer, were economically or politically rational in the minds of local cadres. Economic privileges, food, and the right to a parcel of land may have been key divisive issues in a countryside that simply did not have enough to go around.

If the countryside was increasingly prone to violence provoked by economic desperation, it was also rapidly succumbing to a paranoid, martial outlook that led it to close in on itself. The trauma of wholesale collectivization and fearsome peasant rebellion, along with the economy of scarcity, must have served, to some extent, to atomize villagers and to create a siegelike existence for rural officials much more profound than in earlier periods of Soviet rule. In this context, the term *alien* may have been much more meaningful and much less artificial than traditionally assumed in the West. Outsiders, as well as *byvshie liudi*, may have become glaringly alien and, consequently, politically or socially suspect within the increasingly insular countryside. Alien status, then, could only have been compounded in cases when outsiders were outspoken either in their activism or

(Jan. 1933): 18; and reports of dekulakization of *kustari* in 1930 in *Bashkiriia in Kollektivizatsiia . . . Bashkirskoi ASSR*, 127–129.

[127] *KIu*, no. 1 (Jan. 1931): 8–9. For the 1929 law, see *Sobranie zakonov*, no. 34 (13 June 1929): 641–642.

[128] Iu. A. Moshkov, "Reshaiushchii etap osushchestvleniia Leninskogo kooperativnogo plana i vopros o zakliuchitel'nom etape NEPa v SSSR," *Problemy agrarnoi istorii Sovetskogo obshchestva*, 153.

criticism or when they actually assumed the appearance or demeanor of aliens.[129]

Whatever the case may be, the repression of outsiders suggests the existence of important divisions in the newly collectivized countryside, which were compounded and brutalized by the violence and traumas of the times. These divisions suggest that the repressive actions of local cadres were often played out within and on the basis of local circumstance and need. The divisions also suggest the possibility of a traditional, regressive political culture at work that victimized outsiders as enemies or scapegoats to be expelled from its midst.[130]

Divisions within the village may also explain the repression of another group of unexpected targets among the so-called class enemies of this time. These targets were economically marginal households or individuals, who were needy, incapable of contributing their fair share of work in the collective farm, or entitled to collective farm privileges. This category included Red Army families, the elderly and ill, the families of exiled or rehabilitated kulaks, and women of special repute. These individuals and households were subject to expulsion from the collective farm and taxation as kulaks. Less frequently, they were subject to dekulakization. In all cases, the state condemned their persecution.

The families of Red Army soldiers were of special concern to the Soviet state, because the state was forced to depend on the peasantry for its largest number of conscripts.[131] To offset or prevent a decline in peasant soldier morale, the state attempted to exempt members of Red Army families from dekulakization and, in later years, from expulsion from the collective farm, regardless of the social origin of the family members.[132] Cases of repression of Red Army families were condemned and routinely overturned.[133]

Despite the state's attempts to protect Red Army families from repression, the families experienced frequent persecution, especially in 1932 through

[129] This point may explain why Red Army veterans appear on occasion among the repressed. See, for example, *DIu*, no. 9 (May 1934): 12, 14; no. 15 (Aug. 1934): 13; no. 3 (Feb. 1935): 13–14.

[130] Note that, to some extent, categories of outsiders and *byvshie liudi* were overlapping. The *otrubniki* and owners of economic establishments in the villages (e.g., tavern owners, mill owners) could be included as outsiders as well as *byvshie liudi*.

[131] However, the state endeavored to increase the numbers of working-class soldiers at this time. E. H. Carr, *Foundations of a Planned Economy, 1926–1929*, vol. 2 (New York, 1971): 318.

[132] See n. 101 above; and *SIu*, no. 1 (1934): 21–22. For the impact of collectivization on the morale of peasant soldiers, see Carr, *Foundations*, 330–331; *SIu*, no. 21 (30 July 1932): 11; Fainsod, *Smolensk*, 331; V. I. Varenov, *Pomoshch' krasnoi armii v razvitii kolkhoznogo stroitel'stva* (M, 1978): 40–47.

[133] See cases cited below.

1934.[134] *Sel'kory* often reported cases of persecution among the families of Red Army men who were frequently expelled from the collective farms and incorrectly taxed.[135] Since Red Army families were officially exempt from the repression aimed at kulaks, some Red Army families may have actually qualified for inclusion as kulaks,[136] although there were serious efforts to screen out socially alien elements from the draft.[137] More probably, however, a range of other explanations suggest themselves as factors for the persecution of Red Army families.

Red Army veterans, like *otkhodniki*, are generally considered to have been a politically or culturally progressive force in the village. Activist veterans could have encountered difficulties with corrupt officials or could have been falsely denounced by families whose members had suffered at the activists' hands during dekulakization. There were, in fact, two cases when wives of soldiers were expelled from collective farms for exposing drunkenness and other problems of collective farm administrators.[138] Also, Red Army veterans, as was suggested in the case of the *otkhodniki*, could have expressed their supposedly advanced consciousness through the courage to protest.[139]

In all probability, the basis for the persecution of Red Army families was economic, and prompted by the economy of scarcity at work in the Soviet countryside, especially in the years after 1931. Red Army families formed a special category within the peasantry who were entitled to certain kinds of material aid from the state.[140] Since peasant relatives were apt to write to their menfolk in the army with all manner of complaints and ask them to intercede with the authorities, the correct and timely provisioning of the families was an important concern to the state.[141] However, many complaints indicated that local authorities failed to aid needy Red Army families.[142] It may have been easier for local authorities, especially collec-

---

[134] See *SIu*, no. 4 (Feb. 1933): 12–13; no. 15 (Aug. 1933): 8–10; no. 4 (1934): 17–18; *DIu*, no. 3 (Feb. 1934): 13; no. 12 (June 1934): 12; and Fainsod, *Smolensk*, 244.

[135] *DIu*, no. 11 (Sept. 1933): 18; no. 3 (Feb. 1934): 13; no. 13 (July 1934): 13–14; no. 1 (Jan. 1935): 13–14. In most of these cases, the families affected had members in the army; in several cases, however, persecution was directed at families with veterans, rather than with active soldiers. See *DIu*, no. 9 (May 1934): 12, 14; no. 15 (Aug. 1934): 13; no. 3 (Feb. 1935): 13–14.

[136] In fact, one exceptional case reported the expulsion of a Red Army family from a collective farm to be correct because the father was a kulak. *DIu*, no. 23 (Dec. 1934): 11.

[137] On draft procedures, see *Kiu*, no. 13 (July 1931): 14; Fainsod, *Smolensk*, 326–327; Varenov, *Pomoshch' krasnoi armii*, 42. A soldier faced dismissal if his family was expelled from the collective farm, indicating the seriousness of the issue and suggesting it was not in the state's interest to see Red Army families randomly persecuted. On such dismissal of soldiers, see *SIu*, no. 4 (1934): 17–18.

[138] *DIu*, no. 6 (Mar. 1934): 5; *SIu*, no. 4 (1934): 17–18.

[139] Varenov, *Pomoshch' krasnoi armii*, 40–47.

[140] Fainsod, *Smolensk*, 331–333.

[141] Ibid.

[142] Ibid.; *SIu*, no. 21 (30 July 1932): 11.

tive farm authorities, to expell soldiers' families than to divert scarce resources to them. Moreover, here, as in the case of the outsiders, labor-short Red Army families may have been resented or viewed as a burden for not doing their fair share of work in the collective farm.[143]

In principle, there should not have been "needy" Red Army families. The district military authorities were not supposed to draft peasants from households where there would be no one left to work following the conscription of an able-bodied young man.[144] But such strictures were routinely violated,[145] and the patterns of Soviet conscription continued to follow old village patterns from before the Revolution, resulting in the disproportionate recruitment of poor peasants from small households and "undesirables."[146] Such families may have been particularly vulnerable to repression and expulsion from the collective farm within an economy of scarcity, as "expendables" incapable of doing their fair share of work.

There may also have been another prerevolutionary pattern at work in the persecution of Red Army families. The *soldatka*, or army wife, in prerevolutionary Russia (especially prior to the 1874 military reforms) was often a pariah, as an unattached woman within a still very much patriarchal rural society.[147] During the Civil War, such women were often pressured by their communes to give up their land allotments or were refused help with their work.[148] Such attitudes may have conditioned their treatment in the collective farms.

In addition, labor-short Red Army families, who remained outside the collective farms, sometimes hired labor on a parttime basis to help out during busy agricultural seasons. Hiring labor may have led to their classification as kulaks, despite explicit instructions to the contrary.[149] In

---

[143] See the case of an expulsion from the collective farm of a Red Army wife and her four-month-old child because her husband was in the army, in *DIu*, no. 6 (Mar. 1934): 5; and the case of a Red Army family with few working members who were persecuted in the collective farm, not given food, and taxed as kulaks, in ibid., no. 4 (Feb. 1933): 12. A 1938 decree forbid collective farms to expel a family when one of its members was away (temporarily or permanently) working for a state enterprise. See *Sobranie postanovlenii i rasporiazhenii pravitel'stva SSSR*, no. 18 (29 April 1938): 289–291.

[144] Fainsod, *Smolensk*, 331.

[145] According to Fainsod, ibid., this principle was violated in the Smolensk Region.

[146] For earlier conscription patterns, see Steven L. Hoch, *Serfdom and Social Control in Russia: Petrovskoe, a Village in Tambov* (Chicago, 1986): 151–158; and Rodney D. Bohac, "The Mir and the Military Draft," *Slavic Review*, vol. 47, no. 4 (1988): 657.

[147] Beatrice Farnsworth, "The Soldatka: Folklore and Court Record," *Slavic Review*, vol. 49, no. 1 (1990).

[148] Barbara Evans Clements, "Baba and Bolshevik: Russian Women and Revolutionary Change," *Soviet Union*, vol. 12, pt. 2 (1985): 162; idem., "Working-Class and Peasant Women in the Russian Revolution, 1917–1923," *Signs*, vol. 8, no. 2 (1982): 221–224.

[149] *Kiu*, no. 1 (Jan. 1931): 8–9. See also earlier regional decrees warning against the use of a "formal" approach to households employing hired labor and singling out Red Army families, widows, invalids, families without able-bodied workers, "seasonal" students, and certain types of *kustari* as exceptions to the rules on hiring labor. Similar decrees are in *Kollektivizatsiia sel'skogo khoziaistva Iakutskoi ASSR* (Iakutsk, 1978): 48–50; and

cases when Red Army families were prosecuted for hiring labor, local authorities were following the letter of the law as determined by central definitions of kulak households and ignoring later legal refinements exempting soldiers' families.

Finally, as in the case of the *otkhodniki*, some Red Army families may have used their special status, exempting them from dekulakization and taxation as kulaks, to remain outside of the collective farm. In these cases, local authorities may have simply ignored central directives protecting these families in order to gain new sources of revenue by taxing the families as kulaks.

Along with Red Army families, other types of marginal households and individuals found themselves subject to repression. The elderly and ill, the families of exiled or rehabilitated kulaks, and certain types of women appear very occasionally in the sources. The repression of elderly peasants, apart from any question of social origin, appears to have taken place on occasion. The journal *Sovetskaia iustitsiia* reported that there were many court cases, leading to dekulakization and exile, against elderly peasants in the Central Black Earth Region in 1930 for not fulfilling grain delivery quotas even though these peasants were incapable of fulfilling their quotas.[150] In 1932, N. V. Krylenko criticized legal authorities for cases involving imprisonment of the elderly for failure to fulfill their economic obligations.[151] In 1934, violations were reported during the soviet election campaign in Aleksinkii district where everyone over sixty years of age was disenfranchised.[152] These cases suggest that elderly peasants were occasionally treated like Red Army families on the basis of their marginal economic status, which rendered them economically unproductive and a burden on household and collective farm alike. Elderly peasants living alone may have been particularly vulnerable to repression. The marginal status of the elderly in these years is not an aberration within the context of peasant society where the elderly were often viewed as an economic burden or a source of generational strife.[153] As early as 1927, it was

---

Kollektivizatsiia sel'skogo khoziaistva Turkmenskoi SSR (Ashkhabad, 1968), vol. 2: 632, n. 18. Also see *SIu*, no. 27 (Oct. 1934): 2, for an editorial warning against disenfranchising private farmers, who hired labor in busy seasons when a family member was in the army.

[150] *SIu*, no. 2 (20 Jan. 1931): 21. As late as mid-1936, *SIu* reported that ill and elderly people in the Kursk Region were taxed excessively to force them out of collective farms. These people were then unable to pay taxes and were thrown out into the streets. Neighbors were ordered not to take them in. *SIu*, no. 17 (15 June 1936): 8–9.

[151] Ibid., no. 24 (30 Aug. 1932): 7.

[152] Ibid., no. 27 (Oct. 1934): 1. In the same year, the sixty-two-year-old Evdokiia Seka found herself expelled from her collective farm for being "insufficiently able to work." Her case is in *Istoriia kolektivizatsii sil's'kogo gospodarstva Ukrains'koi RSR* (Kiev, 1971), vol. 3: 373.

[153] For an extreme case of resentment, see the murder of an elderly peasant as reported in *Kiu*, no. 11 (15 June 1929): 10. Also see Hoch, *Serfdom and Social Control*, 16, 40, on the economic dependency and status of the elderly in the days of serfdom.

reported that peasants over age sixty were disenfranchised in parts of the country during rural soviet election campaigns.[154] The ill, as well as the infirm, were also vulnerable to repression, if central decrees warning against their persecution at the hands of local officials are any indication of their vulnerability. During the 1931 campaign to uncover kulaks for taxation purposes and the 1934 soviet election campaigns, officials were warned that not all farms with hired labor should be treated as kulak farms or disenfranchised. These warnings singled out the ill (as well as Red army families) among those exempted from kulak status.[155]

The families of rehabilitated peasants (i.e., incorrectly dekulakized peasants) and of recently exiled kulaks were also vulnerable to repression. A People's Commissariat of Justice report of 1931 noted that there was a "tendency" among officials in the Central Black Earth Region to dekulakize juridically recently rehabilitated households and the wives of exiled kulaks for failure to fulfill grain delivery quotas.[156] In these cases, the households were most certainly economically weak, following the confiscation of their property and, in the case of the rehabilitated, the failure to receive compensation for their confiscated belongings. Consequently, it was impossible for them to fulfill their obligations to the state. It may also be that these households were somehow unusual, if not economic or social outcasts within the village to begin with, given their earlier vulnerability during dekulakization.

Finally, some women, particularly single women who violated the sexual conventions of the countryside, were subject to various forms of repression in this period. In 1931, a rural court charged a collective farm woman with *rasstroistvo* (disorder) of family life and expelled her from her farm for her "lewd" conduct with a married brigadier.[157] In 1933, a collective farm woman was expelled from her farm for divorcing her husband and living with a private farmer.[158] The widow Novikova was dekulakized without any basis in 1933, expropriated, and thrown into the streets with her children.[159] For hiring labor, the de facto head of household, Shpanova, was labeled a kulak, expelled from the collective farm, and later sentenced to one year of hard labor for failure to pay her taxes. Her case was overturned when the center intervened and discovered that her husband was too ill to work and she only hired labor during the busy season.[160] These cases seem to indicate that women who were economically or socially marginal were vulnerable to persecution.[161] Such

[154] Bol'shakov, *Derevnia*, 429.
[155] *Kiu.*, no. 1 (Jan. 1931): 8–9; *SIu*, no. 27 (Oct. 1934): 2.
[156] *SIu*, no. 2 (20 Jan. 1931): 21.
[157] Ibid., no. 29 (20 Oct. 1931): 19–20.
[158] Ibid., no. 1 (Jan. 1933): 19.
[159] Ibid., no. 22 (Sept. 1934): 19. This case, like the others cited above, was dismissed later.
[160] Ibid., no. 17–18 (30 June 1932): 64.
[161] Officials were warned against exiling individuals incapable of working, pregnant women,

a pattern of repression would not be inconsistent with village tradition. Profligate women were often social pariahs in the village and widows often clashed with other villagers over their right to a land allotment before collectivization.[162]

As in the case of the outsiders, the basis for the repression of marginal individuals and households may reside in the economy of scarcity in the Soviet countryside in the 1930s, since most of these cases took place between 1932 and 1934. Economically marginal people may have been viewed as a burden on the collective farm or as a source of untapped revenue, when they remained outside the collective farm. To a much greater extent than outsiders, economically marginal people were "expendable." Incapable of doing their fair share of work, they may have been perceived as a drain on already scarce resources within the economy of scarcity.

The vulnerability of these people may also suggest a reassertion of certain traditional, rural forms of political culture. The groups included among the marginal individuals and households subject to repression had been people on the economic or social periphery of village life, both before and after the Revolution. As such, their life within the village had always been a struggle. In the aftermath of collectivization and the violence and trauma that accompanied it, the traditional exclusivity of the village may have deepened and, with that deepening, the usual oppression of marginal people may have been transformed into more active forms of repression. The brutalization of everyday life may have brought with it a violently antagonistic set of social relations that pitted the strong against the weak and the mainstream against the marginal.

With the exception of most of the *byvshie liudi* and Civil War opponents, the categories of victims discussed in this analysis were not centrally designated targets of repression. The victimization of these categories surely derived in part from the *proizvol* of rural cadres. Just as surely some part of the *byvshie liudi* and Civil War opponents were the object of false denunciation. But the snowballing of repression during this period seems also to have been shaped by the dynamics of a traditional rural political culture and to have resulted in a kind of traditional victimization. The aliens of these times were the aliens of times past. Actual divisions within rural society were more complex than the Marxist-Leninist-Stalinist conception of class struggle between rich and poor peasants, between the rural

and women with children. See *SIu*, no. 22 (10 Aug. 1932): 2. Warnings against exiling families without able-bodied workers were issued in Siberia in 1930 and in Dagestan in 1935 in decrees on dekulakization. See *Istoriia kollektivizatsiia Vostochnoi Sibiri*, 163–164; and *Kollektivizatsiia sel'skogo khoziaistva Dagestanskoi ASSR* (Makhachkala, 1976), vol. 2: 152–156.
[162] Clements, "Working-Class and Peasant Women," 221–224.

capitalist and the rural proletariat. Divisions within the village derived not from capitalist class formations, but from traditional peasant society. Hostility was directed against the village political, social, and economic elite; outsiders caught between the city and countryside; and individuals and households living on the economic and social margins of rural life. Traditional hostilities, particularly during the years of famine, were intensified by the economy of scarcity at work in the countryside and the search for scapegoats. Land, in the form of the *usad'ba*, and food became divisive issues within the newly collectivized countryside. Aliens and economically marginal households became rivals for scarce resources. *Otkhodniki, kustari,* and Red Army families outside of the collective farm system became resources in themselves for land and tax revenues. The countryside closed in on itself in the midst of profound crisis. And in this respect, the dynamics of repression at work in the countryside had much in common with the dynamics of repression to be found in other peasant cultures during other periods of crisis.[163]

The regression of the Soviet countryside in the 1930s can only be understood within the context of an understanding of the dynamics of a country and a countryside experiencing dramatic rates of social and demographic mobility. The social and demographic mobility of the 1930s is generally analyzed from the perspective of its impact upon urban society.[164] From the urban perspective, the impact of such tremendous rates of mobility points in the direction of modernization. From the rural perspective, however, the impact may very well have been quite the opposite. The necessary question becomes *who* was leaving the countryside for the city. The answer, in short, is the young, the skilled and educated, the more enterprising peasant fearful of dekulakization, and, in general, a greater percentage of males than females.[165] These groups represented the social forces in the countryside most likely to be receptive to change. In effect, these groups were potential "modernizers" within the village context. Their loss may have served to stall, if only temporarily, the cultural development of the countryside and to reinforce the traditional political culture of the village.[166] If this suggestion is correct, it may

[163] For example, early modern Europe witnessed similar crises during witch-hunts in which the oppression of traditional categories of elites, outsiders, and marginal people turned into violent repression in the context of political, religious, or economic crisis. See H. R. Trevor-Roper, *The European Witch-Craze of the Sixteenth and Seventeenth Centuries and Other Essays* (New York, 1968): 109–112, 110–111, 114–115, 127; and Joseph Klaits, *Servants of Satan* (Bloomington, 1985), chap. 4. Paul Boyer and Stephen Nissenbaum in *Salem Possessed* (Cambridge, MA, 1974) suggest that village factional strife formed the basis of the Salem witch-hunts.

[164] Fitzpatrick, *Education and Social Mobility.*

[165] Ibid., 158, 177; Viola, *Best Sons,* 181. For percentages of working-age people in the collective farms, see *Istoriia krest'ianstva SSSR* (M, 1986), vol. 2: 368, which notes that in 1935 less than half of the collective farm population was of working age.

[166] See Eklof, *Russian Peasant Schools,* 470, for similar suggestions on the impact of peasant out-migration on the village. For a different view on this issue, see Joseph Bradley, *Muzhik and Muscovite* (Berkeley, 1985): 128–141.

provide another clue to understanding the seemingly regressive nature of politics and repression in the countryside in these years.

The regression of the Soviet countryside to a traditional form of victimization necessarily begs the question of who, precisely, was behind the victimization. The answer to this question is not revealed in the sources, nor will a definitive answer be offered here. This analysis suggests, however, that the categories of victims discussed here appear less frequently in the sources during the period of wholesale collectivization when the countryside was subject to rule by outside forces. Both before and after the most intensive years of collectivization, the village and, after it, the collective farm were granted relative autonomy from the intrusions of urban plenipotentiaries and cadres in the conduct of day-to-day administration. The collective farms and local soviets were staffed by officials who were generally peasants recruited from among the local activists. The basis of the dynamics of repression derived from a compound of political warfare unleashed from on high and traditional antagonisms. The repressive activities of local cadres were at least partially shaped by the same rural political culture in which they themselves had been molded. The images of the enemy hatched in the minds of peasant officials may have been glossed over with a thin veneer of Marxist-Leninist vocabulary, but their construction was in fact determined less by ideology or state edict than by social realities and battles far older than the Revolution of 1917. Rural officials were very much a part of the society and culture in which they operated.

The patterns of victimization at work in this period were neither all-inclusive nor absolute. Although members of the three categories of analysis were highly visible among the victims of repression, not all members of these categories were repressed. Therefore, the question of a triggering mechanism behind the repression comes to the fore. Why were some individuals repressed, while others were left in peace? The answer to this question surely remains hidden in local sources. However, a range of possibilities presents itself, including motives of revenge and jealousy, local power struggles, ideological commitments, and the specific economic conditions of particular collective farms. It could also be argued that the search for enemies, and the thinning out of the number of authentic class aliens (i.e., *byvshie liudi* and critics), especially after 1932, may have made it inevitable that outsiders and marginal people, as the most vulnerable inhabitants of the village, would be served up as scapegoats. If so, this dynamic resembles similar dynamics at work in the early modern European witch-crazes when local investigators ended up scraping the bottom of the barrel in search of witches because this was their job and because they believed. In such cases, the most vulnerable were the most likely to be victimized.

Although the dynamics of repression in the Soviet countryside may have been shaped in part by a traditional rural political culture, the scope and actual forms of repression were determined ultimately by the policies and broader political culture of the times. The country was at war with itself during the period of wholesale collectivization and, to a great extent, had been in endless turmoil from the time of the Revolution, with only a short interval of peace during the 1920s. The general political culture was shaped by intolerance, maximalism, voluntarism, a thirst for revenge against real and perceived enemies, and a blind spot to individual tragedy. The Revolution of the First Five-Year Plan accelerated and compressed the driving forces of the general political culture. The enthusiasm of the period was largely exhausted by 1931. The aftermath of the First Five-Year Plan brought with it a paranoid, martial spirit and profound economic crisis. The trauma of collectivization, the desperation of hunger, and the violence of the times served to brutalize and, perhaps, to atomize the rural populace, leading to a siege mentality and endemic paranoia among officials and peasants alike. Traditional rural political culture, which in normal times may have been merely oppressive, became repressive in this context. The policies of repression came from above; the snowballing of the repression, however, occurred within a context of habitual *proizvol*, an economy of scarcity, a traditional political culture run riot, and the sustained violence of the times.

4

The omnipresent conspiracy:
On Soviet imagery of politics and
social relations in the 1930s

Gábor Tamás Rittersporn

In August 1941 a young NKVD officer was taken captive by the Germans. He pretended to be a peasant's son who had studied agronomy and mathematics, before being "mobilized" to work in the political police in the spring of 1938, at the age of twenty-five. He also pretended to have rendered some services to German intelligence in Riga in 1940. His interrogators were impressed by his willingness to cooperate and to present himself in a favorable light.[1] They were equally impressed by his manifestly sincere conviction that there was hardly any sphere of Soviet society where conspiracies were not present in the 1930s. In some respects the young man was far from being poorly informed. Apparently assigned to the surveillance of Komintern officials and foreign Communists in Moscow, he possessed pertinent information about people who must have been unknown even to police cadres, if they were not specialized in his field.[2]

Nevertheless, the interrogators could not help wondering if he was able to distinguish between his undeniable familiarity with certain facts and rumors stemming from the NKVD's obsession with the ubiquity of spies and plotters.[3] Indeed, the young man reported a profusion of conspiracies in educational institutions, enterprises, and offices as well as in the highest spheres of government in the 1930s. He even presented a chart of the complicated relations among secret organizations of "leftist" and "rightist" groups that included defendants in the show trials, commanders of the army, and leading officials of the Komintern and the NKVD.[4] Despite his

The author wishes to express his gratitude to the Alexander von Humboldt Foundation whose generous support made this research possible.

[1] Political Archive of the Foreign Office, Bonn (hereafter cited as *PA, AA*) Abteilung Pol. 13, Akten betreffend GPU-Funktionär Shigunow, pp. 175755, 176008, 176019, 176023, 176026–7.
[2] Ibid., pp. 175760, 175770, 175779, 175796, 175925.
[3] Ibid., p. 176023.
[4] Ibid., pp. 175761–3, 175862, 175885, 175888.

eagerness to seek the favor of his interrogators, he was ready to enter into dispute with them when they objected to his tendency to see spies in entire ethnic groups and especially when they reminded him that they knew better who had been working for German intelligence in the Soviet Union. So much so that he continued to stick to his opinion concerning an alleged German spy, insisting that he was better informed about the real state of affairs behind the regime's facade.[5]

The young officer's propensity to see a complicated web of conspiracies at the center of Soviet politics had obviously more than a few things to do with his training by the NKVD and proceeded from a consciously cultivated spy mania in the secret police. Nevertheless, everything points to the assumption that Soviet citizens of the epoch were inclined to lend credit to the regime's propaganda about the subversive activities of plotters and foreign agents. Captured officers seemed to believe that there was something behind the accusations against the high command in 1937.[6] At the start of the war, ordinary citizens were ready to accept the idea that the "whole of our country is full of spies" and to attribute the disastrous military situation to "high treason" and "wrecking" in leading circles.[7]

In the course of the 1930s, political and even social relations came to be understood increasingly in terms of conspiratorial intrigues. Plots and wrecking became central paradigms by which the regime sought to explain political processes and social conflicts, and official as well as popular milieux were disposed to suspect the work of subversive machinations behind the apparently inexplicable turmoil that turned into an unmanageable daily reality and represented a permanent threat to the security of virtually any Soviet citizen.

It became routine for the Soviet authorities to ascribe the regime's difficulties to "subversive" activities of "conspirators" during the collectivization and industrialization drives. Well-publicized show trials were staged between 1928 and 1931 to demonstrate that the hardships of the period originated in the "wrecking" by "plotters" among managerial and technical cadres and among members of the scientific and planning establishments.[8] Antisaboteur campaigns focused on specialists who were

[5] Ibid., pp. 176009, 176022.
[6] PA, AA, Abteilung Pol. 13, Allgemeine Akten 12, Teil 2, DIX 221: 'Vernehmung...', 23 September 1941, p. 2; Abteilung Pol. 13, Allgemeine Akten 14: Document 409, p. 2. See also R. V. Ivanov-Razumnik, *Tiurmy i ssylki* (New York, 1953) p. 277 where, writing during the war, the author evokes "Tukhachevskii's well-known conspiracy" and T-4908 of the Trotsky Papers about Moscow rumors of the summer of 1937 concerning the "military plot." (Quoted with the permission of the Houghton Library.)
[7] PA, AA, Abteilung Pol. 13, Allgemeine Akten 13, DIX 322: no. 147, 149, 211, 213; Federal Archive, Koblenz (hereafter cited as *BA*) NS 8, 226, p. 35.
[8] K. Bailes, *Technology and Society under Lenin and Stalin* (Princeton, 1978) pp. 69–121; H. H. Schröder, *Industrialisierung und Parteibürokratie in der Sowjetunion* (Berlin, 1988) pp. 216–230.

identified as leftovers of the Old Regime, and when the last show trial of this wave took place in April 1933 against the background of famine and intense intraparty conflict and in the wake of a major crisis of collectivization and industrialization, its defendants were once again Soviet and foreign engineers.[9]

The identity of the wrecker changed, however, in a matter of less than four years. A new imagery of the "enemy" emerged by the early months of 1937 that applied to veteran members of the party, to high-ranking officials, and to practically all cadres. This imagery could be disregarded as the propaganda of a completely perverted regime, were it not that it reflected real problems of the system and something of the way these problems tended to be seen in leading circles and by the population, and explained a good deal of the regime's perversity.

It became increasingly doubtful after the early 1930s that the hardships the public had to endure were temporary and incidental and that people alien to the regime could alone be blamed for them. This fiction seemed all the more difficult to maintain since it was hardly possible to separate the adversities of daily life from the operation of governmental mechanisms that turned out to be unmanageable. The official discourse acknowledged that collectivization and industrialization had increased the "strength and authority" of the party and state apparatus "to an unprecedented degree" and that "everything or almost everything" depended therefore on the way officeholders fulfilled their "decisive [and] exceptional" role. It had to be admitted, however, that this state of affairs did not mean that the apparatus worked in a uniform, regular, and controllable manner. Hence strict measures were necessary to ensure the implementation of the party's "political line."[10] This line ceased to be the object of open contest by the early years of the decade, but the functioning of the administration, the attempts by top bodies to regulate it, and the response of the apparatus to such attempts were far from making the regime's policy clear and unambiguous.

Governmental mechanisms had a strong tendency to work in an unpredictable way and, whatever the "party line" happened to be, there was every chance that it would be altered through the daily operation of the apparatus. Virtually all important decisions about industrial and agricultural policy or about the screening of party membership were implemented in such a manner that the outcome had little to do with the originally envisaged effects. If officials bothered to carry out major directives, they concentrated their efforts mainly on producing immediate

[9] H. Kuromiya, *Stalin's Industrial Revolution* (Cambridge, 1988) pp. 292–294; Bailes, p. 280; Schröder, pp. 317–323.
[10] *XVII S"ezd VKP(b)* (Moscow, 1934) pp. 33–35, 48, 532–533, 600–601; *KPSS v rezoliutsiiakh i resheniiakh s'ezdov, konferentsii i plenumov CK*, vol. 5 (Moscow, 1971) pp. 152–154, 159–160.

spectacular results that often did not amount to more than the appearance of the projected changes. Far from improving the work of party bodies and rationalizing management and production, nationwide campaigns disorganized the administration and the economy and aggravated social tensions.[11] This phenomenon had nothing to do with alternative programs of reform-minded cadres or oppositional movements within the apparatus. Officials routinely misused their powers in order to make a show of success, and in many cases they hardly had a choice, confronted as they were by the indifference or hostility of the masses, by inadequate resources, and by the prospect of censure, dismissal, or penal sanctions if they could not produce at least the semblance of results or find scapegoats for failures.

The behavior of officials did not deviate from the norms set by higher bodies, including the center, whose incompetent or contradictory measures, scapegoating of subordinates and "hostile" elements, and triumphal reports on dubious successes were merely imitated by the apparatus. However sincere Moscow's warnings against abuses and excesses might have been, insiders had no reason to take them too seriously. Measures to alleviate tensions in the countryside even included a rather parsimonious amnesty for some categories of peasants who had been exiled or imprisoned for their alleged or real resistance to collectivization, and a symbolic amnesty for officials condemned mainly for their liberal attitude during the ruthless food procurement drives of 1932 and 1933.[12] But a multitude of instructions and injunctions concerning the sowing and harvesting campaigns and the delivery of agricultural products showed that there was no illusion in high places about the cooperativeness of the population: If results were to be obtained, the people had to be put under pressure by grass-roots cadres who were themselves under the threat of penal sanctions.[13]

Moscow had every reason to issue repeated calls for restraint in the prosecution of petty rural officeholders[14] who were frequently put on trial

---

[11] J. A. Getty, *Origins of the Great Purges – The Soviet Communist Party Reconsidered, 1933–1938* (Cambridge, 1985) pp. 58–91; L. H. Siegelbaum, *Stakhanovism and the Politics of Productivity in the USSR, 1935–1941* (Cambridge, 1988) pp. 99–144; G. T. Rittersporn, *Stalinist Simplifications and Soviet Complications: Social Tensions and Political Conflicts in the USSR 1933–1953* (Reading, 1991) pp. 31–47.

[12] *Sobranie zakonov i rasporiazhenii Raboche-Krest'ianskogo Pravitel'stva SSSR* part 1 (hereafter cited as *SZ*) (1934) pp. 465–466, (1935) pp. 613–614, 674–675.

[13] *Sovetskaia iustitsiia* (hereafter cited as *SIu*) (1934) no. 8, p. 3, no. 9, p. 25, no. 17, p. 22, (1935) no. 4, p. 17, no. 27, p. 2; *Sotsialisticheskaia zakonnost'/Za sotsialisticheskuiu zakonnost'* (hereafter cited as *SZak*) (1934) no. 4, pp. 36, 39–41, no. 5, p. 11, no. 7, p. 37, no. 8, pp. 3, 31–32, no. 9, p. 44, no. 10, pp. 1–2, 28–30, 34, no. 11, pp. 48–49, no. 12, p. 48, (1935) no. 10, p. 64; *Ugolovnyi kodeks RSFSR* (hereafter cited as *UK*) (Moscow, 1937) pp. 132, 138.

[14] *SIu* (1934) no. 13, p. 13, (1935) no. 2, p. 2, no. 13, p. 5, no. 31, p. 15, (1936) no. 13, p. 5; *SZak* (1934) no. 10, p. 35, (1935) no. 5, pp. 58–59.

by higher-ups if something went wrong with farming and food procurements. More often than not, however, the latter acted in the spirit of directives of the Central Committee and the government that pressed for quick results and emphasized the personal responsibility of all cadres for the success of the agricultural campaigns.[15] In the same way, it was vain to enjoin local authorities to moderate their zeal in purging the party and to refrain from persecuting people merely because of their social origin, if the move came some months after a vigilance drive in the name of the Central Committee that had dispatched lists of "unmasked" people whose guilt was nothing more in most cases than their social origin or their past.[16] Official spokesmen admitted that wholesale repression discredited the regime and that the authority and efficiency of penal provisions would be compromised if used in an inflated and irregular way.[17] Nevertheless, harsh measures against the masses and junior officials seemed justified by instructions that mobilized the judiciary to "contribute to the successes" of agriculture, industry, and transport and to detect "hostile" intentions behind failures and professional errors.[18]

A paradoxical situation developed in which the activities of individual officeholders often deviated from or were in conflict with policies decided by the central authorities, yet were in harmony with a general pattern of action that was hardly ever compatible with the political line fixed by the center. The paradox was intimately related to the contradictory political objectives of the regime: ensuring order among the masses as well as social peace, regular and controllable functioning of the administration and its "decisive and exceptional" role. Maintaining order and the preeminence of the apparatus implied the delegation of large powers and created the danger of transgressions and social tensions. On the other hand, control meant curtailing the authority of officialdom, which tended to encourage popular insubordination, as in the case when Moscow publicly condemned the first excesses of collectivization and triggered a series of riots.[19] When the top bodies tried to regulate the administration's working, they were in fact trying to do away with the logic that their own actions had established and that inevitably reappeared in the operation of the apparatus. A solution to this problem could hardly be found if the dominant

[15] Smolensk Archive (hereafter cited as *WKP*), RS 116/154e, *WKP* 84, p. 42, *WKP* 176, p. 181, *WKP* 186, pp. 178–180.

[16] *Bol'shevik* (hereafter cited as *B*) (1936) no. 13, pp. 9, 12–13, no. 15, pp. 45–48; *Partiinoe stroitel'stvo* (hereafter cited as *PS*) (1936) no. 8, p. 55, no. 14, pp. 52–53, no. 15, p. 36; *SZ* (1936) pp. 473–474; "Ob iskliuchennykh iz partii," *Pravda* (hereafter cited as *P*) 6 June, 1936, p. 3; *116/154e* pp. 44–49, 79–88.

[17] *SIu* (1935) no. 10, pp. 1–2, no. 13, p. 5, no. 25, pp. 2–3, no. 27, p. 2, (1936) no. 6, p. 5, no. 13, p. 13, no. 27, pp. 7–8; *SZak* (1935) no. 5, pp. 7, 9–10, no. 6, pp. 5, 7.

[18] *SIu* (1934) no. 19, p. 25, (1935) no. 5, pp. 24–25, no. 36, p. 3; *SZak* (1934) no. 12, p. 51, (1935) no. 2, pp. 59–60. See also note 13.

[19] L. Viola, *The Best Sons of the Fatherland – Workers in the Vanguard of Soviet Collectivization* (Oxford, 1987) pp. 123–126.

position of the party and state apparatus in society was to be maintained.

Something had to be done, however, since the activities of officialdom manifestly disorganized the regime and brought a deterioration in its relations with the rest of society. The habit of the agricultural administration to furnish false data made a fiction of economic planning, as did the tendency of industrial management to meet plan targets through manufacturing defective goods, raising prices, or refusing to fabricate badly needed products.[20] There could be no question of running a self-contained and highly centralized apparatus if it refused to cooperate with control agencies and, despite repeated warnings, dismissed officials who had been nominated by top bodies.[21] Not even the appearance of a legal order could be maintained where officials extended their powers, especially when they inflicted unauthorized penalties on the population through local ordinances incompatible with statute law.[22] And the state's legitimate monopoly on violence was under serious threat when the regime proved unable to define which officials were entitled to carry out arrests, and when regional administrations had to be reminded that the supreme governing body had the prerogative to make the ultimate decision about the execution of death sentences.[23]

There could be no secret about the involvement of ranking cadres and party veterans in the disorganization of the system's functioning. Authoritative statements emphasized that officials and often high dignitaries with "well-known merits in the past" were responsible for the irregular and uncontrollable working of governmental mechanisms and warned that intractable "bigwigs" would be demoted, dismissed, and punished "without respect of personalities."[24] Actions were taken against a number of transgressing officeholders but, instead of looking for the origins of their misdeeds in the administration's working, there was a notable tendency to attribute them to "criminal" intentions and to the allegedly "alien" social origin of the culprits.[25] Already during collectivization excessively harsh measures as well as reluctance to apply such measures were ascribed to "deviationist" or "hostile" practices of cadres.[26] In this

[20] *XVII S"ezd*, pp. 23, 153–154, 267–268, 289; "O zapasnykh chastiakh," *P*, 16 June 1937, p. 2, "O beloi zhesti," *P*, 17 June 1937, p. 3, "Planovykh del mastera," *P*, 1 July 1937, p. 3.
[21] *PS* (1935) no. 13, pp. 44–45, (1936) no. 20, pp. 37–38, 47, no. 22, p. 48; *B* (1936) no. 6, pp. 76–77; "O rabote upolnomochennykh KPK," *P*, 17 Mar. 1936, p. 2.
[22] *Vlast' sovetov* (hereafter cited as *VS*) (1936) no. 9, pp. 8–9, no. 11, pp. 37–39, no. 16, pp. 23–24, (1937) no. 10, pp. 16–18; *SZak* (1934) no. 5, p. 11; *SIu* (1934) no. 13, pp. 9–10.
[23] *SIu* (1934) no. 13, p. 9–10, (1935) no. 16, p. 9, (1936) no. 27, p. 17; *SZak* (1934) no. 1, pp. 35–36, no. 5, p. 10, no. 7, p. 36; *WKP* 184, p. 16.
[24] *XVII S'ezd*, p. 34; *KPSS v rezoliutsiiakh*, pp. 152–153, 160.
[25] *PS* (1934) no. 13, p. 3, no. 16, p. 48, no. 21, pp. 63–64, no. 22, pp. 3–4, (1935) no. 3, p. 47, no. 14, pp. 45–48.
[26] R. W. Davies, *The Socialist Offensive – The Collectivisation of Soviet Agriculture 1929–1930* (London, 1980) p. 330; N. E. Zelenin, "O nekotorykh 'belykh piatnakh'

respect, threats to censure distinguished officials merely for their abuses represented a remarkable innovation. Nevertheless, when it came to singling out a Central Committee member, the propaganda did not dwell on that person's presumed faults. It highlighted alleged association with "class enemies" and called for vigilance against "kulaks" and "Trotskyists."[27]

The persistence and ubiquity of official abuse does not allow one to explain it as a transitory phenomenon, and the tensions it provoked within the regime were more than rivalry between center and periphery. Even top officials had good reasons to feel insecure in face of charges against unruly bigwigs because malpractice and the ensuing conflicts had broad implications for every echelon, in all agencies and in all branches of the apparatus, just as transgressing officials and their allies were likely to be found everywhere. The interaction of agencies in a huge governmental mechanism and wide networks of solidarity among cadres spread abuses throughout the apparatus, and the party-state itself organized officials in groups and coteries that had members, patrons, and associates on different hierarchical levels and in many institutions and localities. Any officeholder was likely to participate in a systematic and organized obstruction of openly uncontested policies and almost any cross section of the apparatus behaved like a clandestine political opposition with the sole aim of securing the career of the incumbents of responsible positions.

Inclined to equate their career with the strengthening of the regime, officeholders were unlikely to grasp the political implications of this state of affairs and were not disposed to see the disorganizing effect of their activities, especially since they followed a pattern that characterized the working of the highest bodies. Obstruction of the regime's policies was as inseparable from the ordinary functioning of the administration as were periodic attempts to check officialdom, and refusal to submit to control agencies was as necessary in order to remain in responsible positions as it was necessary to ensure the regular and controllable operation of governmental mechanisms. The more it became indispensable to fight official abuse, the more such abuse became an integral part of the everyday realities of the system, and the more difficult it became to recognize its manifestations as results of the ordinary functioning of the regime and its relations with the rest of society. Officialdom saw itself as the best representative of the interests of the working masses. This was not conducive to the realization that the practices of the administration stemmed from unpopular policies. To admit that uncontrollability and abuses were inseparable from the regime's normal universe would cast doubt on the raison d'être of the administration as an agency invested with the prerogative

zavershaiushchego etapa sploshnoi kollektivizatsii," *Istoriia SSSR* (1989) no. 2, pp. 11, 13–14; Viola, pp. 128–129.
[27] Editorials, *P*, June 8 and 16, 1935; *PS* (1935) no. 12, p. 10.

to direct and supervise the system's functioning and its own working. These circumstances made it difficult to avoid attributing the regime's problems to machinations of people alienated from or hostile to the system.

There was a remarkable tendency, already in the 1920s, to avoid searching for the origins of the administration's intractability in the fact that it was accountable only to itself. Characteristically, the consequences of this state of affairs were debated mainly in terms of an analogy with the French Revolution, and even oppositionists were reluctant to acknowledge that the system had not evolved according to the promises of October.[28] Besides the scapegoating of "bourgeois specialists," the late 1920s also saw the criminalization of factional activities in the party, and alleged deviations from the sinuous "General Line" were identified with a negative stereotype that ended with the top leadership creating the image of an organized "Right Opposition" that never existed in reality.[29] A succession of party purges accustomed the membership to suspect wrongdoing by "class-alien elements,"[30] and this certainly helped to strengthen the conviction of cadres that the regime's ills had hardly anything to do with the mode of operation of the apparatus. This conviction must have been shaken by attacks against "bigwigs, braggarts and petty tyrants" and on "their disregard for the decisions of higher bodies."[31] But the "discovery" in June 1936 of widespread "subversion" by former oppositionists must have reassured officials that the origins of the regime's problems would not be sought in the everyday work of the administration. Very soon, however, the pretexts of "Trotskyism" or "sabotage" could also be used to clamp down on cadres who had never belonged to the opposition and whose eventual "wrecking" consisted only in their working in accordance with the usual pattern of the apparatus.[32]

Difficult to believe as it seems today, the monstrous accusations of "subversion," "high treason," or "conspiracy" against leading officials were not necessarily incredible in the 1930s, especially for insiders of the administration. They were likely to remember strictures like those of a secret circular of late 1927 that complained about the surfacing of confidential party and government instructions in foreign capitals shortly after their enactment, a circular that also happened to find its way abroad. At the time the leaking of state secrets was attributed to oppositionists, and apparatchiki might also have known about an unsuccessful attempt to

[28] T. Kondrateva, *Bolcheviks et Jacobins* (Paris, 1989) pp. 113–170.

[29] M. Reiman, *Die Geburt des Stalinismus* (Frankfort, 1979) pp. 42–70; Schröder, pp. 172–179.

[30] Cf. the reasons for expulsion during the 1929, 1933, and 1935 purges in Getty, pp. 47, 54, 83; Schröder, pp. 183, 345.

[31] "Kommunist i sovetskii zakon," *P*, 1 April 1936, p. 2; editorial, *P*, 9 May 1936.

[32] Rittersporn, pp. 77–83, 92–103.

set up an oppositional "bloc" in 1932. It was this bloc that was referred to when the "Trotskyist" threat was "rediscovered."[33] In all probability it was only from hearsay that most officials could learn something about Trotsky's attempts to mobilize followers in the early 1930s by sending postcards to the USSR.[34] On the other hand, a multitude of official documents and declarations mentioned "anti-Party" groups of militants who were highly critical of the policies prevailing in the first years of the decade and among whom figured a certain number of leading cadres and former "deviationists."[35] In one form or another, insiders were likely to have been acquainted with the call of one of these groups to remove the "gravedigger of the Revolution," Stalin, or with rumors about the dissatisfaction of certain delegates of the Seventeenth Party Congress with Stalin and about their intention to replace him.[36] And accustomed to reason according to the principle of analogy that was a cornerstone of the period's legal practice,[37] officeholders might be tempted to explain the regime's repressed problems in terms of similar phenomena.

Beyond these circumstances, the credibility of charges against wrecking and conspiring officials was certainly reinforced by the experience of those who were involved in the political processes of the 1930s. Many of them would have known about obscure maneuvers, like an abortive attempt by the secret police in 1933–4 to stage a show trial.[38] They might wonder if similar machinations were behind the manifestly contradictory moves that followed Kirov's murder, when for about three weeks the authorities could not decide if the assassin had acted alone or in concert with a White plot or with the former Left Opposition, but nevertheless ordered the execution of dozens of people on the basis of a law that was promulgated in three versions within a week. Since it was finally decided that the murderer belonged to a "leftist conspiracy," the mass shootings could not be taken even for retaliation because their victims had been identified as White Guards. Insiders may have been even more bewildered by the inconsistency of the version implicating the Left Opposition whose former leaders were originally cleared from suspicion but nonetheless slated for banishment,

---

[33] Reiman, pp. 244–245. For the "bloc" see Getty, pp. 119–122; Idem., "Trotsky in Exile: The Founding of the Fourth International," *Soviet Studies* (1986) no. 1, pp. 28–29; P. Broué, "Trotsky et le bloc des oppositions de 1932," *Cahiers Léon Trotsky* (1980) no. 5, pp. 5–37.

[34] Trotsky Papers, T-10248 (quoted by the permission of the Houghton Library).

[35] R. W. Davies, "The Syrtsov-Lominadze Affair," *Soviet Studies* (1981) no. 1, pp. 29–50; Schröder, pp. 320–322.

[36] *Izvestiia TsK KPSS* (1989) no. 6, pp. 103–106; *Istoriia KPSS* (Moscow, 1963) p. 486; Schröder, pp. 325–326. For data casting doubt on rumors about the Seventeenth Congress, see *Izvestiia TsK KPSS* (1989) no. 7, pp. 114–121.

[37] P. H. Solomon, *Soviet Criminologists and Criminal Policy* (New York, 1978) pp. 22–26.

[38] For the relevant documents see *PA*, *AA* Botschaft Moskau, A 14d, Verhaftungen bei Controll Co.; Abt. IV Rußland, R15, Verhaftungen bei Angestellten der Controll Co. M. b. H. in Sowjetrußland and Strafverfolgung, Begnadigung, vol. 4.

and later were condemned to heavy prison terms after a trial at which they were found not guilty of being involved in the alleged plot.[39]

"Revelations" about "clandestine machinations" in high places were not entirely unbelievable for people who had some reason to suspect obscure intrigues among top policymakers, and the number of such people must have been considerable in an apparatus that experienced notable political turnabouts at the time when organized wrecking was discovered in the party-state. Changes in industrial policy could not go unnoticed for cadres who had been accused of sabotaging Stakhanovism, before being officially cleared from suspicion[40] at the moment when Trotskyist subversion became a major theme of the propaganda. A year after the noisy vigilance campaign that followed Kirov's assassination, it was decreed unlawful to discriminate and fire people solely on the grounds of an alien or suspect background and, in striking departure from past practice, the Central Committee warned that the fact of having concealed one's social origin was not necessarily a sufficient reason for expulsion from the party.[41] Although these moves hardly squared with the drive against "hidden" Trotskyists, officeholders could see an obvious contradiction between the line mobilizing merely a hunt for ex-oppositionists and efforts to draw a profile of the "enemy" that could apply to everyone answerable for any failure of the administration.

Constantly threatened to become victims of the eagerness of higher-ups to choose scapegoats for shortcomings, grass-roots cadres were not necessarily reluctant to accept the idea that their superiors acted with ulterior motives. And increasingly exposed to punishment for any deficiency in their administrations, leading officials were by no means impervious to the reasoning that the actions of unruly subordinates brought about their misfortunes and that these actions proceeded from harmful intentions. Nevertheless, the metaphors of wrecking and conspiracy denoted more than pervasive suspicion within the apparatus. They expressed something that was well beyond the regime's official self-image: the fact that the political process consisted of behind-the-scenes intrigues to manipulate governmental mechanisms and potentially unmanageable chain reactions of maneuvers and countermoves with unforeseeable consequences. Ever since the 1920s, Soviet politics had been characterized by intricate covert maneuvering in the highest milieux.[42] But a new situation arose in the wake of collectivization and industrialization, when the "decisive and

[39] Getty, *Origins*, pp. 209–210; G. T. Rittersporn, "Soviet Politics in the 1930s," *Studies in Comparative Communism* (1986) no. 2, p. 112.
[40] F. Benvenuti "Stakhanovism and Stalinism, 1934–38," *CREES Discussion Papers*, Series SIPS, no. 30, pp. 40–47; Siegelbaum, pp. 117–120, 127–135.
[41] See note 16.
[42] R. Service, *The Bolshevik Party in Revolution* (London, 1979) pp. 175–199; Reiman, pp. 118–171.

exceptional" role of the administration and the extraordinary breadth of officialdom's responsibilities had a strong tendency to make obscure machinations of the entire apparatus inseparable from the regime's policies.

The only legitimate agency of decision making and action, the party-state ensured its predominance through trying to assume the direction of all essential activities of society. The everyday functioning of the administration had an immediate impact on the political process, even if this was by no means clear for those who happened to be involved in the petty intrigues of this or that institution, agency, or locality. Irregular and uncontrollable working patterns brought disruptions whose agents were genuinely subversive from the point of view of the regime's quasi-military ideal of order, and the disorganization and social conflicts their actions brought about represented a real threat to the efficiency, popularity, and stability of the system. Attempts to impose control were in fact efforts to do away with politics as it came to be practiced by the 1930s. The failure of these attempts was an integral part of the political process and liable to appear as the result of wrecking and conspiracies, especially since control was entrusted to the very administration whose ills were to be cured, and officialdom was not inclined to see these ills in the fact that it was accountable only to itself.

The system's logic appeared in the imagery of sabotage and plots, so much so that it is questionable if insiders were able to keep entirely away from rationalizing the regime's internal conflicts through the representation of a "struggle" with "enemies". It is beyond reasonable doubt that this imagery was cynically manipulated by top politicians who directly participated in the fabrication of "proofs" against highly placed "plotters,"[43] and it is more than probable that a great number of dignitaries imitated their example at lower levels of the hierarchy. But even these people seem to have acted in order to avert something that appeared to them as the threat of potential conspiracy, be it in the form of their censure by dissenting militants or their attempted ouster at the Seventeenth Congress, in the form of the sheer existence, even at their places of exile and detention, of old oppositionists,[44] or in that of unpredictable machinations by rivals under the pretext of the fight against subversion.

Although Bukharin could not help wondering if the high leadership believed Kamenev's "monstrous [and] mean accusations" against him, he had no doubt about Kamenev's culpability and reckoned with the possibility that Tomskii was also "enmeshed" in his "plot."[45] People did know that they were not enemies or conspirators. On the other hand, they

[43] *Izvestiia TsK KPSS* (1989) no. 4, pp. 49, 51–55, no. 5, pp. 71, 73–74, 76, no. 8, pp. 91–92, no. 9, pp. 36–39, 42.

[44] Ibid. (1989) no. 5, p. 72, no. 6, pp. 112–115, no. 9, pp. 35–36.

[45] See his letter to Voroshilov in D. Volkogonov, "Triumf i tragediia," *Oktiabr'* (1988) no. 12, pp. 118–119.

knew how disorderly the functioning of the regime was and they also had information about all sorts of irregularities and abuses. The secretive character of dealings within the party-state made uncertain the stand and actions of colleagues, and therefore virtually anything could be supposed about anyone and especially about a priori "suspect" people, like former oppositionists. These circumstances must have weighed heavily when a commission of the Central Committee found convincing statements by detainees against Bukharin and Rykov and decided "unanimously" to refer their affair to the secret police because of their alleged connivance with "plotters."[46]

Few members of this commission could have been unaware of the way in which such confessions were obtained. One of these people, P. P. Postyshev, was one of those regional leaders whose apparatus suddenly "discovered" that "terrorist acts" had been in preparation against them at the time of the Kirov murder by "counterrevolutionary groups" whose alleged participants were pressed to admit their "guilt."[47] Another member, V. Ia. Chubar', suspected a "torrent of slander and intrigues by enemies of the people" when his turn came in the wake of denunciations he himself had helped to set in motion.[48] A third participant, R. I. Eikhe, headed a region that had distinguished itself in the launching of the purge: He too was presumably in danger after the "evidence" given by the victims of a show trial.[49] He did not seem to doubt that people arrested with his sanction were "real Trotskyists," even when he was already in the hands of the NKVD, though he maintained that their confessions against him had been dictated by "conspiratorial" intentions and that other "proofs" of his "guilt" were "dirty falsifications" of the interrogators.[50] His conviction was shared by a purged candidate member of the Politburo, Ia. E. Rudzutak, who wanted to inform the Central Committee that "there is in the NKVD an as yet unliquidated center skillfully fabricating cases and forcing innocent people to admit crimes they did not commit."[51]

It is hardly surprising if cadres "discovered" that "what appeared... before to be occasional shortcomings in the work of the Party apparatus... were [in fact] a systematic subversive work conducted over the years [to achieve] the political corruption of the apparatus... [and] its transformation into a blind instrument."[52] Everything points to the assumption that, unable to deny their share of responsibility in measures contributing to the deterioration of the living conditions of the population, fallen officials

[46] *Izvestiia TsK KPSS* (1989) no. 5, pp. 79–81, 84.
[47] See two documents quoted to this effect in Volkogonov, pp. 52–53.
[48] Ibid. p. 159.
[49] Rittersporn, *Stalinist Simplifications and Soviet Complications*, p. 93.
[50] Volkogonov, p. 161; *Izvestiia TsK KPSS* (1989) no. 3, p. 141.
[51] Volkogonov, pp. 161–162; *Izvestiia TsK KPSS* (1989) no. 3, p. 142. The two editions reproduce this document and Eikhe's letter in slightly different wording.
[52] WKP 392, pp. 96–97; WKP 103, p. 126.

were probably sincerely claiming to be ignorant of "the behind-the-scenes life" of their "unmasked" superiors and "blind executors of the whole work of wrecking."[53] Inexplicably contradictory directives became easily understandable as parts of the "sabotage" that might be suspected even behind the overburdening of the courts by the purge.[54] Omnipresent as it appeared, "subversion" was imputable to any officeholder, and since cadres were under heavy pressure to reveal culprits in their ranks, they did their best to deflect the offensive onto the most vulnerable: against people whose office or affiliations became a priori "suspicious" in the new conditions and, as usual, against people whose past or personal relations furnished pretexts to designate them as "hostile elements."[55] Everyone could become suspect virtually for anything and the circumstances were ideal for settling old accounts, regardless of the consequences and often perhaps in anticipation of intrigues by rivals.

The manipulation of the purge and its unexpected turns had every chance to appear as the work of conspiracies, the more so since there was no difference between the muddled and confusing schemes to single out enemies and the usual machinations of the apparatus. As zealous purgers were no less exposed to arrest than officials reluctant to hunt down wreckers, devout implementation of the rather uncertain line was as likely to arouse suspicion as attempts to protect hard-pressed associates. Both tendencies could be detected in the actions of the high leadership, therefore people had good reason to feel reassured that they were following Moscow's policies, even if they happened to deviate from them at any particular moment. The understanding of the struggle against the regime's ills in terms of fighting subversion amounted to taking the problems of the system for their solution. No wonder then that these problems were only aggravated in the wake of the purge. The threat intensified the activity of solidarity networks among cadres whose attempts to save each other reinforced the imagery of omnipresent "plots."[56] The overzealous hunt for enemies was often nothing more than application of policies according to the momentary career interests of officials who purged the institutions under their jurisdiction in order to prove their political trustworthiness.[57] Energetic "cleansing" also could be taken for "wrecking," especially after January 1938 when the decimated Central Committee warned that the campaign was distorted by "hostile" maneuvers.[58]

---

[53] *WKP* 109, pp. 67, 72; *WKP* 321, pp. 194–195.

[54] *WKP* 103, p. 133; *SIu* (1937) no. 8, pp. 11, 16, no. 23, pp. 37–38.

[55] Rittersporn, *Stalinist Simplifications and Soviet Complications*, pp. 142–157.

[56] "Dela sverdlovskogo obkoma," *P*, 22 May 1937, p. 4; "K chemu privodit politicheskaia slepota," *P*, 31 May 1937, p. 2; "Dela krasnoiarskogo kraikoma," *P*, 11 July 1937; "Vragi i ikh pokroviteli," *P*, 17 July 1937, p. 3; *B* (1937) no. 14, pp. 5–8; *PS* (1937) no. 15, pp. 40–43; *WKP* 111, pp. 229, 151–152, 176; *WKP* 163, p. 131, *WKP* 321, p. 165.

[57] Rittersporn, *Stalinist Simplifications and Soviet Complications*, pp. 158–164.

[58] *KPSS v rezoliutsiiakh*, pp. 303–312.

There was scarcely any need to convince the population about the existence of subversive activities among higher-ups. Allusions to acts of sabotage by grass-roots cadres were already multiplying in letters of complaint from peasants and workers at a time when the propaganda was still concentrating its fire merely on "hidden Trotskyists."[59] Routinely comparing their superiors to gendarmes or rough bosses of the Old Regime and indignant to see that they were often shielded from prosecution by local potentates even when guilty of obviously criminal offenses,[60] ordinary citizens were inclined to suspect the worst machinations of the powers-that-be. The masses were ready to attribute all hardships of their working and living conditions to premeditated wrongdoing by officeholders and even to demand the shooting of their "wrecking" superiors.[61] The show trials seemed to suggest that "it is impossible to trust Party members," though people could also believe that purged "conspirators" wanted to "liberate" peasants and workers.[62] Rumors about intricate scheming among top leaders[63] indicate that the turbulent events of 1936–8 convinced the public that everything was possible in high places. Politics could easily be seen in terms of conspiratorial intrigues by citizens constantly threatened to become victims of unpredictable reversals of a confused struggle of each against all among higher-ups, by people who thought that every party member was a police informer and that the "country is ruled by a small bunch of people."[64]

Not only the masses were inclined to suspect officeholders of plotting against them. Officialdom was also disposed to see clumsy "cabals" among the population and obsessed about their potentially hostile acts. When, in the wake of the first revelations about the Trotskyist threat, a group of workers wrote to a regional secretary that Kirov could be murdered only because of people like the managers of their factory, the secretary noted on this letter that it represented "the enemy's method of discrediting the leadership."[65] There was a remarkable tendency to look for subversive intentions behind the reluctance of the masses to comply with official orders, especially in the rural world where the judiciary was

[59] WKP 195, p. 182; WKP 197, pp. 77, 89, 230; WKP 355, p. 220.
[60] WKP 195, pp. 52, 182; WKP 197, pp. 77, 89, 230; WKP 201, p. 246; WKP 335, p. 187.
[61] WKP 195, pp. 21–23.
[62] WKP 87, p. 6; WKP 199, pp. 46, 55.
[63] See, e.g., PA, AA, Botschaft Moskau, A2c Innere Politik der UdSSR (Verwaltung . . .): the embassy to the Foreign Office, 28 Sept. 1936; Pol. Abt. V Po. 5 Ukraine, Innere Politik . . ., vol. 1: the Kiev consulate to the embassy, 1 April 1937, pp. 1–2; Botschaft Moskau, A4 Militär- und Marineangelegenheiten, vol. 6: telegrams of the embassy to the Foreign Office, 11 and 12 June 1937; Pol. Abt. V Po. 5 Rußland, Innere Politik . . ., vol. 3: "Lagebericht," 7 July 1937, p. 3, vol. 5: v. Tippelskirch to v. Welck, 10 January 1938; Pol. Abt. V Po. 7 Ministerien, Rußland: v. Tippelskirch to Schliep, 1 August 1938.
[64] WKP 87, p. 7; WKP 199, p. 72.
[65] WKP 355, p. 114.

regularly reminded that even negligent work could conceal wrecking or counterrevolutionary acts.[66] One of the most widespread manifestations of popular unruliness, theft of public property, was also declared a counterrevolutionary crime and ascribed to "enemies of the people."[67]

Officialdom felt beleaguered by a hostile population whose unpredictable moves motivated local cadres to impose punishments for the use of "indecent expressions" by their "subjects" and to restrict their right to assemble or to enter and leave villages.[68] Preconceived notions about proletarian virtues prompted questions about the supposedly class-alien origins of counterrevolutionary attitudes among workers whose close surveillance was nevertheless strongly recommended in order to prevent their political trouble making.[69] Kirov's assassination revealed dark hatred toward high dignitaries: People often rejoiced at the killing and prophesied that others too would be killed, including Stalin.[70] In the following weeks an attempted murder of Stalin was persistently rumored, so that the public believed that he had died when Kuibyshev's death was announced in a Leningrad theater.[71] But it was by far more than megalomaniac fear from lèse majesté that dictated a nationwide clampdown on "counterrevolutionary expressions in connection with comrade Kirov's assassination."[72] The population's respect for the system's most publicized symbol was in question and ultimately its loyalty to the state, especially in view of the pervasive war psychosis of the period and apparently frequent manifestations among the masses of a willingness to oppose the regime in case of armed conflict.[73] Simple citizens formed the overwhelming majority of the purge victims, subjected to wholesale repression in an increasingly chaotic and murderous attempt to root out the omnipresent danger of popular insubordination that coalesced with a centrally sponsored drive of the wholesale purge of "former kulaks, members of anti-Soviet parties, White

---

[66] *SIu* (1934) no. 8, p. 3, (1935) no. 11, p. 33, no. 20, p. 24; *SZak* (1934) no. 4, p. 41, no. 11, p. 48, no. 12, p. 48, (1935) no. 2, p. 63; *UK*, pp. 135, 138–139.

[67] *SZ* (1932) pp. 583–584; *SIu* (1935) no. 5, pp. 2–3, no. 13, p. 3; *SZak* (1937) p. 3; I. V. Stalin, *Sochineniia*, vol. 13 (Moscow, 1951) pp. 207–212.

[68] *SIu* (1935) no. 13, p. 5; *VS* (1936) no. 16, p. 24; *SZak* (1938) no. 3, p. 125, no. 6, p. 12.

[69] *WKP* 87, p. 7; *WKP* 109, pp. 19, 21, 36.

[70] *WKP* 109, p. 73; *WKP* 252, pp. 37–40; *WKP* 316, pp. 6–7; *WKP* 352, p. 115; *WKP* 415, pp. 22, 132; *RS* 921, pp. 133, 294.

[71] *PA, AA*, Abt. IV Ru. Po. No. 3, Rußland, Personalien . . . vol. 5: the Leningrad consulate to the embassy, 26 Jan. 1935.

[72] *SIu* (1935) no. 18, p. 10.

[73] *RS* 921, pp. 294, 300; *WKP* 199, p. 46; *WKP* 362, p. 340; *PA, AA*, Botschaft Moskau, A2 Innerpolitische Verhältnisse . . . vol. 8: the Kiev consulate to the embassy, 10 April 1935; Botschaft Moskau A2a, UdSSR – Parteiwesen: "Politischer Bericht", 4 July 1935, pp. 2–3; Botschaft Moskau A24e, Zweifelhafte Persönlichkeiten . . . vol. 2: letter in Russian received on 30 Dec. 1936; Botschaft Moskau, A39b Jahres- und Halbjahresberichte . . . Charkow: the consulate to the embassy, 12 January 1937, p. 11 and 10 June 1937, p. 14; *BA, NS* 43, 17, p. 533.

Guards, gendarmes and officials of tsarist Russia, bandits, returned émigrés, participants of anti-Soviet organizations, churchmen and sectarians [and] recidivist criminals."[74]

There were many possibilities of "unmasking enemies" among the masses. Nothing was easier than cleansing kolkhozes and enterprises from people of allegedly kulak background or from sons and daughters of class-alien elements, though such actions whose victims were sometimes denounced to the police could also hit "disorganizers" of production who had a corrupting effect on work discipline.[75] The number of these enemies could be high because, taking advantage of the disarray of the purged apparatus, peasants worked less and less in the kolkhoz, illegally enlarged their household plots, and avoided paying taxes and making compulsory food deliveries.[76] As the purge unfolded, workers began to defy cadres under the pretext that the cadres were potential wreckers and more and more often absented themselves from the enterprises.[77] Characteristically, calls for mobilizing the judiciary to fight these practices pretended that they were encouraged by "enemies of the people" and stopped short of imputing "sabotage" to workers.[78]

The purge ended with a mobilization drive to enforce harsh disciplinary and penal measures against workers and peasants.[79] No wonder then that a poll among wartime refugees showed that they were more likely than other social groups to characterize their work environment as "hostile" or "frightening."[80] No wonder also that the powers-that-be felt threatened by the reaction of the masses who, when the war came, could feel betrayed by "parasitic" bosses whose determination to save only their own skin seemed to confirm forebodings about the disastrous consequences of wrecking and plots of higher-ups.[81]

The imagery of omnipresent subversion and conspiracy denoted a dark feeling of suspicion and threat among leaders and the populace. This feeling did not necessarily appear as fear of a specific danger, and the

---

[74] For the relevant directive dated July 1937 and stipulating that the "most hostile . . . [of these] elements" had to be shot and others were to be sentenced to long terms of detention, see *Izvestiia TsK KPSS* (1989) no. 10, pp. 81–82.

[75] See, e.g., *WKP 516*, pp. 2–77, in particular pp. 12–13, 22, 27, 39, 41, 45, 47, 55, 57.

[76] *VS* (1938) no. 10–11, pp. 52–53; editorials, *P*, 17 April and 12 Aug. 1938; *Istoriia KPSS*, t. 4, kniga 2-ia (Moscow, 1971) p. 428; *Istoriia SSSR s drevneishikh vremen do nashikh dnei*, vol. 9 (Moscow, 1971) p. 352.

[77] Editorials, *P*, 29 April, 11 May, 24 June, and 14 and 25 Aug., 1937; *SZ* (1937) p. 246; *B* (1937) no. 16, p. 19, no. 19, p. 7.

[78] *SIu* (1938) no. 17, pp. 10, 12; *B* (1938) no. 23–24, p. 10; "Lishit" lodyrei," *P*, 14 Dec. 1938, p. 3; "Komandiry proizvodstva i trudovaia distsiplina," *P*, 25 Dec. 1938, p. 2.

[79] Rittersporn, *Stalinist Simplifications and Soviet Complications*, pp. 256–258.

[80] A. Rossi, *Generational Differences in the Soviet Union* (New York, 1980) pp. 216–219, 228–230.

[81] *PA, AA*, Abteilung Pol. 13, Allgemeine Akten 13, DIX 322: no. 120.

underlying experience of anxiousness varied according to age, personal background, and social status.[82] It nevertheless permeated the relationships of social categories to each other and to the regime. As social groups define themselves in their relations to each other and to the state, the representation of ubiquitous wrecking and plots revealed a strong inclination of officialdom and the masses alike to identify themselves as potential victims of impenetrable machinations.

Given the omnipresence of misgovernment and official abuse as well as social tensions and political conflict, the imagery of ubiquitous subversion was by no means ungrounded. It seems difficult to escape the conclusion that the unpredictable, incomprehensible, and treacherous daily reality of the system fed perceptions of omnipresent conspiracy. From the point of view of those who were inclined to see concerted action by a monolithic party-state as the *primum movens* of the period's turmoil, it was natural to attribute every event and every twist and turn of the sinuous political line to machinations of an all-powerful center and its supreme leader, whereas the work of a multitude of competing forces could be suspected by those who had doubts about the regime's ability to control and regiment everything.

In both cases, the representation of wrecking and plots located a paradigmatic feature of the entire system in merely one or some of its parts. The allegorization of an ineffable evil that came to possess the world of every social category, the projection of the regime's elusive and hostile universe in identifiable deeds and agents, tallied with traditional popular rural folkloric beliefs that attributed everyday misfortunes to the activities of evil spirits.[83] But such a projection could never have taken the form of sabotage and conspiracies without the regime's unwillingness to explain its problems in terms of the administration's ordinary working and social conflict, and it could hardly ever have had murderous consequences without officialdom's attempt to exorcise the system's ills through the use of an apparatus that happened to provoke and embody them. Collective representations of the omnipresent conspiracy were captive of the everyday reality of a system that became colonized by the party-state's political practice and discourse.[84]

[82] R. W. Thurston, "Fear and Belief in the USSR's 'Great Terror': Response to Arrest, 1935–1939," *Slavic Review* (1986) no. 2, pp. 213–234; R. A. Bauer, A. Inkeles, C. Cluckhohn, *How the Soviet System Works* (Cambridge, MA, 1956) pp. 178–179; A. Inkeles, R. A. Bauer, *The Soviet Citizen* (Cambridge, MA, 1959) pp. 23, 108, 245; Rossi, pp. 184, 186, 217, 229, 239, 324.

[83] M. Lewin, *The Making of the Soviet System: Essays in the Social History of Interwar Russia* (New York, 1985) pp. 275–276, 310.

[84] For a similar impact of elite concepts and practices on popular beliefs and behavior see N. Cohn, *Europe's Inner Demons* (London, 1975) pp. 225–255; R. Kieckfeber, *European Witch Trials* (London, 1976) pp. 73–92.

5

The Soviet economic crisis of 1936–1940 and the Great Purges

Roberta T. Manning

Scholars have long noted that the Soviet economy experienced considerable difficulties after 1936, as the high economic growth rates of the mid-thirties suddenly gave way to what Naum Jasny called "snail-like crawl, stagnation and even declines" that persisted right up to the Nazi invasion of the USSR.[1] This development has traditionally been attributed to the impact of the Great Purges of 1936–1938, which decimated economic planners and administrators, both nationally and locally.[2] A close reading of the contemporary Soviet press, available collections of economic statistics, and archival materials would suggest, however, that the falloff in Soviet growth rates was a cause as well as a consequence of the purges.

Key areas of the Soviet economy were already encountering major problems or stagnating growth rates in the first half of 1936, *before* the June 1936 arrest of Kamenev and Zinoviev heralded the onset of a new upsurge of political terror that resulted in the arrest of growing numbers of former Party Oppositionists throughout the nation by July and August.[3] Agricultural production fell precipitously in 1936, due to climatic conditions

The author wishes to express her gratitude to the John Simon Guggenheim Memorial Foundation, the Harvard Russian Research Center, and the administration of Boston College for supporting this research.

1 Naum Jasny, *Soviet Industrialization* (Chicago, 1961), 177. According to some scholars, the drop in overall industrial production was quite substantial, from 10–12% per year between 1928 and 1937 to only 2–3% a year from 1937 to 1940. Norman Kaplan and Richard Moorstein, "An Index of Soviet Industrial Output," *American Economic Review*, vol. 50, no. 2 (June 1960), 307 and Warren G. Nutter, *The Growth of Industrial Production in the Soviet Union* (Princeton, 1962), 198.

2 Jasny, 132–179; Alec Nove, *An Economic History of the USSR* (New York, 1982), 236–9, 256–68; Roy Medvedev, *Let History Judge: The Origins and Consequences of Stalinism* (New York, 1971), 485–90; and Barbara G. Katz, *Journal of Economic History*, vol. 35, no. 3 (Sept. 1975), 567–90.

3 For this, see J. Arch Getty, *Origins of the Great Purges: The Soviet Communist Party Reconsidered, 1933–1938* (Cambridge, 1985), 119–222; The Smolensk Archive, WKP 499, pp. 322–8; *Rabochii put* (Smolensk) Sept. 6, 1936, p. 1.

that had already manifested themselves before the arrest of Kamenev and Zinoviev; and industrial growth rates began to falter in some vital areas of the economy. Indeed, the output of vital fuels and construction materials like coal, oil, and timber grew more slowly than the remainder of the economy in the mid-thirties and then stagnated or even declined in the first half of 1936. The resulting shortfall in fuel and construction materials began to cause havoc in other sectors of the economy by the end of the year.

These economic difficulties contributed substantially to the expansion of political terror. In the summer of 1936, mass arrests appear to have been politically motivated and largely confined to former members of the small and long defunct Left Opposition within the Communist Party and persons who supported, defended, or refused to disassociate themselves from former Oppositionists, either in the past or present. Most of those arrested had long been excluded from influential positions in the government and the economy. On September 26, 1936, however, in the wake of the Kemerovo Coal Mine explosion of September 23, Stalin ordered Nikolai Ezhov, who headed the Party Control Commission and the Industrial Department of the Central Committee, to take over the leadership of the political police, the NKVD. Under Ezhov's direction, the focus of the terror expanded to include growing numbers of industrial managers, administrators, and engineers,[4] and the main accusations leveled against purge victims also changed from conspiracy to assassinate Soviet leaders to economic sabotage or "wrecking."[5]

Evidence of wrecking was found in abundance in the real-life problems of the Soviet economy, which were attributed to malevolent human design rather than the result of economic forces out of anyone's control, pressures from above to achieve the impossible, and human error, ignorance, or sheer incompetency. In the course of the following year, agricultural administrators and provincial and district political leaders in charge of overseeing the operation of the economy would also fall prey to similar charges, as the nation's economic problems grew ever more grave, under the impetus

---

[4] Robert Conquest, *The Great Terror: Stalin's Purges of the Thirties* (New York, 1973), 217–28; Getty, 116–28 and Medvedev, 167–72.

[5] One can find this shift both in charges leveled against local Communists expelled from the Party and arrested for counterrevolutionary crimes in the Western Oblast in the summer and fall of 1936 and those raised against the defendants in the major show trials covered in the Soviet press in 1936 and 1937. The assassination and attempted assassination of Soviet leaders was the main charge against the defendants in the Kamenev-Zinoviev trial of August 1936, whereas wrecking or economic sabotage became the prime charge in major show trials thereafter, like the Novosibirsk trial of the Kemerovo conspirators in November 1936, the trial of the Orenburg Railway officials in December 1937, and the Piatakov-Radek trial of January 1937. The Smolensk Archive, WKP 538, pp. 346, 371, 376, 382, 387, 397, 399–401, 407, 438, 442, 452–4, 467–8, 485, 502–3, 512, 517, 541–6, 553–5; *Pravda*, Aug. 15–24, 1936, Oct. 8, 1936, Oct. 10, 1936, Nov. 20–24, 1936, Dec. 28, 1936, and Jan. 21–30, 1937.

of both spontaneous economic forces unleashed earlier and the ever-expanding terror.

Eugene Zaleski, in his monumental study of Stalinist planning, suggests that problems endemic to "the administrative-command system" figured prominently in the charges against the purge victims:

Disproportions that appeared [in the economy] in 1936 became the most common accusations in the trials of people that Stalin wanted liquidated (for example, former Deputy Commissar of Heavy Industry Piatakov). A few examples of such accusations, cited by Lokshin in 1937, show the chronic defects of the Stalinist planning system were simply presented as sabotage: incorrect use of equipment, failure to carry out capital repairs, reluctance to introduce new techniques, delays in installations of imported equipment, ordering equipment not corresponding to needs, failure to declare real productive capacities, frequent changing and poor drafting of specifications, dispersion of resources on multiple construction projects, extension of construction schedules, reductions of investment efficiency, disproportions among various workshops and putting into operation blast furnaces not completely finished. These facts appear to be confirmed and indisputable. The accusations of sabotage and the language of repression, however, make it impossible to discuss true responsibility.[6]

To be sure, such phenomena are an enduring feature of the administrative-command or Stalinist economic system and have come to be recognized as such by Soviet leaders and economists and foreign specialists alike. But in the 1930s, when this system was new and the nation had yet to accumulate much experience with it and its shortcomings, such systematic failings were attributed to deliberate economic sabotage. Soviet political leaders and many ordinary citizens of the 1930s were inclined to attribute adversity to the machinations of malevolent forces, as Gábor Rittersporn has argued.[7] This was especially true of the years of the Great Purges (1936–8), when the double digit industrial growth rates of the early- to mid-thirties suddenly and unexpectedly plummeted.

The economic problems that started to set in by the middle of 1936 and their origins have yet to be fully explored. As usual, the hardest hit area of the economy was agriculture, which still employed about two thirds of the Soviet populace. The 1936 agricultural year began with great expectations, kindled by the good harvest of 1935 and the successes of the Soviet government in mechanizing agriculture in recent years, as Table 5.1 demonstrates. Stalin confidently predicted a 7 to 8 billion *pud* grain harvest in the near future, almost twice prerevolutionary production levels.[8] But 1936 ended instead with a massive crop failure, the worse harvest since the 1932–3 famine, as Table 5.2 indicates.

As usual in Russia, capricious weather, particularly drought, accounted

---

[6] Eugene Zaleski, *Stalinist Planning for Economic Growth, 1933–1952*, (Chapel Hill, NC, 1980), 248–9.
[7] Rittersporn, this volume.
[8] *Pravda*, Jan. 29, 1936 and Feb. 11, 1936.

Table 5.1. *The mechanization of Soviet agriculture, 1930–1940*

Year	No. of MTSs	No. of tractors	No. of combines
1930	158	72,100	1,700
1931	1,228	125,300	6,400
1932	2,446	148,500	14,500
1933	2,916	210,900	25,400
1934	3,533	276,400	32,300
1935	4,375	360,300	50,300
1936	5,000	422,700	87,800
1937	5,818	454,500	128,800
1938	6,358	483,500	153,500
1939	6,501	495,800	n.d.
1940	6,980	523,000	182,000

Source: Alexander Baykov, *The Development of the Soviet Economic System* (Cambridge, 1947), p. 331.

largely for the short harvest, which was global in scope, as the crops failed in 1936 in Europe, Canada, Australia, the Near East, India, Northern China, Japan, and even the United States.[9] In the USSR, the autumn of 1935 was dry and little snow fell in winter, always an ominous sign. The spring of 1936 was cold and late, with sharp oscillations of cold and warm weather. In many areas, freezes set in after the new crops had sprouted. A spell of intense heat and a drought that lasted up to forty days in many areas then ensued. The result was stunted crops and peculiar growing patterns. All crops, both winter and spring, were affected, with the exception perhaps of cotton and sugar beets. Crops that usually ripened in succession ripened simultaneously, putting considerable strain on the Soviets' newly acquired agricultural equipment and inexperienced machine operators. To make matters worse, most regions experienced violent, heavy thunderstorms on the eve of the harvest, flattening the grain crop in many areas so it could not be mechanically harvested.[10]

By July 1936, the Soviet press began to hint at the possibility of "great losses" and to note that the machine tractor stations were not coping well

[9] *Sotsialisticheskoe zemledelie*, Dec. 19, 1936; *Pravda*, Aug. 3, 1936, Nov. 17, 1936; *Sotsialisticheskaia rekonstruktsiia sel'skogo khoziaistva*, 1936 no. 8 (Aug.) pp. 215–16, no. 10 (Oct.) pp. 217–21; 1937 no. 4 (April) pp. 193–202, no. 11–12 (Nov.–Dec.) pp. 217–23; 1938 no. 9 (Sept.) pp. 135–48.

[10] *Pravda*, Mar. 15, 1936, July 4, 1936, July 9, 1936, Mar. 15, 1937; *Sovetskoe stroitel'stvo*, no. 7 (July 1936) p. 49 and no. 11 (Nov. 1936); *Bolshevik*, no. 12 (June 15, 1936) pp. 90–2, 95 and no. 20 (Oct. 15, 1936) p. 19–31; *Vlast sovetov*, no. 23 (Dec. 15, 1936) p. 52; *Sotsialisticheskoe zemledelie*, July 21, 1936, p. 1.

Table 5.2. *Soviet grain crop estimates by year (in millions of metric tons)*

Year	Jasny	Johnson-Kahan	Official Soviet data (Clarke) (new)	Wheatcroft
1909–13				72.0
1913			80.1	84.0
1920			45.2	50.0
1921			36.2–42.3	42.0
1922			56.3	54.0
1923			57.4	56.6
1924			51.4	51.4
1925			74.7	72.5
1926			78.3	76.8
1927			72.8	72.3
1928	73.3	73.3	73.3	73.3
1929	71.7	71.7	71.7	71.7
1930	83.5	83.5	83.5	78.0
1931	66.0	66.0	69.5	68.0
1932[a]	66.4	63.0	69.6	67.0
1933	70.1	67.1	68.4	69.0
1934	72.2	67.3	67.6	72.0
1935	76.6	69.3	75.0	77.0
1936	63.6	60.0	56.1	59.0
1937	96.0	91.9	97.4	98.0
1938	75.9	70.7	n.d.	75.0
1939	82.9		n.d.	75.0
1940			95.6	86.2

[a] A recent article by Mark Tauger in *Slavic Review* argues that all earlier estimates, both Western and Soviet, greatly overstate 1932 harvest yields that may have run as low as 50 million metric tons of grain. Mark B. Tauger, "The 1932 Harvest and the Famine of 1933," *Slavic Review*, vol. 50, no. 1 (spring 1991), pp. 70–89.
Source: Naum Jasny, *The Socialized Agriculture of the USSR* (Stanford, 1949), p. 793; D. Gale Johnson and Arcadius Kahan, in U.S. Congress, Joint Economic Committee, *Comparisons of the United States and Soviet Economies* (Washington, DC, 1959), Part 1, p. 231; Roger A. Clarke, *Soviet Economic Facts, 1917–1970* (New York, 1972), pp. 111–112; and S. G. Wheatcroft, "Grain Production Statistics in the USSR in the 1920s and 1930s," *CREES Discussion Papers: Soviet Industrialization Project Series*, SIPS No. 13, p. 9.

with the harvest, due to acute fuel and spare parts shortages, the poor organization of work on the part of both the MTSs (machine tractor stations) and collective farms, bad repair work, and horrendous living and working conditions for the nation's tractor and combine drivers.[11] *Pravda*

[11] *Krest'ianskaia gazeta*, Mar. 6, 1936, Mar. 18, 1936, April 18, 1936, May 12, 1936, May 14, 1936, June 10, 1936, June 28, 1936, June 30, 1936, July 4, 1936, July 8, 1936, July

in retrospect some months later compared the weather conditions of 1936 with those of 1891, a well-known famine year. *Sotsialisticheskoe zemledelie,* the organ of the All-Union Commissariat of Agriculture, subsequently insisted that in "many places" climatic conditions in 1936 were "more difficult than in 1921," when one of the all-time worse crop failures on record in Russia occurred.[12] At the time, however, the Soviet press actively sought to create the impression that the crops had not failed by stressing individual Stakhanovite achievements and developments in regions that did not experience a crop failure that year, like the Ukraine.[13] Secret communiques of local party agencies, however, admitted outright in May 1936 that the crops were threatened by drought and assessed the ensuing harvest losses as "great" by early August.[14]

Growing official malaise about the state of the harvest surfaced in press articles that began to express concern for the 1937 crop, articles that started to appear long before the 1936 harvest was all in.[15] Fears of serious fodder shortages also surfaced in the press by the end of July, for the simultaneous ripening of food and technical crops and dry weather threatened the hay harvest, which always took second place to these other crops. A shortage of hay, traditionally the main source of livestock fodder, would jeopardize the nation's livestock herds, which had almost finally recovered from the mass slaughtering of the collectivization period. Reports of new outbreaks of mass slaughtering, the usual peasant response to crop failures and fodder shortages, began to trickle into the press by the end of 1936 and became ever more commonplace in the winter and spring of 1937 as remaining fodder stocks were exhausted.[16]

By the time the new bumper crop of 1937 was gathered in, Soviet

10, 1936, July 16, 1936; *Pravda,* Jan. 21, 1936, Jan. 31, 1936, Aug. 5, 1936; *Sotsialisticheskoe zemledelie,* June 8, 1936, June 27, 1936, June 30, 1936, July 15, 1936; *Sovetskoe stroitel'stvo,* no. 7 (20) July 1936, p. 49.

[12] *Pravda,* Mar. 15, 1937 and *Sotsialisticheskoe zemledelie,* Oct. 17, 1936. These remarks were made in passing in the context of articles that were on the whole remarkedly upbeat, entitled respectively "The Successes of Socialist Sugar Beet Production" and "Collective Farm Victory Over Drought."

[13] See, for example, *Pravda,* Sept. 26, 1936, Oct. 2, 1936, Oct. 20, 1936, Nov. 15, 1936 and *Vlast sovetov,* no. 23 (Dec. 15, 1936) p. 52.

[14] See, for example, the resolutions of the Western obkom bureau. The Smolensk Archive, WKP 538, pp. 217, 363, 393, 408–9.

[15] Beginning in August 1936, the Soviet press started to follow the course of field work on the 1937 crop more closely than work on the current harvest still underway, by running numerous stories on the planting of winter crops and the fall plowing of spring crop lands. These accounts indicated that the same fuel and spare parts shortages and sloppy repair work that had earlier plagued the 1936 crop continued to prevail. *Sotsialisticheskoe zemledelie,* Aug. 1, 1936, Aug. 2, 1936, Oct. 2, 1936, Oct. 6, 1936, Oct. 12, 1936, Oct. 14, 1936; *Krest'ianskaia gazeta,* Sept. 24, 1936, Sept. 28, 1936, Oct. 12, 1936, Oct. 14, 1936, Oct. 16, 1936, Oct. 18, 1936.

[16] *Sotsialisticheskoe zemledelie,* July 30, 1936, Sept. 9, 1936, Feb. 15, 1937; *Sovetskoe stroitel'stvo,* no. 10 (Oct. 1936) pp. 41–2; *Krest'ianskaia gazeta,* Aug. 10, 1936; *Rabochii put* (Smolensk) May 29, 1937; and *Pravda,* Dec. 20, 1936.

Table 5.3. *The impact of the 1936 crop failure on Soviet livestock herds*
1936–1938

Type of livestock	No. of livestock (millions of heads)			
	1/1/36	6/1/36	1/1/37	1/1/38
cattle	50	56.7	47.5	50.9
sheep and goats	58	73.5	53.8	66.6
pigs	23.3	24.3	20.0	25.7
horses	16.3	16.6	15.9	16.2

Source: *British Foreign Office Russia Correspondance* 1936, reel 3, vol. 20341,
p. 33; 1938, reel 4, vol. 22293, p. 142, and reel 5, vol. 22298, pp. 131–133;
Izvestia, April 17, 1938; and *Sotsialisticheskoe zemledelie*, April 21, 1938.

livestock herds had declined substantially from the levels that prevailed on
the eve of the 1936 harvest, as Table 5.3 indicates.[17] In many regions of
the country, epidemics of livestock diseases raged unchecked among surviving malnourished animals,[18] inspiring widespread charges that a number
of provincial and district political leaders and agricultural administrators,
both national and local, had deliberately infected the beasts with diseases
in order to "wreck" the collective farm economy.[19]

Despite the loss of substantial numbers of livestock and efforts to keep
the crop failure secret, the Soviet government managed to cope with the
1936 crop failure much better than it or its tsarist predecessors had coped
with earlier periods of short harvests and acute food shortages, as in 1891,
1905–6, 1921–2, and 1932–3.[20] Exports of grain and fodder were sharply
curtailed from August 1936 on and then ceased altogether in January and

[17] The national data in Table 5.3 conceal substantial regional variations. In the Western
Oblast, cattle herds declined by 14.4% in 1937, but the decline was much greater in
individual raions, since the numbers of cattle declined by 24.4% in Belyi Raion and by
38% in Andreevo Raion. *Rabochii put* (Smolensk) June 21, 1938.

[18] For example, in the Western Oblast, the number of cattle infected with brucellosis rose
from 946 in March 1936 to 5930 in March 1937. Tsentral'nyi Gosudarstvennyi Arkhiv
Narodnogo Khoziaistva SSSR, fond 7486, op 16, del 745, 1936, p. 30 and del 1063,
1937, p. 9. (Hereafter cited as TsGANKh.)

[19] *Pravda*, April 2, 1937, June 30, 1937; *Sotsialisticheskoe zemledelie*, June 23, 1937, July
16, 1937, July 17, 1937, July 20, 1937, July 21, 1937, July 22, 1937, July 24, 1937, Aug.
3, 1937; *Rabochii put* (Smolensk) May 10, 1937, July 4, 1937, Nov. 22, 1937, Nov. 29,
1937; and TsGANKh, fond 7486, op 16, del 1056, 1937, pp. 3–37 and del 1105, 1937,
pp. 1–38 and fond 9477, op 1, del 419, 1937, pp. 1–22.

[20] Richard G. Robbins Jr., *Famine in Russia, 1891–1892: The Imperial Russian Government
Responds to a Crisis* (New York/London, 1975); Roberta T. Manning, *The Crisis of the
Old Order in Russia: Gentry and Government* (Princeton, 1982), 167–9; Charles M.
Edmondson, "An Inquiry into the Termination of Soviet Famine Relief Programmes and
the Renewal of Grain Exports, 1922–23," *Soviet Studies*, vol. 33, no. 3 (July, 1981) pp.
353–69; Robert Conquest, *Harvest of Sorrow: Soviet Collectivization and the Terror
Famine*; and S. G. Wheatcroft, "More Light on the Scale of Repression and Excess

February 1937, as top government officials assimilated the magnitude of the crop failure.[21] The government also delved into its now sufficient food reserves in the fall of 1936 and spring of 1937 to provide famine relief on a massive scale, mainly in the form of food and fodder loans on generous terms to collective farmers.[22]

Nonetheless, food supplies remained severely strained throughout the first half of 1937 until the new year's harvest began to come in. By February 1937, Soviet employees of foreign embassies who visited relatives in villages near Moscow reported that bread was sold only a few hours each night, long lines formed "hours before the stores opened," and purchases were restricted to one kilogram (2.2 pounds) per customer. British diplomats noted that more peasants than usual were coming into Moscow to buy bread, and the number of street beggars noticeably increased.[23] By April, Leningraders, whose food supplies came from central stocks, were forbidden to buy more than two kilograms of black bread at a time, and what passed for white bread locally was diluted with a hefty quantity of rye meal.[24] The major cities from August 1936 on also experienced chronic shortages of vegetables and potatoes, essential components of a great variety of soups, which along with bread, cereals, and boiled potatoes were the dietary staples of most Soviets at this time.[25] In the often restive Donbas coal-mining region, the quality and quantity of available food supplies deteriorated sharply by the end of 1936, resulting in the closing of 450 of the area's 860 workplace canteens.[26]

Viscount Chilston, the British ambassador to the USSR, attributed the upsurge of arrests of industrial managers in late 1936 and early 1937 to popular discontent over the strained food supplies, pointing out in a letter to Foreign Minister Antony Eden shortly after the Piatakov show trial at the end of January 1937:

Mortality in the Soviet Union in the 1930s," *Soviet Studies*, vol. 42, no. 2 (April, 1990) pp. 355–67.

[21] *Pravda* April 4, 1937 and *British Foreign Office Russia Correspondence*, 1937, reel 3, vol. 21096, pp. 191–2. Earlier, however, some high officials, like Soviet President Kalinin and N. Lisitsyn, Deputy Commissar of Agriculture of the RSFSR, had publicly assessed the harvest as "good," although "not the best," despite climatic conditions. See, for example, *Sovetskoe stroitel'stvo*, no. 11 (Nov. 1936) p. 7 and N. Lisitsyn, "Obespechit vysokii urozhai 1937 g.," *Vlast sovetov*, no. 24 (Dec. 30, 1936) pp. 19–20.

[22] In the case of Belyi raion (Western Oblast), these loans amounted to 8,700 metric tons of grain – 741.1 kilograms for every collective farm family. Substantial seed loans were also given the raion to plant the next year's crop. The Smolensk Archive WKP 238, pp. 21, 43, 56–57, 66, 71, 79, 82, 96, 215–16 and WKP 321, p. 127.

[23] *British Foreign Office Russia Correspondence*, 1937, reel 3, vol. 21096, pp. 210–11.

[24] Yet meat became more abundant and meat prices fell, due to the upsurge in the slaughtering of livestock, which could no longer be adequately fed on many collective farms. Ibid., reel 6, vol. 21106, pp. 131–4.

[25] *Pravda*, Aug. 21, 1937 and Aug. 24, 1937. Reports of these shortages were delayed for a year and combined with reports of the abundant 1937 harvest!

[26] *British Foreign Office Russia Correspondence*, 1937, reel 3, vol. 21096, p. 211.

There seems little doubt that anxiety for food supplies is a contributory cause of the present state of nervousness. It is believed that grain reserves are sufficient to prevent a definite famine, but the government would certainly be loth to use them on a large scale in the present state of international relations, and are probably sailing as close as they dare to the wind of popular discontent.[27]

Not surprisingly the purges in the hard-hit Donbas were among the most severe in the nation, as central authorities felt compelled to intervene repeatedly to limit the number of engineers and managers arrested.[28] Political shake-ups in local government and the Commissariat of Agriculture began in earnest in June 1937, when scant food supplies caused by the 1936 crop failure reached their zenith on the eve of the new harvest. Policymakers, administrators, and specialists responsible for policies and practices that contributed to the short 1936 harvest – like the absence of any crop rotation whatsoever on most collective farms, the chronic inability of the MTSs to balance their account books and keep their tractors and combines in working order, and foul-ups in the production and distribution of selected seeds – began to be arrested en masse for wrecking agriculture and/or creating food shortages in order to increase popular discontent against the government.[29]

Concern for the 1937 crop surfaced early and persisted long after it became apparent that the 1937 crop was likely to be best yet, exceeding even the highest prerevolutionary harvest on record, as Table 5.2 demonstrates.[30] The 1936 crop failure exhausted the nation's food reserves, and actual famine, like the one that occurred in 1932–3, remained a distinct possibility should the harvest fall short once again before government food stocks were replenished.[31] Moreover, the fuel and spare parts problems

---

[27] Ibid., 1937, reel 4, vol. 21099, p. 206.

[28] See, for example, the *Pravda* article of September 17, 1936, criticizing the excessive expulsions of party members in the Donbas, the SNK/CC Resolution of April 28, 1937, that warned against wholesale repressions of managers and engineers in the Donbas mines and required that all cases prosecuted in the Donbas be reviewed by Moscow prosecutors so that cases based on insufficient evidence could be dropped; and Stalin's speech to a delegation of mining and metallurgy workers from the Donbas on October 29, 1937, lauding the importance of leaders. *Pravda*, Sept. 17, 1936, p. 2, May 15, 1937, p. 2, and Oct. 31, 1937, p. 1. For a discussion of the Great Purges in the Donbas, see Hiroaki Kuromiya in Chapter 10 of this volume.

[29] Such charges were leveled against the leaders of the Western Oblast and of the Grain Administration of the All-Union Commissariat of Agriculture (NKZ) when they were arrested in June, 1937. The Smolensk Archive, WKP 111, pp. 152–65, 170–5 and *Pravda*, June 29, 1937, July 15, 1937; *Sotsialisticheskoe zemledelie*, May 12, 1937, May 14, 1937, May 27, 1937, July 2, 1937. In Smolensk, the first of the local show trials on July 31, 1937, involved the director of the local bakery trust, who was convicted of wrecking and given a ten-year prison sentence for creating local bread shortages. Subsequently the head of the oblast trade department and the managers of two major bakeries were also tried and convicted on identical charges. Boris Gregorievich Men'shagin, *Vospominaniia Smolensk . . . Khatyn' . . . Vladimirskaia tiur'ma* (Paris, 1988), 31–33.

[30] See Table 5.2 for the 1937 harvest.

[31] For example, Belyi Raion (Western Oblast) received the last of a series of substantial food loans from the government on May 28, 1937, and was informed that no further aid was

plaguing the MTSs proved even greater in 1937 than in 1936, due to the continuing deterioration or stagnation of key areas of the economy.[32] The escalation of terror in the summer and fall of 1937, when mass arrests peaked, appears in part to have been directly related to efforts to prod local officials – from collective farm and rural soviet chairmen to raikom party secretaries – into harvesting and turning over to the state as much of the bumper 1937 harvest as possible, while correcting a series of existing administrative policies and practices detrimental to agriculture, which higher authorities evidently blamed for the previous year's crop failure.[33]

By the second half of 1936, however, Soviet economic problems were by no means limited to agriculture. In some sectors of the economy, a general slowdown, stagnation, and occasionally even decline in production had clearly set in and began to spread to the remainder of the economy. This situation persisted until well into 1940, if not until the German invasion of the USSR in June 1941.[34] The slowdown was masked by an improvement in the performance of agriculture after 1936, by runaway inflation, which consistently allowed the ruble output targets of the Five-Year Plan to be met or even exceeded, and by outright government censorship of unfavorable economic news, which extended to ever larger areas of the economy, as Soviet industry failed to make decisive progress and the onset of World War II drew near.

Nonetheless, the Soviet press noted early in 1936 that the physical output of key fuels and construction materials – coal, oil, and timber – were lagging considerably behind plan, failing to keep up with the high growth rates of the rest of the economy,[35] as Table 5.4 indicates. In the Donbas coal mines, for example, throughout 1936 and much of 1937 the

available. In June, the town of Belyi was 2.5 metric tons short of the 500 tons of grain required by the populace, and grain to fill the deficit could not be purchased anywhere. The Smolensk Archive, WKP 238, p. 82 and WKP 111, pp. 8, 169.

[32] For the press alarm about the state of the new harvest even after it was clear a record harvest was in the making, see, for example, *Pravda*, June 2, 1937, June 4, 1937, June 11, 1937, July 17, 1937, July 18, 1937, July 20, 1937, July 29, 1937, Aug. 21, 1937, Sept. 2, 1937, Sept. 18, 1937, Sept. 23, 1937. In general all the Soviet press, especially the agricultural press (*Sotsialisticheskoe zemledelie* and *Krest'ianskaia gaezta*), expressed much more concern and alarm about the 1937 crops than was true of the 1936 crops, possibly because stakes were higher, given the depletion of food reserves by the summer of 1937.

[33] Robert W. Thurston, "Fear and Belief in the USSR's 'Great Terror': Response to Arrest, 1935–1939," *Slavic Review*, vol. 45, no. 2 (summer, 1986), 229 and Roberta T. Manning, "The Great Purges in a Rural District: Belyi Raion Revisited," *Russian History*, vol. 16, nos. 2–4 (1989), 409–33. See also the resolutions of the Commission on Soviet Control on the poor preparations for the 1937 harvest and the June 1937 Central Committee Plenum on agriculture. *Rabochii put* (Smolensk) June 15, 1937; *Sotsialisticheskoe zemledelie*, May 12, 1937; *Sotsialisticheskaia rekonstruktsiia sel'skogo khoziaistva*, 1937, no. 7 (July), 1–33; and *Pravda*, July 5, 1937.

[34] Jasny, 177–200 and Zaleski, *Stalinist Planning* 160, 172–8, 186–7, 248–56, 265–79.

[35] *Bolshevik*, no. 11 (June 1, 1936) pp. 8–29, 62–68; no. 13 (July 5, 1936) pp. 35–48; no. 20 (Oct. 15, 1936) pp. 9–18; *Pravda*, July 4, 1936, July 14, 1936, July 29, 1936, Aug. 29, 1936, Oct. 22, 1936, Dec. 13, 1936, Dec. 19, 1936; *British Foreign Office Russia Correspondence*, 1936, reel 2, vol. 20341, pp. 6, 233; and Lewis H. Siegelbaum,

Table 5.4. *Annual production in key bottleneck areas of the economy during the Soviet economic crisis/slowdown of 1936–1940: Output of fuels and construction materials (as of January 1 of the year given)*

Product	1913	1928	1935	1936	1937	1938	1939	1940
Coal[a]	29.1	35.5	109.6	126.8	128	133.3	146.2	165.9
Coke[a]				19.9	20.0	19.6	20.2	20.2
Oil[a]	9.2	11.6	25.2	27.4	28.5	30.2	30.2	31.1
Manganese ore[a]				3.0	2.8	2.3	2.3	
Iron ore[a]	9.2	6.1	26.8	27.8	27.8	26.6	26.9	29.9
Pig iron[a]	4.2	3.3	12.5	14.4	14.5	14.7	14.5	14.9
Steel[a]	4.3	4.3	12.6	16.4	17.7	18.1	17.6	18.3
Rolled steel[a]	3.5	3.4	9.4	12.5	13.0	13.3	12.7	13.1
Steel pipes[b]	77.7	171	639	859	923	909	917	966
Cement[a]	1,777	1,850	4,488	5,872	5,454	5,688	5,197	5,675
Timber (including firewood)[c]	67	61.7	210.1	221.9	209	223	264.1	246.1
Commercial timber[c] (exclusive of firewood)	30.5	36	117	128.1	114.2	114.7	126.1	117.9
Sawed timber[c]				40.9	28.8	34.5	34.5	

Note: The output levels listed are those prevailing January 1 of the given year, so the figures listed under 1936 reflect the progress made in 1935 rather than problems emerging in 1936. For the latter, see the figures given under 1937.

[a] Measured in millions of metric tons
[b] Measured in thousands of metric tons
[c] Measured in millions of cubic meters

Source: Roger A. Clarke, *Soviet Economic Facts, 1917–1970* (New York, 1972), pp. 53–54, 59–61, 76, and 79; and Naum Jasny, *Soviet Industrialization, 1928–1952* (Chicago, 1961), p. 199.

production of coal declined from month to month from the record output levels set at the height of Stakhanovite enthusiasm in December 1935.[36] This development enhanced existing strains throughout the economy, caused by unrealistic planning, and accounted for the inability of ever larger numbers of industries to meet the ambitious physical output targets of the annual 1936 plan.[37]

Fuel shortages also rendered the poor harvest of 1936 poorer than it might otherwise have been by inhibiting the use of combines and tractors, while the shortage of timber contributed to the spread of livestock diseases by preventing the construction of much needed barns to house the nation's growing livestock herds, which had increased significantly since 1933. As a result, many animals were either left outside or in semicompleted structures to confront the Russian winter, or farm administrators were compelled to ignore government quarantine regulations and house sick and healthy animals together, practices that were subsequently regarded as manifestations of wrecking.[38] The simultaneous "motorizing" of both agriculture and the armed forces and the coming of many mammoth new industries on line in the mid-1930s had stimulated domestic demand for fuels as never before in Russian history, at the very time their production slowed and finally stagnated.[39] The shortfall in timber production, which was used as both a fuel and construction material, threatened to curtail the future expansion of the economy.

By early 1937, the crisis extended to ferrous and nonferrous metals and cement, essential building blocks of an industrial civilization along with coal and oil, and to water and river transport. The latter was severely hurt by the 1936 drought that rendered many rivers unnavigable for much of 1936 and 1937, thus hindering deliveries of available fuels and raw materials and augmenting the strain on the railroads.[40] The railroads, by the way, were already experiencing difficulties in supplying the economy with the increasing amounts of fuel that it required, despite the growing volume of railroad freight carried daily.[41] Moreover, the railroads themselves,

Stakhanovism and the Politics of Productivity in the USSR, 1935–1941 (Cambridge, 1988) pp. 118–20, 128–9, 138–9.

[36] *Pravda*, June 7, 1936.

[37] Zaleski, *Stalinist Planning*, 267.

[38] For example, see The Smolensk Archive, WKP 362, 502–6 and TsGANKh, fond 7486, op 16, del 1956, 1937, 4–27 and fond 9477, op 1, del 1105, 1937, 17 and 82–3.

[39] See Tables 5.1 and 5.11 and *British Foreign Office Russia Correspondence*, 1939, reel 1, vol. 23677, 246.

[40] *Bolshevik*, no. 13 (July 15, 1937) pp. 42–8, no. 16 (Aug. 15, 1937) pp. 11–22; *Pravda*, Feb. 17, 1937, Mar. 30, 1937, April 2, 1937, April 4, 1937, April 29, 1937, May 11, 1937, June 6, 1937, Aug. 14, 1937, Sept. 21, 1936, Oct. 24, 1936, Nov. 11, 1937, Nov. 27, 1937, Dec. 12, 1936; "Annual Economic Report for 1937," *British Foreign Office Russia Correspondence*, 1938, reel 4, vol. 22293, pp. 138–45; 1937, reel 2, vol. 21094, part iii, pp. 63–5, 91–2, 152–8; 1937, reel 4, vol. 21110, pp. 159–65.

[41] See, for example, *Pravda*, Feb. 20, 1936, July 30, 1938 and *British Foreign Office Russia Correspondence* 1938, reel 4, vol. 22293, pp. 39–46.

along with other forms of transportation, were not immune to the fuel shortage. General G. S. Liushkov, NKVD chief of the Far Eastern *krai*, who defected to the Japanese in the summer of 1938 to avoid arrest, testified that reserves of coal were so limited on the Far Eastern railroad in 1937 and 1938 that railway authorities were frequently compelled to seize coal addressed to other industries so the trains could continue to function.[42]

By the summer of 1937, few industries appeared to escape the effects of the new crisis. On July 28, 1937, the U.S. Ambassador to the USSR, Joseph E. Davies, informed Secretary of State Cordell Hull that "the criticisms by the Soviet press of conditions in industry have been so insistent and so drastic that the impression has become general among observers here that a serious breakdown of the economic industrial structure is imminent."[43] Such a breakdown failed to occur as Davies went on to predict, but many, if not most, areas of the economy experienced a significant drop in growth rates, stagnation, or even occasional declines for the next several years, notwithstanding considerable efforts to reverse the situation.[44] To be sure, the Soviet press claimed that a recovery set in midway through 1938, but output statistics of key fuels and construction materials contained in Table 5.4 and isolated Soviet press reports of continued problems belie such claims.[45]

The economic slowdown of 1937–41, although conditioned by the terror, began in some key sectors of the economy, as we have seen, before the onset of mass arrests in August and September 1936, and the slowdown continued after mass arrests subsided in 1938 and early 1939. The slowdown set in at a time when Soviet leaders, especially Stalin, expected "great breakthroughs" and new "miracles" in the economy, based on the real achievements of 1934 and 1935.[46] But no such miracles occurred. The

[42] *British Foreign Office Russia Correspondence*, 1939, reel 10, vol. 2398, p. 329. The British somehow managed to obtain a transcript of the November 1938 interrogation of Liushkov by the Japanese.

[43] Joseph E. Davies, *Mission to Moscow* (New York, 1941) pp. 179–80.

[44] Jasny, *Soviet Industrialization*, 177.

[45] *Pravda*, June 1, 1938, June 2, 1938, June 4, 1938, June 11, 1938, June 23, 1938, July 39, 1938, Aug. 31, 1938, Oct. 21, 1938, Oct. 22, 1938, Nov. 11, 1938, Nov. 9, 1938, Nov. 24, 1938. See also Zaleski, *Stalinist Planning*, 279 and *British Foreign Office Russia Correspondence*, 1938, reel 4, vol. 22293, pp. 38–46, 216–17.

[46] For this, see the speeches of Stalin and other Soviet leaders, like Molotov, Kalinin, Peoples' Commissiar of Agriculture Chernov, the head of the Central Committee Agricultural Department Iakovlev, and others, at meetings of Stakhanovites in various areas of the economy at the end of 1935 and early 1936 and at the December 1935 Central Committee Plenum and the January 1936 meeting of the Central Executive Committee, reported in various press organs. For examples of such sentiments, which vanish after March 1936, see *Sotsialisticheskoe zemledelie*, Nov. 23, 1935, p. 1; *Krest'ianskaia gazeta*, Jan. 2, 1936, p. 1, Jan. 4, 1936, p. 1, Jan. 10, 1936, p. 1, Jan. 12, 1936, p. 1, and Jan. 16, 1936, p. 1; *Sovetskaia stroitel'stvo*, no. 1 (Jan. 1936) pp. 1–13, no. 2 (Feb. 1936) pp. 1–2 and no. 3 (Mar. 1936) pp. 11–16; *Bolshevik*, no. 5 (Mar. 1 1936) p. 7; *Sotsialisticheskaia rekonstruktsiia sel'skogo khoziaistva*, 1935, no. 11 (Nov.) pp. 5–14 and 1936, no. 1 (Jan.) pp. 3–22.

economic conditions of the late thirties were less conducive to the very rapid industrial growth of the sort that the nation had experienced earlier, even in the absence of terror, although the terror, provoked by real-life economic problems, greatly disrupted and impeded the operation of the economy.

In the first half of the thirties the Soviet economy grew in an extensive fashion, through the application of imported technology and increasing amounts of domestic labor power and raw materials. To obtain machinery from abroad, the Soviets exported large quantities of foodstuffs and raw materials in 1929–30, as Tables 5.5, 5.6, and 5.7 indicate. After 1930, however, Soviet foreign trade declined sharply under the impetus of adverse terms of trade after the onset of the Great Depression and acute and mounting domestic need, as agriculture and the armed forces were mechanized and the large-scale industries created by the First Five-Year Plan went into operation. The curtailment of Soviet exports in turn prevented the nation from acquiring the foreign currency necessary to purchase machines and equipment abroad. Each year between 1933 and 1940, the USSR was able to spend at most in real terms only one-fourth to one-half the amount spent on machine imports by tsarist Russia in 1913, compared to two to two and one-half times as much in 1930–1![47] (See Tables 5.6 and 5.7.) The Soviets, however, had accumulated an enormous backlog of unutilized and underutilized equipment by 1930–2, due to construction delays on the gigantic projects of the First Five-Year Plan, so the impact of the curtailment of foreign trade was only felt in full several years later, in 1936 and 1937.

By then, however, the number of new recruits entering the industrial labor force each year had also declined by close to two-thirds (see Table 5.8), because of the improvement of living conditions on the collective farms[48] and the expansion of Soviet draft calls.[49] Industries like mining and lumbering, which were plagued by particularly dangerous working conditions, unusually poor living conditions, and excessive rates of labor turnover, began to suffer an acute and growing labor shortage. The chronic labor shortage in mining and lumbering contributed to the stagnation and even decline in the output of vital raw materials – oil, coal, timber, and ferrous and nonferrous metals – at the very time that domestic consumption of these materials was rapidly expanding.[50] In the process, ever smaller

---

[47] For this, see Franklyn D. Holzman, *Foreign Trade Under Central Planning* (Cambridge, MA, 1974) p. 41 and Roger A. Clarke, *Soviet Economic Facts, 1917–1970* (New York, 1972) p. 48.

[48] M. A. Vyltsan, *Zavershaiushchii etap sozdaniia kolkhoznogo stroi (1935–1937g.g.)* (Moscow, 1978), 172–84.

[49] For this, see Table 5.9.

[50] *Pravda*, Sept. 10, 1937, Oct. 27, 1938, Nov. 24, 1938; *Sovetskoe stroitel'stvo*, no. 2(127) Feb. 1937, P. 80; *Bolshevik*, no. 16 (Aug. 15, 1937) pp. 14–22; *British Foreign Office Russia Correspondence*, 1937, reel 2, vol. 21094, part iii, pp. 63–5, 83–7, 91–4, 136–40, 154–8, 1939, reel 10, vol. 23698, pp. 299 and reel 11, vol. 23699, pp. 84.

Table 5.5. *Soviet foreign trade I: Exports and imports, 1913–1940 (measured in old rubles at 1950 exchange rates)*

Year	Exports	Imports
1913	5,298	4,792
1927–8	2,759	3,295
1929	3,219	3,069
1930	3,612	3,690
1931	2,827	3,851
1932	2,004	2,454
1933	1,727	1,214
1934	1,458	810
1935	1,281	841
1936	1,082	1,077
1937	1,312	1,016
1938	1,021	1,090
1939	462	745
1940	1,066	1,091

Source: Roger A. Clarke, *Soviet Economic Facts, 1917–1970* (New York, 1972), p. 37.

Table 5.6. *Soviet foreign trade II: Exports and imports, 1913–1940 (measured in volume indexes in 1913 and 1929 price weights)*

Year	Exports		Imports	
	1913 price weights	1929 price weights	1913 price weights	1929 price weights
1913	100.0		100.0	
1928	37.7		49.4	
1929	44.4	100.0	48.3	100.00
1930	56.6	135.7	65.7	141.3
1931	54.3	146.1	85.3	161.5
1932	52.2	127.8	71.2	115.8
1933	48.8	118.5	37.9	62.5
1934	42.9	102.9	26.3	47.1
1935		90.5		51.5
1936		68.2		59.4
1937		71.5		54.5
1938 (9 mo.)		62.4		63.4

Source: Franklyn D. Holzman, *Foreign Trade Under Central Planning* (Cambridge, MA, 1974), p. 41.

Table 5.7. *Soviet foreign trade III: Selected exports and imports,*
1913–1940 (measured in physical indexes)

		Exports		Imports
Year	Oil (000 tons)	Round and sawed timber (000 tons)	Grain (metric tons)	Machinery and equipment (m. rubles[a])
1913	925.5	7,353.6	9.182	796.8
1927–8	2,782.8	2,912.9	0.289	788.0
1929	3,858.6	5,376.6	0.178	923.3
1930	4,713.0	7,229.8	4.764	1,726.6
1931	5,225.5	5,914.6	5.056	2,076.2
1932	6,117.7	5,546.1	1.727	1,366.9
1933	4,930.1	6,115.7	1.684	521.9
1934	4,315.2	6,323.5	0.769	202.3
1935	3,368.6	6,605.8	1.517	198.1
1936	2,665.6	5,888.4	0.321	419.4
1937	1,929.3	4,994.3	1.277	278.5
1938	1,388.4	3,151.7	2.054	376.4
1939	474.2	1,715.6	0.277	288.3
1940	874.3	1,006.9	1.155	353.6

[a] Measured in current, not weighted rubles
Source: Roger A. Clarke, *Soviet Economic Facts, 1917–1970* (New York, 1972),
p. 23.

Table 5.8. *The Soviet industrial labor force, 1928–1940*

Year	Numbers employed	Period	Average yearly increase
1928	4,339,000		
1932	9,374,000	1928–32	1,258,750
1937	11,641,000	1932–7	453,400
1940	13,079,000	1937–40	479,333

Source: Roger A. Clarke, *Soviet Economic Facts, 1917–1970*
(New York, 1972), p. 23.

surpluses of these commodities remained for export abroad in exchange
for the foreign technology on which Soviet economic progress still
rested.[51]

[51] See, for example, Table 5.7.

Table 5.9. *Size of the Russian and Soviet armed forces, 1913–1941*

Year	Number of troops
1913	1,400,000
1921	5,500,000
1924 to 3/15/34	562,000
1/1/35	940,000
1/1/36	1,300,000
1/1/37	1,433,000
1/1/41	4,207,000
1/1/42 (planned)	5,500,000

Source: A. L. Narochnitskii (ed.), *SSSR v bor'be protiv fashistskoi agressii, 1933–1945*, 2d expanded edition (Moscow, 1986), pp. 5, 150–151; Abram Bergson, *The Real National Income of Soviet Russia Since 1928* (Cambridge, 1961), p. 365; Michel Gardner, *A History of the Soviet Army* (London, 1966), p. 358; Paul Gregory *Russian National Income, 1885–1913* (Cambridge, 1982), p. 247; and L. G. Beskrovnyi, *Russkaia armiia i flot v XIX veke voenno-ekonomicheskii potential Rossii* (Moscow, 1973), pp. 31, 55, 61.

Table 5.10. *The relationship between investment and defense spending in the USSR, 1928–1940*

Year	Defense[a]	Defense as percentage of total budget (%)	Investment[a]	Investment as percentage of total budget (%)
1928–9	0.9	10.2	3.7	42
1929–30	1.0	7.5	6.7	50.4
1931	1.3	5.1	16.0	63.7
1932	1.3	3.4	24.8	65.2
1933	1.4	3.3	25.0	59.3
1934	5.0	9.0	31.2	56.2
1935	8.2	11.1	39.4	53.5
1936	14.9	16.1	41.9	45.3
1937	17.5	16.5	43.4	40.8
1938	23.3	18.7	51.7	41.7
1939	39.2	25.6	60.4	39.4
1940	56.7	32.5	58.3	33.4

[a] Measured in billions of current rubles
Source: F. D. Holzman, "The Soviet Budget, 1928–1952," *National Tax Journal*, Sept. 1953, vol. 6, no. 31, p. 242.

Also, by the mid-thirties on, the burdens of military spending came to weigh ever more heavily upon the Soviet economy, as Tables 5.9, 5.10, and 5.11 indicate, with the onset of Japanese and German expansionism. Between 1932 and 1936, the rate with which the Red Army was able to provide its forces with new technology was most impressive.[52] By the start of 1936, the USSR had become the world's leading military power (see Table 5.12) with 1,300,000 men under arms, 5,000 tanks, 100,000 trucks, 150,000 tractors, 112 submarines, and over 3,500 military aircraft.[53] Soviet military spending, however, grew even more rapidly from 1936 on, when minor, chronic border skirmishes between Soviet and Japanese troops along the Soviet-Manchurian border escalated sharply, giving rise to what David Dallin called "a state of semi-war" that prevailed from 1936 until September 1939, when the Soviets decisively defeated the Japanese at the Battle of Khalkin Gol.[54] In 1936, too, Germany and Japan concluded the Anti-Comintern Pact, an alliance to halt the spread of international Communism that contained a secret protocol known to the Soviets, directed explicitly against the USSR;[55] and both nations adopted ambitious four- and five-year plans to build up their military and military-related industries in preparation for a major war.[56] The USSR thus confronted the bane of any landlocked nation: the prospect of a two-front war. And Russia faced not just any two-front war but a two-front war with two powers that had already singlehandedly defeated Russia in major wars in this century – the Japanese in the Russo-Japanese War of 1904–5 and the Germans in World War I (1914–18).

Soviet military spending consequently quadrupled between 1936 and 1940, even when one consults only the official state budget that consistently

---

[52] Katz, 578.
[53] *Sovetskoe stroitel'stvo*, no. 1 (126) Jan. 1937, p. 43; *Bolshevik*, no. 5–6 (Mar. 15, 1937) p. 56; *Vlast sovetov*, no. 23 (Dec. 15, 1936) pp. 45–7; B. H. Hart (ed.) *The Red Army* (New York, 1956) pp. 59–60; Malcolm Mackintosh, *Juggernaut: a History of the Soviet Armed Forces* (London, 1967) pp. 68, 77 and John Erickson, *The Soviet High Command* (London, 1962) p. 304.
[54] David J. Dallin, *Soviet Russia and the Far East* (New Haven, 1948), 23–44 and James William Morley (ed.) *Japan's Road to the Pacific War: Deterrent Diplomacy: Japan, Germany, and the USSR, 1935–1940: Selected Translations from Taiheiyo senso e no michi kaisen gaiko shi* (New York, 1976), 113–78.
[55] For the text of the Anti-Comintern Pact and secret protocol, which were originally initialed on June 23, 1936, but only made public the following November, see Morley, 261–4. To be sure, the secret protocol stopped short of committing either party to military action, stipulating only that if either Germany or Japan became involved in a war with the USSR, they would confer together on measures to take in order to safeguard their mutual interests. The terms of the alliances that helped trigger the First World War, however, were equally vague. For this, see Sidney Bradshaw Fay, *The Origins of the World War* (New York, 1959) pp. 68–71, 105–24, 152–67.
[56] Gerhard L. Weinberg, *The Foreign Policy of Hitler's Germany: Diplomatic Revolution in Europe, 1933–1936* (Chicago, 1970), 310–15, 352–5; *Bolshevik*, no. 18 (Sept. 15, 1936) pp. 79–88 and no. 23 (Dec. 1, 1936) p. 66; and James P. Crowley, *Japan's Quest for Autonomy: National Security and Foreign Policy, 1930–1938* (Princeton, 1966), 285–6.

Table 5.11. *Annual average production of basic types of armaments in the USSR, 1930–1940*

Armament type	1930–1	1932–4	1935–7	1938–40
aircraft[a]	869	2,595	3,758	8,805
tanks	740	3,371	3,139	2,672
artillery pieces	1,911	3,778	5,020	14,996
rifles	174,000	256,000	397,000	1,379,000
naval shipbuilding (tons displacement)	2,400[b]	14,000[c]		30,460[d]

[a] Includes civilian aircraft as well as military aircraft
[b] Figure given is for the years 1928–32.
[c] Figure given is for the years 1933–6.
[d] Figure given is for the year 1939.
Source: David Holloway, *The Soviet Union and the Arms Race* (New Haven, CT, 1983), p. 6.

Table 5.12. *The balance of military power, 1933–1936 (as of January 1 of the year given)*

	No. of troops		No. of aircraft		
Nation	1933	1936	1934	1936	1938
USSR	562,000	1,300,000		over 3,500	
Germany	100,000	650,000		2,000	
Japan	285,000	345,000		1,280	
Italy		500,000	931		2,161
France	400,000	400,000	1,970		4,000
Great Britain	135,000	360,000	1,072		2,238
United States	135,000	150,000			

Source: *Pravda*, Feb. 23, 1936, Mar. 7, 1936, Aug. 31, 1936; *Bolshevik*, no. 5 (Mar. 5, 1936); Gerhard Weinberg, *The Foreign Policy of Hitler's Germany, 1933–36*, pp. 41, 162; Malcolm Mackintosh, *Juggernaut: A History of the Soviet Armed Forces* (London, 1967), pp. 68, 77; *Pravda*, Mar. 15, 1939, p. 3.

understated the real weight of military spending on the Soviet economy. Funding available for investment in all other areas of the economy was thereby curtailed, contributing to the industrial slowdown of 1936–40. As Stanley H. Cohn has pointed out about the Soviet economy:

The consumer is not alone in sacrificing for defense spending; the growth potential of the economy is also restrained. Those periods in Soviet history which have seen sharp increases in defense spending, such as 1937–1940, 1951–1952 and

1960–1963, have also been periods in which rates of increase in investment have sharply declined.[57]

This was certainly true in the case of the USSR in the late thirties. In 1932, 3.4% of the Soviet state budget went to the military, while 65.2% was invested in the economy; by 1940, defense accounted for 32.5% of the budget and investment for little more – 33.4%. Indeed, by then rising military expenditures forced the Soviets to reduce the amount of investment in absolute terms for the first time since the onset of the five-year plans in 1928, as Table 5.10 demonstrates.

Long before 1940, however, investment in real terms declined in much of the Soviet economy more than these figures, derived from the official Soviet state budget and expressed in rubles, indicate. In the political climate of the mid- to late thirties, the armed forces and armaments production received prior claim over civilian industry to resources in short supply and to use of the nation's overburdened transportation system. In 1936–40, repeated unplanned and unforeseen increases in military spending, undertaken in response to the changing international situation, disrupted efforts at economic planning and severely strained an already overtaut economy. The results were growing supply problems throughout industry and agriculture.[58] Moreover, heavy military stockpiling and repeated partial military mobilizations on the part of the Soviets between 1938 and 1940 sapped the vitality of the economy by disrupting transportation in large areas of the nation and diverting vital raw materials in short supply, including oil, to the armed forces.[59]

---

[57] Stanley H. Cohn, *Economic Development in the Soviet Union* (Lexington, MA, 1970) pp. 75–6. Cohn went on to suggest that growth is also sapped by sharp rises in capital–output ratios caused by the drain of "highly trained scientists, engineers, and managers" into the defense industry and research, depriving civilian industry of vital inputs. Ibid., 76.

[58] The Second Five-Year Plan (1933–7) sought to increase military spending substantially by 150%. But changes in the international situation provoked an increase in planned military spending on the part of the USSR in 1935, 1936, and 1937 as well as chronic cost overruns that helped fuel the runaway inflation of these years. In 1936, the Soviet Union spent 20.2 billion rubles on defense, considerably more than the 4.3 billion earmarked for 1936 by the original version of the Second Five-Year Plan or the 14.9 billion listed in the annual budget for 1936 at the start of the year. Between 1938 and 1940, defense spending rose 141.6% instead of the 127.5% planned; and by the start of 1940, it was scheduled to grow 200–250% within the next year and one-half to two years. Maurice Dobb, *Soviet Economic Development Since 1917* (New York, 1948) pp. 275–90; Nove, 227–8, 236; Zaleski, *Stalinist Planning*, 150–2, 189, 191–4, 198–9, 203, 228–32; and *SSSR v bor'be protiv fashistskoi agressii, 1933–1945* (Moscow, 1976) 1st edition, pp. 4, 161–4.

[59] Major mobilizations occurred during the Battle of Lake Khasan (July 18 to August 10, 1938), the Munich Crisis of August and September 1938, the Battle of Khalkin Gol (April through mid-September 1939), on the eve of the Soviet invasion of Poland on September 17, 1939, during the Finnish War (November 1939 to March 1940), and during the Soviet annexations of the Baltic states in May and June 1940. *British Foreign Office Russia Correspondence*, 1938, reel 2, vol. 22288, p. 145; 1938, reel 5, vol. 23687, pp. 194–202, 263; 1939, reel 11, vol. 23699, pp. 204–8, 213–14, 259; 1940, reel 6, vol. 24850, pp. 133–42, 182–3.

Rising international tensions also overheated the domestic political climate in the USSR, creating a political situation in which mass terror could and did occur. By 1936 and 1937, Soviet foreign news coverage in the daily press was dominated by news of the tense situation prevailing on Soviet borders, especially the lengthy border with Japan in Manchuria, and by stories about German and Italian intervention in the Spanish War and Japan's war of aggression against China. Readers could not help but come away with the impression that the "big war" everyone was expecting had already begun.[60] The press also periodically engaged in graphic descriptions of the deadly and "dirty" war of the future, extrapolated from the experiences of World War I and from the ongoing "little wars" launched by Italy, Germany, and Japan, in Abyssinia, Spain, and China. Readers were repeatedly told that war in the future would extend to the entire land area of nations, thanks to recent developments in aviation. In such a war, no one would be spared, because chemical and bacteriological weapons as well as air raids on the civilian population with incendiary bombs far more powerful than any used in World War I had become an integral part of modern warfare, along with sabotage and espionage by undercover agents working far behind enemy lines.[61] The frequency with which the press published photographs of bombed out cities and suffering civilians in Spain and China[62] and news reports about the use of poison gas in Abyssinia by the Italians and in China by the Japanese, rendered such dire predictions believable.[63] Such reports also made widespread accusations of espionage and sabotage plausible, if not likely, and thereby contributed to

---

[60] This was just as true of the provincial press, like *Rabochii put* (Smolensk), published in the Western Oblast, as it was for national periodicals like *Pravda, Izvestiia, Bolshevik, Sotsialisticheskoe zemledelie,* and *Krestianskaia gazeta.* Such reports were also more likely to appear on the front page in 1936 and 1937 than either earlier or later.

[61] For examples of such articles, see *Pravda,* May 11, 1936, May 20, 1936, July 14, 1936, July 29, 1936, Aug. 1, 1936, May 4, 1937, Mar. 30, 1938; *Vlast sovetov,* no. 21 (Nov. 18, 1936) pp. 22–3; *Bolshevik,* no. 11 (June 1, 1937) pp. 38–50 and no. 15 (Aug. 1, 1937) pp. 1–5. See also the popular brochures of Uranov and Khamadan. Uranov, *O nekotorykh kovarnyi priemakh verbovochnoi raboty inostrannye razvedok* (Moscow 1937) and Al. Khamadan, *Iaponskii shpionazh* (Moscow, 1937).

[62] See, for example, *Pravda,* Mar. 30, 1936, April 4, 1936, April 7, 1936, April 23, 1936, April 21, 1936, April 25, 1936, May 26, 1936, Aug. 10, 1936, Aug. 13, 1936, Aug. 14, 1936, Sept. 3, 1936, Sept. 16, 1936, Nov. 15, 1936, Nov. 16, 1936, Dec. 12, 1936, Dec. 25, 1936.

[63] For Soviet reports of the use of poison gas, see, for example, *Bolshevik,* no. 23 (Dec. 1, 1936) p. 67; *Pravda,* Feb. 24, 1936, Feb. 27, 1936, Mar. 10, 1936, April 4, 1936, Aug. 16, 1936, Aug. 19, 1936, Sept. 2, 1936, May 6, 1938. *Pravda* also published a number of photographs in 1936 showing antigas defense measures taken in other lands, like Abyssinia, France, and Great Britain. *Pravda,* Jan. 28, 1936, Feb. 9, 1936, April 15, 1936. Although the use of poison gas by the Italians in Abyssinia was well documented in the 1930s, use of such gases and biological warfare by the Japanese in China has only recently been definitely established. For this, see Yuki Tanaka, "Poison Gas: The Story Japan Would Like to Forget," *Bulletin of the Atomic Scientists,* vol. 44, no. 8 (Oct. 1988) pp. 10–19; and Peter Williams and David Wallace, *Unit 731: Japan's Secret Biological Warfare in World War II* (New York, 1989).

the political persecution of a significant number of Soviet citizens, especially those in positions of authority, as "masked" (i.e., covert) agents of German and Japanese intelligence services, participants in a new and awful form of warfare that failed to distinguish between front and rear but engulfed entire nations.

The Soviet industrial slowdown of 1936–40 coincided, as is usually the case of perturbations in the Soviet economy, with a downturn in the global business cycle that set in during 1937 and affected industry throughout the world, which had just recovered to pre-Depression levels of output at the end of 1936.[64] Between the first quarter of 1937 and the first quarter of 1938, world trade dropped by 12%, while the industrial output of the United States, the world's leading industrial power, where the new downturn began, fell by 34% between May and December 1937, a period in which much of Soviet industry, too, experienced a significant decline.[65] Elsewhere the effects of the new crisis appeared more muted, although everywhere heavy industry or producers' goods, the mainstay of the Stalinist economy, appeared to be the economic sector most adversely affected by the new downswing.[66] Contemporary Soviet analyses of the world economy noted with dismay that nations that were furthest along with rearmament, like Germany, Italy, Japan, and Great Britain, fared better in the new crisis than was true of the United States, which still resisted pressures for large-scale peacetime military spending and consequently only regained pre-Depression levels of industrial output after its involvement in World War II. Yet all nations, even the United States, responded to the crisis by increasing defense spending, and hence goverment orders to hard-hit heavy industry, in 1937 and subsequent years.[67] In this way, the effects of the crisis were magnified for the USSR, which felt compelled to match the combined build-up of its two major rivals – Germany and Japan – with yet another new, massive military buildup of its own.

The Soviet industrial slowdown of 1936–41 was rooted in several simultaneous developments: the nation's inability to continue to import large amounts of technology from abroad at the high rates of the early thirties, a simultaneous sharp falloff in the number of recruits entering the urban workforce, and the overburdening of the economy with defense spending, which escalated out of control after 1935. This does not mean

---

[64] *Bolshevik*, no. 10 (May 15, 1937) p. 47 and Zaleski, *Planning for Economic Growth*, xxi, xxxii–xxxiii, 104–6, 145–7, 252–6, 267–9, 300–4.

[65] *Pravda*, June 8, 1938 and *Bolshevik*, nos. 23–24 (Dec. 15, 1937) pp. 48–63.

[66] *Pravda*, April 6, 1938, April 16, 1938, June 8, 1938, p. 5

[67] *Bolshevik*, nos. 23–24 (Dec. 15, 1937) pp. 43–8, nos. 4–5 (Mar. 15, 1937) p. 106 and *Sotsialisticheskoe zemledelie*, Jan. 1, 1939, p. 4. However, the Soviets failed to note that the Scandinavian states, which had made the most progress of any nations at this time toward the creation of a cradle-to-grave welfare state, also fared as well during the new crisis.

that the Great Purges did not contribute to the nation's economic woes by an across-the-board replacement of experienced economic managers with inexperienced ones at a time when the economic climate and pressures on managers were growing ever more unfavorable and difficult. At any rate, the Great Purges resulted in considerable industrial disorganization in 1937 and 1938, when industry performed the most poorly, and when, as the British ambassador Lord Chilston put it, there were "few industrial enterprises of which the managing staff has not changed several times during the last twelve months as a result of arrests and executions."[68] Soviet government leaders, especially Stalin, expected new "economic miracles" and "great breakthroughs" in the economy and attributed the economic problems that set in midway through 1936 to sabotage and espionage by a vast conspiracy, led by former Party Oppositionists in league with the USSR's real-life enemies – Germany and Japan.[69]

Terror was also fueled paradoxically by government efforts to address the nation's economic problems by purely economic means, without new major infusions of imported technology, labor power, or natural resources. In 1935–7, the Soviet government moved to increase economic efficiency on the part of enterprises and workers alike, by the promotion of Stakhanovism, the repeated introduction of new, higher work norms for workers, the encouragement of economic inequality as an incentive, and the establishment of economic accountability and self-financing in much of heavy industry, the machine tractor stations, and state farms. All of these moves eventually contributed to the expanding terror.

Stakhanovitism, which developed in the fall of 1935 and spread throughout industry and agriculture by the end of the year, was endorsed by the government in hopes of increasing productivity by encouraging workers to use and master new technology, adopt new work techniques, and force such practices upon recalcitrant managerial and engineering personnel, who were often reluctant to accept high plan targets or individual record setting that might temporarily interfere with continuously increasing production on the part of the enterprise as a whole, because superiors judged managers' work on the gross output of their enterprises.[70] The Stakhanovite movement consequently provoked conflicts between managers and workers over the organization of labor and gave rise already by the end of 1935 and early 1936 to increasing complaints of bad working conditions and numerous charges of sabotage raised by workers against managers and engineers.[71] The topmost Soviet leaders initially sought to

---

[68] Lord Chilston to Antony Eden, *British Foreign Office Russia Correspondence*, 1973, reel 3, vol. 21095, 173.

[69] These views are expressed clearly in the only major speech made by Stalin during the Great Purges of 1936–8, his report to the February–March 1937 Central Committee Plenum. *Pravda*, March 29, 1937.

[70] Siegelbaum, 6, 74–5, 81–6, 116–20, 129, 141–4, 152–3, 206–8.

[71] Ibid., 82–5, 99, 119–20, 127, 130, 132.

ignore or play down such accusations until the lag in production of vital fuels and construction materials began to impinge upon other areas of the economy. In September 1936, Stalin, possibly alarmed by mounting economic difficulties, placed at the helm of the NKVD N. I. Ezhov, who tended to heed worker complaints against managers and regard economic troubles as manifestations of wrecking.

Stakhanovite "storming" also contributed to growing imbalances and supply problems in industry and agriculture characteristic of the late thirties and a simultaneous increase in mechanical failures and the accident rate, which would subsequently be attributed to sabotage or wrecking. Stakhanovite achievements could rarely be maintained for long and "Stakhanovite periods" were usually followed by a decline in output to previous levels, if not lower, feeding the suspicions of Soviet leaders, like Stalin, and of some ordinary citizens that "hostile elements," not objective economic forces, were behind the falloff in production.[72]

Finally, the Stakhanovite movement enormously increased the wage fund and forced an ever more cost conscious government, faced with rising military spending, to raise work norms significantly in both industry and the MTSs in the spring of 1936 and again in May 1937. Since the new norms were anywhere from 14% to 50% greater than the old ones, a substantial proportion of workers – from 9.6% to 44.9%, depending on industry – proved incapable of fulfilling the new quotas, which increased bad feelings among workers toward managers and technical personnel responsible for introducing the new norms. Many workers suffered wage cuts as the result of the new norms, and the numbers of Stakhanovites declined noticeably, thus depriving many who had become accustomed to being considered Stakhanovites of their expected bonuses, access to consumer goods in short supply and apartments, as well as public recognition and awards, like the much coveted Order of Lenin, dispensed in large numbers to the nation's leading Stakhanovites in late 1935 and early 1936.[73] No wonder that charges of wrecking, particularly wrecking the work of Stakhanovites, proliferated each time the work norms were revised upward, especially after the hikes of May 1937 significantly reduced the numbers of Stakhanovites.[74]

The introduction of new work norms coincided with the abolition of rationing, the growing availability of consumer goods for those with the money and influence to acquire them, and the food shortages and rising bread prices resulting from the 1936 crop failure. These developments

---

[72] Ibid., 104–8.
[73] Ibid., 88–9, 94–5, 156–60, 227–35 and *Pravda*, Oct. 21, 1936, p. 1 and Dec. 4, 1936, p. 4.
[74] Siegelbaum, 158–60 and *Krest'ianskaia*, July 8, 1937, p. 6, July 12, 1937, p. 4, July 20, 1937, p. 3, July 22, 1937, p. 4, July 24, 1937, pp. 1–2, July 26, 1937, pp. 1, 3, July 30, 1937, pp. 3–4, Aug. 2, 1937, p. 3.

rendered wages more meaningful to workers, while reducing their ability to earn higher wages.[75] The increase in labor norms for workers also took place at a time when the salaries of professionals, like teachers, doctors, engineers, managers, and technicians, were being raised, rendering increasingly visible socioeconomic differences between managers and professionals on the one hand and ordinary workers on the other.[76]

At the same time, economic pressures on managers grew as the government sought to combine higher rates of military spending with a balanced budget. On April 11, 1936, a joint decree of the Party Central Committee and the Council of Peoples' Commissars eliminated state subsidies to a large number of industries and the MTS, while state subsidies to other industries were substantially reduced. In this way, many key industries became self-financing for the first time since the onset of the Five-Year Plans. Already by 1937, state subsidies to economic enterprises were cut by half the 1936 level, and most of the remaining subsidies went to ailing agricultural institutions, like state farms and MTSs, not to industries as was earlier the case.[77] Simultaneously, industrial *glavki*, subdivisions of industrial commissariats that oversaw the operation of particular industries, were empowered to acquire their own supplies, as allocations from central stocks were reduced.[78] Not surprisingly, the industries affected by this measure included many of those experiencing major problems by the end of 1936 and the opening months of 1937, like coal and iron mining, ferrous and nonferrous metals, cement, and the forest industry. By the end of 1936, growing numbers of factories and machine tractor stations found themselves unable to pay for needed fuel, supplies, and raw materials. Others, including many of the nation's best known enterprises, like the Stalingrad Tractor Works, the Kirov Works, and the Red Profintern Machine Building Plant, found themselves chronically indebted and their "careerist leaders" accused by *Pravda* of "anti-government practices," like deceiving the government and wasting state funds, ominous charges that were regarded at the time as manifestations of wrecking.[79]

In this way, the economic problems of 1936–41 and the Great Purges appear to be inexorably linked. The industrial slowdown, which set in at a time when the USSR could least afford it, when a two-front war without allies seemed to be the Soviets' inevitable fate, shaped the course of the Great Purges at least as much, if not more so, as the terror in turn

[75] Siegelbaum, 185–9 and Davies, 383.
[76] *British Foreign Office Russia Correspondence*, 1937, reel 6, vol. 21106, p. 123 and Baykov, 341–2.
[77] *British Foreign Office Russia Correspondence*, 1936, reel 2, vol. 20341, p. 71, reel 3, vol. 20344, p. 87, reel 6, vol. 20352, p. 47; *Pravda*, July 16, 1936, p. 1, July 18, 1936, p. 1; Abram Bergson, *Soviet National Income and Product in 1937* (New York, 1953) pp. 14–15, and 118–19.
[78] *Pravda*, July 18, 1936, p. 1.
[79] See, for example, *Pravda*, Oct. 9, 1936, p. 6 and April 2, 1938, p. 1.

influenced the operation of the economy. In 1936–8, as veteran journalist William Henry Chamberlain has pointed out in regard to Soviet political persecutions of the First Five-Year Plan period, "When plans went awry, when deprivations, instead of disappearing, became more severe, when promised improvements in food supply did not materialize, the subconscious temptation to seek scapegoats became almost irresistible."[80]

To be sure, the economic problems that surfaced in the second half of the 1930s would not have in and of themselves resulted in political terror. Other factors were also required: a suspicious and volunteerist leadership that expected "miracles" and refused to accept economic constraints, a political culture and populace accustomed to blame hardship on demonic forces and conspiracies, and social and political tensions created by the prospect of a two-front war with two nations that had already vanquished Russia individually in recent wars.

In the end, however, the economic problems that contributed to the upsurge in terror in 1936–8 ultimately worked to temper the repression. Several years of continuous repression and the replacement of economic and political leaders several times over failed to revive the nation's sagging growth rates, while resulting in ever-declining educational levels on the part of those in charge of the economy, as the supply of adequately educated managers ran out. This situation prompted top Soviet leaders to seek to rein in the terror for fear of creating even more problems for the hard-pressed economy.[81] In December 1938, the Soviet leadership replaced the conspiracy-minded Ezhov as NKVD chief with Lavrenti Beria, who pointed out to the Eighteenth Party Congress in March 1939 shortly after taking office that it was a mistake to regard all malfunctionings in different sectors of the economy as the work of "wreckers" and "enemies of the people," when some of these problems were simply the result of incompetent work on the part of persons in positions of authority.[82] With such views entrenched in the leadership of the political police, political terror on the scale of 1936–8 temporarily abated, notwithstanding continuing difficulties in the overtaxed economy.

[80] William Henry Chamberlin, *Russia's Iron Age* (Boston, 1934), 167.
[81] For this, see Boris Starkov, Chapter 1 in this volume.
[82] *Pravda*, March 15, 1939, p. 6.

6

The Stakhanovite movement: Background to the Great Terror in the factories, 1935–1938

Robert Thurston

Recent studies have considerably deepened our understanding of Stakhanovism, the movement of model workers intended to spur others to greater productivity, which began in September 1935.[1] However, archival materials and obscure local sources opened even more recently have provided new evidence on the dynamics and results of Stakhanovism within the factories. This chapter looks at how the movement produced new tensions or exacerbated old ones at the point of production, particularly among various strata of people on the job. These strains will then be linked much more directly than other inquiries have done to the Great Terror as it developed from the fall of 1936 on. The Stakhanovites' story and its connection to the coming of mass arrests reveal new aspects of a two-way relationship between state and society. Finally, I will also discuss the fate of workers in the terror in more detail than previous writers have done.

Stakhanovism had a wide range of unsettling effects on factory life. First, the movement broadened and/or revived workers' opportunities to criticize management and to offer suggestions about production organization and processes. This wave of criticism enhanced old tensions and provoked new ones within the factories. Second, additional demands on managers and technical personnel (ITR, *inzhenernye-tekhnicheskie rabotniki* or engineering-technical employees) now arose. Supervisors' reactions to these

---

[1] Francesco Benvenuti, "Stakhanovism and Stalinism, 1934–1938," CREES Discussion Papers, SIPS, no. 30, the University of Birmingham, 1989; Lewis H. Siegelbaum, *Stakhanovism and the Politics of Productivity in the USSR, 1935–1941* (New York: Cambridge University Press, 1988); Donald Filtzer, *Soviet Workers and Stalinist Industrialization: The Formation of Modern Soviet Production Relations, 1928–1941* (Armonk, NY: M. E. Sharpe, 1986); Vladimir Andrle, *Workers in Stalin's Russia: Industrialization and Social Change in a Planned Economy* (New York: St. Martin's, 1988); and Henry Norr, "The Stakhanovite Movement and the Great Purges," paper delivered at the Workshop on State Coercion and Soviet Society in the 1930s, Austin, Texas, Mar. 1986.

demands caused further problems between levels of people involved in industrial production. Such interaction within enterprises, unleashed or deepened by Stakhanovism, led at least a significant part of the Stalinist leadership to suspect managers and ITR of sabotage. All of these factors played a part in engendering the Great Terror.

Most treatments of Stakhanovism argue that it caused major tensions between workers, as the less capable deeply resented the raising of job norms – production rates for specific tasks – that followed the Stakhanovites' spectacular feats. Although this feeling undoubtedly appeared for a time, it is likely that problems between workers were considerably less important after early 1936 than strains between workers and managers.

In looking at this last set of tensions, we approach the outbreak of the Great Terror in an unorthodox way. New research on the terror among specific groups suggests that a kind of unholy interaction between state and society helped to produce a spate of violence. In the cases of both astronomers and architects, antagonisms and denunciations began within their ranks, and the secret police (NKVD) entered the picture only after trouble started from below.[2] Of course, the national leadership, which set the general tone for events, bears responsibility for encouraging denunciations and directing the police to make arrests on the merest suspicion of disloyalty. But in fact people were not only victims of the state, they were participants in repression. Workers' frustrations and desires thrust them into this role.

The list of problems plaguing Soviet industry in the mid-1930s is long and well known. Among major difficulties were labor shortages, especially of experienced foremen and skilled workers; high turnover; bottlenecks in production; shortages in tools, materials, and transportation; tension between managers and workers; and relentless pressure to produce at virtually any cost. Stakhanovism strongly exacerbated all of these problems.

The fall of 1935 marked a meteoric rise of the movement in both official rhetoric and the number of workers dubbed Stakhanovites. With this upsurge, a sharp change occurred in the tone and direction of workers' criticisms. Clothed in their new status as heroes of production, early Stakhanovites voiced demands for improvement in their own and all workers' situations. Indeed, the vast majority of the exemplars' calls for changes in the workplace necessarily involved all hands. The leading workers' statements thus had broad implications from the beginning of the movement. These spokesmen and women did not represent a new "labor

---

[2] Robert A. McCutcheon, "The 1936–1937 Purge of Soviet Astronomers," *Slavic Review* 50, no. 1 (1991); and Hugh D. Hudson. Jr., "The Murder of Mikhail Okhitovich and the Terror in Architecture," paper delivered to the 23d National AAASS Convention in Miami, Florida, November 1991.

aristocracy," contrary to the assertions made in older studies;[3] rather, they articulated aspirations of workers in general. For example, in December 1935 Stakhanovites employed in the glass and chemicals industries of Moscow Oblast (the rough equivalent of a province) spoke up about the failure of managers and technical personnel to supply production materials adequately, make timely repairs, and conduct "correct accounting," which referred to underpayment of wages to all workers. Noting these problems, the Oblast administration of local industry remarked that it was "necessary to end the insufficient development of work on the penetration of Stakhanovite methods."[4] In other words, managers were told to get busy and enable more workers to achieve the new status conferred by the movement.

At a meeting of executives and Stakhanovites of the ceramics industry, also held in December 1935, a molder insisted in his own rambling way that six months before,

our bosses lived, but the workers got by (*pozhivali*). . . . [Now the bosses] will look after us at the factory as they should. This is correct. But we don't believe it. We believe it when the director curses – well, okay, you live well, but we live badly.[5]

Mistrust and resentment of superiors had quickly found outlets through Stakhanovites. Perhaps some of these proletarian critics deliberately chose to reproach management, in the hope that they could deflect other workers' resentment away from themselves. A little class solidarity in the factories might save bruised egos and heads.

In February 1936 a group of Murmansk workers joined in the chorus of complaints. During a general meeting of all three shifts at the city railroad depot, that is, a session attended by Stakhanovites and non-Stakhanovites alike, workers charged that union leaders and the railroad management had not helped ordinary hands to join the new movement. Some workers alleged that, "Whatever you say, however many suggestions you make about removing the defects and disorders in production, no one does anything. On the contrary, later they pressure those who spoke up with criticisms. It's better to keep quiet."[6]

Published in the national trade union journal, the report was one of many indications that the Stalinist leadership expected managers and ITR

---

[3] See, for example, Leon Trotsky, *The Revolution Betrayed* (New York: Merit, 1965 [1937]), pp. 124–125; and Isaac Deutscher, *Soviet Trade Unions: Their Place in Soviet Labour Policy* (London: Royal Institute of International Affairs, 1950), pp. 113–114.

[4] Tsentral'nyi Gosudarstvennyi Arkhiv Moskovskoi Oblasti [hereafter TsGAMO], f. 6852, o. 1. d. 290, l. 40; the Moscow Oblast administration of local industry, a meeting of Stakhanovites and managers in the glass-chemical sector, 17 Dec. 1935.

[5] Tsentral'nyi Gosudarstvennyi Arkhiv RSFSR [hereafter TsGA RSFSR], f. 52, o. 1, ed. khr. 14, l. 60; stenographic record of a meeting of Stakhanovites in the porcelain industry, 8 Dec. 1935.

[6] F. Voropaev, "Profrabotu na transporte – na uroven' stakhanovskogo dvizheniia," *Voprosy profdvizheniia*, no. 2 (Feb. 1936), p. 17.

to pay close attention to workers' demands and suggestions, now coming steadily from below. The article also points to the fact that national leaders were receptive to workers' criticisms, whereas local officials, often directly affected by complaints, were not.[7] Workers could feel that the regime was in some sense on their side but that local administrators were against them.

A related campaign now developed from above and below to make vast numbers of workers Stakhanovites. At the movement's first national conference, held in November, Stalin called for Stakhanovism to spread "widely and deeply" across the entire Soviet Union.[8] In a typical resolution of the period, the Leningrad Oblast and city party organizations together declared that all managers and ITR in the area had the responsibility to provide Stakhanovites with a constant supply of tools and materials, to organize work properly, and to help the development of the movement.[9]

Occasionally the pressure for improvement expanded so much that managers felt obliged to restructure production thoroughly. In the fall of 1935 the director of the VOTI Machine-Building Factory, for example, responded to Stakhanovites' demands by ordering "a whole series of measures" regarding technical questions.[10]

Workers, seeing the remarkable privileges and pay provided for some by early Stakhanovism, and understanding that it was to become a very broad program, did not always resist it; instead, they often pressed for their own chance to share the wealth. A. Kh. Busygin, second in stature in the movement only to Stakhanov himself, echoed the sentiments of other, lesser known workers:[11] Every worker wanted to be a Stakhanovite. He presented to his commander the question Why do you give my neighbor, a Stakhanovite, a good tool? I too want to have a good tool. Then under the new pressure from the working masses the commanders began to move faster.[12]

---

[7] For more on this tendency, see my "Reassessing the History of Soviet Workers: Opportunities to Criticize and Participate in Decision-making, 1935–1941," in Stephen White, ed., *New Directions in Soviet History* (Cambridge: Cambridge University Press, 1991).

[8] I. V. Stalin, *Sochineniia*, tom 1 [14], 1934–1940, ed. Robert H. McNeal (Stanford, 1967), p. 97.

[9] *Pokoleniia udarnikov. Sbornik dokumentov i materialov o sotsialisticheskom sorevnovanii na predpriiatiiakh Leningrada v 1928–1961 gg.* (Leningrad, Lenizdat, 1936), pp. 93–94, a resolution of 26 Oct. 1935.

[10] Tsentral'nyi Gosudarstvennyi Arkhiv Narodnogo Khoziaistva [hereafter TsGANKh], f. 7297, o. 42, d. 28, l. 42; Svodnye svedeniia o stakhanovskom dvizhenii na predpriiatiiakh sektora podchinennykh narkomu tiazhelogo mashinostroeniia, 1935 (from the VOTI factory). And see TsGA RSFSR f. 52, o. 1, ed. khr. 14, l. 54, for an account by a worker in the Rechitskaia porcelain factory of a similar response from management.

[11] TsGA RSFSR f. 52, o. 1, ed. khr. 18, l. 10; Stenogramma I otraslevoi konferentsii rabotnikov farforno-faiansevoi promyshlennosti, April 1936. The speaker was party organizer of a shop, but nonetheless he made quite a bitter remark in his speech about workers' housing.

[12] A. Kh. Busygin, *Zhizn' moia i moikh druzei* (Moscow: Profizdat, 1939), pp. 27–28.

Since there were rarely enough good tools to go around, and shortages of materials were endemic in the system, workers were bound to be frustrated at the failures of managers to help them become Stakhanovites. This is the thrust of articles like "They are hindering us from working in Stakhanovite fashion" in the Far Eastern newspaper *Tikhookeanskaia zvezda (Pacific Star)*, for instance, toward the end of 1935 and into 1936. Workers' letters to the paper made the same point.[13] Authentic or staged, such complaints expressed the same mood found in archival sources and in statements by some emigres.

When managers were able to arrange conditions so that higher levels of production followed, workers may then have wondered why that could not happen regularly. This was the implication of a worker's remark at the so-called branch conference of the porcelain industry, held in April 1936. "In the very first days of the Stakhanovite movement, the [factory] administration fully supplied us with auxiliary materials, so that we did not have one minute of idle time. My brigade fulfilled [the production plan by] 140%."[14] Surely if the next week the managers could not duplicate this supply of materials, so that fulfillment and pay declined, workers would have felt resentment and looked for scapegoats. This attitude is suggested by another Far Eastern newspaper article, published in October 1936. The writer criticized managerial performance at the Kirov Factory because "the director had all opportunities, [and] everything necessary, to organize labor correctly at the plant. . . . But the director didn't succeed in doing this. He works the way he worked three years ago, when there was no Stakhanovite movement."[15]

A further source of tension developed as workers responded to another key aspect of the new program, its emphasis on innovation,[16] by experimenting on the machinery. This practice could lead not only to decreases in output, at least in the short run, but also to damage to the equipment.[17] Managers frequently opposed such tinkering by workers, who then tried out new techniques in secret. One used his power saw in the old manner whenever supervisors were around because for them any departure from standard practice was a "disaster."[18] In such cases workers tried to dodge

---

[13] *Tikhookeanskaia zvezda* [hereafter *TZ*], 28 Nov. 1935, p. 1; and 28 April 1936, p. 3.

[14] TsGA RSFSR f. 52, o. 1, ed. khr. 19, l. 44.

[15] *TZ*, 11 Oct. 1936, p. 3.

[16] See Stalin, *Sochineniia*, tom 1 [14], p. 85; and S. Iashin, "Eksperimentirovat', itti vpered," *Stakhanovets*, no. 2 (1936), p. 19, for typical exhortations to workers to experiment.

[17] Kviatkovskii, "Kak rabotaiut tovarishcheskie sudy kuznetskogo metallurgicheskogo kombinata," *Sovetskaia iustitsiia* [hereafter *SIu*], no. 2 (Jan. 1935), p. 12; and see Siegelbaum, *Stakhanovism*, p. 143, for the story of workers who ruined a blast furnace while trying for a record in 1937.

[18] O. A. Ermanskii, *Stakhanovskoe dvizhenie i stakhanovskie metody* (Moscow: Gosudarstvennoe Sotsial'no-ekonomicheskoe Izdatel'stvo, 1940), p. 294. Stalin repeated a similar story in *Sochineniia*, tom 1 [14], p. 87, where he also mentioned that Busygin had almost lost his job at one factory for experimenting.

supervision, and management tried to spy on them to catch violations of the rules. Under these conditions mistrust clearly mounted on both sides. Thus the pressure for the expansion of Stakhanovism from both workers and the national leadership created extraordinarily difficult tasks for Soviet managers, already beset with a host of demands on their time and energy. At the Vostokostal' (Eastern Steel) Plant, for example, workers proposed 87% more changes in production in 1936 than they had in 1935.[19] Because arrests among managers and ITR in the fall of 1935 on charges of sabotaging the Stakhanovite movement showed that it was dangerous not to follow up on such suggestions,[20] supervisors moved quickly to listen to workers. Sometimes this took a great deal of time: S. S. D'iakonov, director of the Gor'kii Auto Factory, estimated that at the end of 1935 and the beginning of the next year, he spent 15–30% of his time on "issues of the organization of the Stakhanovite movement."[21] Late in 1935, under strong pressure from its *glavk*, a higher level of industrial organization, the Ordzhonikidze Lathe Factory organized a special brigade of the "best normers and technologists" to spread Stakhanovite experience among the workers.[22] In addition, Stakhanovite training courses were now to be arranged on a vast scale, but without removing workers from production.[23] Of course, all these changes did in fact deflect attention not only from production but from safety issues as well,[24] with no lessening of pressure for high output. Because the best of the ITR were sometimes assigned to

[19] M. Voskresenskaia and L. Novoselov, *Proizvodstvennye soveshchaniia – shkola upravleniia (1921–1965 gg.)* (Moscow: VTsSPS Profizdat, 1965), p. 94.

[20] See, for example, TsGANKh f. 7566 o. 1, ed. khr. 2816, ll. 4–5. Commissariat of Heavy Industry, Materialy po podmoskovkomu basseinu. Stakhanovskoe dvizhenie; and *Slu*, no. 1 (Jan. 1936), p. 3.

[21] V. A. Sakharov, *Zarozhdenie i razvitie stakhanovskogo dvizheniia (na materialiakh avtotraktornoi promyshlennosti)* (Moscow: Izdatel'stvo Moskovskogo universiteta, 1985), p. 56. By the second half of Nov. 1935 the Stalin auto factory in Moscow had fifty engineers involved in special bureaus for consultation with workers; ibid., p. 41. For a good example of the massive paperwork required by Stakhanovism, see TsGANKh f. 7622, o. 1, d. 493, ll. 26–36, where measures taken at the Khar'kov tractor factory to improve production are outlined.

[22] TsGANKh f. 7995, o. 1, d. 333, l. 153; Materialy otraslevoi konferentsii stankoinstrumental'noi promyshlennosti, 1936.

[23] *Kommunisticheskaia partiia Sovetskogo Soiuza v rezoliutsiiakh i resheniiakh s'ezdov, konferentsii i plenumov TsK. Chast' III, 1930–1954.* (Moscow: Gos. Izdatel'stvo Politicheskoi Literatury, 1954), p. 271; from the Central Committee Plenum 21–25 Dec. 1935.

[24] TsGA RSFSR f. 52, o. 1, ed. khr. 19, ll. 47–48. Stenogramma I otraslevoi konferentsii rabotnikov farforno-faiansevoi promyshlennosti, 9 aprelia 1936 g. Nikotin, president of the factory union committee at the Kalinin factory, reported that at the end of 1935 in the whole industry, expenditures on protecting labor (*okhrana truda*) were reduced 50%, and in his factory by 18 million rubles. But the People's Commissar of the industry and the union central committee got the funds restored. But Nikotin reported that he had learned at the conference that all such funds had been taken away from his factory. The president of the meeting then remarked, "This interests us least of all. Tell how you help the Stakhanovite movement." Nikotin was unmoved: "But this interests us," he replied, and went on to describe unsafe conditions at his plant.

help workers become Stakhanovites, the risk increased that an enterprise would not fulfill its plan, leading to unpleasantness for its administrators.

Some accounts indicate that management's new receptivity to workers' ideas improved morale and brought the two sides closer, for instance at the Stalin Auto Plant.[25] But other practices probably irritated supervisors considerably. In one shop of the Voroshilovgrad Locomotive Factory, Stakhanovites raised small flags if they needed tools or materials. A foreman or special "duty officer" (*dezhurnyi*) then went to find out the worker's needs and bring the desired items.[26] It is easy to imagine the resentment that foremen would have felt at being made the Stakhanovites' flunkies. This problem is evident in a source from 1938 that undoubtedly reflects earlier friction as well. At the Mikoian Meat-Packing Plant in Moscow, three foremen reportedly told workers that they did not want to organize production for the Stakhanovite movement, saying, "Work in the old way. We are sick of being nurses for you."[27] Lower-level managerial personnel already had reason to resent some workers: Paid little more than the hands below them before Stakhanovism, now they were sometimes far behind, as leading Stakhanovites amassed thousands of rubles per month in wages and bonuses.[28] Yet foremen and ITR always bore much more responsibility than workers. In this setting the new demands and status of leading toilers had to increase antagonism between the two sides.

Upper-level management sometimes responded to lesser administrators' lack of enthusiasm for the new trends by firing or demoting them, as at the Cheliabinsk Tractor Factory in October 1935.[29] Although this may have soothed workers' feelings at the time, it could also have made them more suspicious in general of those with higher rank in the factories. For their part, managers certainly resented having to fire experienced people, especially given the conditions of a general labor shortage and the difficulty of attracting reliable foremen to begin with.

[25] R. Sabirov, "Kak profgruppa stala sploshnoi Stakhanovskoi," *Voprosy Profdvizheniia*, no. 1 (Jan. 1936), pp. 66–67. Former workers of the Likhachev auto factory in Moscow told me that Ivan Alekseevich Likhachev, for whom the plant is now named and who directed it from 1926 to 1956, had close personal rapport with the labor force. He frequently circulated through the works, always had an open door at his office, listened personally to complaints, and would direct aides to follow up on workers' proposals the moment they were made. Interview with Nikolai Alekseevich Avdeev, Nikita Ivanovich Chepel', Evgenii Leont'evich Gorushitel', and Konstantin Vasil'evich Pushkin, Moscow, April 12, 1988.

[26] *Profrabota po-novomu: rasskazy predfabzavkomov, tsekhorgov i gruporgov* (Moscow: Profizdat, 1936), pp. 17–18.

[27] B. Usachev, "Bogateishie rezervy," *Stakhanovets*, no. 1 (1938), p. 45.

[28] TsGANKh f. 4086, o. 2. ed. khr. 3365, ll. 77–78; Protokol zasedaniia presiduma TsB ITS metallurgov iuga ot 19.IV.36; ibid., l. 125, Direktoram metallurgicheskikh zavodov, 25.V.36, from the head of the main administration for metal production (GUMP), Gurevich.

[29] TsGANKh f. 7622, o. 1, d. 493, ll. 3, 5. Narodnyi kommissariat tiazheloi promyshlennosti. Glavnoe upravlenie avtotraktornoi promyshlennost. Otchety i svedeniia o razvitii stakhanovskogo dvizheniia po zavodam GUTAP. 1935–1936.

Moreover, there was no guarantee that the Stakhanovite movement would improve a plant's overall performance. As Siegelbaum has shown, the campaign often created bottlenecks and other problems in production.[30] The special attention given to leading workers also contributed to this situation. Although there were 1,140 Stakhanovites at the Iakovlevskii weaving mill by the end of 1935, many did not make their norms per loom, and the mill as a whole had produced only 66% of the plan for the past eleven months.[31] Trying to work on too many machines at once gave rise to various difficulties, leading to increased tension all around. At the Gudok Printing Plant, the "old skilled foremen" opposed the efforts of a female worker to operate two machines at once, because when she turned her back on one, it would make defective products.[32] In such situations, it was not the worker but the supervisors who bore responsibility for the problem; they had to answer for failure to meet the plan targets.

All of these new or heightened frictions in industry occurred in a context already fraught with difficult relations, given the immense pressure on everyone to produce and the poverty of most workers. Ivan Gudov, a leading early Stakhanovite, probably spoke for many of his peers when he wrote this at the beginning of the movement:

The supremacy of the engineers over the workers was underscored in every way. It was as though on the faces of some engineers it was written "I am an engineer, I am an elder master, I know better, don't give me useless questions, don't stick your nose in my business, do as you're ordered."

But we, the Stakhanovites, ruptured this authority with our practical experience, we corrected and basically broke up the technical processes and methods of organization of work developed in the technical bureau. This did not please some engineers.[33]

Even allowing for some exaggeration on Gudov's part, surely this "rupture of authority" did not merely displease some engineers but appeared as a grave threat to their positions in general. Having spent years acquiring an education, then facing immense responsibilities and dangers in a nearly impossible situation, they must have regarded their right to direct production as one of the few concrete prerogatives they enjoyed. This point alone goes far to explain managers' resistance to the Stakhanovite movement.

It was now easier for workers to conceive of these supervisors as wreckers, a charge that quickly surfaced. In the Moscow Coal Basin seventeen men,

[30] Siegelbaum, *Stakhanovism*, p. 104.
[31] Ermanskii, *Stakhanovskoe dvizhenie*, pp. 306–307, citing a speech by the Politburo member A. A. Andreev at the Dec. 1935 Central Committee Plenum.
[32] V. A. Kozlov and O. V. Khlevniuk, "Stakhanovskoi dvizhenie: vremia i liudi," in *Istoriia. Podpisnaia nauchno-populiarnaia seriia* (Moscow: Znanie, 1984), no. 12.
[33] I. Gudov, *Put' stakhanovtsa. Rasskaz o moei zhizni*. (Moscow: Gosudarstvennoe Sotsial'no-ekonomicheskoe Izdatel'stvo, 1938), p. 30. In the early 1930s Busygin also resented his bosses: *Zhizn'*, p. 19.

ranging from directors of mines down to brigade foremen, were fired, demoted, warned, and even put on trial in the last few months of 1935 alone for "sabotage" of the Stakhanovite movement.[34] At the end of November, the Supreme Court of the Russian Republic announced that "resistance to the development of the Stakhanovite movement on the part of administrative-technical personnel" would be tried under notorious article 58 of the criminal code whenever such crimes were carried out with "counter-revolutionary goals."[35] Managers now had to support and broaden Stakhanovism or face dire consequences. News of the policy could not have failed to reach workers, adding to their suspicions.

Arrests and threats along this line marked the high point of tension produced by the movement. Yet within a few months new developments, first the rapid broadening of the movement, began to ease the situation. Nor were the new norms, or subsequent rises that came later in the prewar period, generally difficult to meet.[36] After early 1936, workers were at least somewhat reassured that they would not be pushed intolerably by higher norms.[37]

A key change in regime policy toward workers who spoke against Stakhanovism occurred at the same time. In March 1936 the Presidium of the Supreme Court of the USSR announced that worker-critics were no longer to be brought to trial. "In many cases courts have incorrectly judged individual backward workers as enemies of the people for incorrect remarks," the Presidium stated. Such comments reflected the inability of some workers to cope with the new situation, said the court, which we may take to mean that they could not fulfill the raised norms. But workers' negative remarks do not "indicate their opposition to the Stakhanovite movement or sabotage" and should be countered not with court action but "mass explanatory work."[38] In April the official journal of the Commissariat of Justice denounced the prosecution of workers and technical personnel for opposition to Stakhanovism, arguing that this practice was a direct violation of Stalin's words in November 1935.[39] What Stalin had said was in fact not quite so mild: He had remarked that the "conservative elements of industry" who were not helping the movement should be persuaded to fall in line. Failing that, "more decisive measures" should be taken.[40] Nevertheless, his words did lend themselves to the clear change in

---

[34] TsGANKh f. 7566 o. 1, ed. khr. 2816, ll. 4–5.

[35] "O zadachakh sudebnykh organov," *Slu*, no. 36 (1935), p. 2.

[36] Siegelbaum, *Stakhanovism*, p. 262; Thurston, "Reassessing," p. 168.

[37] The subject of norms has been very poorly understood in Western literature, and their importance has generally been vastly overstated. Only about 32% of all industrial workers were particularly strongly affected by norms as of early 1938. For a fuller treatment of this knotty area, see my "Reassessing."

[38] Degot', "Dela, sviazannye s soprotivleniem stakhanovskogo dvizheniiu," *Slu*, no. 14 (May 1936), p. 3.

[39] Ibid., no. 11 (April 1936), pp. 8–9.

[40] Stalin, *Sochineniia*, tom I [14], p. 98.

court policy in the spring of the next year, when the Commissariat of Justice instructed its judges and prosecutors in no uncertain terms that coercion was not to be applied to critics of Stakhanovism, especially when they were workers.

With the bearable increases in norms and the change in the regime's response to criticism in early 1936, Stakhanovism's impact on workers' lives became considerably more benign than during its first months. Thereafter the movement appears to have caused less trouble among workers than between workers and managers. In the second sphere ominous harbingers of the Great Terror, to come just a few months later, now appeared.

Although the atmosphere of suspicion linked to Stakhanovism thus registered an up-and-down pattern, it definitely left a legacy that lent itself to dark interpretations of problems in industry, which worsened as stagnating production of key fuels and raw materials began to impede the development of other areas of the economy midway through 1936. In addition, the crop failure of the same year curtailed urban food supplies,[41] no doubt increasing social tensions in the factories.

Charges of sabotage in industry dated back to 1917 and figured prominently in 1928–31, but the scale and tensions of the Stakhanovite movement meant that a great wave of such allegations now arose, as noted for the fall of 1935. Within several months, the emphasis in these accusations shifted from holding back the growth of the movement to more serious "wrecking," leveled against managers and technical personnel. In May of 1936, prefiguring and preparing the way for the charges of sabotage that followed the Kemerovo mine explosion in the fall, often cited as a key event in the opening of the Great Terror, the national press reported a similar incident near Cheliabinsk. A mine shaft had collapsed, burying the "best Stakhanovite brigade" and killing nine of fourteen workers. Six managers were convicted of wrecking, and the assistant technical director of the mine was shot.[42]

At almost the same time, the national press attacked union central committees in Donbas mines for lack of vigilance regarding "enemies" and linked the problem to Stakhanovism. Mining output had fallen below the record levels achieved in December 1935,[43] a decline blamed on the union leaders' failure to uncover sabotage of Stakhanovite methods. In the previous

---

[41] For these developments, see Chapter 5 in this volume by Roberta T. Manning.

[42] Degot', "Dela," p. 3. Note that this case was mentioned in the same article that emphasized not sending workers to courts for criticism of the Stakhanovite movement (see note 38). If the central leadership offered a "truce" to managers regarding the movement and criminal responsibility for accidents, it did not last long. In Jan. 1936 managers had also suffered for their "crimes" in this respect. A. Krasnosel'skii, "V bor'be za tekhniku bezopasnosti," *SIu*, no. 3 (Jan. 1936), pp. 8–9, published a long list of jail terms given to supervisors after accidents.

[43] *Pravda*, 7 June 1936. I am grateful to Roberta Manning for this citation.

four to five months, an article in the labor union newspaper *Trud* charged
in May 1936 that the central committee of the miners' union "has not
considered one concrete fact of sabotage and *has not brought one saboteur
to justice.*"[44] The hunt for wreckers was on, in these cases months before
Stalin's infamous telegram of September 1936 recommending N. I. Ezhov
to head the NKVD and prodding the police to greater activity. Probably
many workers, in light of other evidence and all the tensions on the job,
believed that industrial sabotage had in fact occurred.[45]

As for Stalin's entourage, the rash of workers' complaints and rising
factory tensions made national leaders suspicious of managers and ITR as
the Stakhanovite movement developed. Though important central figures
wavered back and forth on the issue of whether supervisors widely sabotaged
the movement,[46] suspicion appears in accounts of meetings between
prominent Stakhanovites and G. K. Ordzhonikidze, Commissar of Heavy
Industry.[47] One reason for such mistrust was widespread violations of
rules on wages, as administrators scrambled to find money to pay the
leading workers, supply them with special goods and services, and keep
them on the job.[48] Such manipulations occasionally became apparent to
higher levels, particularly when a factory did not meet its production plan,
an increasing phenomenon as the economic problems of 1936 worsened.
Investigations of the factory's books typically resulted. Given the callousness
of the central leadership toward managers, its tendency to blame problems
on anyone except itself, and Stalin's oft-noted suspiciousness,[49] justifications
for finagling pay were not accepted during the terror. Thus in the Far

[44] *Trud*, 6 May 1936, p. 2. Italics in the original.
[45] See my "Fear and Belief in the USSR's 'Great Terror': Response to Arrest, 1935–1939," *Slavic Review* 45, no. 2 (1986), especially 221–222; and my "Reassessing."
[46] See Benvenuti, "Stakhanovism," and Norr, "Stakhanovite Movement."
[47] Such conversations are recounted in Makar Mazai, *Zapiski stalevara* (Moscow: Sotsekgiz, 1940), p. 53, in the fall of 1936 with Ordzhonikidze; M. I. Vinogradova, *Riadom s legendoi. Povest'*. (Moscow: Profizdat, 1981), p. 67, with Postyshev and Ordzhonikidze, 13 Nov. 1935; and TsGANKh f. 7622 o. 1, ed. khr. 604, i. 87, Slet stakhanovtsev-Busygintsev avtomobil'noi promyshlennosti, 19 Oct. 1935, Busygin and Dybets, head of the main administration for auto and tractor production (GUTAP).
[48] TsGANKh f. 7622, o. 1, d. 251, l. 3; a report from the Stalin Auto Factory in Moscow for 1937, noting that the plant was losing millions of rubles from labor turnover. "Lowering the loss of production from turnover would justify supplementary expenditures for housing construction," the report noted. Managers were prone to taking any funds they could in order to stop the hemorrhage of workers. And see ibid., f. 7566, o. 1, ed. khr. 2816, ll. 8–9, a report from coal mines in the Podmoskovnyi basin that related that in two mines in 1934–6 turnover ranged from 256% to 355%. This was linked to "poor organization" of the workplace, housing, clubs, kindergartens, and other amenities.
[49] The best treatment of Stalin's paranoia is by Robert C. Tucker, *Stalin in Power: The Revolution from Above, 1928–1941* (New York: Norton, 1990). Dmitrii Volkogonov, author of the first ever serious Soviet biography of Stalin, found in many archival documents that he repeatedly ordered the police to investigate any and all denunciations. "Stalin always believed" police reports of such investigations, Volkogonov commented. In his *Triumf i tragediia: I. V. Stalin. Politicheskii portret* (Moscow: Novosti, 1989), book 1, part 1, p. 274.

Eastern Steel Trust, "wreckers" were found in 1937 who had "distorted pay" in that and the previous year, amounting to an overexpenditure of 22.6 million rubles in 1936 alone.[50]

As noted, the Stakhanovite movement entailed increases in labor norms throughout Soviet industry in early 1936, from 10% on average in certain industries to 55% in others.[51] In some cases managers now found that if they followed the new norms, workers would leave for other positions.[52] However, if factory administrators devised ways to get around the new standards, they again ran the risk of discovery and prosecution. One example of the outcome occurred at the Stalinogorsk Coal Trust; wrecking during the setting of new norms in February 1936 had supposedly produced distortions in pay from mine to mine, causing workers to move about in search of better pay.[53] The story between the lines is certainly that individual managers had tried to boost miners' income in order to attract or hold them. In any event, the result was increased labor turnover and disruption.

Attempting to stabilize their labor force during 1937 and 1938, executives at the trust level and below sometimes petitioned their supervisors in the *glavki* to allow reductions in norms. This too happened at the Stalinogorsk Coal Trust, and the *glavk* responded positively. All concerned tried to protect themselves by referring to wrecking as the cause of the problem in the first place.[54] Executives of two weaving trusts sent at least thirty-eight requests to have norms lowered to the Commissariat of Light Industry in 1938. In a few cases the Commissariat allowed the changes.[55] Acting completely on their own, managers in the Donbas in "very many" cases raised job pay rates (*rastsenki*) and lowered norms; in one group of mines this happened four times in 1937 alone.[56] The central leadership could not have been pleased at any attempt to roll back a key feature of Stakhanovism, and suspicion of wrecking by executives undoubtedly rose.

All this occurred in a context of massive, habitual lying from lower to

---

[50] TsGANKh f. 4086, o. 2, ed. khr. 4205, l. 2, Materialy po trudu Vostokostali, Magnitke i Kuznetsku/K s'ezdu metallurgov Vostoka 28.VII.37. And see ibid., f. 4806, o. 2, d. 4173, l. 34; in this GUMP informed the metal plant "Svobodnyi sokol" that the former director of the Makeev metal plant, Gvakhariia, was an enemy of the people. He had broken the law on pay in various ways. The document is dated 7 June 1937.

[51] Filtzer, *Soviet Workers*, p. 184.

[52] Sakharov, *Zarozhdenie*, p. 36, referring to the situation in the Gor'kii auto factory in late 1935.

[53] TsGANKh f. 7566, o. 1, d. 2821, l. 10. Narodnyi komissariat tiazheloi promyshlennosti SSSR. Glavnoe upravlenie ugol'noi promyshlennosti "Glavugol." Feb. to Aug. 1937.

[54] Ibid. and l. 12.

[55] TsGANKh, f. 7604, o. 8, ed. khr. 117, passim. Narkom legkoi promyshlennosti SSSR otdel rabochikh kadrov i zaplaty. Materialy po peresmotru norm vyrabotki i rasstenkov tkachei Aleksandrovskogo i Ivankovskogo trestov i dr. 1938.

[56] Ermanskii, *Stakhanovskoe dvizhenie*, p. 330; A. Minevich, "Uporiadochit' zarabotnuiu platu v kamennougol'noi promyshlennosti," *Profsoiuzy SSSR*, no. 8–9 (Aug.–Sep. 1939), pp. 73–74, reports that at one Donbas mine in 1938, thirty-five norms were lowered even though the old ones were being filled by 150–160%.

higher levels of industry. In the Donbas mines, the newspaper *Za industrializatsiiu* reported in August 1937, "The practice of [providing] incorrect, false information about the state of work is very widespread. Mutual deception in production – this is the curse of the Donbas."[57] Soviet managers even had a saying for the general situation: "It's necessary not to work well but to account well."[58] Stalin and his cronies undoubtedly knew of this pattern, though they were hardly prepared to remedy its root causes, which were built into the economy across the country. But the leadership would have been equally unlikely to sympathize with overt law breaking.

Most of the practices and problems outlined here existed in Soviet industry before the Stakhanovite movement began. However, that phenomenon greatly exacerbated a host of sore points in factory life, from tensions between managers and workers to labor turnover, bypassing norms, and lying about production. As Henry Norr has pointed out, Soviet leaders complained in the fall of 1935 about the resistance of managers in general to Stakhanovism; the center did not distinguish between "old" or "bourgeois" specialists and the new, "Red" executives.[59] As far as I am aware, this was the first time that the Stalinist chiefs spoke about the newly trained industrial elite in this manner. Thus one major result of Stakhanovism's early period was to draw the national leadership and workers somewhat closer together in their views of industrial supervisors; another outcome was to contribute to some of the tensions that fed wholesale arrests of managers and engineers in 1937–8.

Several Western writers have asserted that all *glasnost'*-era revelations from the USSR support the argument that the terror affected the entire populace and effectively frightened everyone into complete submission to the regime.[60] This claim about new evidence is simply not true. In fact,

[57] *Za industrializatsiiu*, 17 Aug. 1937, quoted in Ermanskii, *Stakhanovskoe dvizhenie*, p. 329. And see the favorable comment on breaking laws at a conference of *glavki* of the Commissariat of Heavy Industry in ibid., pp. 331–332. No date is given, but it came before the preface to the book was written in Dec. 1938.
[58] I. V. Paramonov, *Uchit'sia upravliat': mysli i opyt starogo khoziaistvennika*, izdanie 3-e (Moscow: Ekonomika, 1977), p. 118. Tsentral'nyi Gosudarstvennyi Arkhiv Oktiabr'skoi Revoliutsii (hereafter TsGAOR), f. 7952, o. 5, d. 67, l. 84, has an interview with Chernousov, head of the laboratory at the Kuznetsk metal plant; he described Bardin, the director, as "a very decisive person, a person capable of going past the letter of the law, if the interests of the cause, if the essence [of the matter] demanded it, a person capable of going farther." In Jan. 1935 Ordzhonikidze spoke with a group of factory directors in heavy industry and told one that he should fulfill a promise about production "no matter what." This was an open invitation to break the law and cook the books. G. K. Ordzhonikidze, *Stati i rechi*, 2 vol. (Moscow: Gospolitizdat, 1956–1957), 2, pp. 632–633.
[59] Norr, *Stakhanovite Movement*, p. 5.
[60] Robert Conquest, *The Great Terror: A Reassessment* (New York: Oxford University Press, 1990); and Walter Laqueur, *Stalin: The Glasnost Revelations* (New York: Charles Scribner's Sons, 1990).

almost all the statistical data released from the USSR in recent years indicates that the toll of arrests and unnatural deaths was *lower* than many writers of the totalitarian school have suggested. No moral issue is at stake here; we are still speaking of millions of victims, and linked to them millions of others who suffered. But the numbers make a considerable difference in our analysis of how the regime ruled and how people responded to it. If, as some works maintain, seven, eight, or even fifteen million people were prisoners in jails and the Gulag system by the end of the 1930s, we might justifiably speak of a "system of terror."[61] But recent Soviet publications, citing archival sources, mention 1.5 million in the labor camps on the eve of World War II and about 2.3 million altogether in places of detention or administrative exile. Of the camp prisoners, the portion sentenced for "counter-revolutionary crimes" ran this way: 12.6% in 1936, 12.8% in 1937, 18.6% in 1938, 34.5% in 1939, and 33.1% in 1940.[62] Thus the vast majority of prisoners were arrested for other, more "normal" criminal activity. Of course, crime is socially and culturally defined to a considerable extent in any society, and we may be speaking of a political coloration to many arrests, for example, the detention of collective farm chairpersons who found it necessary to juggle the books and were caught.[63] Nevertheless, the clear thrust of these and many other figures released under *glasnost'* is that the scope of repression was dramatically less than numerous old-school writers have believed.

Even with *glasnost'*, information on the fate of Stakhanovites and workers in general during the Great Terror is scanty. Painstaking research in recent Soviet periodicals, especially local newspapers, which have been publishing lists of victims and their occupations,[64] will help in filling out the picture. Ultimately we need access to secret police archives, which has been discussed by Soviet officials in the wake of the failed coup of August 1991, but at the moment of this writing does not seem imminent. In the meantime, we must fall back on impressionistic evidence and some less than systematic data on arrests that have appeared in the last few years.

When detentions of workers occurred in the worst part of the Great

---

[61] For such estimates of the camp population, see Conquest, *Great Terror*, 485–486; and David J. Dallin and Boris I. Nicolaevsky, *Forced Labour in the Soviet Union* (London, Hollis and Carter, 1948), p. 62, who estimate 15 million in the camps by 1940–2 as a conservative figure.

[62] "Arkhipelag GULAG glazami pisatel'ia i statistika," *Argumenty i fakty*, no. 45, (1989), p. 5. Corroboration has recently been provided in articles by Aleksandr Dugin, for example, in *Sotsial'no-politicheskie nauki*, no. 7, 1990, cited in Vera Tolz, "Archives Yield New Statistics on the Stalin Terror," Radio Liberty, *Report on the USSR* 2, no. 36, 1990, p. 1. For a broader treatment of arrests and demographics in the 1930s, see S. G. Wheatcroft, "More Light on the Scale of Repression and Excess Mortality in the Soviet Union in the 1930s," *Soviet Studies* 42, no. 2 (1990).

[63] See Stephan Merl, *Sozialer Aufstieg im sowjetischen Kolchossystem der 30er Jahre?* (Berlin: Duncker & Humblot, 1990).

[64] See Tolz, "Archives."

Terror, 1937–8, various factors were involved. First, workers might be pulled in as the lowest elements in a chain of acquaintances that began with someone higher up. Probably this is what happened in an incident described by the former chief of construction for the Donbas Mine Trust. He listed sixteen people arrested in 1937, beginning with the chief before him, then the first secretary of the regional party committee, the director of the trust, and finally "a few rank-and-file workers, about two or three."[65] Second, there were the "babblers," mentioned for example by Evgeniia Ginzburg.[66] These were people who had made the wrong kind of criticism, one too strident in reproaching the regime or socialism in general, before the wrong audience. However, workers did express various kinds of criticisms before, during, and after the terror with no ill effects.[67] And, as noted, the Supreme Court ordered that workers who criticized Stakhanovism were not to be arrested. Third, some sources cite workers in prisons or camps during the Great Terror but do not specify the reasons for arrest. In these cases charges of sabotage may have figured.[68] Finally, simple theft or other criminal activity could land workers in jail.

As the terror subsided in late 1938 and early 1939,[69] a new campaign began to improve discipline among workers. Now managers and ITR were relatively well protected, while workers found themselves under arrest for violating laws on lateness or slack discipline. These incarcerations were qualitatively different from those of the Great Terror, since they had a clear and limited goal and did not usually result in dispatch to the labor camps, let alone in death.[70]

Hiroaki Kuromiya has examined recent local newspaper accounts of the terror in the Donbas that list several hundred workers as "repressed."[71] It is of course extremely difficult to know what such data mean; were some of these people arrested and later released, as occasionally happened even in the worst period?[72] What proportion of all workers suffered in this

[65] [Harvard] Project on the Soviet Social System [hereafter HP], respondent number 470, A series, vol. 23, p. 25. This man was a Russian engineer born about 1913. These interviews with ex-Soviet citizens, conducted in displaced persons camps in Germany in 1950–1, with a few in the New York area, were translated into English by the interviewers.

[66] Eugenia Ginzburg, *Journey into the Whirlwind*, trans. Paul Stevenson and Max Hayward (New York: Harcourt Brace Jovanovich, 1967), p. 180.

[67] See my "Reassessing."

[68] Ivan N. Minishki, "Illiuzii i deistvitel'nost'," Bakhmeteff Archive of Russian and East European History and Culture, Columbia University [hereafter BA], p. 135.

[69] See my articles "Fear and Belief"; "The Soviet Family During the 'Great Terror,' 1935–1941," *Soviet Studies* 43, no. 3 (1991); and "Social Dimensions of Stalinist Rule: Humor and Terror in the USSR, 1935–1941," *The Journal of Social History* 24, no. 3 (1991).

[70] See Filtzer, *Soviet Workers*.

[71] Private communications, 25 Nov. 1991 and 13 Jan. 1992.

[72] In "Arkhipelag Gulag" Zemskov gives a figure of 364,437 people released from places of confinement in 1937, though we do not know how many were freed as a result of investigations and how many because they had completed their sentences. I have recorded

way? Was the Donbas story a typical one, or did the fact that coal production represented a particularly vital and troubled part of the economy make police activity more widespread there?[73]

Vera Tolz has recently reported on similar lists published in the newspaper *Vechernii Leningrad*. This evidence concerns a mass grave near the city with about 46,000 bodies, all of people supposedly executed in 1937–8. Of 1,663 people identified in the newspaper as of the time Tolz wrote, "the majority were peasants and workers." Tolz goes on to state that "the Stalin terror touched all strata of Soviet society, not just Party officials and the intelligentsia, as some people have believed."[74]

A number of questions about the meaning of this information must immediately arise. How many peasants, how many workers? How many of all the victims were shot for counter-revolutionary crimes? If less than 20% of those arrested in the Great Terror were charged with such offenses, the question becomes critical in assessing the significance of any information on aggregate death tolls. The 1,663 bodies identified in the Leningrad grave represent only 3.6% of the total buried there, and in turn that total is only 7.6% of the minimum Tolz estimates were executed in 1937–8. This is clearly not large enough to be a particularly useful sample. Moreover, it seems difficult to be sure that the bodies date only from those two years; that has been a problem in determining the meaning of the well-known Kuropaty graves, for example. The point is not that Tolz is wrong, though there are problems in her work.[75] Rather, there is not yet enough statistical data available to judge the social composition of terror victims.

Other sources provide a broader picture. Comments on the social status of arrestees throughout the thirties by fellow prisoners largely suggest that workers were not frequently arrested on political charges. For example, one account speaks of a prison in 1938 with a high NKVD official, professors, party workers, economic employees, and finally "simple people."[76] A survivor of the terror in the Kalmyk Autonomous Republic mentioned carnage among journalists, writers, and leaders of the party and government; he said not a word about ordinary people.[77] One might argue that these comments reflect only the concerns or snobbishness of the observers, but

a number of people arrested but then released in 1937–9, for example, in a story related by HP number 532, A, vol. 28, p. 23, a Russian male economist born about 1900, speaking of an assistant director of a resort trust in the Urals arrested in 1937 but released six months later.

[73] On difficulties of production in the Donbas, see Manning, Chapter 5 in this volume.

[74] Tolz, "Archives," p. 4.

[75] For example, she states that "most of those arrested spent three to four months in prison before being sent to the camps – as the camp literature suggests." Tolz, "Archives," p. 3. But in fact memoirists frequently reported much longer stays in prison; see my "Fear and Belief," p. 231n, for a small sample of such recollections.

[76] A. T., "Tipy zakliuchennykh NKVD," (also called "Galleriia tipov zakliuchennykh NKVD"), A. T. Manuscript, BA, p. 1.

[77] HP number 71, B5, p. 34. No biographical data are available.

remarks specifically emphasizing the tendency of arrests to fall on people in positions of responsibility are frequent.[78] Regarding 1937–8, an emigre interviewed after the war recalled that "those who were arrested were not peasants but [white-collar] employees and mostly Party people. I was glad that they were cutting each other's throats."[79] A former timekeeper in a factory reported that "there were less [sic] repressions of course upon the working class, but there were arrests among them."[80] In the Harvard Project survey of "non-returnees" after the war, 2,718 respondents completed questionnaires. Those with "administrative responsibility were twice as likely as their nonadministrative peers to report having been personally arrested." Respondents considered factory managers and engineers to be in a particularly arrest-prone category, but they believed that workers were at relatively low risk.[81] When an interviewer asked one nonreturnee how a Soviet citizen could avoid trouble with the regime, he replied that "he should be an average worker so that no one will bother him."[82] It may be worth mentioning that in the dozens of memoirs I have read, the 764 long interviews in the Harvard Project, and a great variety of other sources, I have encountered exactly one arrest of a Stakhanovite, in 1938, reportedly "for spending money foolishly."[83] On the other hand, Stakhanovites rose during the terror, in many cases to replace those who had been arrested.[84]

In light of the numerous comments from survivors about the relatively low incidence of arrests among workers, it seems difficult to accept Tolz's suggestion that they comprised a high proportion of all those swept up by the NKVD. At present the statistical material is not enough to replace the impressionistic evidence. In any event, to state an obvious point, arrests were much more concentrated among the relatively small number of supervisory personnel than among the millions of workers.

Various accounts portray workers more as actors in the Great Terror of 1936–8 than as victims. Even allowing for exaggeration and personal bitterness, the statement of an engineer who worked in Soviet plants in the worst years of arrests is indicative. He characterized the title *engineer* as a

[78] "A. Dneprovets," Untitled ms. in the Aleksandr Vozniuk-Burmin file, BA, pp. 7, 16. "Dneprovets" worked in the local *militsiia* in Dnepropetrovsk.
[79] HP number 415, A, vol. 20, p. 67. This respondent was a male Russian born about 1907 who had worked as a foreman in a milk plant.
[80] HP number 421, A, vol. 21, p. 22; a female Russian born about 1906 who had worked as a timekeeper in a factory.
[81] Raymond Bauer and Alex Inkeles, *The Soviet Citizen: Daily Life in a Totalitarian Society* (Cambridge, MA: Harvard University Press, 1959), pp. 48–49, 108.
[82] HP number 165, A, vol. 10, p. 13. No biographical data available.
[83] Mikhail Boikov, *Liudi sovetskoi tiur'my* (Buenos Aires: Seiatel', 1957), vol. 2, p. 260.
[84] I. Kuz'minov, *Stakhanovskoe dvizhenie – vysshii etap sotsialisticheskogo sorevnovaniia* (Moscow: Gos. Sotsial'no-ekonomicheskoe Izdatel'stvo, 1940), p. 139, gives details on promotions of Stakhanovites in three factories. Of course, he does not specify that they rose because people above them were repressed.

"synonym for candidate for concentration camp or execution." The NKVD, he believed, accepted "all denunciations of engineers . . . whether they were written or anonymous or in whatever form they were. Workers took advantage of this to settle their own personal accounts."[85] The American John Scott worked as a welder in Magnitogorsk during the terror. There Soviet workers jeered at their supervisors: "You're a wrecker yourself. Tomorrow they'll come and arrest you. All you engineers and technicians are wreckers."[86]

Some of these grudges and accusations stemmed from superiors' handling of Stakhanovism. In Factory Number 35, Smolensk Oblast, "light cavaliers" (probably members of the Komsomol, the Young Communist League) "unmasked" saboteurs of the Stakhanovite movement in one shop toward the end of 1936. A normer, responsible for setting wage rates on specific tasks, had supposedly deliberately cut Stakhanovites' pay. The offended workers took their case to the factory party committee, whereupon the normer was fired, and the shop chief and a foreman were turned over to the courts for prosecution.[87] On the Stakhanovite movement's second anniversary, its namesake journal announced that the former director of a chemical plant had been an enemy. Among his crimes was sloppy use of Stakhanovites, so that their number increased but the quality of work declined.[88] Reports of this type, published in the midst of national hysteria about enemies, probably further encouraged workers to think of their bosses as potential wreckers. All this by no means suggests that the hunt for enemies came only from below; far from it. Rather, workers' aspirations, grievances, and suspicions constituted an important part of the forces that drove the pursuit forward.

Charges of wrecking from the factory floor may have found a particular resonance at high levels from September 1936 to the end of 1938, during N. I. Ezhov's tenure as head of the NKVD. Born in 1895, he became a metalworker in the highly politicized Putliov Works in St. Petersburg at the age of 14. Apparently he remained an ordinary metalworker until at least 1917.[89] Thus he came of age as a member of one of Russia's most radical occupations, at a time of sharp and increasing tension between

---

[85] HP number 403, B10, p. 18. No biographical data available.

[86] John Scott, *Behind the Urals: An American Worker in Russia's City of Steel* (Bloomington: Indiana University Press, 1973, reprint of 1942 edition), p. 195.

[87] Vsesoiuznaia kommunisticheskaia partiia (bol'shevikov). Smolenskii oblastnoi komitet. The Smolensk Archives [Hereafter SA]. Microfilm Series T87, box 28, reel 37, WKP 318, list 8, Dec. 9, 1936. A report from Factory Number 35; to whom is unclear.

[88] "Vtoraia godovshchina," *Stakhanovets*, no. 8, 1937, p. 3; and see *Pokoleniia udarnikov*, p. 106, "Iz otcheta Krasnogvardeiskogo raikoma [Leningrad]," a document from Jan. 1937 recounting the removal of a shop head by the local raikom (district party committee) for sabotage of the Stakhanovite movement. Two factory directors were similarly removed for failing to lead the movement.

[89] J. Arch Getty, *Origins of the Great Purges: The Soviet Communist Party Reconsidered, 1933–1938* (New York: Cambridge University Press, 1985), p. 116.

workers and employers in the metal-processing industry.[90] It is difficult to imagine that Ezhov did not vividly recall eight turbulent, hard years of work in the mills, together with all the tensions that went with them. These experiences may have predisposed him to accept workers' complaints against managers as perfectly valid. As we have seen in several examples, the NKVD began investigations in factories in response to workers' charges, a pattern found in police practice in other milieux as well.[91]

Whatever its scope, as the terror unfolded the resentments and demands fostered by early Stakhanovism heightened tensions in industry. Now managers and ITR could be identified by both the regime and workers as convenient scapegoats for the failure to raise pay and living standards. They could be held responsible for slumps in production and difficulties in meeting the plan. A whole host of factors, among them availability of housing, the quality of other services, and the general willingness of supervisors to listen to factory hands, determined whether workers regarded managers favorably. But Stakhanovism's tangled impact encouraged both Soviet leaders and workers to regard factory administrators with suspicion, an attitude that helped lead all too neatly and quickly to the explosion of the Great Terror.

[90] See Heather J. Hogan, "Labor and Management in Conflict: The St. Petersburg Metal-Working Industry, 1900–1914," Ph.D. dissertation, the University of Michigan, 1981.

[91] See note 2 above and, among many examples, HP 111, A, v. 9, pp. 32–33; HP 99, A, v. 7, p. 22; HP 338, A, v. 17, p. 6 on kolkhozniki denouncing chairmen of the farms, which would invariably bring in the NKVD. Also A. T., "Tipy," p. 1; and SA, T87, box 44, reel 43, WKP 386, ll. 132–133.

Part III: Case studies

7

The Great Terror on the local level: Purges in Moscow factories, 1936–1938

David L. Hoffmann

Memoirs and accounts written by victims of Stalinist repressions have described the horrifying human toll of the Great Terror.[1] In building upon these histories – in seeking to understand not only the suffering of victims but also the impetus, unfolding, scope, and consequences of the purges – it is particularly useful to examine the Great Terror on the local level. Whereas records from the Smolensk Party Archive have provided Western historians with valuable information on the purges in a largely agrarian oblast, materials depicting the purges in Soviet factories have previously remained quite scarce. Just recently, however, Western scholars have for the first time received access to party archives in the Soviet Union.[2] Party documents held at the Moscow Party Archive (including *obkom*, *gorkom*, *raikom*, and factory *partkom* records) furnish a detailed picture of the purges and their impact upon Moscow workers, managers, and party officials. This research note will discuss the catalyst initiating the purges in Moscow factories, the charges brought against purge victims, the spread and scope of arrests, a social profile of those purged, and the consequences of the purges for factory management and party membership.

The initial impetus for the purges came from the Central Committee in the form of a July 29, 1936, top-secret letter directing local party committees to root out all Trotskyists. In turn the Moscow city and oblast party committees sent a secret letter to all factory party committees on August 16, 1936, advising them to do the same. Upon receipt of this letter, the tone of party committee meetings at factories changed overnight –

---

[1] The most exhaustive work on Stalinist repressions is of course Aleksandr I. Solzhenitsyn, *The Gulag Archipelago 1918–1956* (New York, 1973); other invaluable accounts include Evgeniia Ginzburg, *Journey into the Whirlwind* (New York, 1967), and Nadezhda Mandelstam, *Hope against Hope* (New York, 1983).

[2] In the summer of 1990, I conducted research for two months in the Moscow Party Archive, thereby becoming the first Western scholar to gain access to local party archives in the Soviet Union.

accusations and counteraccusations proliferated, as party members suddenly began to blame preexisting problems of lagging production on the presence of Trotskyists in the factory.[3]

Party committees quickly expelled a number of officials and managers, and charged them with Trotskyism, wrecking, espionage, and sabotage. A number of purged managers were also charged with aloofness toward workers, failure to visit the shop floor regularly, and mistreatment of workers.[4] Such charges were frequently connected with managers' failure to promote Stakhanovism and with their neglect or abuse of Stakhanovites. For example, one "Trotskyist" was accused of impeding a Stakhanovite ten-day campaign (*dekada*) by mistreating workers, and one engineer was purged for calling Stakhanovites "self-seekers" (*rvacha*).[5] Indeed the language of charges brought against purge victims often echoed the antimanagerial tone of Stakhanovism, as purged managers were denounced for "conservatism and sluggishness" and for "sabotaging the Stakhanovite movement or ignoring it."[6]

During the Great Terror, the NKVD investigated and commonly arrested party members who had been purged from the party. Once the NKVD had made a number of arrests, party members having any association with those arrested were called before the party committee for questioning. At one Moscow textile mill, all party members with relatives, friends, co-workers, or any other associates who had been arrested were themselves subject to questioning, expulsion from the party, and arrest.[7] This principle of guilt-by-association led to the arrest of large numbers of officials from the same departments of party organizations. Arrests at the Dinamo plant, for example, were concentrated in the party's agitation and propaganda department, where officials were accused of "spreading Trotskyist ideas."[8] Once the purges gathered momentum, denunciations

[3] MPA (Moskovskii Partiinyi Arkhiv) f. 432, op. 1, d. 165, ll. 125–126; f. 468, op. 1, d. 155, l. 207.
[4] MPA f. 432, op. 1, d. 176, ll. 138–139; d. 178, ll. 35, 71–76.
[5] MPA f. 432, op. 1, d. 165, l. 126; d. 180, l. 16. On the relationship between Stakhanovism and the purges, see also Francesco Benvenuti, "Stakhanovism and Stalinism, 1934–1938," Discussion Paper (Soviet Industrialization Project Series #30), Centre for Russian and East European Studies, University of Birmingham (July 1989), pp. 52–54.
[6] MPA f. 69, op. 1, d. 947, ll. 10–12; f. 432, op. 1, d. 176, l. 23. Compare these charges with the antimanagerial tone of Stakhanovism, as exemplified by Stalin's speech at a conference to honor Stakhanovites, *Labour in the Land of the Soviets. Stakhanovites in Conference* (Moscow, 1936), pp. 17–18; and by the memoir of Stakhanovite Ivan Gudov, *Sud'ba rabochego* (Moscow, 1974), pp. 25–29. In a few instances, Stakhanovites (who commanded salaries and prestige above that of managers) played a leading role in the denunciation and purging of managerial personnel. On the superior status of Stakhanovites, see TsGAORgM (Tsentral'nyi Gosudarstvennyi Arkhiv Oktiabr'skoi Revoliutsii goroda Moskvy) f. 415, op. 2, d. 448, ll. 10–13. For an account of a Stakhanovite who led the removal of his factory director during the purges, see Aleksandr Busygin, *Zhizn' moia i moikh druzhei* (Moscow, 1939).
[7] MPA f. 262, op. 1, d. 115, l. 140. See also f. 432, op. 1, d. 165, ll. 188–190.
[8] MPA f. 432, op. 1, d. 176, l. 31.

and counterdenunciations multiplied as party members hastened to im-
plicate others before they themselves could be denounced for Trotskyism
or for lack of vigilance. In one plant after the NKVD had arrested a number of party functionaries, the factory director stood accused of having
failed to uncover these Trotskyists himself.[9]

How broad was the scope of the purges in Moscow factories, and which
social groups did they victimize? Evidence from the Moscow Party Archive
suggests that the purges remained very much an elite phenomenon, with
party officials and high-level technical personnel subject to arrest, while
few rank-and-file workers were victimized. Party archives, of course, do
not provide a complete record of purge victims; workers who were not
party members may have been arrested without mention in party documents,
and NKVD archives are needed for definitive study of this question.[10] But
although the operations of the NKVD remain to be studied, it is clear that
factory party organizations directed all their energies to purging their own
membership and to purging leading technical specialists.[11]

Some rank-and-file workers belonged to factory party organizations
(and might have been subject to party purges), but they accounted for a
small percentage of the party's members in 1937. The bloodless party
purge of 1933–4 had expelled many workers recently inducted into the
party, while most workers of long-standing party membership had risen to
managerial positions. Of nearly 700 full and candidate party members of
working-class origin at one Moscow plant in early 1937, only 163 still
worked "at the bench" (*u stanka*). In fact, almost all purge victims at this
factory had joined the party in the early 1920s or before, and a large
percentage were high-level party officials and "Old Bolsheviks" (whose
party membership predated the Revolution); virtually no rank-and-file
workers numbered among purged party members.[12]

Also noteworthy in party documents is the large proportion of Jewish
names among those arrested – perhaps simply a reflection of the large

---

. [9] The report added that in addition to trusting Trotskyists, the director's offenses included
    failure to fulfill the plan, and aloofness toward workers; MPA f. 432, op. 1, d. 178, l. 34.
[10] It does appear that one subgroup of nonparty workers was at risk during the purges –
    workers who had previously been persecuted as "class aliens" (e.g., those who had been
    dispossessed as "kulaks" during collectivization). See Janucy K. Zawodny, "Twenty-six
    Interviews with Former Soviet Factory Workers," (Hoover Archives), II/24. The party
    committee of the Elektrozavod plant, in response to a secret directive from the Moscow
    party committee, concluded in late Aug. 1936, that "class-alien elements" had penetrated
    the factory and that concrete measures were needed against them; MPA f. 468, op. 1, d.
    155, l. 207.
[11] MPA f. 429, op. 1, d. 109, l. 51. The antimanagerial character of the purges is reflected in
    Moscow factory newspapers that urged workers to uncover Trotskyists and spies among
    managers, and to "join the battle against enemies of the people." *Martenovka*, 24 Jan.
    1937, pp. 1–3; 30 Jan. 1937, pp. 1–8; *Kirovets*, 7 Apr. 1938, p. 1.
[12] MPA f. 432, op. 1, d. 176, l. 10; d. 178, ll. 70–87. On the 1933–4 party purge, see
    Leonard Schapiro, *The Communist Party of the Soviet Union* (New York, 1960), pp.
    435–436.

percentage of party members and technical intelligentsia who were Jewish, but perhaps also an indication of anti-Semitism fueling the purges.[13] For example, one engineer arrested for his association with Trotskyists was also denounced for being the son of "the leader of a Jewish religious cult."[14] Such evidence turns upside-down current claims by anti-Semitic groups in the Soviet Union that the purges represent a crime perpetrated by Jews against ethnic Russians.

What consequences did the purges have on the local level? The most direct result of the purges was of course the arrest and incarceration or execution of purge victims, but consequences extended to factory production, party work, and personnel changes as well. Labor discipline deteriorated rapidly with the onset of the purges (as shown by a marked increase in worker absenteeism and tardiness), and resulted in a substantial fall in factory production. The purges not only decimated the ranks of managers and party officials, but also severely eroded managerial authority. Workers became emboldened to criticize their foremen, whereas managers were reluctant to discipline workers for fear of antagonizing them and provoking denunciations. The lingering effects of the purges are reflected in the fact that labor discipline had still not recovered in 1939.[15]

The purges disrupted party work in other spheres as well. As the sole focus of party meetings came to be rooting out Trotskyists, members devoted all their time to denouncing one another, questioning suspects, and checking party personnel. The purges stifled initiative and frank discussion, and attention to nonpurge matters virtually ceased. During this period, factory party organizations neglected or abandoned altogether routine party functions such as promoting labor productivity, conducting political propaganda, and organizing cultural and educational programs.[16]

The purges caused large-scale personnel changes both in party membership and in industrial management. With the depletion of the party's ranks during the purges, Moscow factory party committees recruited many new members, especially in 1938. Most new inductees into the party were young (often in their twenties) and had only worked in Moscow factories since the early 1930s.[17] Selection of new members in 1937 and 1938 focused more on the nominees' lack of liabilities than upon their attributes.

---

[13] MPA f. 432, op. 1, d. 176, l. 14; d. 178, ll. 72–75. It may simply have proven easier to denounce someone with a Jewish name as being a Trotskyist, but for other evidence of anti-Semitism in Moscow factories, see MPA f. 468, op. 1, d. 83, l. 57; f. 667, op. 1, d. 4, l. 69.

[14] MPA f. 432, op. 1, d. 180, l. 16.

[15] MPA f. 432, op. 1, d. 180, l. 9; d. 205, t. 2, l. 58; d. 226, l. 47; f. 468, op. 1, d. 157, ll. 30–31.

[16] MPA f. 432, op. 1, d. 178, l. 15; d. 187, l. 7.

[17] MPA f. 432, op. 1, d. 180, l. 125; d. 191, ll. 96–97; d. 191a, l. 33. For a discussion of changes in party composition nationwide, see Schapiro, pp. 435–440; T. H. Rigby, *Communist Party Membership in the USSR 1917–1967* (Princeton, 1968), pp. 217–227.

Usually the first question posed to nominees for candidate or full party membership was whether they had any relative or associate who had been arrested or who had traveled abroad; an affirmative response would disqualify them.[18]

Nominees with no black mark on their record stood a good chance of acceptance if they had attended political discussion circles and could correctly answer simple questions about the writings of Lenin and Stalin. Technical education at a technicum, factory-apprenticeship school (*FZU*), or workers' school (*rabfak*) further increased their chances for acceptance. In fact, many of the nominees were newly educated specialists of working-class origin. The party also favored Stakhanovites for admission, as nominees' production records were scrutinized prior to their admittance into the party.[19]

Newly educated specialists and Stakhanovites also received promotions into managerial positions vacated by purge victims; as managerial personnel from plant directors to engineers to shop foremen were arrested, *vydvizhentsy* took their places.[20] In this way the purges created a new elite not only at the highest echelons of the party but also at the local and factory levels. The purges thus represent the bloody and tumultuous realization of Stalin's 1935 speech, "Cadres Decide Everything" – his call for technically competent and politically loyal cadres.[21] This is not to say that the purges solved problems of lagging production. On the contrary, the purges disrupted production and left a legacy of embitterment and fear terribly detrimental to normal industrial and societal function.[22] But a tremendous change in personnel undeniably occurred in Moscow factories, both among party officials and the managerial elite.

The enormous impact of the Great Terror on Moscow factories is indisputable. As a short-term consequence, the purges caused a drop in labor discipline and in industrial production. As a more permanent consequence, the purges decapitated the party and managerial elite and led to the promotion of new personnel. Hopefully, archival access will continue to broaden, allowing further investigation of the purges in other regions of the country. Also needed is access to NKVD archives to determine more definitively the scope and character of purge victims. Nonetheless, new perspectives and understandings of the Great Terror are possible based on archival material now becoming available.

---

[18] Nominees of peasant origin were also asked if any relative had ever been dekulakized, as this was also grounds for rejection. MPA f. 432, op. 1, d. 178, l. 174; d. 191, ll. 96–97; d. 220, ll. 144–145.

[19] MPA f. 432, op. 1, d. 178, l. 174; d. 191, ll. 96–97; d. 191a, l. 33; d. 216, l. 2.

[20] MPA f. 432, op. 1, d. 204, l. 231.

[21] Iosif V. Stalin, *Sochineniia*, vol. 14, ed. Robert McNeal (Stanford, 1967), pp. 61–62. Sheila Fitzpatrick first made this argument in "Stalin and the Making of a New Elite, 1928–1939," *Slavic Review* 38 (Sept., 1979), pp. 394–395, 400–402.

[22] O. V. Khlevniuk, "1937 god: protivodeistvie repressiiam," *Kommunist* 1989 #18, p. 107.

8

The Great Purges in a rural district: Belyi Raion revisited

Roberta T. Manning

Half a century now separates us from the Great Purges of 1936–8. Yet the causes of these political persecutions remain obscure, for many key sources for the study of the purges are only now beginning to be explored in any systematic fashion by historians. The manner in which scholars have traditionally approached the Great Purges accounts for the failure to explore thoroughly all available sources. Until recently, the Great Purges have been studied from the top down, from the vantage point of the apex of the Soviet political system, usually with an emphasis on the role of Soviet dictator Joseph Stalin, to whose personal predilections and political needs the purges have often been exclusively attributed.[1]

Thus viewed, available source materials on the purges were rapidly exhausted, since the archives of the higher councils of the Communist party were closed until quite recently to scholars. Stalin's few public pronouncements at the time of the Great Purges, which is all we had to go on before the Central Party Archives became freely available to researchers, offered little insight into the causes of the purges or Stalin's own role in these events.[2] As a result, scholars tended to rely for large part on sources not generally accepted by historians, like rumor, gossip, and second- and third-hand accounts of developments within the Kremlin, even those of

The author would like to thank the Harvard Russian Research Center for supporting the research on which this paper rests.

[1] Major empirical studies of the Great Purges that portray the impetus of the purges as coming from above include Robert Conquest, *The Great Terror: Stalin's Purge of the Thirties* (New York: Macmillan, 1968); Merle Fainsod, *Smolensk Under Soviet Rule* (Cambridge: Harvard University Press, 1958), 132–37, 222–37; Zbigniew K. Brzezinski, *The Permanent Purge: Politics in Soviet Totalitarianism* (Cambridge: Harvard University Press, 1956); Roy Medvedev, *Let History Judge: The Origins and Consequences of Stalinism* (New York: Random House, 1971); and Alexander Solzhenitsyn, *Gulag Archipelago: An Experiment in Literary Investigation*, 3 vols. (New York: Harper & Row, 1973).

[2] For this, see J. Arch Getty, *The Origins of the Great Purges: the Soviet Communist Party Reconsidered, 1933–1938* (Cambridge: Cambridge University Press, 1985), 137–49, 179.

individuals who were outside the USSR altogether at the time of the Great Purges.[3]

Among the most valuable of the many underexplored sources on the Great Purges are the files of the Belyi Raion party organization found in the Smolensk Archive.[4] These materials from an overwhelmingly rural administrative district located to the northwest of Moscow contain discussions and formal reviews of the cases of party members in political trouble for much of the duration of the purges. The materials on Belyi cover the critical period between the July 29, 1936, Central Committee letter on the Kamenev-Zinoviev trial,[5] which triggered the persecution of former party oppositionists in a number of local party organizations,[6] and the January 19, 1938, Central Committee resolution condemning excessive repression of local Communists, which is generally regarded as the first major step in winding down the purges.[7] To be sure, the final stage of the Great Purges (between the January 1938 Central Committee letter and the immediate aftermath of the removal of national NKVD chief Nikolai Ezhov on December 8, 1938) is not covered by the available documents. In this period, many of those persecuted earlier were rehabilitated and the more zealous purgers fell victim to the purges.[8] But the purges were already waning in Belyi Raion at the end of 1937 (as Table 8.9 indicates), even before the intervention of the Central Committee. Viewed from lower levels of the Soviet political system, like Belyi, the Great Purges appear a far different, more complex political phenomenon than we have hitherto assumed, fueled by input from below as well as pressures from above.

Although incomplete, the Belyi documents are unique in that they provide

[3] For discussions of the use of sources in existing studies of the Great Purges, see Getty, *The Origins of the Great Purges*, 207–20 and Gábor Tamás Rittersporn, *Simplifications staliniennes et complications soviétiques: Tensions sociales et conflicts politiques en URSS 1933–1953* (Paris: Editions des Archives Contemporaines, 1988), 261–365.

[4] For a guide to the archive, see *Guide to the Records of the Smolensk Oblast of the All-Union Communist Party of the Soviet Union, 1917–1941* (Washington, DC: 1980). For studies of Belyi Raion that draw on these materials, see Roberta T. Manning, "Government in the Soviet Countryside in the Stalinist Thirties: The Case of Belyi Raion in 1937," *The Carl Beck Papers in Russian and East European Studies* (Pittsburgh, Russian and East European Studies, University of Pittsburgh, 1984), no. 301, 1–71 and Fainsod, *Smolensk Under Soviet Rule*, 122–37.

[5] The Smolensk Archive, WKP 499: 322–28 (henceforth the archive will be referred to by file number only).

[6] WKP 538: 346, 371, 376, 382, 387, 397, 399–401, 407, 438, 442, 452–54, 467–68, 485, 502–9, 512, 517, 541–46, 553–55.

[7] *Pravda*, Jan. 19, 1938.

[8] Between the January 1938 Central Committee Plenum and early August 1938, oblast party committees throughout the nation reviewed 85,271 of the 154,933 pending appeals of expelled Communists and overturned 54% of these expulsions. The January 1938 Central Committee resolution explicitly called for the reversal of all expulsions in which party procedures had been violated as well as the readmission of the many expelled Communists who had been cleared by NKVD of committing any legal offenses. *Pravda*, Aug. 7, 1938, and Jan. 19, 1938.

insight into the reasons why ordinary Communist party members in Belyi Raion supported, promoted, and accepted the persecution of their fellow Communists. According to existing party procedures, the cases of all party members in political trouble in the raion were subjected to two reviews, first in the member's primary party organization (ppo) and then again at the raion level, usually by the raion party committee (raikom) bureau, the executive organ of the local party organization. Only after review at the raion level did any party sanctions imposed take legal force.[9]

Transcripts of the raion-level reviews of the cases of all Communists expelled from the Belyi Raion party organization in the course of 1937 exist in the Smolensk Archive, along with the formal charges leveled against these party members by their ppo's. Many of the cases of these expelled Communists, particularly those most highly placed in the raion political heirarchy, were also discussed by the raion party membership at general raion party conferences that met several times in the course of 1937.[10]

Oblast materials and periodic raion party censuses indicate that no members of the Belyi Raion party organization were expelled in the second half of 1936, when the Great Purges first began to make inroads among Communists in the Western Oblast, the larger territorial entity of which Belyi was then part, with its capital in Smolensk.[11] Between January 1, 1937, and January 5, 1938, however, 37 members of the 239 member raion party organization were expelled from the Communist party on the votes of raion-level bodies.[12] This amounted to 11.7% of the members of the local party organization. The rate of expulsions from the Communist Party in 1937 ran somewhat lower in Belyi Raion than in Smolensk Oblast and the nation as a whole. Between June 18, 1937, and January 27, 1938, 2,168 Communists (12.5% of the members and candidates of the oblast party organization) were expelled.[13] Nationwide, approximately 100,000

---

[9] The party procedures followed in expelling members from the Communist party in the late 1930s and in processing appeals against such decisions are outlined in *Krest'ianskaia gazeta*, Mar. 18, 1936.

[10] WKP 321: 1–304 and WKP 111: 1–232.

[11] WKP 538: 307, 346–555 and WKP 321: 139.

[12] WKP 321: 63–64, 154, 157–62, 189, 192, 194–98, 200–22, 228, 238, 240–41, 252–60, 272–76, 284, 292–93, 297–300; WKP 111: 92–114, 186–90, 193–206, 211–18; WKP 362: 517 and WKP 203: 176. Actually the raion party organization never formally voted to expel raikom secretary T. I. Kovalev, who has been included in this group of thirty-seven, because his case was so central to the Great Purges in the raion. Kovalev was removed as raikom secretary by the March 1937 raion party conference. Another raion party conference in June 1937 petitioned the obkom to initiate criminal proceedings against Kovalev on charges of wrecking. By then, however, Kovalev had left the raion to work in the oblast control commission in Smolensk, overseeing the oblast land department. He was expelled from the party in Smolensk upon the fall of his political patrons in the oblast leadership in June, shortly before the adoption of this resolution in Belyi. WKP 111: 3–81, 152–75 and WKP 103: 131.

[13] *Tsentr dokumentatsii noveishei istorii Smolenskoi oblasti* (formerly *Partiinyi arkhiv Smolenskoi oblasti*), hereafter cited as TsDNISO (PASO), fond 6, op. 1, del 120, p. 1.

Communists (14.5%) were expelled in 1937 – 24,000 in the first half of the year and 76,000 in the second half[14] – in a party that numbered 1,453,828 members and candidates at the start of 1937.[15] The highest purge rates were apparently found in the Ukraine, where 30 out of the 66 party *raikoms* (raion party committees) were dissolved, because they were deemed "hostile, from top to bottom," according to the minutes of the January 1938 Central Committee Plenum that condemned these developments.[16]

Expelled Communists were usually removed from their official positions in party, government, and economic organizations upon their expulsion from the party.[17] A major exception to this practice in Belyi was the local NKVD chief Vinogradov who initially remained at the helm of the raion NKVD after he was expelled from the party by the raion party conference of September 19–20 over the opposition of oblast representatives at the conference and the oblast NKVD organization. But Vinogradov too was eventually removed.[18] Communists and other Soviet citizens who lost their jobs in 1937 experienced enormous difficulties in finding new positions, and considerable stretches of unemployment were not uncommon.[19]

Expulsion from the party and loss of one's job, however, was often only the first step in a lengthy "purge process." For all too many victims, this process resulted in arrest; mistreatment, if not actual torture, at the hands of the police; lengthy imprisonment in appalling conditions; and – for some of them – even mass execution and burial in unmarked trenches, most likely in Krasnyi Bor in the Katyn Forest near Smolensk, where most of the 4,500 people from the Smolensk region who were sentenced to be shot in 1937 apparently met their tragic end.[20]

By the end of 1937, at least eight Belyi Communists were known to have been arrested in the main for embezzlement and "wrecking" (*vreditel'stvo*),

---

[14] *Rossiiskii tsentr khraneniia i izucheniia dokumentov noveishei istorii* (formerly *Tsentral'nyi Partiinyi Arkhiv, Institut Marksizma-Leninizma*), hereafter cited as RTsKhIDNI (TsPA), fond 17, op. 2, del 639, p. 4.

[15] T. H. Rigby, *Communist Party Membership in the U.S.S.R. 1917–1967* (Princeton: Princeton University Press, 1968), 52.

[16] RTsKhIDNI (TsPA) fond 17, op. 2, del 639, pp. 4–37.

[17] In addition, twenty-two Belyi Communists who were neither expelled nor investigated lost their official positions for various misdeeds. WKP 111: 67, 114 and WKP 321: 300.

[18] WKP 111: 95–114; WKP 362: 356, 450, 510; and WKP 241: 8. Merle Fainsod in his classic study of the Smolensk Archive maintained that Vinogradov was subsequently restored to party membership upon appeal because "in this case too...the NKVD succeeded in taking care of its own." Fainsod, *Smolensk Under Soviet Rule*, 170. But there is no evidence in the Smolensk Archive that indicates that this was the case. The last archival references to Vinogradov said that he had been replaced as raion NKVD chief and had left the raion. The review of his case by the obkom bureau was scheduled for January 3, 1938, before the January Central Committee Plenum resolution provided a substantial chance of clemency for party members in Vinogradov's position.

[19] For the employment problems of expelled Communists, see the January 1938 Central Committee resolution, *Pravda*, Jan. 19, 1938.

[20] *Moscow News*, no. 32 (Aug. 13–20, 1989), 15.

as chronic mismanagement was then called.[21] In addition, the local raikom bureau explicitly called for the prosecution of eight other expelled Communists, turning evidence against them over to the prosecutor to facilitate their conviction.[22] Such action was redundant, however, for expelled Communists were automatically investigated by the police at this time; expulsion from the party meant essentially to turn the party member in question over to the mercies of the NKVD.[23] Those investigated in Belyi also included seven men who had not yet been formally expelled from the party who were investigated on the request of the local party organization.[24] The ultimate fate of those investigated cannot be determined from the Party Archives examined here alone. One would also have to consult local NKVD archives, which were often destroyed in the Smolensk area at the onset of the Nazi invasion to prevent their falling into German hands,[25] and the archives of the special collegia (*spetkollegiia*) of the Western Oblast court and the *troikas*, administrative boards consisting of three officials, which tried the local purge victims. These archives were not yet open to scholars as late as the summer of 1992.[26]

Party archives indicate that at least twenty-four non-Communists were arrested in Belyi Raion in 1937, although data on non-Communists is by no means complete and information from the oblast and other Smolensk raions indicate far more non-Communists were arrested and executed than Communists.[27] In Belyi arrested non-Communists appear to have been to a significant degree employees of three particularly troubled raion institutions – the lumber industry, the Shamilovo sovkhoz, and the Belyi MTS

---

[21] WKP 111: 175, 178, 181, 193–206 and WKP 321: 232, 242, 260, 273, 298.

[22] WKP 321: 101, 195–98, 220, 228–29, 253, 292; WKP 111: 104, 204; and WKP 362: 517.

[23] For this, see the January 1938 Central Committee resolution. *Pravda*, Jan. 19, 1938.

[24] WKP 111: 90, 110–11; WKP 321: 300; WKP 203: 181–88; WKP 440: 113–14, 120; and WKP 363: 517.

[25] At any rate, this was the case of local NKVD archives in Sychevka Raion, which bordered on Belyi to the east. However, oblast NKVD archives appear to have survived (down to 1938) but were still uncatalogued and unavailable to scholars in the summer of 1992. N. Pavlov, *Ispolnenie dolga* (Moscow: Moskovskii rabochii, 1973), 23–28.

[26] WKP 103: 77, 80, 140, 177, 207–10 and *Rabochii put* (Smolensk), Aug. 29–31, 1937; Sept. 3–7, 1937; Oct. 13–18, 1937; Oct. 21–28, 1937; Nov. 13–16, 1937; and Nov. 24–28, 1937. The archives of the *spetkollegiia* should be found in the State Archive of Smolensk Oblast (Gosudarstvennyi arkhiv Smolenskoi oblasti or GASO). For a guide to this archive, see *Katalog arkhivnykn fondov gosarkhiva Smolenskoi oblasti i ego filiala v g. Viaz'me (sovetskoi period)* (Smolensk: Gosizdat, 1987).

[27] WKP 111: 99, 178 and WKP 321: 283–84. Most of these arrests, however, occurred before the fall of NKVD chief Vinogradov, and evidence in the archives indicates that the arrests of non-Communists increased after his expulsion from the party. For this, see WKP 321: 281–84, 293 and WKP 111: 213–14, 220. According to the Smolensk Oblast NKVD chief in 1989, 4,500 persons were sentenced to be shot in the oblast in 1937. Since only 2,168 Communists were expelled from the oblast party organization between June 18, 1937, and January 27, 1938, when the terror peaked and 796 of these were still alive and protesting their expulsions in January 1938, the executions of non-Communists outran those of Communists several times over. *Moscow News* no. 32 (Aug. 13–20, 1989), 15 and TsDNISO (PASO) fond 6, op. 1, del 120, 1.

(machine tractor station) – that experienced major financial losses, with tens or even hundreds of thousands of rubles unaccounted for.[28]

The arrest of Communists in Belyi Raion in 1937 in all but two cases followed, not preceded, their expulsion from the party.[29] The exceptions to this general rule involved the embezzlement of significant amounts of public funds. In most other instances the party, not the police, appeared to take the political initiative. Indeed, criticism of the laxity of the local NKVD chief, prosecutor, and raion judge on the part of rank-and-file rural Communists, local procurements and forestry officials, and low-level police officers in the summer and fall of 1937 served as a major impetus to the Great Purges within the raion party organization.[30] To be sure, obkom representatives joined in these attacks at the end of the summer after the collection of procurements in the raion faltered for a second year in a row, due to a substantial crop failure throughout much of the non-black-soil region, amid what was otherwise a bumper crop elsewhere in the nation.[31] Only rarely in the 1930s did procurements campaigns proceed without the arrest of a few low-level rural officials or at the very least without threatening such officials with arrest, removal from office, or expulsion from the Communist party unless the pace of procurements picked up.[32]

The only clearcut case in which the police and higher authorities outside the raion took the initiative in pushing for the expulsion of a Belyi Communist without substantial local backing was that of raikom secretary Karpovskii. Karpovskii happened to be unfortunate enough to have received a letter from an aunt in Rumania, a fascist nation, which was intercepted by the NKVD on September 5,[33] just as national anxiety about "fascist spies and saboteurs" peaked after the arrest of the national military leadership and the local oblast leadership as "masked" (i.e., covert agents of German and Japanese intelligence services).[34] As a result, the discussion of the Karpovskii case within the Belyi Raion party organization appeared far less spontaneous and enthusiastic and more contrived than the discussions preceding the expulsions of other local leaders. Indeed, much of the discussion focused on the failings of other officials.[35]

[28] For the troubles of these institutions, see WKP 321: 155, 281–84, 297–98, 302 and WKP 111: 98–99, 159, 161, 183.

[29] The exceptions were N. A. Barabonov, the chairman of the Iskra Collective Farm; S. M. Marchenkov, director of the October Lumber Association; and director of the local linen factory Arkhipov. WKP 321: 232, 260, 273.

[30] See, for example, WKP 111: 74, 76–78, 86–95, 97, 100, 106–12, 155–58, 179, 273.

[31] Ibid., 179–80; *Sotsialiticheskoe zemledelie* July 24, 1937; *Bolshevik*, no. 18 (Sept. 15, 1937) p. 10; and Tsentral'nyi Gosudarstvennyi Arkhiv Narodnogo Khoziaĭstvo SSSR fond 9477, op. 1, del 473 1937–1938, p. 2 and del 626 1938, p. 32.

[32] This, indeed, was how former raikom secretary Kovalev had traditionally operated. WKP 111: 3, 6, 27, 30, 34, 41.

[33] Ibid., 114, 193–94, 197, 204–5.

[34] Getty, *Origins of the Great Purges*, 163–71.

[35] Compare, for example, the discussion that preceded Karpovskii's expulsion (WKP 111: 92–114, 193–206) with that which preceded the removal of Kovalev as raikom secretary (ibid., 3–81) or NKVD chief Vinogradov's expulsion (ibid., 105–14, 186–90).

Except for the Karpovskii case, the police appeared to follow the lead of the local party in dealing with Belyi Communists. The party occasionally called in the police and prosecutor to investigate the cases of Communists in trouble who had not yet been expelled from the party, especially at the height of the Great Purges in the raion in the fall of 1937. But moves to expel Communists and calls for judicial investigations on the part of the party were generally preceded by citizens' complaints to the local or national press[36] or by substantial criticism of the party member concerned by rank-and-file Communists. In this process, the expellees' subordinants and peers usually played a more prominent role than their superiors.[37]

Indeed, raion leaders often lagged behind rank-and-file party members in their zeal to oust their fellow Communists. The tide of expulsions in the raion's ppo's outran those accepted by local party leaders in the raikom bureau by over 40% in 1937,[38] although in a few cases ppo's proved more reluctant than higher level party bodies to push for expulsions.[39] Raion leaders finally responded to the rising tide of expulsions in the fall of 1937 by suspending all party meetings in the raion for over a month, first at the raion level and then in the ppo's, in hopes of impeding further expulsions.[40]

Although the local party organization responded to pressures from below in 1937, it did not always respond to pressures from outside the

[36] Citizen complaints played a role in the political troubles of Kovalev, Usachev, Shelaev, Makarov, T. F. Zhukov, and those expelled Communists connected with the Nikulenkova Affair (Vinogradov, Antipov, Malofeev, Petrov, and Usachev). This affair revolved around a Communist milkmaid, Nikulenkova, whose production record was altered by several highly placed Belyi officials so the local party organization could be represented by a party member at a conference of the nation's leading Stakhanovite livestock tenders in Moscow attended by Stalin and other top dignitaries. The wide publicity surrounding this conference and awards, including *ordeny*, given Nikulenkova for her false achivements, prompted complaints from her fellow collective farmers to the raion newspaper. For this, see WKP 111: 186–90, 213–14; WKP 321: 68–69, 204–25, 228–29; WKP 239: 152, and WKP 362: 64–67.

[37] This was particularly true in the cases of the most highly placed local Communists, like raikom secretary Kovalev, raion soviet executive committee chairman P. I. Stogov, and raion NKVD chief Vinogradov. WKP 111: 3–81, 105–11, 152–75, 186–98.

[38] In addition to the thirty-seven local Communists whose expulsions were upheld by raion-level party bodies, sixteen other party members in the raion were expelled by their ppo's in 1937. The party raikom, however, overturned these expulsions in thirteen cases, substituting lesser penalties, like reproofs, warnings, and demotions. All but two of these cases (raion soviet executive committes chairman F. M. Shitov and P. I. Frolov, editor of the raion newspaper) involved low-level rural officials (collective farm or rural soviet chairmen) or ordinary workers, as the Belyi party organization generally dealt more leniently with its less influential members than its more highly placed members in 1937. WKP 321: 79, 191, 198–99, 219–20, 255, 274, 276, 284–85, 300; WKP 111: 97, 206, 300; WKP 362: 535; and WKP 263: 249.

[39] This was true in the cases of T. F. Zhukov (the head of the raion education department); A. F. Belov, the director of the local agricultural technicum; S. F. Rodchenkov, chairman of the raion consumers' cooperative; and A. M. Pavlov, a local procurements official. WKP 321: 157–62, 221, 255, 258, 260; and WKP 111: 214, 218.

[40] WKP 321: 258 and WKP 111: 92, 117, 193, 207, 213.

raion. Obkom representatives assigned to oversee the operation of the raion party organization encountered considerable difficulties in directing the flow of local events in 1937. To be sure, obkom representatives managed to persuade the March 1937 raion party conference in Belyi to drop charges of Trotskyism against raikom secretary Kovalev when Kovalev was removed from office by the conference.[41] But popular revulsion against Kovalev's methods of government, fueled by the February 1937 Central Committee Plenum resolution that stressed intraparty democracy and introduced secret ballot elections with multiple candidates for party officials,[42] prevented the obkom from keeping Kovalev in office. Yet oblast leaders retained considerable confidence in Kovalev's administrative abilities. Indeed, they appointed him to a high position as a representative of the Western Oblast Party Control Commission, entrusted with overseeing the operation of the oblast land department, the local affiliate of the Commissariat of Agriculture, immediately upon his ouster as raikom secretary.[43] Moreover, the obkom did not prove successful in securing the election of its own candidate to replace Kovalev. Rumors circulated among Belyi Communists that the obkom's candidate was "even worse than Kovalev" in his treatment of subordinates, prompting the local party *aktiv* to insist on a raikom secretary of their own choice.[44]

The obkom representatives at the September 1937 raion party conference also failed in their efforts to prevent the expulsion of NKVD chief Vinogradov from the party by diverting the purges in the raion in the main toward low-level rural officials who had failed to deliver agricultural procurements. Although procurements-related expulsions did increase under pressure from the obkom in August and September 1937, the number of expulsions of high Belyi officials, including Vinogradov, escalated even more rapidly.[45] The intervention of the obkom on behalf of Kovalev and Vinogradov provoked considerable resentment. Belyi party members responded by denouncing the "improper behavior" of the obkom representatives and calling for the prosecution of several long-time obkom representatives, or "instructors" as they were called, responsible for overseeing the operations of the raion party organization – Makarov, Chausov, and Nesterov – who were now accused of being part of the now discredited political machine of former obkom secretary Rumantsev.[46]

---

[41] WKP 111: 58–67. In his account of the 1937 events in Belyi, Fainsod insisted erroneously that the impetus for the removal of Kovalev came from above, from the Western obkom that intended to make Belyi the scapegoat for the antidemocratic practices denounced at the February 1937 Central Committee Plenum when no evidence in the archive would indicate this. Fainsod, *Smolensk Under Soviet Rule*, 132.

[42] For this, see Getty, *The Origins of the Great Purges*, 141–44.

[43] WKP 111: 228–32 and *Partiets* (Smolensk) 1937, no. 4, pp. 19–25.

[44] WKP 111: 174 and WKP 103: 131.

[45] WKP 111: 96, 100, 103, 113.

[46] Ibid., 7, 25, 96, 100, 114, 154–56, 158, 166, 168, 171, 174–75, 196, 200, 205 and WKP 321: 166.

Table 8.1. *Occupational status of Party expellees compared to the*
members of the raion party organization who were not expelled
(1/1/37 to 1/5/38)

Occupational status	Number expelled	Number not expelled
Heads or assistant heads of raion-level institutions	14 (40.5%)	23 (13.1%)
Lesser raion-level officials	4 (10.8%)	55 (31.4%)
Heads of educational institutions	3 (8.1%)	2 (1.1%)
Directors of local industries	4 (10.8%)	12 (6.9%)
Rural soviet chairmen	4 (10.8%)	24 (13.7%)
Collective farm chairmen	5 (13.5%)	17 (9.7%)
Lesser party members	3 (8.1%)	42 (24.0%)
Total	37 (100%)	175 (199%)

Note: The proportion of rural soviet chairmen, collective farm chairmen, and lesser party members among the raion membership not expelled is understated, since occupational data was available for only 175 of the 202 Belyi party members who were not expelled in 1937 (86.2%). Missing cases consist disproportionately of rank-and-file party members and low-level officials, because the occupants of all major posts in the raion were known.
Sources: WKP 321, pp. 63, 139–140, 158–162, 175–176, 189, 192, 194–198, 220–222, 228–229, 232, 238–250, 252–256, 258–260, 272–276, 291, 298–300 and WKP 111, pp. 92–114, 193–206.

The main target of the Great Purges in Belyi Raion at least insofar as the local party organization was concerned appears to have been local leaders or "bosses," individuals who wielded considerable influence and power in the raion, as Table 8.1 demonstrates. Among those expelled from the party in Belyi Raion in 1937 were two first secretaries of the party raikom, the chairman and assistant chairman of the raion soviet executive committee, the raion NKVD chief, the raion prosecutor, the secretary of the Komsomol raikom, the head of the raion land department (the local affiliate of the Commissariat of Agriculture), the director of the Belyi MTS, the chairman of the town soviet, the head of the raion education department (the local affiliate of the Commissariat of Enlightenment), the chairman of the raion consumers' cooperative, and the director of the raion store. Indeed, the only top-ranking local officials spared as of the start of 1938 were the editor of the raion newspaper, P. I. Frolov, who was under a political cloud for much of the last four months of 1937, and Ia. P. Senin, the head of the political section of the Shamilovo sovkhoz, who was about to be indicted on charges of wrecking as 1937 wound to an end. Although Frolov was cleared of the charges raised against him, both men were removed from the raikom bureau in December 1937, rendering the personnel turnover on that key executive body since the start of the year complete.[47]

The directors of industrial establishments and the more important educational establishments in the raion appear to have been particularly hard-hit. In addition, five collective farm chairmen, five rural soviet chairmen, and the head of one of the two major procurements agencies in the raion were expelled. At least eight of these expulsions seemed to have resulted from the pressures placed by oblast officials on the local party organization and judiciary to speed up the collection of procurements.[48] Procurements-related cases also accounted for three of the eight Communists known to have been arrested.[49] Interestingly enough, however, several of the rural officials expelled at the height of the 1937 procurements campaign were already in trouble with the local party organization as a result of earlier, repeated complaints filed by rural schoolteachers and ordinary peasants.[50]

Expelled officials were generally replaced by low-level local officials, selected in the main from the minor staff members of the party raikom (raikom instructors, the manager of the raion party office, and the raikom librarian); employees of the raion financial department, the only major local institution untouched by the Great Purges; and local rural soviet chairmen who were overwhelmingly if not exclusively recruited from Belyi peasants.[51] S. L. Galkin, Belyi's third and last raikom secretary in 1937, appears to be the only exception to this general practice of appointing local people to replace the expellees, coming to the raion from without as the obkom's candidate to replace Karpovskii. Galkin earlier served as raikom secretary in Kozelsk in the south of the Western Oblast.[52]

Contrary to popular impressions, the most vocal local purgers, who were in the main associated with the party's ideological apparatus, did not benefit to any significant degree from the purges. To be sure, M. V. Martynov, the raikom *kul'tprop*, who had been persecuted for criticism by Kovalev by being removed from office and expelled from the party, was

---

[47] WKP 321: 12, 110, 284–87, 300.

[48] Ibid., 219–20, 228, 231, 255, 260, 273.

[49] This was true of F. D. Petrov, head of the raion land department; collective farm chairman N. A. Barabonov; and D. M. Makarov, chairman of the Medvedevskii rural soviet. WKP 111: 179, 181 and WKP 321: 219.

[50] This was true, for example, of D. M. Makarov, G. I. Shelaev, and N. A. Beliaev. WKP 362: 14, 20–26, 44–47, 82–97, 129–31, 177–82, 238–41, 280–81, 330–31, 394. In addition, N. A. Barabanov, chairman of the Iskra collective farm, had repeatedly been charged with embezzlement and drunkeness since 1935 and had been given frequent warnings by the party to alter his behavior. WKP 385: 79 and WKP 321: 26.

[51] For these promotions, see WKP 321: 168, 191, 217, 239, 246, 278–79, 280–83, 289, 295–96, 301, 304, 321; WKP 111: 110, 198, 220; WKP 440: 9–10, 21; WKP 235: 336; and WKP 362: 450. Fainsod is wrong when he asserted that all the new appointees were strangers to the raion. Fainsod, *Smolensk Under Soviet Rule*, 137. Evidently he failed to check to see if those who replaced the old raion leadership attended the raion party conferences earlier in the year.

[52] WKP 111: 117–18.

able to exact his revenge. Martynov, the only local party member to mention or quote Stalin in party debates, initiated the local attack on Kovalev's leadership and regained his old position for his pains. He also continued to pursue the expulsion of Kovalev's chief associates. Although he was occasionally mentioned as a possible candidate for a first or second secretaryship, such appointments were not forthcoming. By the year's end, Belyi's new businesslike raikom secretary Galkin increasingly occupied Martynov with routine assignments correcting the deficiencies in his own work, like organizing collective farm wall newspapers or investigating why the party educational network functioned so poorly.[53]

E. F. Zaitsev, the local representative of OBLIT, the censorship agency, who went even further than Martynov in attacking the old raion leadership, was quietly transferred out of the raion, no doudt at Galkin's behest.[54] Several other local party members, who were particularly vocal in calling for expulsions and making accusations against their fellow party members (Prokunin, the director of the local industrial combinat, and Iakushkin and Goliashev who headed the raion military command), ceased to speak out after being charged with possible corruption.[55] Officials at this time were particularly vulnerable to such accusations, given the dearth of adequate accounting and record-keeping skills among the undereducated Soviet officials of the 1930s, which left many of them unable to account for the public funds at their disposal before a court of law.

When biographical profiles of the thirty-six Belyi Communists expelled from the party in 1937 are compared to the results of a raion party census taken on May 17, 1937, just before the expulsions began in earnest in the raion, a number of interesting tendencies emerge, which are summed up in Tables 8.2 through 8.8.[56] Men and women were represented among the expellees in proportions virtually identical to their representation among the raion party membership at large, as shown in Table 8.2. Female expellees, as might be expected, tended to occupy less important positions than their male counterparts, accounting for both of the "lesser party members" listed in Table 8.1, although both of the top-ranking women Communists in the raion – D. M. Shatseva, chairman of the town soviet, and S. M. Dymshits, director of the raion store – were expelled from the party in 1937.[57] Women Communists, however, were more likely than their male peers to have been judged by their relations. All four of the

---

[53] See WKP 111: 3–6, 71, 109, 110–12, 157, 173–74, 177–78, 187–88, 202–3, 215–16, 218, 229 and WKP 321: 212–15.
[54] WKP 111: 105, 199, 201–3, 213–14, 219 and WKP 321: 239, 279.
[55] WKP 111: 28, 37, 100, 109–10, 155–56, 197, 216 and WKP 321: 95, 197, 293–94.
[56] T. F. Zhukov, head of the raion education department, who was expelled from the party January 5, 1938, had been excluded from this analysis, because no transcripts of the raion-level hearing on his case are available and biographical and other information on him is incomplete.
[57] WKP 321: 272, 257, 252; WKP 111: 96; WKP 385: 178–81.

Table 8.2. *Sexual composition of Belyi party members expelled in 1937 compared to the raion party organization as a whole (as of 5/17/37)*

Sex	Number expelled	Raion party organization members
Male	32 (88.9%)	209 (87.4%)
Female	4 (11.1%)	30 (12.6%)
Total	36 (100%)	239 (100%)

Sources: WKP 321, pp. 63, 139–140, 158–162, 175–176, 189, 192, 194–198, 220–222, 228–229, 232, 238–250, 252–256, 258–260, 272–276, 291, 298–300 and WKP 111, pp. 92–114, 193–206.

Table 8.3. *Party status of the 1937 expellees compared to the raion party organization as a whole (as of 5/17/37)*

Party status	Expellees	Raion party organization
Members	24 (75%)	148 (61.9%)
Candidates	8 (25%)	91 (38.1%)

Note: Party status was not available for four expellees.
Sources: WKP 321, pp. 63, 139–140, 158–162, 175–176, 189, 192, 194–198, 220–222, 228–229, 232, 238–250, 252–256, 258–260, 272–276, 291, 298–300 and WKP 111, pp. 92–114, 193–206.

expelled women Communists in Belyi possessed male relatives – a husband, brother, or father – who were charged with Trotskyism, arrested on criminal charges, or practiced occupations like trade that were deemed politically untrustworthy by the Soviets in the 1920s and 1930s. This was the case of only three of the thirty-two male expellees.[58]

Party members and town-based Communists were more likely to have been expelled than candidate members and Communists who worked in the countryside, as Tables 8.3 and 8.4 indicate, notwithstanding the spate of expulsions connected with procurements.[59] Communists of working-

[58] WKP 111: 92–114 and WKP 321: 158, 163, 189, 250.
[59] This pattern of persecution may explain Evgeniia Ginzburg's otherwise curious assertion that had she left town for the countryside, she could have escaped arrest. For this, see Evgeniia Ginzburg, *Into the Whirlwind* (New York: Harcourt, Brace Jovanovich, 1975), 21–24.

Table 8.4. *Place of residence of the 1937 Belyi expellees compared to the party organization as a whole (as of 5/17/37)*

Place of residence	Expellees	Raion party organization members
Town	25 (69.4%)	133 (55.6%)
Rural	11 (30.6%)	106 (44.4%)
Total	36 (100%)	239 (100%)

Sources: WKP 321, pp. 63, 139–140, 158–162, 175–176, 189, 192, 194–198, 220–222, 228–229, 232, 238–250, 252–256, 258–260, 272–276, 291, 298–300 and WKP 111, pp. 92–114, 193–206.

Table 8.5. *Social origins of the 1937 Belyi expellees compared to the raion party organization as a whole (as of 5/17/37)*

Social origin	Expellees	Raion party organization members
Worker	8 (22.9%)	76 (31.8%)
Peasant	23 (63.9%)	146 (61.1%)
Other	5 (14.3%)	17 (7.1%)
Total	36 (100%)	239 (100%)

Sources: WKP 321, pp. 63, 139–140, 158–162, 175–176, 189, 192, 194–198, 220–222, 228–229, 232, 238–250, 252–256, 258–260, 272–276, 291, 298–300 and WKP 111, pp. 92–114, 193–206.

class antecedents, as can be seen in Table 8.5, were less represented among the expellees than they were within the raion party organization, indicating perhaps that party claims of favoring the proletarian were not entirely unfounded. Party members of peasant background were represented among expellees and the party organization as a whole in similar proportions, whereas Communists who came from other, more socially elevated origins were substantially more likely to have been expelled in 1937 than were former workers and peasants. Communists under the age of thirty were significantly less likely to have been ousted from the party than members over thirty, as Table 8.6 demonstrates.[60] The Great Purges in the raion also fell disproportionately on the better educated local Communists, as

---

[60] For works that come to similar conclusions, see Conquest, *The Great Terror*, 534–35 and Jerry Hough and Merle Fainsod, *How the Soviet Union is Governed* (Cambridge: Harvard University Press, 1979), 176–77.

Table 8.6. *Age structure of the 1937 Belyi*
expellees compared to the raion party
organization as a whole (as of 5/17/37)

Age group	Expellees	Raion party organization members
25–29	2 (5.9%)	46 (19.6%)
30–39	22 (64.7%)	144 (60.3%)
Over 40	10 (29.4%)	49 (20.5%)

Note: Age data was not available for two of the thirty-six expellees, raikom secretaries Kovalev and Karpovskii.
Sources: WKP 321, pp. 63, 139–140, 158–162, 175–176, 189, 192, 194–198, 220–222, 228–229, 232, 238–250, 252–256, 258–260, 272–276, 291, 298–300 and WKP 111, pp. 92–114, 193–206.

Table 8.7. *Educational level of the 1937 Belyi*
expellees compared to the raion party
organization as a whole (as of 5/17/37)

Educational level (maximum attained)	Expellees	Raion party organization members
Primary or less	15 (71.4%)	222 (92.8%)
Secondary	6 (28.6%)	17 (7.1%)
Higher	0 (0%)	0 (0%)

Note: The education of fifteen of the thirty-six expellees was not recorded in their party records.
Sources: WKP 321, pp. 63, 139–140, 158–162, 175–176, 189, 192, 194–198, 220–222, 228–229, 232, 238–250, 252–256, 258–260, 272–276, 291, 298–300 and WKP 111, pp. 92–114, 193–206.

Table 8.7 illustrates. Among the expellees could be found all five of the members of the raion party organization with over six years of formal schooling.[61]

---

[61] WKP 385: 296. The exceedingly low educational levels of Belyi officials are typical of Soviet rural raions in the 1930s and immediately after World War II. For this, see *Ocherki istorii Smolenskoi organizatsii KPSS* (Moscow: Moskovskii rabochii, 1985), I, 205; D. I. Budaev (ed.), *Sotsial'no-ekonomicheskoe razitie Rossii i zarubezhnykh stran* (Smolensk: Smolenskii pedagogicheskii institut, 1974), 85; T. H. Rigby, *Communist Party Membership in the USSR, 1917–1967* (Princeton: Princeton University Press, 1968), 401–7.

Table 8.8. *Date when the 1937 Belyi expellees joined the Communist
party compared to the raion party organization as a whole (as of 5/17/37)*

When party was joined	Expellees	Raion party organization
1904–1917	1 (2.8%)	6 (2.5%)
1918–1922	8 (22.2%)	21 (8.8%)
1923–1927	9 (25%)	45 (18.8%)
1928–1933	18 (50%)	164 (68.6%)
1936	0 (0%)	3 (1.3%)
Total	36 (100%)	239 (100%)

Sources: WKP 321, pp. 63, 139–140, 158–162, 175–176, 189, 192, 194–198,
220–222, 228–229, 232, 238–250, 252–256, 258–260, 272–276, 291,
298–300 and WKP 111, pp. 92–114, 193–206.

Contrary to popular belief, Old Bolsheviks of prerevolutionary vintage
did not appear to be the main target of the Great Purges, at least insofar as
Belyi Raion was concerned, as Table 8.8 indicates. Old Bolsheviks in Belyi
were no more prominently represented among the expellees than among
the party organization at large. Local party members who joined during
the New Economic Policy (NEP) of 1921–7 were more likely to have been
expelled in 1937 than those who joined the party during the Stalin
Revolution (1928–33), as one might expect. But the brunt of the purges
fell most heavily on Communists who joined the party during the Civil
War, as Nikita Khrushchev pointed out in his "secret speech" to the
Twentieth Party Congress of the Communist Party of the Soviet Union
(CPSU) on the persecutions of the Stalin era.[62]
The prominence of the Civil War generation among those expelled from
the party and arrested at the time of the Great Purges was in part a
consequence of the many high positions held by this generation of
Communists. The Civil War generation tended to outnumber by far the
Old Bolsheviks among the party membership and to dominate raion-level
positions, which often were reserved only for persons with at least ten
years of party membership.[63] Raion-level officials enjoyed a number of
advantages over lesser Communists and the population at large, like consumer
goods in short supply and better housing, if only through semilegal "self-
supply" or under-the-counter treatment allotted them informally by local
trade and housing officials. Although such advantages were often surpris-

[62] Nikita Sergeyevich Khrushchev, *The Secret Speech* (Nottingham, Eng.: Spokesman Books,
1976), 26.
[63] Moshe Lewin, *The Making of the Soviet System: Essays on the Social History of Interwar
Russia* (New York: Pantheon, 1985), 23–24 and Rigby, 68–69, 78, 83.

ingly modest by foreign standards,[64] such perquisites were deeply resented by rank-and-file Communists.[65] Especially resented was the fact that rare shipments of new goods to the raion were offered first to the wives of three important officals – NKVD chief Vinogradov, chairman of the raion soviet executive committee Stogov, and assistant chairman of the raion soviet executive committee Vasiunin, whose wife was said to be raikom secretary Kovalev's mistress.[66] These "privileges" were no doubt particularly resented by rank-and-file Communists in 1937, given the strained food supplies that prevailed in the first half of the year in the wake of the previous years' crop failure.[67]

Belyi materials strongly suggest, however, that animosity against the Civil War generation was also engendered by the militarylike leadership style of many of these Communists, rooted in their wartime experiences. Long time Belyi raikom secretary Kovalev, who appears to have been genuinely hated for his abusive treatment of his subordinates, provides an extreme example of such "civil war" methods of government. Kovalev governed Belyi like the former noncommissioned officer he once was by giving and following orders. He expected orders to be carried out as at the front in wartime, without discussion, criticism, or questioning of either his own initiatives or directives from above.[68] This was true even in the case of erroneous orders, like sowing plans based on inaccurate estimates of the amount of arable land in the raion that completely disrupted efforts at crop rotation and contributed to the 1936 crop failure.[69] When policies failed, Kovalev responded by berating officials like a drill sergeant, showering them with threats and calling them derogatory names, like "sheep," "oxen," "mice," "blockheads," "addlepates," "windbags," and "beachbums," not to mention more off-colored terms not listed in the party minutes. Communists were said to "shoot out of his office like bullets," under the weight of his caustic tongue. Many dreaded their encounters with him, for he was known on occasion to arrest low-level party members on charges

---

[64] For a discussion of the impoverished living conditions of many rank-and-file Communists as well as the raion leadership, see Manning, "Government in the Soviet Countryside in the Stalinist Thirties," 19–22.

[65] For such sentiments, see WKP 111: 28, 32, 36, 39, 44, 47–49, 63, 105, 109, 165, 169, 188–89, 196.

[66] Ibid., 14, 39, 52, 79, 101–2, 162, 167, 175. Vasiunin was removed from office and left the raion in disgrace after Kovalev's fall from power.

[67] For this, see Chapter 5 in this volume.

[68] For a devastating portrait of such methods of government outside of Belyi, see the evolution of the character Misha Koshevoi in books six and seven of the second volume of Mikhail Sholokhov's *The Quiet Don*, which was published at the time of the Great Purges. Mikhail Sholokov, *The Don Flows Home to the Sea* (New York: Vintage, 1960), 517–688 and D. H. Stewart, *Mikhail Sholokhov: A Critical Investigation* (Ann Arbor: University of Michigan, 1967), 98–103, 179–83.

[69] For the disruption of crop rotation, which was a national, not purely local problem, see WKP 111: 19–20, 40, 44, 81, 83, 94, 152, 159–60, 165, 170, 194 and WKP 321: 93, 165–66.

of embezzlement and wrecking even though he possessed no legal power to make arrests.[70]

Complaints against Kovalev therefore mounted, especially in the fall of 1936, after he forced his subordinates to falsify flax harvest statistics by threatening otherwise to take away their party cards. His standing with his superiors in the oblast party leadership, however, remained strong, even after Kovalev was removed from office by a rank-and-file insurgency against his leadership at the March 1937 raion party conference, for Kovalev was immediately appointed to an influential position in the oblast party administration. The continued support given Kovalev by oblast leaders, especially Western obkom secretary I. P. Rumantsev, stemmed from Kovalev's ability to publicize the exploits of his raion. Rarely did a week pass in 1936 without a major article in a national or oblast press organ about the accomplishments of Belyi Raion's limited stock of Stakhanovites.[71] Of course, Belyi's high reputation as a leading flax producer often rested on fraudulent or misleading claims that merely rendered Kovalev's subordinates ever more dissatisfied with his leadership, since lower-level Belyi officials were fearful that the truth would inevitably come to light, given the raion's growing renown.

Such fears finally prompted Kovalev's subordinates to leave the raion or to complain of these practices to the All-Union Party Control Commission. One such complaint – that of V. N. Antipov, senior surveyor in the raion land department, who maintained that Kovalev had coerced him to falsify harvest statistics – attracted the attention of Lenin's sister, Mariia Ulianova, who served as a deputy chairman of the control agency. Ulianova immediately dispatched a series of letters to Kovalev's superiors in the Western obkom, who ignored her inquiries, possibly because Kovalev had falsified harvest results at the behest of oblast leaders, desperate for some success to show the center admist the 1936 crop failure.[72]

Finally the Party Control Commission sent an emissary, Golovashchenko, to Belyi to investigate matters by organizing a discussion of Kovalev's leadership methods, first in the raikom bureau on March 15 and then at the raion party conference of March 19–22, 1937, the first of a series of raion party meetings sanctioned by the February–March 1937 Central Committee Plenum as a means to "democratize" the operations of the party in connection with the introduction of the new Stalin Constitution, widely proclaimed by Soviet leaders to be "the world's most democratic." Golovashchenko carried out his task by seeking out Kovalev's local critics

[70] See WKP 111: 1–79 and *Rabochii put* (Smolensk), April 4, 1937.
[71] See, for example, *Krest'ianskaia gazeta*, Mar. 14, 1936; *Vlast sovetov*, no. 9 (May 15, 1936); *Rabochii put* (Smolensk), Jan. 25, 1936, Jan. 27, 1936, Feb. 15, 1936, April 2, 1936, April 4, 1936, April 10, 1936, April 16, 1936, April .17, 1936, May 20, 1936, May 22, 1936, May 28, 1936, etc.
[72] For evidence that the obkom tried to ignore complaints against Kovalev, including Antipov's, see WKP 355: 248; WKP 538: 423; and WKP 239: 152.

and persuading the most bold and articulate of them – former raion *kul'tprop* Martynov – to launch an attack on Kovalev at the raion party meeting. Martynov did this with relish and the resulting "frank" and "freewheeling" debate resulted in Kovalev's ouster as party secretary, even before the new party elections scheduled for April. Obkom representatives at the meeting intervened only to defend Kovalev from charges of Trotskyism, raised by Martynov.[73]

Although local grievances against leaders like Kovalev fueled the Great Purges in the raion, outside developments greatly influenced the timing of these events, as we can see from Table 8.9, which outlines month by month the expulsions from the Belyi Raion party organization in 1937. The expulsions began after the ouster of long-time raikom secretary Kovalev in March, escalated sharply with the arrest of the military high command and the fall of the oblast leadership in June, and peaked in September as a mass campaign to arrest "anti-Soviet" elements sanctioned by the Politburo in July got underway locally. The terror in Belyi tapered off thereafter as the raion's top leaders were replaced. The interplay of three key, unrelated developments appears to account for this pattern of expulsions. These developments were the (1) party's democracy campaign launched in the wake of the introduction of the Stalin Constitution, (2) the 1936 crop failure, and (3) the decisions taken at the center, possibly by Stalin personally, to settle political accounts with the old party opposition, military leaders, individuals arrested earlier who had served out their prison terms, and oblast political machines, including that of long-time Western obkom secretary I. P. Rumantsev.[74]

The democracy campaign, which began at the end of 1936 with the adoption of the new Stalin constitution, took on new relevancy for the party after the February–March 1937 Central Committee Plenum called for periodic party conferences in the raions and oblasts and introduced secret ballot elections with multiple candidates for party secretaries and party organizers.[75] Periodic raion party conferences, which occurred four times in 1937, provided Belyi party members with the opportunity to oust raikom secretary Kovalev even before the general party elections scheduled for April 1937 and to launch attacks on other local officials and the All-Union Commissariat of Agriculture. Belyi, however, was the only Smolensk raion (out of ninety-one at the time) that replaced its raikom secretary before the April party elections. Two other Smolensk area raions managed to replace their secretaries in the April elections, before the fall of the oblast party leadership. Elsewhere the Rumantsev machine held firm.[76]

[73] For these developments, see WKP 111: 3–67, 108, 173–74.
[74] Getty, *The Origins of the Great Purges*, 119–36, and 163–71 and *Trud*, June 4, 1992, p. 1.
[75] *Pravda*, Mar. 11, 1937.
[76] WKP 111: 1–124. *Partiets* (Smolensk), 1937, no. 4, pp. 19–25 and *Rabochii put* (Smolensk), May 18, 1937.

Table 8.9. *Timing of the expulsions from the Belyi Raion party organization (1/1/37 to 1/5/38)*

Year/month	Number of expulsions
1937 January	0
February	0
March	0
April	1
May	0
June	3[a]
July	3
August	5
September 1–20[b]	14
October 21–31[b]	3
November	4
December	3
1938 January 1–5	1
Total	37

[a] Includes former raikom secretary Kovalev who was expelled by the obkom sometime between the fall of the oblast leadership June 19–21, 1937, and July, 2, 1937, when he turned up as a brigade leader on the Shooting Star Collective Farm in Belyi Raion but was not listed as a member of the farm ppo.
[b] No raion-level party bodies met between September 20 and October 21.
Sources: WKP 321, pp. 63, 139–140, 158–162, 175–176, 189, 192, 194–198, 220–222, 228–229, 232, 238–250, 252–256, 258–260, 272–276, 291, 298–300 and WKP 111, pp. 92–114, 193–206.

On occasion the party conferences in Belyi sanctioned the expulsion of party leaders, like NKVD chief Vinogradov, when party executive organs, like the raikom and raikom bureau, refused to do so.[77] The extension of secret ballot elections to party organizers, which was somehow delayed in Belyi until August, resulted in the complete turnover of these officials who had hitherto been appointed by the raikom secretary.[78] Since party organizers had the power to call and set the agenda of ppo meetings, elections of these officials by the ppo's undermined the raion leadership's control of the workplace ppo's, setting the scene for the expulsion of almost all remaining "bosses" and raion leaders.[79]

The 1936 crop failure also contributed to the persecution of local elites.

[77] WKP 111: 105–14.
[78] Ibid., 150 and WKP 321: 226, 239.
[79] WKP 111: 7–8, 15, 17–18, 30, 39, 48–49, 56.

It is no accident that political shakeups in the localities began in earnest in June, as short food supplies caused by the crop failure reached their zenith on the eve of the new harvest.[80] As food and fodder supplies grew more strained in the first half of 1937, existing grievances among rank-and-file Communists of elite living standards grew more acute and a search was launched for scapegoats, at both the national and local levels. Policymakers and administrators responsible for bad agricultural policies that seemingly contributed to the crop failure, like the disruption of crop rotation and inability of the MTSs to keep their tractors in working order and operate within their budgets, began to be charged with the "wrecking of agriculture," a charge leveled against leaders of the Western Oblast, when they fell from power at the end of June.[81] Interestingly enough, such charges were first raised by party members in Belyi against oblast and national agricultural administrators as early as the March 1937 party conference, long before such accusations were reiterated at the national level at the June 1937 Central Committee Plenum devoted to agriculture.[82]

The depletion of food reserves in town and countryside alike contributed to the reluctance of local collective farmers to turn in procurements in the wake of a second bad harvest in a row throughout the non-black-soil region.[83] Fearing famine in the towns and cities and under pressure from higher authorities to replenish exhausted food reserves, desperate oblast officials joined in local attacks on raion leaders, especially the judiciary, the raion land department, and the raion soviet executive committee, which played important roles in the collection of procurements, thereby contributing to the peaking of the local terror in September 1937.[84]

National decisions to prosecute the party opposition, military high command, and oblast leaders as agents of German and Japanese intelligence services, who sought to undermine the Soviet economy and defense potential, created a political climate in which lesser leaders lost authority and their good intentions were increasingly doubted. The major show trials of the Old Bolsheviks seem to have had less of an impact on Belyi Raion than

---

[80] Belyi received the last of a series of substantial food loans for needy collective farmers from the government on May 28, 1937. The town of Belyi, however, received no government food aid in 1937, because local officials failed to deliver 1,000 metric tons of grain collected in procurements in 1936 for shipment to other parts of the country. In June 1937, the town was 2.5 metric tons short of the 500 tons of grain required by the populace, and grain to fill the deficit could not be purchased anywhere. The town's grain supply was also said to be badly adulterated with mud and other filth. WKP 238: 82 and WKP 111: 8, 169.

[81] WKP 111: 152–65, 170–75; *Krest'ianskaia gazeta*, Mar. 22, 1937, April 18, 1937, and July 16, 1937; and *Pravda*, June 29, 1937 and July 15, 1937.

[82] WKP 111: 18, 20, 37–38, 40, 44, 57.

[83] *Bolshevik*, no. 18 (Sept. 15, 1937) p. 10 and *Sotsialiticheskoe zemledelie*, July 24, 1937.

[84] WKP 111: 85, 177–84 and Manning, "Government in the Soviet Countryside," 35–40. Areas that did not fulfill their procurements could not expect to receive food supplies from central stocks.

they did on more urban, industrialized areas.[85] Nevertheless, in early 1937 in the wake of the Kamenev and Zinoviev and Piatakov trials, the senior zootechnician on the Shamilovo sovkhoz, Gaidukevich, was arrested on charges of wrecking, after 799 piglets in his care perished from swine cholera and being wintered over in a barn without a roof under conditions of chronic fodder shortages, caused by the 1936 crop failure. Gaidukevich, who had been expelled from the party in Leningrad for Trotskyism in the late 1920s, was subsequently sentenced to five years in prison.[86] The arrest of the oblast leadership and military high command in June 1937 had a more dramatic, immediate effect on local politics, as Table 8.9 demonstrates, leading rapidly to a strong upsurge in expulsions from the Communist party.

Whereas the fall of the military and oblast leadership influenced developments in Belyi Raion, the accusations made against local Communists differed from those raised against oblast leaders and the military high command, as Table 8.10 indicates. This table outlines in an abbreviated form the formal charges contained in the resolutions passed by raion-level party bodies in expelling party members in 1937. Absent entirely were the implausible accusations of treason, espionage, and links with foreign intelligence services that proliferated at the national and, to a lesser extent, oblast levels of government. The absence of such charges in Belyi does not mean that the raion party organization was not affected by the national spy mania and fears of Fascist infiltration, whipped up by the Soviet press in the late thirties as German and Japanese expansionism got well underway.[87] The mood of suspicion and fear engendered by such journalism accounts for the inclusion of a non-Communist "Polish spy," most likely an immigrant from Poland (or someone of Polish descent), among those arrested in September in the Belyi lumber industry.[88] It also accounts for the reluctance of local party members to come to the defense of raikom secretary Karpovskii once it was known that he was receiving mail from his aunt in Fascist Rumania, although Karpovskii appears to have been personally well regarded among the local party *aktiv*, unlike Kovalev.[89]

Political offenses in general occupied a relatively modest place in the

[85] The obkom bureau review of cases of Communists expelled in the wake of the Kamenev-Zinov'ev trial indicates that they came disproportionately from the more industrialized and urbanized areas of the oblast. WKP 538: 346–555.

[86] WKP 321: 284; WKP 111: 108, 161, 163, 200, 216, 220, 225; WKP 440: 102–5; and WKP 362: 496–506.

[87] For an example of this mania, see Stalin's speech to the February 1937 Central Committee Plenum and the article by A. Uranov in *Pravda*, May 22, 1937. These materials were required reading for all Belyi Communists in the summer of 1937. The Uranov article was also distributed to the raion population at large at the end of August, on the eve of the upsurge in local expulsions from the party. *Pravda*, Mar. 29, 1937; WKP 440: 20, 34, 63, 97, 160; and WKP 321: 225.

[88] WKP 111: 99.

[89] WKP 321: 92–96, 193–205.

Table 8.10. *Grounds on which Belyi party members were expelled in 1937*

Charge	Numbers accused	Percentage accused
Misgovernment (total number accused)	29	80.5
violations of citizens' rights and democratic procedures[a]	21	58.3
violations of government directives and policies set above[b]	18	50
Mismanagement and neglect of official responsibilities	23	63.8
Systematic drunkenness[c]	9	25
Corruption	7	19.4
Bad connections (total number accused)	16	44.4
with enemies of the people[d]	8	22.2
with alien relations	4	11.1
with alien employees	13	36.1
with persons living abroad	1	2.7
Wrecking	5	13.8
Political opposition[e]	5	13.8
Pursued rightist or right-Trotskyist policies[f]	5	13.8
Pursued misguided policies that served the enemy's cause	4	11.1
Politically erroneous views	2	5.5
Alien origins	3	8.3
Violations of party regulations and procedures[g]	11	30.5

Note: The totals here add up to more than thirty-six because a variety of charges were leveled against each person expelled. The majority of the charges raised fit into two categories: misgovernment and mismanagement.

[a] Of these, ten persons were charged with administrative-bureaucratic methods of government; five with rudeness to toilers and subordinates; three with suppression of criticism; three with ignoring toilers' complaints; four with neglecting public services or denying toilers the rights and benefits due them; five with nepotism as part of a "family circle;" four with acts that outraged public opinion (like the failure to prosecute cases of rape and the affair of the false Stakhanovite milkmaid Nekulenkova); four with violations of the law on the eternal use of land; and one with abuse of office.

[b] Of these, ten persons were charged with false reports; eight with laxity in enforcing the law, particularly in the countryside; five with failure to collect procurements; three with failure to fulfill the plan; and three with giving illegal tax advantages to individual peasants.

[c] Five persons thus charged were also accused of committing offenses, like wife beating, attempted rape of collective farm women, "degenerate behavior," "acts discrediting Soviet power," and slander while "under the influence of alcohol."

[d] Said to be Trotskyists or "the former hostile leadership" of the raion or oblast.

[e] Subsequently charges of Trotskyism were dropped against one of these expellees, the "Trotskyist Belov," after the obkom overturned his expulsion on procedural grounds; Belov's ppo refused to accept such charges, insisting that Belov maintained connections with Trotskyists and expressed Trotskyist views but was not himself an active Trotskyist. The raikom bureau responded by expelling Belov once again on these lesser charges that were acceptable to his ppo.

[f] Of these, two persons were specifically charged with pursuing rightist policies and three with right-Trotskyist policies.

[g] Of these, six persons were charged with having deceived the party about their social origins, political past, or activities of their relatives; four were charged with refusal to implement orders of the raikom or to heed past warnings; two left the raion without the permission of the raikom; two were said to be passive; and one failed to pay his party dues for eight months.

Sources: WKP 321, pp. 63, 139–140, 158–162, 175–176, 189, 192, 194–198, 220–222, 228–229, 232, 238–250, 252–256, 258–260, 272–276, 291, 298–300 and WKP 111, pp. 92–114, 193–206.

accusations made against local Communists in 1937, as Table 8.10 indicates, and such charges figured even less in party debates and discussions. Indeed, no political accusations whatsoever were leveled against ten of the thirty-six local party members expelled in 1937.[90] Only one expellee, a newcomer to the raion, was charged with political offenses alone. This man was excluded from the party for "wrecking" and "hostile work" as a recently dismissed soviet executive committee chairman in another raion, presumably as a result of accusations originally raised there.[91]

Although charges of "political opposition" and wrecking were commonplace at higher levels of government, such accusations account for relatively few of the formal charges raised against the Belyi expellees. Yet the term *wrecking* was utilized throughout local party debates as a synonym for mismanagement. Five local Communists, including Kovalev, two high officials in the raion land department, and the director of a local lumber mill, were charged with wrecking in the form of chronic mismanagement and misguided policies that disrupted the functioning of a large part of the raion's economy.[92] Five Communists (13.6%) were accused of political opposition. But such charges covered a range of offenses, from "Trotskyism," "right opposition," and "right Trotskyism" to "Menshevism" and "banditry," a term applied to the activities of both outright criminals and anti-Soviet rebels who continued to function after the end of the Civil War. In all cases, the political opposition referred to had occurred in the past, ten to twenty years earlier.[93] In addition, three local leaders (Stogov, Karpovskii, and Vinogradov) were charged with pursuing "right-Trotskyist policies" and two lesser officials with following "rightist policies."[94] A number of lesser political charges were also made against Belyi Communists, as Table 8.10 indicates, like the pursuit of politically misguided policies that served "the enemy's cause," the expression of politically erroneous views, the possession of "alien" social origins, and violations of party regulations and procedures, like failure to pay party dues or to report one's social origins accurately to the party.

---

[90] Ibid., 63, 175–76, 228, 254–55, 259–60, 300. Many of these cases appear to have been procurements-related cases in which political intervention of higher authorities played a role.

[91] Ibid., 273–74.

[92] Ibid., 189, 252–54, 273–74, 298 and WKP 111: 175. In addition, the director of the October Lumber Industry Association, S. M. Marchenkov, was charged with "wrecking" by his ppo but the raikom bureau reduced this charge to "allowed conscious abuse." WKP 321: 273.

[93] WKP 321: 157–62, 189, 193–205, 272 and WKP 111: 175. However, the obkom subsequently overturned on review the expulsion of the one local Communist who was charged with being a "Trotskyist," A. F. Belov, the director of the local agricultural technicum, on procedural grounds. Belov's ppo was willing to expel him for "connections with Trotskyists" and expressing Trotskyist views but not for being a Trotskyist. The Belyi raikom responded to this impasse by expelling Belov once again on these lesser charges that were acceptable to his ppo. WKP 321: 261.

[94] WKP 111: 204 and WKP 321: 232, 238.

The most common political charge leveled against Belyi Communists in 1937, however, and the only political charge discussed to any extent in local party meetings was the charge of possessing "bad connections," in the form of politically suspect friends, associates, relatives, and subordinates, particularly the latter. Such charges were leveled against 44.4% of the local Communists expelled in 1937. A broad range of social and political categories figured in such accusations in Belyi. In party resolutions, local Communists were variously condemned for association with *pomeshchiki*, priests, merchants of the first guild, kulaks, tsarist or White military officers, old regime policemen and volost elders, the old "hostile" leadership of the oblast, convicted Trotskyists, former Mensheviks or SRs, church psalm readers, civil war deserters, persons disenfranchised under the NEP, and those earlier convicted of embezzlement.

Most of the Communists accused of bad connections were charged with hiring prerevolutionary elites or the offspring thereof in the government or economic institutions that they directed.[95] The frequency of such charges and the passion with which they were discussed in the Belyi Raion party organization in 1937 indicate the strength of the social and political hatreds that spawned the Revolution and continued to influence Soviet politics twenty years later. Such charges also indicate the survival of notions of social class characteristic of the soslovie-based ancien regime, in which social-legal status and political rights were usually passed on from parents to children, unlike a modern industrial society, in which one's own occupation and achievements determines one's social status and all citizens are considered equal before the law.

Accusations of bad connections against party members in positions of authority peaked in the fall of 1937, as the result of a secret Politburo resolution of July 2, 1937, signed by Stalin. This resolution directed the NKVD and local party committees to arrest en masse "former kulaks and criminals exiled at one time,...who returned to their oblasts upon completing their sentences" and who, it was alleged, were "instigators of all sorts of anti-Soviet diversionary crimes, both on collective farms and sovkhozes and in certain areas of industry."[96] Those arrestees deemed "most dangerous" were to be immediately executed. To speed up the processing of large numbers of arrests that surely would result from this decree, *troikas*, administrative boards consisting of three local officials, were established in the raions and oblasts to handle such cases in order to avoid overloading the already overburdened judiciary.

A second Politburo resolution of July 31 established explicit quotas by oblast for both arrests and executions, and localities were admonished not

---

[95] WKP 321: 98–104, 158–63, 193–205, 220–22, 238, 249–50, 252, 257, 261, 272–73, 291–92, 298 and WKP 111: 175.
[96] *Trud*, June 4, 1992, pp. 1, 4.

to exceed these quotas and to leave the families of those arrested alone, save in border areas or in the cases of the "most dangerous" arrestees, that is, those slated for execution.[97] Smolensk Oblast received orders to arrest a total of 7,000 individuals and to execute 1,000 of them. Nationwide, the Politburo sanctioned 270,450 arrests and 60,450 executions, a total of 330,900 victims, excluding any family members affected. The Politburo ordered that this arrest operation should begin on August 5 and run for four months.[98] Consequently, in Belyi Raion it coincided with the 1937 harvest and procurements campaigns and the crescendo of the local terror.

Local NKVD organs selected victims for arrest from "enemy lists," drawn up in mass meetings in workplaces and on collective farms, rather than from lists or orders compiled at higher levels of government.[99] Given such local input into the selection of victims, it is not surprising that the persecutions that resulted from these decrees were by no means confined to the categories targeted by the Politburo – former kulaks and criminals who had served out their sentences. As earlier during collectivization, a broad array of old elites and their offspring as well as persons who had allegedly opposed Soviet power in the past, often dating back to the Civil War, appeared on the enemy lists. Very few of the individuals included on these lists had been arrested or imprisoned earlier, contrary to the Politburo's orders.[100] At mass meetings, convened in workplaces to discuss measures to liquidate the consequences of wrecking in the oblast, individuals were included on the enemy lists on the basis of little more than accusations or hearsay evidence. Two-thirds of the individuals included on such enemy lists in neighboring Sychevka Raion, which bordered on Belyi, were specialists or officials by occupation. Many of them appear to occupy positions with salaries higher than the average accorded ordinary citizens or rank-and-file party members.[101] Perhaps social tensions rooted in the failure of Soviet society to live up to the egalitarian ideals of the Revolution and the strained economic conditions of the times account for the prevalence of such persecutions. Also, although a majority of those included on enemy lists in Sychevka were local people, persons who came from outside the raion appear to have been disproportionately represented, indicating

[97] Ibid.
[98] Ibid.
[99] These conclusions are based on an analysis of the most extensive lists of alien and hostile elements drawn up at this time, which can be found in the Smolensk Archive – those from Sychevka Raion, which bordered on Belyi. Until NKVD archives in the Smolensk region become freely available to scholars, the Sychevka enemy lists must remain our best source for this phase of the terror. WKP 516: 1–79. On these lists, arrests were noted in marginalia, which indicates that the lists antedated the arrests.
[100] Ibid. Previous arrests and convictions were noted on the Sychevka enemy lists.
[101] Ibid. The Sychevka enemy lists noted the occupations of those arrested, which have been compared to the distribution of salaries within the Belyi Raion party organization and the relative wage scales paid to selected groups of officials and specialists at this time. For this, see Manning, "Government in the Soviet Countryside," 18–21.

perhaps that localist resentment of the large numbers of specialists and administrators recruited from outside the raion helped to fuel these persecutions.[102]

In any case, the results far exceeded the original intentions, quotas, and categories of the Politburo. In addition to the arrests and executions sanctioned by the Politburo, hundreds of individuals in the raion lost their jobs or were expelled with their entire families from their collective farms in a two- to three-month period in the fall of 1937. Responsible officials who resisted pressures to dismiss individuals accused of being class aliens en masse from the institutions that they headed were warned by the local party organization to mend their ways or were expelled from the Communist party or even arrested.[103] Consequently, employment opportunities for those who lost their jobs or were expelled from their collective farms remained quite dismal if not nonexistent. Local party leaders who were not content to attribute all that was wrong on the collective farms to kulak machinations, as occurred in neighboring Sychevka Raion, where raion leaders proved most reluctant to implement the Politburo's decrees, were themselves placed on trial as enemies of the people, charged with allowing kulaks to rise to positions of authority in order to wreck livestock production on the collective farms.[104]

As persecutions outran by far the Politburo's original intentions, the January 1938 Central Committee Plenum intervened and ordered an immediate half to the persecution of class aliens, because mass dismissals of officials charged with possessing alien origins had come to impair quite seriously the functioning of local government institutions, particularly the public schools. Local party and Komsomol organizations were ordered to review cases of all those excluded or dismissed from work as class aliens and to restore to their previous positions those persecuted who had not committed other offenses. In the wake of this resolution, officials deemed responsible for such excesses were themselves to be expelled from the party and Komsomol as "overinsurers," and many of their victims were to have their memberships restored.[105] For example, eleven of the thirty-nine party members who were expelled in 1937 in nearby Sychevka had their party membership restored by May 1, 1938.[106] Mass expulsions of families from collective farms in the autumn of 1937 on similar charges was also declared to be illegal, because these expulsions were often undertaken in violation of the collective farm charter by collective farm chairmen acting unilaterally or in meetings without the two-thirds quorum of farm members

[102] WKP 516: 1–79. Those who came from outside the raion were noted on the enemy lists.
[103] WKP 321: 264, 272, 281–2, 285, 297 and WKP 111: 95–102, 105–8, 195–6, 198–200, 205–7, 224–50.
[104] *Rabochii put* (Smolensk), Oct. 16, 1937, p. 1.
[105] *Pravda*, Jan. 19, 1938.
[106] TsDNISO fond 67, op. 1, del 495, p. 3.

required for such decisions.[107] The extent of unsanctioned persecutions
of categories of individuals not mentioned in the Politburo decree,
particularly class aliens and Civil War foes, indicate that the "enemies"
that most troubled many Communists and politically active citizens outside
the party were the traditional foes of the regime and Revolution rather
than Fascist agents and former Party Oppositionists that figured so
prominently in the national show trials and in the statements of central
party leaders.[108]

Political charges of any nature, however, played a relatively minor role
in the reasons why party members were expelled in Belyi Raion in 1937.
Local party members appeared more concerned with matters that affected
them immediately and directly, like mismanagement, misgovernment,
chronic alcoholism, and the corruption of key party members. Such charges
collectively account for the bulk of the accusations made against Communists who were expelled from the Belyi Raion party organization in
1937, dominating the party resolutions sanctioning expulsions and figuring
even more prominently in debates among party members. Of special concern
were specific acts of mismanagement that contributed to the 1936 crop
failure, like faulty planning and land surveying that disrupted the practice
of crop rotation, the inability of the Belyi MTS to keep its accounts in
order and its tractors functioning, and the overly enthusiastic promotion
of flax growing, a labor-intensive crop that exhausts the soil and occupied
land earlier cultivated in much-needed grain and fodder crops.[109] These
deficiencies persisted throughout 1937 and no doubt figured in the second
bad harvest in a row that occurred in the non-black-soil region amid the
bumper harvest of 1937.

Most of the accusations of mismanagement made against Belyi officials
can be verified by other source materials as valid or quite likely. Official
malingering or simple incompetence on the part of officials, most of whom
lacked the education that their posts would seem to require, contributed
substantially to the raion's problems. Yet many incidents of mismanagement
also seemed rooted in erroneous, contradictory, or uncoordinated national
policies, which may explain the greater incidence of political persecutions
at higher levels of government. At fault, too, were circumstances outside

[107] This was the result of a Council of Peoples Commissars/Central Committee resolution
signed by Stalin and Molotov. *Krestianskaia gazeta*, April 20, 1938, p. 1 and
Sotsialisticheskoe zemledelie, April 20, 1938, p. 1. This resolution was preceded by a
report made by the Smolensk Oblast land department on December 4, 1937, that
complained about excessive illegal expulsions of peasants from local collective farms and
indicated that efforts were already being made to stem the tide of these expulsions. For
this, see TsDNISO (PASO) fond 6, op. 1, del 39, pp. 41–135.
[108] For the latter, see the speeches of Stalin and Molotov to the February–March 1937
Central Committee Plenum. *Pravda*, Mar. 29, 1937, April 1, 1937, April 21, 1937.
[109] For this, see WKP 111: 6, 11–13, 18, 21, 25, 40, 44, 50, 53, 57, 72, 75, 77, 83, 94,
159–60, 170, 178, 194–99 and WKP 321: 93, 163–67, 196, 253–54, 265, 281–83,
301.

the control of many accused officials – like unusually bad weather and national shortages of fuel and spare parts for the nation's growing tractor fleet – and the refusal of many collective farms to make their natural payments to the MTSs, which inhibited the purchases of fuel and spare parts by the MTSs when these were available.[110]

In addition to mismanagement, local Belyi party members, judging from their debates and resolutions, were equally concerned with bureaucratic and nondemocratic methods of government: violations of democratic procedures, Soviet laws, and citizens' rights; the suppression of criticism; neglect of citizens' complaints and social services; and the habitual rudeness of many officials toward citizens and toilers as well as their subordinates within the bureaucracy. Such methods of government had long inhibited the revelation of the disastrous economic practices of many raion institutions and delayed necessary changes in national policies, like the correction of faulty land balance statistics, on which faulty agricultural planning rested.[111] Violations of government directives and policies set from above also figured in the charges leveled against the Belyi expellees in local party debates and resolutions, although such charges were less common than charges of violations of citizens' rights and democratic procedures.

Violations of national policies and accounting procedures contributed to the raion's economic troubles and the "bad mood" on local collective farms frequently mentioned in party debates.[112] This was particularly true of the widespread, chronic falsification of reports, production records, and statistics by Kovalev and his closest political associates and their tendency to favor individual peasants over collective farmers in the collection of taxes and procurements. To be sure, they only did so because it was easier to collect such payments from collective farms than from individual peasants, who generally lived isolated, on widely scattered khutora, amid the raion's many impenetrable forests and bogs.[113]

The charges made against Belyi Communists upon their expulsion from the party in 1937 would indicate that the Great Purges were caused at

---

[110] For this, see *Pravda*, Mar. 15, 1937; *Kollektivizatsiia sel'skogo khoziaistva v zapadnom raione RSFSR (1927–1937 g.g.)* (Smolensk: Tipografiia im. Smirnova Smolenskogo oblupravleniie po pechati, 1968), 626; WKP 111: 152, 194, 208, 213–14. For press reports indicating that the MTS fuel and spare parts problems were not confined to Belyi, see *Krest'ianskaia gazeta*, April 28, 1936, May 6, 1936, May 12, 1936, May 14, 1936, June 10, 1936, June 30, 1936, July 4, 1936, July 16, 1936, July 30, 1936, Sept. 24, 1936, Oct. 14, 1936, July 20, 1937, July 24, 1937, July 26, 1937, July 30, 1937, and Sept. 28, 1937. Such shortages were perceived as shortages in 1936, but in 1937, after the 1936 crop failure, such shortages were perceived as wrecking on the part of MTS directors and specialists.

[111] WKP 111: 1–79, 128, 198 and WKP 321: 89–96, 125, 155, 159, 166, 170, 195, 254, 259, 282–83.

[112] For this, see WKP 111: 23, 27, 153–54, 169, 175 and WKP 321: 97.

[113] For the falsification of statistics, see WKP 111: 13–14, 26–28, 47, 55, 57, 98, 107–8, 153–54, 165, 171, 187–88 and WKP 321: 93, 195, 204–5, 228. For the favoring of individual peasants, see WKP 111: 106–8 and WKP 321: 195–96, 231.

least in part by premature efforts to allow more citizen involvement in the
Soviet political system, clean up official corruption, combat alcoholism,
encourage citizen complaints against bad government, and improve the
operation of the Soviet economy. The goals of these efforts do not seem all
that dissimilar from some of the very early stages of *perestroika*. Moreover,
perestroika was a common political slogan in 1936 and 1937,[114] and
democratization remained an official goal of the Stalinist regime until the
fall of 1937, when plans to hold contested elections to the new Supreme
Soviet were suddenly abandoned without any explanation,[115] resulting in
one-candidate elections for the next fifty-two years.

   In the late 1930s, reformist efforts gave way to terror under the impact
of the desperate conditions of the times. Political, social, and economic
tensions, aggravated by the onset of German expansionism, the sudden
escalation of ongoing border conflicts with the Japanese in Manchuria,[116]
the 1936 crop failure, and national decisions to prosecute former members
of defunct opposition movements within the Communist Party as traitors
created a tense political climate. Under these conditions, the politically
active at all levels of the Soviet government came to regard abuses uncovered
through reform efforts, like alcoholism, corruption, incompetency, and
mismanagement, in a sinister light as manifestations of suspected foreign
and domestic enemies or at the very least as acts that furthered "the
enemy's cause."[117] Such attitudes explain but do not justify the exceedingly

---

[114] See, for example, the use of the term *perestroika* in Zhdanov's speech to the
February–March 1937 Central Committee Plenum, in the title of the resolution adopted
by this plenum as a result of Zhdanov's report, in a discussion of political developments
in 1936–7 in a recently published local history of the Smolensk Oblast party organization,
and in the titles of numerous articles published in the journal *Sovetskoe stroitel'stvo*
between July 1936 and August 1937. *Pravda*, Mar. 6, 1937; and *Ocherki istorii
Smolenskoi organizatsii KPSS* (Moscow: Moskovskii rabochii, 1985), I, 202–3; S.
Vlasenko, "O perestroike raboty organov kommunal'nogo khoziaistva," *Sovetskoe
stroitel'stvo*, no. 7 (120) (July 1936), 69–76; Ia. Zakharin, "O perestroike raboty
sovetov i ispolkomov (Chuvashchaia ASSR)," ibid., 77–78; I. Mironov, "O perestroike
raboty sovetov," ibid., no. 8 (121) (Aug. 1936), 67–73; A. Luzhin, "O perestroike
raboty sovetov," ibid., no. 5 (May 1937), 38–45; A. Ianovskii, "Perestroike raboty
gorsovetov po kommunal'nomu khoziaistvu," ibid., no. 6 (June 1937), 39–44; I. Mironov,
"Perestroika raboty sovetov Udmurtskoi ASSR," ibid., 52–57; A. S-n, "Perestroika
organizatsionnoi i massovoi raboty sovetov," ibid., 72–79; and G. Vainshtein, "O
perestroike raboty finorganov," ibid., nos. 7–8 (Jul.–Aug. 1937), 87–93. In addition,
several issues of *Sovetskoe stroitel'stvo* (no. 5, May 1937; no. 6, June 1937; and nos.
7–8, Jul.–Aug. 1937) carried sections entitled "*perestroika raboty sovetov*" and
"*perestroika raboty gosapparata*," each containing several articles about various reforms
underway in the operation of local soviets and organs of government, including closer
attention to citizens' complaints, to bring these institutions in line with the new 1936
Constitution.
[115] Getty, 180–82.
[116] J. Dallin, *Soviet Russia and the Far East* (New Haven: Yale University Press, 1948),
22–43.
[117] A good example of such changes in attitudes is the attitude toward the lack of crop
rotation on 80% of the nation's collective farms. This situation was mentioned in passing
as a problem in early 1936 by high officials, like Iakov Iakovlev, the head of the Central

harsh fate accorded many suspected offenders. When viewed from localities like Belyi, the Great Purges appear to be a far more complicated set of events than earlier scholarship and belles lettres alike would have us believe, marked by considerable input from below as well as intervention from above.

Committee Agriculture Department, but it came to be regarded quite differently, as a manifestation of "wrecking in agriculture" after the 1936 crop failure. See *Krest'ianskaia gazeta*, Feb. 4, 1936, Mar. 10, 1937, June 28, 1937, July 8, 1937, and July 28, 1937. Another example is the changed attitude toward fuel and spare parts shortages on the MTSs discussed in footnote 99 above.

9

The Red Army and the Great Purges

Roger R. Reese

To date the study of the purge of the Red Army officer corps from 1937–9 has focused exclusively on the terror of the *Ezhovshchina*, that is, the arrest and execution of officers by the secret police of the People's Commissariat of Internal Affairs (NKVD) headed by Nikolai Ezhov for whom the period is named. Several articles and documents on the Red Army purge published in *Voenno-istoricheskii zhurnal* and *Izvestiia TsK KPSS* in 1989 and 1990 have revealed that the terror was only one of two extraordinary processes that eliminated officers from the army in those years. The other, heretofore unrecognized, was expelling officers from the army and discharging them from the Communist party for associations with enemies of the people and, in 1938, for associations with foreigners, which did not necessarily result in death or imprisonment. Thousands of officers were expelled from the party as the result of independent actions by primary party organizations, and subsequently discharged from the army in an orgy of denunciations at the local level out of Moscow's control. As these two processes became interrelated, confusion added to fear and magnified the effect of the terror. Simultaneously, thousands of officers were reinstated and tens of thousands new officers commissioned, more than making up for the purged officers numerically, but not in experience, and making it extremely difficult to assess the impact of the *Ezhovshchina* on military cadres. This new information suggests a need to reexamine our understanding of the purge of the Red Army, because before the publishing of the aforementioned materials and documents, it was assumed that all officers removed from the armed forces in the years 1937–9 had been arrested and either executed or imprisoned by the NKVD. Table 9.1 from a report by E. A. Shchadenko, Chief of the Commanding Personnel section of the People's Commissariat of Defense, however, shows that a minority of army officers and political leaders were removed from the army by arrest, and the majority were discharged from the army through expulsion from the party.

Table 9.1 shows, first of all, how the process of cleaning the army of "enemies of the people" actually was part of an informal party membership purge or *chistka*. Some officers were arrested and some just expelled from the party and discharged from the army. The NKVD, which arrested officers for being enemies of the people, was indirectly involved in the membership purge of the party, but played a wider role in terrorizing Soviet society and the party purge was a component of that, but not one that the NKVD controlled or orchestrated.

What the table does not tell, however, is the subsequent fate of those men expelled from the party and discharged from the army and not later reinstated. In the civilian sector expulsion from the party was often the prelude to arrest, and we can assume the same for the armed forces. Table 9.1 only shows why an individual was removed from the army. Once out of the army, unless rehabilitated, their fates are unknown. Therefore, the table allows us to assess the number of leaders eliminated from the army between 1937 and May 1940 for political reasons, but not to determine simply how many men were arrested in the *Ezhovshchina*. All told, 34,301 army, air force, and Political Administration of the Red Army (PUR) leaders were discharged from the army either through arrest or expulsion from the party during the *Ezhovshchina*. Of these, 11,596 were reinstated by May 1940. This leaves the fate of 22,705 men unknown. These men could have faced a variety of ends after their discharge. Those discharged because of arrest could have remained in the Gulag under arrest, or later been freed but not reinstated to the army, or even been shot; those expelled and not rehabilitated may later have been arrested and sent to the Gulag or possibly executed. The most extreme possibilities would be for all to have been shot or for all to have been set free to go home. Neither extreme is likely. If the NKVD was out to arrest someone, it does not seem plausible that just because people had been discharged from the army and party they would not be arrested; quite the opposite would seem to apply. We know those discharged were not all killed because officers continued to be released and rehabilitated after May 1940.

The numbers also show a more limited impact on the military than previously thought. Before the publication of the figures in Table 9.1, it had been variously estimated that between 25% and 50% of the Red Army officer corps was repressed in the *Ezhovshchina*. Conveniently, Shchadenko's office gave the percentage of the leadership permanently discharged in the purge, which allows a calculation of the total strength of the *nachal'sostav* in the purge years. In 1937, the *nachal'sostav* numbered 144,300, of whom 11,034 discharged for political reasons remained discharged as of May 1940, equalling 7.7% of the *nachal'sostav*. In 1938 there were 179,000 leaders, of whom 6,742 political dischargees were still discharged in May 1940, which equalled 3.7% of the *nachal'sostav*; and in 1939 the army had 282,300 leaders, 205 or 0.08% of whom were dis-

Table 9.1. *Cleaning out the army and reconsidering discharges, 1937–1939 (excluding the air force)*

Reason for discharge	Discharged in 1937	Reinstated in 1938–9	Remained discharged	Discharged in 1938	Reinstated in 1939	Remained discharged	Discharged in 1939	Reinstated by 5/1/40	Remained discharged
Arrested (by NKVD)	4,474	206	4,268	5,032	1,225	3,807	73	26	47
Discharged (expelled from the KPSS for associations with conspirators)	11,104	4,338	6,766	3,580	2,864	716	284	126	158
Discharged for political-moral reasons (drunkenness, moral depravity)	1,139	109	1,030	2,671	321	2,350	238	23	215
Discharged by directive of NKO of 24 June 1938 for associations with Poles, Germans, Latvians, Lithuanians, Finns, Estonians, Koreans, and others				4,138	1,919	2,219			
Dropped from the rolls due to death or medical discharge	1,941	8	1,933	941	4	937	1,283	9	1,274
Total	18,658	4,661	13,997	16,362	6,333	10,029	1,878	184	1,694
Percent of *nachal'sostav*	13.1	—	9.7	9.2	—	5.6	0.7	—	0.6

Note: Nachal'sostav is the term that defines the military leadership and includes officers and political leaders.
Source: "O rabote za 1939 god: Iz otcheta nachal'nika Upravleniia po nachal'stvuiushchemu sostavu RKKA Narkomata Oborony SSSR, E. A. Shchadenko, 5 Maia 1940," *Izvestiia TsK KPSS,* vol. 2, no. 1 (1990), 188.

charged for political reasons and remained discharged in May 1940. Because the army stepped up officer procurement during the *Ezhovshchina*, and at a rate that outpaced discharges, it is extremely difficult to invent a statistic to describe the cumulative impact of the purge on the military, and Shchadenko's annual figures are probably the most definitive we will ever have. We face the same situation with the Red Air Force, which in 1937 had approximately 13,000 officers, lost 4,724 in the purge, but had about 60,000 officers in 1940.[1]

The reason for the earlier high estimates of the percentage of repressed officers and PUR men by Western historians was not so much the erroneous estimates of the number of repressed officers, but tremendously low estimates of the size of the *nachal'sostav*. John Erickson and Robert Conquest estimated the officer corps to number 80,000 and 70,000 respectively, so whereas Erickson's estimates of between 20,000 and 30,000 men discharged is very near the mark, his estimate of the impact is very far off, as is Conquest's estimate of 35,000 arrested officers out of a corps of 70,000. His estimate of a minimum of 20,000 arrested PUR men is 300% off.[2] Both of these historians considered the majority of victims of the *Ezhovshchina* to have been arrested, not expelled and discharged, and did not realize how quickly and in what large numbers men were rehabilitated.

The following descriptions of party membership purges and comparison of previous *chistki* in the military and civilian sectors makes clearer how the events of 1937–9 were abnormal. On orders from Moscow, the Communist Party purged itself frequently between 1921 and 1939. Some *chistki* were conducted on a unionwide basis, others were restricted to selected areas, all were to rid the party of self-serving opportunists, people from social classes ineligible for party membership, the politically unreliable, those of bad moral character, and even those incompetent at their posts. The *chistki* were supposed to strengthen the party and make it a more efficient tool of the center.

Civilian *chistki* were not always conducted according to a uniform pattern. Victor Kravchenko described a *chistka* at his technical institute in 1933, which was a public affair:

In the presence of a large audience the party member to be examined stood before the *chistka* verification committee, which was armed with information supplied by the primary party organization; handed over his party card; and then recited his political life history. The commission gave back the party cards to those who passed the subsequent examination of their social origins and past political behavior.

---

[1] F. B. Komal, "Voennye Kadry Nakanune Voiny," *Voenno-istoricheskii zhurnal*, no. 2 (1990), 21; "O Nakoplenii Nachal'stvuiushchego sostava i popolnenii im Raboche-Krest'ianskoi Krasnoi Armii 20 Marta 1940 g." *Izvestiia TsK KPSS*, vol. 2, no. 1 (1990), 178–180.

[2] Robert Conquest, *The Great Terror* (New York: Macmillan, 1968), 228, 485; John Erickson, *The Soviet High Command* (New York: St. Martin's Press, 1962), 449, 451–452.

People suspected of being in political trouble were often taunted by members of the audience who urged the commission to expel them. Those who failed the test were expelled from the party on the spot.[3]

According to Roberta Manning the *chistka* procedure in rural Belyi Raion was more methodical in 1937. The primary party organizations recommended their own members for dismissal from the party. These recommendations were forwarded to the raion party organization, which then decided whether or not to expel the party members in question.[4]

Civilians in managerial positions who were expelled from the party often lost their jobs and students in higher education were expelled from their school, because it usually took party credentials to attain a managerial position or to enter higher education from the period of the First Five-Year Plan and afterwards. The trauma of the ordeal could be so great and the consequences so severe that those purged sometimes committed suicide.[5]

Chistki procedures in the Red Army were actually not very different from those in civilian party organs. On orders from the People's Commissariat of Defense (NKO) and the PUR, military district headquarters formed verification commissions composed of men from outside the unit being examined. Prior to its arrival, regimental party bureaus prepared by having party cells (the military's primary party organization) in the battalions engage in self-criticism (*samokritika*) to identify the unfit, thus facilitating the commissions' work. At *samokritika* sessions company-level political leaders (*politruki*) encouraged the men to express opinions not of their own, but of other party members' behavior, which the *politruki* dutifully recorded for future use.[6] Arriving at the regiment, the commission met with the party bureau composed of the regimental party secretary, his assistants, and the regimental commissar, and read the results of the self-criticism sessions. Then, sitting behind a table, they called individuals to be examined into a private room one at a time. The person being examined usually stood alone opposite them and recited his story, then the commission asked him questions and delivered a verdict on his membership in the party, sometimes immediately, but often after short deliberations.[7] The army's *chistki* seem, then, to have been well organized and private, which

---

[3] Victor Kravchenko, *I Chose Freedom* (New York: Charles Scribner's Sons, 1946), 134.

[4] Roberta T. Manning, "The Great Purges in a Rural District: Belyi Raion Revisited," *Russian History*, vol. 16, nos. 2–4 (1989), 410, 411.

[5] Kravchenko, 134; Roberta T. Manning, "Government in the Soviet Countryside in the Stalinist Thirties: The Case of the Belyi Raion in 1937," *The Carl Beck Papers in Russian and East European Studies* (Pittsburgh: Russian and East European Studies, University of Pittsburgh, 1984), no. 301, 16; Manning, "The Great Purges in a Rural District," 411.

[6] Boris I. Balinskii, *Memoir*, unpublished manuscript, Record Series 15/35/57, University of Illinois Archives.

[7] *Krasnaia zvezda*, 6 Sept. 1929, 17 Oct. 1933, 17 May 1934; Nikolai G. Liashchenko, *Gody v shineli* (Frunze: Kyrgyzstan, 1974), 144–145.

helped maintain discipline in the unit and the authority of the officers during the proceedings.

The most significant difference between civilian and military party purges until mid-1937, was that soldiers and officers expelled from the party were not ousted from the military. Because there were no party membership requirements in the army for enlisted men or officers, there was no reason to discharge men from the army for no longer being in the party. Yet expulsion from the party could hold some serious consequences for officers as promotions to the higher levels of the army were often linked to party membership. Losing one's party card could mean the stifling of a career and it was, paradoxically, actually worse for an officer to have been a Communist and been expelled from the party than to have never been in the party at all. Officers who lost their party cards carried the stigma of being distrusted by the party. Those who had never been party members still had the potential of becoming such.

Chistki should not be viewed as antimilitary actions on the part of the party, or as attempts to subvert the leadership of the army; in fact, they reflected a genuine concern for the moral health of the Red Army just as civilian *chistki* were to strengthen, not punish, those party organs. In the military *chistki* men were expelled not only for political reasons; failure in one's military duties could also result in being booted out of the party. In the 1933 *chistka*, for example, the particular stress was on discipline. Those who did not maintain it in their units, or were personally undisciplined, were subject to expulsion from the party. In one instance a commission investigating the Third Rifle Regiment determined that "member of the party Kozlov serves as the commander of a signals detachment and does not appear able to create the conditions required for iron military discipline. As a result his detachment has infringements of discipline." The commission asked him a series of elementary political questions, which he could not answer, and they decided that "Kozlov did not fulfill party tasks," so he therefore "was cut loose from the party cell."[8] *Chistka* commissions also often uncovered men from ineligible social classes serving in the army not only as enlisted men, but even as officers.[9] Despite the apparent practical effects of *chistki*, there is no doubt that they were intended to insure conformity to the policies and ideology of the center by party members and the institutions they were part of, and under Stalin this was far more important than job performance.

What appears to have happened in 1937−9 is that the call to unmask "enemies of the people," a function of the *Ezhovshchina*, was accompanied

[8] *Krasnaia zvezda*, 17 Oct. 1933.
[9] Former White guardists, nobles, sons of nobles, the bourgeois and sons of the bourgeois, kulaks and their sons were not allowed to serve in the Red Army, yet many did in order to establish proper Soviet credentials and social status.

by an informal *chistka*, one not organized by the People's Commissariat of Defense or PUR, but by the primary party organizations themselves. There were important differences between this informal *chistka* and normal membership purges. The primary party organs from company cell to regimental party bureau now looked for enemies of the people (wreckers and spies) instead of politically unacceptable, morally corrupt, or incompetent individuals. Of course it is conceivable that some of the incompetent and corrupt were classified as enemies of the people, yet a large number of officers, although fewer than in previous years, continued to be discharged under the category "political-moral reasons." Anyone discharged for other than moral or medical reasons was expelled from the party without benefit of a hearing. And, of course, anyone arrested by the NKVD was expelled from the party. More than paralleling each other, the two processes of expulsion and arrest became intertwined.

To better appreciate the dynamics of the *Ezhovshchina* it is useful to examine similarities and differences between the *Ezhovshchina* of 1937–9 and the *chistki* of previous years. Like *chistki*, the terror did not come unannounced, and there was some attempt at mental conditioning of the intended victims beforehand. Certain clues could have tipped off the astute observer, such as the trials of the former Right Oppositionists Zinoviev and Kamenev, highly publicized in 1936 and early 1937, which served to alert the Soviet population at large that enemies of the people, namely Trotskyists and Fascists, were being found at the highest levels of the party and government, and with seemingly impeccable Revolutionary, Civil War, or Bolshevik credentials. In fact, the name of Field Marshal Mikhail Tukhachevskii, who was later accused of being the ringleader of a Fascist-Trotskyist group in the army, was ominously brought out in the Radek-Piatakov trial in January 1937. Other portents were that between January 1 and June 10, 1937, 577 officers were discharged for political reasons and that in March, the NKVD began to make arrests of Red Army officers serving as advisors to the Republican forces in Spain.[10]

During the Radek-Piatakov trial in early 1937, the political officers of military units organized the soldiers to pass resolutions to root out Fascist-Trotskyist centers everywhere and resolved further that death was the only just punishment for such traitors. The soldiers also vowed increased vigilance to uncover enemies of the people. In the two weeks before the arrests of the first officers in the Soviet Union proper, numerous articles in the military press called for more vigilance against enemies of the people. Therefore, when the arrests of the high-ranking military officers Tukhachevskii, Iakir, Uborevich, Kork, Eideman, Feld'man, Primakov, and Putna were announced, the shock was less than it might otherwise have been.

[10] Erickson, 449, 451–452; Oleg F. Suvenirov, "Narkomat oborony i NKVD v predvoennye gody," *Voprosy Istorii*, no. 6 (1991), 29.

Another factor that led to general acceptance of their treason by the rank and file was that the "traitors" were said to have been tried by a military tribunal of high-ranking officers, albeit in secret, which was normal for serious military crimes.

The mass of the military, led by PUR, accordingly called for the death penalty for such Fascist-Trotskyist traitors after the arrest of Tukhachevskii just as had been done after the Radek-Piatakov trial. Three days after the arrests of military leaders were announced, all battalion-sized units and larger in the Red Army, Navy, and Air Force had passed resolutions calling for the traitors to be shot, which they were.[11]

Unlike a *chistka*, the *Ezhovshchina* had no unit hearings. Arrested men simply disappeared into the Gulag or the grave. Another important distinction is that unlike the *chistki*, the *Ezhovshchina* was not limited to Communists. Although aimed mostly at party members, some non-Communists were repressed in the terror as well, although nonparty members had the advantage of not having to fear expulsion and subsequent discharge. A third difference was that in previous *chistki* enlisted men and officers seem to have been equally as susceptible to expulsion, whereas in the *Ezhovshchina*, with rare exception, only officers were expelled. Just as after each *chistka* the party claimed it was strengthened, the RKKA (*Raboche-Krest'ianskaia Krasnia Armiia*, the Workers-Peasants Red Army) claimed it was bolstered by the purge of Fascist-Trotskyist traitors, which enabled it to promote younger, loyal, and deserving Communists, and even nonparty officers.[12]

Although the *Ezhovshchina* in the army was launched not as a party purge but as a campaign to root out enemies of the people everywhere, party members suffered the most, most likely because party organs, initially encouraged to expose enemies of the people, turned inward to examine themselves as they had been conditioned to do, thus creating the informal *chistka*. Second, people of high rank and responsibility suffered the most and they were overwhelmingly party members. Because associations with such people became grounds for expulsion and discharge, their associates, other party members, and ranking officers were more vulnerable to terror and expulsion than lower ranking nonparty members.

An especially important difference between the informal *chistka* of 1937–8 and previous formal *chistki* was the consequence of expulsion. Prior to June 1937, servicemen expelled from the party only lost their party cards, but during the *Ezhovshchina* they were most often, but not always, discharged from the military and marked as likely candidates for arrests. No longer was the worst result of military discharge the stifling of a career, but the end of a career and possibly doom. Beyond that, the

[11] *Krasnaia zvezda*, 26 Jan.–1 Feb. 1937, 11, 12, 14 June 1937.
[12] *Krasnaia zvezda*, 16 June 1937.

proceedings that led to expulsion contributed to the feeling of helplessness of both victims and potential victims. Usually, at an excited meeting of the primary party organization with mixed ranks and without formal procedures and clouded by emotion, the accused was set upon by most of those at the meetings with little chance for defense. How such a threat of unwarranted and often capricious discharge must have contributed to the rise in suicides and alcoholism in the army at this time must be considered when assessing the total impact of the purge years.[13]

How expulsions became part of the *Ezhovshchina* is partially explained by the following incidents related by Lev Mekhlis, appointed by Stalin to head PUR in 1938 after Jan Gamarnik committed suicide rather than be arrested. Mekhlis offered the following incident of absurdity:

> The party organization of the 301st Transport Company of the 48th Rifle Division submitted the following resolution. "Our horses are in a poor state, they do not have cover, their oats are poured out on the ground, and they appear ill on account of it, do we not have here, on the part of the commanding personnel, enemies of the people?"[14]

The resolution said nothing about expelling or arresting the company leaders, but was submitted to the regimental party bureau for consideration. In prefacing this episode in his report submitted to the Central Committee, Mekhlis said the party cells in failing to understand what was meant or intended by the terms criticism (*kritika*) and self-criticism (*samokritika*) – both intended to increase military discipline – actually had undermined the authority of the commanders. This indicates that primary party organizations, from regimental party bureaus down to company cells felt themselves under pressure to make denunciations of some sort and therefore concocted accusations such as this.[15] In many cases, however, cases of wrecking did not have to be concocted. Because of the rapid expansion of the army, terror, and discharges, many men were elevated to positions for which they were not prepared and naturally made errors in judgment and performed poorly before gaining mastery of their responsibilities. Any of their mistakes could be labeled wrecking and used against them for either expulsion or arrest.

In a speech to the Eighteenth Party Congress in March 1939, as a part of Moscow's move to end the *Ezhovshchina*, Mekhlis described the following instance of someone suspected of being tainted politically being unjustly expelled by the primary party organization expeditiously and without hesitation.

---

[13] O. F. Suvenirov, "Vsearmeiskaia Tragediia," *Voenno-istoricheskii zhurnal*, no. 3 (1989), 43–44; "O rabote Politicheskogo Upravleniia Krasnoi Armii," *Izvestiia TsK KPSS*, no. 3 (1990), 200.

[14] "O rabote Politicheskogo Upravleniia Krasnoi Armii 23 May 1940 g." *Izvestiia TsK KPSS*, vol. 2, no. 3 (1990), 195.

[15] Lev Mekhlis, *Rech' na XVIII s'ezde VKP(b) 14 Marta 1939 g.* (Moscow: Gosvoenizdat, 1939), 14.

There was even a bizarre case of expulsion like the following. The representative of the special department in a certain regiment told the commissar, Gashinskii, that he was after the club superintendent, a *politruk* by the name of Rybnikov. Gashinskii passed this on in confidence to the party organization, and Rybnikov was expelled by the primary party organization. It soon turned out that Rybnikov was not a bad Bolshevik and that the special department was after him ... to get him to work in their department. The mistake was corrected, but only after comrade Rybnikov had been put to a lot of mental suffering.[16]

From this example, it would appear that the military party organizations had weakly understood their minimal role in the NKVD's work, but tried to play a major role in exposing enemies of the people. At least this is what Mekhlis may have wanted to convey as the center sought to blame the "excesses" of the *Ezhovshchina* on the primary party organizations. In comparing the above two examples we see a contrast in purge procedures by primary party organizations. In the 301st Transport Company they referred their finding to the next higher level for action, just as did civilians in Belyi Raion, but in the Gashinskii case the primary party organization itself expelled the "enemy of the people" suggesting there were local variations in the *Ezhovshchina*, just as in normal *chistki*.

The connection between expelling party members and exposing enemies of the people is reflected in an internal document of the Kiev Military Soviet titled "*Materialy k Protokolu zasedaniia Voennogo Soveta Kievskogo Voennogo Okruga No. 2 ot 26 Marta 1938 goda.*," which gives details of both expulsions and terror in the Kiev Military District. It states that the directive to the Kiev Military District to "clean out the army of enemies of the people" came directly from Stalin and Kliment Voroshilov, the Commissar of Defense. It also ordered members of the district's military soviet to make lists of candidates, both party and nonparty, to fill positions vacated by purged officers.[17] Therefore it would appear that the center, by the use of vague phrases, wanted the lower levels to stir things up in the units, and left them to their own devices.

The orders to the military districts to stir things up were preceded by an article in the military daily *Krasnaia zvezda*, published on 14 June 1937, which called on all army party organs to assist the NKVD in "exposing enemies of the people." Yet after the military purge was underway, only the arrests of Marshal Tukhachevskii and other high-ranting officers were ever mentioned in the military press. Beyond that the military press did not encourage denunciations or any sort of witch-hunt, quite the opposite of the civilian press, which was full of exhortations for uncovering enemies of the people, spies, wreckers, and their protectors. Because the *Ezhovshchina* was virtually never mentioned or even referred to in the military press after June 1937, it would seem that their reading of the civilian press kept the

[16] Ibid., 14.
[17] Suvenirov, "Vsearmeiskaia Tragediia," 47–48.

lower military party organs (the company and battalion cells) active in expelling their members, both in conjunction with and independently of directives from PUR and the People's Commissariat of Defense.

Just as the NKVD's net widened to include associates of enemies of the people, primary party organs also expelled officers they accused of being associated with enemies of the people. For example, I. T. Starinov, a field grade officer, reported the following:

> Soon after my arrival Dmitrii Ivanovich Vorob'ev, my assistant for material and technical supplies, was accused of having connections with Trotskyists. The only pretext for this accusation was Vorob'ev's friendship with Colonel N. M. Ipatov . . . who had been declared an enemy of the people not long before. Engineer P. I. Martsinkevich and Vorob'ev's assistant, V. N. Nikitin, . . . tried to defend him at the party meeting. But there were ill-wishers present; Vorob'ev was expelled from the party.[18]

What makes this a particularly apt example is that Vorob'ev was reinstated to the party nine months later, showing that his association with an enemy of the people was inconsequential and that the primary party organization had overstepped its bounds.

Not every primary party organization got caught up in the whirlwind of denunciations, however. A. T. Stuchenko, a student officer in the Frunze Military Academy during the *Ezhovshchina* said:

> Our party group held together. We did not look for "enemies of the people" among ourselves and firmly resisted all attacks from outside. We even began to be accused of a loss of revolutionary vigilance, and our sectional party organization was threatened with disbandment.

Their lack of "vigilance" did not sit very well with the class commissar, but the group leader held firm against denouncing men in his group. When the purge was ended he and his group were praised. The same class commissar said, "Now those are fine communists in the cavalry section! A close-knit bunch, they held together."[19] It seems that being in a close-knit group was one of the better ways of avoiding denunciation and that it was the average party member who made the *Ezhovshchina* irrational and unpredictable.

The ambiguity of the purpose of the purge was reflected in the terminology used in official documents relating to the purge. In Table 9.2, taken from the aforementioned Kiev report, of the top ten leadership positions in the Kiev Military District, the number of officers authorized and the percentage replaced, the word *replaced* was used, not the word *arrested*. The document reveals that, as of 25 March 1938, of 2,922 men dismissed from their

---

[18] I. T. Starinov, "Homecoming," in Bialer, *Stalin and His Generals* (New York: Pegasus, 1969), 78.
[19] A. T. Stuchenko, "In the Frunze Military Academy," in Bialer, 81.

Table 9.2. *Replacement of top officers in the Kiev Military District,*
1937–1938

Duty position	Authorized	Replaced	Percentage replaced
Corps commander	9	9	100
Division commander	25	24	96
Brigade commander	9	5	55
Regiment commander	135	87	64
Commander of a fortified area	4	4	100
Corps chief of staff	9	6	67
Division chief of staff	25	18	72
Regiment chief of staff	135	78	58
Fortified area chief of staff	4	3	75
Separate district chief of staff	24	19	84

Source: O. F. Suvenirov, "Vsearmeiskaia Tragediia," *Voenno-istoricheskii zhurnal*, no. 3 (1989), 47–48.

positions and discharged from the RKKA, 1,066 had been arrested by the NKVD. This is important as an indicator that terror and expulsions were part of the same process. In the report the operation in the Kiev Military District was referred to as a *chistka*; not a *chistka* of the party, however, but a purge of the army just as Shchadenko's report called it "cleaning out the army" (*Ochistka armii i peresmotr uvalennykh*). The use of the word *chistka* in the Kiev Military District report may have confused the people responsible for conducting the operation about just what Moscow intended, and led to their doing what was familiar in a purge (*chistka*) – cleaning their ranks through expulsion while the NKVD went about making arrests.

Knowing that being replaced in the purges did not necessarily mean being arrested makes the figures in Table 9.2 less meaningful now than was previously thought. It is unclear how many of the 253 officers reported removed in the Kiev Military District were expelled, discharged, arrested and shot or sent to the Gulag, or eventually reinstated. It does not necessarily mean they were all killed, although that is possible, however unlikely.

A third example of the convergence of terror and party purge is a report by Lev Mekhlis to the Central Committee in May 1940 in which he gave the status of post-purge PUR. The report included discussions and figures of both arrests and expulsions from the party and discharges from the army in exactly the same format as Shchadenko's report. Thus, in the mind of the chief of PUR, the whole cataclysm of 1937–9 was one event. This, coupled with the fact that only 265 of the 3,176 men discharged from PUR in 1938 were discharged as a result of arrest, testifies to a more limited than previously thought involvement of the NKVD in the overall

Table 9.3. *Reinstatement of commanding personnel discharged in 1937–1939 (army only, including those discharged for political-moral and medical reasons)*

| | | Had been discharged | |
Year discharged	Total reinstated by 5/1/40	by NKO	at military district level or below
1937	4,661	1,703	2,958
1938	6,333	2,202	4,131
1939	184	125	59
Total	11,178	4,030	7,148

Source: "O rabote za 1939 god: Iz otcheta nachal'nika Upravleniia po nachal'stvuiushchemu sostavu RKKA Narkomata Oborony SSSR, E. A. Shchadenko, 5 May 1940," *Izvestiia TsK KPSS*, vol. 2, no. 1 (1990), 189.

disruption of the armed forces during the *Ezhovshchina*.[20] In the report Mekhlis lamented the "gross errors" that took place while cleaning the cadre of the political administration of enemies of the people, again blaming the excesses on the primary party organizations.

As Table 9.3 shows, quite a number of discharged men were reinstated. Most of the men reinstated had been discharged at or below the military district level, suggesting that those expulsions were just local matters.

Table 9.1 shows that 25% of those arrested and discharged in 1937 were reinstated, 38% in 1938, and nearly 10% in 1939. In all, 30% of army officers arrested or discharged between 1937 and 1939 were reinstated. In the air force, the odds were distinctly greater against purge victims. Of the 5,616 air force officers who were victims of the purge, only 892, or less than 16%, were reinstated by the end of 1939.[21] This may be related to the fact that the Red Air Force had a higher percentage of Communists in the officer corps than did the ground forces.

The figures also suggest that the combined processes only got really out of hand in 1938. In 1937, less than 5% of those arrested were reinstated, indicating that the NKVD was initially methodical about targeting "enemies of the people," but eventually was equally susceptible to the hysteria that in 1938 gripped the whole armed forces. The next year 24% of those arrested were reinstated. In 1937, nearly 40% of those discharged were reinstated, and in 1938, 80%.

Most rehabilitations took place at the local level and were granted by

---

[20] Lev Mekhlis, "Iz doklada Politicheskogo Upravleniia Krasnoi Armii Tsentral'nomu Komitetu VKP (b) o rabote Politicheskogo Upravleniia Krasnoi Armii, 23 Maia 1940 g." *Izvestiia TsK KPSS*, no. 3 (1990), 193.

[21] F. B. Komal, "Voennye Kadry Nakanune Voiny," 24.

the primary party organizations, the political/military chain of command, and special appeals commissions. Still others, though fewer and mainly of higher rank, were rehabilitated by higher authorities, which was what it took to get out of the Gulag. Some of those purged were reinstated rather quickly. The report from Kiev cited earlier showed thirty officers had successfully appealed their expulsions and discharges, and were reinstated by a commission established to hear requests for reinstatement. At the same time central control of the purge was impossible to enforce, and in the case of Kiev things were not wrapped up completely by the end of May as projected, with men still making denunciations in the autumn of that year.[22]

The denunciations and expulsions may have spread so quickly because officers and the rank and file were conditioned through *chistki* to see class enemies and wreckers in all walks of life. The *chistki* of the late twenties and early thirties proved that the Red Army could be penetrated by enemies in all categories of personnel: enlisted, officer, and political. The purposefulness, thoroughness, and apparent impartiality of the *chistka* verification committees legitimized the process and result of such party purges. It is possible that the *chistka* created trust in party- and army-sponsored "cleansing" activities in the minds of the future victims so that when the blood purge came along they were helpless before it. Their trust in the system was so strong that some of those purged still professed faith in the system and believed for years afterward that their arrests were mistakes made by local people, but that the terror itself was justified.[23]

The *Ezhovshchina* does not seem to have alienated the army from the party. During 1937, 10,341 military party members were expelled from the Communist party and simultaneously 23,599 officers and men were admitted to the party; 17,496 of them joined after the purge began.[24] In contrast to the low numbers admitted to the party before the purges, 101,310 soldiers and officers were admitted to the party in 1938. More than ten thousand more members of the military joined the party in the first month of 1939. Civilian party admissions also picked up. In 1939 over a million persons were admitted to the party.[25] Therefore, we must assume that a good many people retained faith in the party and continued to see it as a positive force, or at least as an avenue to advancement despite the apparent hazards of terror and *chistka*.

[22] Kalinin, *Razmyshliaia o minuvshem*, 120–122.
[23] Aleksandr V. Gorbatov, *Years Of My Life* (New York: W. W. Norton & Co. Inc., 1965), 103, 108–151.
[24] O. F. Suvenirov, "Esli b ne ta vakkhanaliia," *Voenno-istoricheskii zhurnal*, no. 2 (1989), 57–58.
[25] Voroshilov, et al., *The Red Army Today, Speeches Delivered at the Eighteenth Congress of the CPSU (B) March 10–21, 1939* (Moscow, 1939), 46; T. H. Rigby, *Communist Party Membership in the USSR 1917–1967*, (Princeton: Princeton University Press, 1967), 217–219, 249.

Although the purge was begun by the center for a specific purpose, most of the turmoil during the purge resulted from a distorted understanding by primary party organizations and local NKVD units of what they were supposed to do, which may have been just what the center wanted. In other words, Stalin wanted to eliminate particular high-ranking officers, and in order to get at them without a military revolt, he unleashed fear, frustration, and even ambition in the ranks with perfectly predictable results. As long as the army was divided against itself, it could not oppose Stalin.

By the end of 1938 Stalin and his collaborators had purged those they wanted and sought to get the army back to normal. It took some effort by the center to end the Red Army purge, showing that Moscow had indeed allowed the purge to run amok in the units, because it could with the proper amount of pressure stop the entire process. Yet this seems to have defined the center's role; it could start and stop the *Ezhovshchina* and eliminate selected victims, but could not guide effectively the primary party organs. The main effort to end the purge in the armed forces came in early February 1939 when *Krasnaia zvezda* published an article stating that, in the interest of discipline, criticism of defects in a commander's and commissar's party discipline would no longer be allowed at *samokritika* sessions at their unit level, but would instead be considered and discussed at the next higher level of command. In effect, Moscow took away the power of the primary party organizations to expel their members. The article stated that the old method of *samokritika* undermined the authority of the commander and commissar.[26] Unit level *samokritika*, in existence for over a decade, was only ended in 1939 because it had become an uncontrollable mechanism for expelling party members during the purge of the military, and something had to be done to stop denunciations and restore the authority of the chain of command over normal military functions.

Moscow took another step to end the rampant expulsions by publicizing in *Krasnaia zvezda* the trial of an army *politruk* charged with falsely denouncing a unit member as an enemy of the people. He was found guilty of slander and sentenced to five years in the camps.[27] Because publicizing military trials was rare, it seems likely that this was a signal to the army that the purge was over. Anyone who could read between the lines knew, thereafter, before denouncing anyone in his unit, he had better be sure of his facts and support from the political organs.

Finally, at the Eighteenth Party Congress in March 1939, Mekhlis made it explicit that the mindless expulsions were to stop. He said:

Political organs and party organizations often expel party members far too light-heartedly. The party commissions of the Political Administration of the Red Army

---

[26] *British Foreign Office Files 371: Russia Correspondence 1939*, vol. 23688, 209–210.
[27] *Krasnaia zvezda*, 15 Jan., 14 Feb. 1939.

finds it necessary to reinstate about 50% of the expelled men because the expulsions were unjustified.[28]

This and the previous two examples illustrate the extensive role the primary party organs played in the *Ezhovshchina*, and that the key to ending the purge was stifling the power and initiative of the lower party organs in the army.

Officers who had been expelled from the party in 1937 and 1938 intensified their petitioning to be reinstated to the party and army in 1938, blaming their unjust expulsions on true enemies of the people, that is, those who had been arrested in the terror. Party organizations held meetings in the units to discuss unjust expulsions and, in the words of Mekhlis, "to act on the basis of facts and documents, not rumors and whispers."[29] The success of these efforts to end the purge is reflected in Table 9.1 for 1939, which shows a tremendous drop in the number of arrests and expulsions, even in discharges for incompetence.

To summarize, terror purges, directed against all sectors of Soviet society at various times throughout the thirties, began in earnest against civilians in 1935, but did not reach the military until 1937 as a new wave of repression hit the civilian sector as well. The terror was begun at the center, but at the local level some people took advantage of it to settle personal scores; there was also a panic response in the primary party organizations to expel and "expose" people in order to protect oneself and to show "vigilance." On the other hand, we have to recognize that the whole process relied on most of the NKVD and party members' belief in what they were doing, and the army's credulity.

Although it lasted until 1941, after 1938 repression within the military was virtually negligible. In the years of the *Ezhovshchina*, 34,301 Red Army and Red Air Force officers and political personnel were removed from the military for political reasons. As of 1 May 1940, 11,596 victims of arrest and expulsion in the army and air force had been reinstated in rank, but as a rule not to their former positions, leaving as a direct result of the purge, 22,705 personnel of the RKKA (of which about 13,000 were from the army, 4,700 from the air force, and 5,000 from PUR) either dead, in the Gulag, or cast into civilian society in disgrace.[30] Although in its worst year approximately only 7.7% of the Red Army's leadership was discharged for political reasons, versus the 20% to 25% suggested by John Erickson and 50% claimed by Robert Conquest, this does not diminish the seriousness of the purge; the higher ranks of the army officer corps literally were decimated and a great deal of experience was lost.[31] And now, knowing

---

[28] Lev Mekhlis, *Rech' na XVIII s"ezde VKP (b) 14 Marta 1939 g.*, 14.

[29] Ibid., 15.

[30] "O rabote Politicheskogo Upravleniia Krasnoi Armii," *Izvestiia TsK KPSS*, vol. 2, no. 3 (1990), 193.

[31] Komal, "Voennye Kadry Nakanune Voiny," 24; Conquest, 485; Erickson, 451–452.

Roger R. Reese

that an unregulated party membership purge became inextricably mixed with the *Ezhovshchina*, but was moderated by prompt mass reinstatements, Western scholars need to reevaluate the extent of the terror in the army, consider the extensive role of the primary party organizations, and rethink the role of the center.

10

Stalinist terror in the Donbas: A note

Hiroaki Kuromiya

In the history of the Soviet Union, political terror is undoubtedly one of the most incendiary issues.[1] This issue has provoked an outburst of national emotion, unleashed by Gorbachev's *glasnost'* campaign. Even the hitherto sacred years of Lenin's rule are no longer immune to harsh criticism and condemnation. Indeed, the Central Committee of the Soviet Communist Party has made known Lenin's extreme cruelty toward the church and believers. This revelation is tantamount to dismantling "the Soviet myth that it was Stalin who initiated repression against the clergy and believers."[2]

There are still limits to the availability of sources, however. As V. V. Tsaplin, the director of the Central State Archive of the National Economy of the Soviet Union (TsGANKh SSSR) in Moscow, admits, the documents on political repression in the Soviet state archives have not been declassified.[3] Consequently, all sorts of speculation on this hitherto forbidden subject circulate in the Soviet press and even scholarly publications, often drawing on Western scholars' work. In the West, in turn, one may be tempted to believe that citations by the Soviets are authoritative.

Although access to archival documents on terror is limited, the Soviet archives are not closed altogether. Soviet historians, who have had access to classified archival material, have published some informative articles on

---

[1] For the terror in the Stalin years, see Robert Conquest, *The Great Terror: Stalin's Purge of the Thirties* (New York, 1973), the second edition of the same book (New York, 1990), J. Arch Getty, *The Origins of the Great Purges: The Soviet Communist Party Reconsidered, 1933–1938* (New York, 1985), Nicolas Werth, *Les proces de Moscou* (Brussels, 1987), and Gábor Tamás Rittersporn, *Simplifications staliniennes et complications sovietiques. Tensions sociales et conflits politiques en U.R.S.S. (1933–1953)* (Paris, 1988).

[2] See, Vera Tolz, "Another Blow to Lenin's Image," Radio Liberty, *Report on the USSR*, 2: 18 (4 May 1990), pp. 4–6. Lenin's 19 March 1922 letter to the Politbureau, which proposed to crush the church by taking advantage of the famine crisis, was published in *Izvestiia TsK KPSS*, 1990, no. 4, pp. 190–193.

[3] "Perestroika v arkhivnom dele: po puti revoliutsii ili reform?" *Voprosy istorii KPSS*, 1990, no. 1, p. 57.

the extent of the terror under Stalin.[4] The Committee for State Security (KGB), the successor to the notorious security police (OGPU-NKVD), also has recently published data on the victims of the state terror under Stalin. Its task force, working "carefully and painstakingly" with archival materials, has declared that from 1930 to 1953, 3,778,234 people (including foreigners) were indicted by judicial and extrajudicial organs for "counter-revolutionary and other state crimes;" of those, 786,098 people were sentenced to capital punishment and shot.[5] As the KGB task force admits, these figures are still incomplete. Nor is it clear who is included in these figures. (For example, are all the dekulakized included?) The KGB announcement thus raises more questions than it answers.

This chapter is intended to provide some concrete data on the scale of terror in one particular area – the Donbas (Donets Basin) coal-mining industry. These data are found in local newspapers and open archives of the TsGANKh SSSR in Moscow. How representative the Donbas is in this respect is open to question. Nor are these data likely to make a direct contribution to the ongoing controversy over "excess mortality" under Stalin.[6] Yet they do afford a concrete view of the Stalinist purge in a locality in 1936–8.

The Donbas was the major coal-mining area located in the Donets region of the Ukrainian Republic and the Northern Caucasus of the Russian Republic. It accounted for 77.3% of the country's coal production in 1929 and 60.8% in 1938.[7] Political and social violence was not new to the Donbas. In the prerevolutionary period, the Donbas witnessed large-scale anti-Jewish pogroms, and during the Civil War of 1918–20 terror was

---

[4] Note, for example, V. V. Tsaplin, "Statistika zhertv stalinizma v 30-e gody," *Voprosy istorii*, 1989, no. 4; V. Zemskov's series of articles in the form of responses to readers' questions in *Argumenty i fakty*, 1989, no. 38, no. 40, 1990, no. 5, and interviews with Zemskov, "'Arkhipelag Gulag': glazami pisatelei i statistika"), ibid., 1989, no. 45, and "Dokumenty tragicheskogo vremeni: arkhivy otkryvaiut tainy," ibid., 1990, no. 35; V. Nekrasov, "Desiat' 'zheleznykh' narkomov," *Komsomol'skaia pravda*, 29 September 1989; A. Dugin, "Gulag: otkryvaia arkhivy," *Na boevom postu*, 27 December 1989 (an abridged version appeared as "Gulag. Glazami istorika," *Soiuz* (Moscow), 1990, no. 9, p. 16); idem., "Govoriat arkhivy: neizvestnye stranitsy GULAGa," *Sotsial'no-politicheskie nauki*, 1990, no. 7 (an abridged edition is "Stalinizm. Legendy i fakty," *Slovo*, 1990, no. 7.); and F. B. Komal, "Voennye kadry nakanune voiny," *Voenno-istoricheskii zhurnal*, 1990, no. 2. Most of these articles are analyzed by Vera Tolz: "Publication of Archive Materials on Stalin's Terror," Radio Liberty, *Report on the USSR*, 2: 32 (10 August 1990), and "Archives Yield New Statistics on the Stalin Terror," ibid., 2: 36 (7 September 1990). Information from closed (secret) funds is usually cited without any reference or as, for example, "kollektsiia TsGAORa." D. A. Volkogonov, *Triumf i tragediia. Politicheskii portret I. V. Stalina*, 2 vols. (Moscow, 1989) also contains new information on the terror culled from various Soviet archives.
[5] "Reabilitatsiia," *Pravitel'stvenny vestnik*, 1990, no. 7 (30), p. 11.
[6] For the most recent contributions, see note 28.
[7] *Sotsialisticheskoe stroitel'stvo soiuza SSR (1933–1938 gg.). Statisticheskii sbornik* (Moscow, 1939), pp. 47–48.

perpetrated by both the Reds and the Whites. Even during the years of the
New Economic Policy, there were staged show trials of "wreckers" in the
mines. The famous Shakhty affair of 1928 led by mid-1931 to the arrests
of half of the Donbas engineers and technicians.[8] The campaign for collectivization and dekulakization resulted in the dispossession and deportation
or murder of untold numbers of peasants.[9] In the grave famine crisis of
1932–3, extraordinarily harsh punishments were again meted out to the
Donbas population. According to the notorious 7 August 1932 law on
"socialist property," 301 people were shot and 8,728 were sentenced to
various terms of imprisonment or forced labor between 7 August 1932
and 1 May 1933.[10] Simultaneously, the slump in coal production resulted
in a savage attack against Communist managers ("saboteurs"), including
expulsion from the party and arrest.[11] The onset of the Stakhanovite
movement in 1935 contributed to the creation of a political atmosphere in
which unprecedented political terror reigned in 1936–8.[12]

A perusal of the Donbas newspaper, *Sotsialisticheskii Donbass*, suggests
that massive terror (arrests, deportations, executions) lasted approximately
from the summer of 1936 to the autumn of 1938, accentuated by several
waves of an intensive campaign against "enemies of the people." Of
course, this does not imply that terror did not begin until the summer of
1936, or that it ended in the autumn of 1938, but rather that it was a
distinctively violent period and came to be known generally as the time of
the Great Terror.

In this period, the Donbas party leadership (which was politically responsible, among others, for the performance of the most important industry
of the region – coal-mining) seems to have been virtually decimated. S. A.
Sarkisov, since 1933 the first secretary of the Donetsk party obkom, was
transferred in April 1937 to head Donbas Coal, the very organization he

[8] See L. I. Brodskii, "Ideino-politicheskoe vospitanie tekhnicheskikh spetsialistov dorevo-
liutsionnoi shkoly v gody pervoi piatiletki," *Trudy Leningradskogo politekhnicheskogo
instituta im. Kalinina*, no. 261 (Leningrad, 1966), p. 73.
[9] Little work has been done on this subject both in the Soviet Union and in the West.
[10] Gosudarstvennyi arkhiv Donetskoi oblasti (GADO), R-920, op. 1, d. 9, l. 50. As is well
known, "socialist property" included a watermelon in the collective farm fields. There
were cases in which hungry peasants and workers who stole a watermelon from the
collective farms were shot.
[11] See Hiroaki Kuromiya, "The Commander and the Rank and File: Managing the Soviet
Coalmining Industry, 1928–1933," in William G. Rosenberg and Lewis Siegelbaum
(eds.), *The Social Dimensions of Soviet Industrialization* (Indiana University Press,
forthcoming).
[12] For this movement and terror, see Lewis H. Siegelbaum, *Stakhanovism and the Politics of
Productivity in the USSR, 1935–1941* (New York, 1988), Gábor Tamás Rittersporn,
"Heros du travail et commandants de la production. La campagne stakhanoviste et les
strategies fractionelles en U.R.S.S. (1935–1936)," *Recherches*, no. 32–33 (1978), and
Robert Maier, *Die Stachanov-Bewegung 1935–1938. Der Stachanovismus als tragendes
und versharfendes Moment der Stalinisierung der sowjetischen Gesellschaft* (Stuttgart,
1990). Francesco Benvenuti has also published *Fuoco sui sabotatori! Stachanovismo e
organizzazione industriale in URSS, 1934–1938* (Roma, 1988).

had savagely attacked for unsatisfactory work. Soon thereafter, in July 1937, he was expelled from the party and shot as an "enemy of the people" and a "Fascist spy;" A. U. Kholokholenko, the second secretary of the obkom, was subjected to the same fate.[13] The new first secretary, E. K. Pramnek, who expelled Sarkisov and Kholokholenko, was in turn removed in April 1938 and was shot in July 1938.[14] With these leaders the majority of obkom members disappeared. There are no accurate statistics available, but of the seventy-six full members in May 1937, only six remained in that capacity in June 1938.[15] It may not be that all of those seventy who disappeared fell victims to the terror. Given the ferocious press campaign against the obkom as a nest of "enemies of people,"[16] however, one may reasonably assume that a large number of them did. Like the party leadership in other regions and provinces,[17] the Donbas obkom was thus annihilated. This scale of terror may be comparable to that inflicted upon the party central leadership.[18]

The scale of terror against coal-mining managers in the Donbas seems to have been less extensive, although the information available is fragmentary. In no way, however, was the terror insignificant. The long-time doyen of the Soviet coal-mining industry, V. M. Bazhanov, who had directly headed Donbas Coal, was demoted in April 1937 in connection with the appointment of Sarkisov. In September Bazhanov was removed from the chief editorship of the journal *Ugol'*, which he had occupied for many years, and soon perished at the age of forty-eight as a "counterrevolutionary wrecker."[19] In September 1937, the People's Commissar of Heavy Industry, L. M. Kaganovich, toured around "all trusts and mines" in the Donbas, discovered "wrecking activities," and attacked and removed managers and engineers en masse.[20] Many of those removed were simultaneously or subsequently arrested by the NKVD.

[13] *Promyshlennost' i rabochie Donbassa. Sbornik dokumentov. Oktiabr' 1917–iiun' 1941* (Donetsk, 1989), pp. 174–175. See also the editorial in *Sotsialisticheskii Donbass*, 28 July 1937, and *Izvestiia TsK KPSS*, 1989, no. 12, pp. 86, 110.

[14] See *Sotsialisticheskii Donbass*, 9 April 1938, *Moscow News*, 1988, no. 22, p. 16, and *Izvestiia TsK KPSS*, 1989, no. 12, pp. 86, 109.

[15] *Sotsialisticheskii Donbass*, 26 May 1937 and 8 June 1938. In June 1938 the Donetsk *obkom* split in two: the Stalino and the Voroshilovgrad obkoms. Seventy of the original seventy-six members appeared on the list of neither obkom membership in June 1938.

[16] See, for example, ibid., 28 July 1938 (ed.) and 24 May 1938 (speech by A. S. Shcherbakov who replaced Pramnek).

[17] For the decimation of provincial party leaders, see J. Arch Getty, "Party and Purge in Smolensk: 1933–1937," *Slavic Review*, 42: 1 (Spring 1983), p. 75.

[18] The Central Committee of the All-Union Communist Party lost the majority of its members to the terror: forty-four of the seventy-one full members and fifty-three of the sixty-eight candidate members (97% of the victims were shot in 1937–9). See *Izvestiia TsK KPSS*, 1989, no. 12, pp. 82–87.

[19] *Sotsialisticheskii Donbass*, 29 April and 1 November 1937, and Tsentral'nyi gosudarstvennyi arkhiv natsional'nogo khoziaistva SSSR (hereafter cited as TsGANKh SSSR), f. 7566, op. 1, d. 2750, l. 3. For a brief biography of Bazhanov, see I. V. Paramonov, *Komandarm ugol'nogo fronta* (Moscow, 1977).

[20] See TsGANKh SSSR, f. 7297, op. 1, d. 232, ll. 1–10, 23, 29, 30–37, 38–44, 45–57,

No aggregate data on this or other waves of terror are available. However, according to one document ("Directory of Senior Officials in the Mines and Trusts of Donbas Coal") by the Chief Coal Administration of the People's Commissariat of Heavy Industry (NKTP), between late 1936 and April 1938, at least 56 (or 26.7%) of the 210 listed were arrested, and two more were indicted for "wrecking."[21] Clearly, these data are far from complete, owing to the massive arrests that created administrative confusion and chaos in bookkeeping. In fact, three documents on the "senior officials" of Donbas Coal, compiled by Donbas Coal itself at that time, list an additional twenty-six managers and engineers as arrested or repressed (*repressirovan*).[22] Nor were the six officials of Donbas Coal's Budennovskii Coal Trust, who were put on a show trial in November 1937 and then executed, included in this directory.[23] For what purposes this directory was compiled is unclear. What is clear from the archival material is that Donbas Coal, under pressure for ever higher production outputs, impatiently and frantically removed its subordinate mine and trust officials from their posts without clearing it with the NKTP or its Chief Coal Administration. (This was a violation of the *nomenklatura* system.)[24] The NKVD, for its part, independently intervened and arrested people. The NKTP or the Chief Coal Administration thus could not control the appointment and removal of important officials. The directory seems to have reflected the effort of the Chief Coal Administration to come to grips with the chaotic state of affairs within personnel management. If one assumes that those senior officials whom the Chief Coal Administration failed to trace were at least as likely to have been repressed as those listed in the directory, then at least a quarter of the senior officials in the Donbas coal-mining industry may have fallen victim to the state terror.

63–67, 68–73, 74–83, 84–94, 95–101, 102–110, 111–118, 128–129, 130–135, 136–139, 140–146, 147–155, 156–161, 215–223, 224–230. Before he went out to the Donbas, Kaganovich had "purged" his commissariat's Chief Coal Administration. See *Pravda*, 2 October 1937 (ed.), and TsGANKh SSSR, f. 7566, op. 2, d. 110, ll. 8–14, which suggest that the great majority of new staff arrived in September and October 1937.

[21] TsGANKh SSSR, f. 7566, op. 2, d. 79, ll. 60–69 ("Spravka o rukovodiashchikh rabotnikakh shakht i trestov 'Donbassuglia.'" In this directory, "senior officials" refer mostly to mine directors and chief engineers. This document is undated but signed in pencil by two officials: I. Fesenko, the director of Donbas Coal who in June 1938 was removed by L. M. Kaganovich, and Savitskii, the head of Donbas Coal's Registration and Allocation Department.) Donbas Coal was a giant industrial organization that in 1938 consisted of some 22 trusts and 277 mines. An almost identical document is also found in ibid., f. 7566, op. 2, d. 114, ll. 15–24.

[22] TsGANKh SSSR, f. 7566, op. 2, d. 79, ll. 32–40, 42–49, and d. 114, ll. 37–43. "Repressed" meant arrest, deportation to labor camps, or execution.

[23] For the trial and executions, see *Sotsialisticheskii Donbass*, 1–10 November, 3 December 1937.

[24] See, for example, the lists of people thus removed in TsGANKh SSSR, f. 7566, op. 2, d. 114, ll. 25–28. For this reason, Donbas Coal was repeatedly threatened with punishment by Kaganovich and the Chief Coal Administration. See ibid., f. 7566, op. 1, d. 3422, l. 1, d. 3514, l. 129, and op. 2, d. 105, l. 127.

Soon after the directory of Donbas Coal senior officials was compiled, the Donbas Coal apparatus itself was "purged" as a nest of "enemies of the people." In this case, too, Kaganovich took the trouble to travel to the Donbas in May and June 1938 to "unmask" these "enemies," "wreckers," and "saboteurs."[25] A list of those dismissed from Donbas Coal between 20 May and 1 August 1938 reveals the following:[26]

1. Morgunov, G. V., chief engineer: repressed.
2. Fesenko, I. A., director: repressed.
3. Zuev, K. I., engineer, Emergency Management Group: [current] place of work unknown.
4. Polissarov, M. A., chief, Dept. of Mining Technology Supply: place of work unknown.
5. Karnets, I. I., socialist competition officer: place of work unknown.
6. Glushenkov, F. F., officer, Mining System Group: place of work unknown.
7. Evdokimov, G. S., motor transport engineer: place of work unknown.
8. Freidis, A. M., controller engineer: place of work unknown.
9. Kogan, A. E., mining system engineer: place of work unknown.
10. Iakushev, A. I., controller engineer: place of work unknown.
11. Zakutskii, A. P., controller engineer: place of work unknown.
12. Polstianoi, G. N., chief, Planning Department: repressed.
13. Levin, L. E., mining system senior engineer: place of work unknown.
14. Iatskikh, V. G., supervisor, Mechanization Group: place of work unknown.
15. Arkhipov, Ia. F., assistant director: repressed.
16. Popov, V. S., geologist: repressed.
17. Belikov, V. P., chief, Technology Dept.: repressed.
18. Khokhlov, I. A., chief, Administrative Dept.: repressed.
19. Bondar', Kh. N., chief, Major Repair Dept.: repressed.
20. Kharchenko, V. N., deputy chief, Labour Force Dept.: repressed.
21. Vasilenko, B. V., engineer in energy and electric mechanics: repressed.
22. Sukhovenko, M. I., chief, Housing and Services Dept.: repressed.
23. Shifman, M. I., engineer, Major Repair Dept.: repressed.
24. Kalinin, chief, Finance [and Accounting] Dept.: repressed.
25. Chaplenko, I. A., supervisor, Organized Recruitment Group: repressed.
26. Sibarov, A. D., deputy chief, Finance and Accounting Dept.: chief accountant, OGPU mine, Prosvetai Anthracite Trust.
27. Iglitsyn, O. A., chief, Special Dept.: repressed.
28. Poliakov, V. A., chief, Cadre Dept.: repressed.
29. Radiakhin, Z. D., chief, Underground Transport Dept.: repressed.
30. Chumichev, V. D., chief, Equipment Supply Dept.: repressed.
31. Sirenko, Mining System Group: repressed.
32. Reznikov, A. M., supervisor, Cadre Training Group: does not work.

Thus, nineteen (or 59.4%) out of the thirty-two dismissed were "repressed;" eleven seem to have disappeared altogether; one no longer worked; and only one was demoted to another job. It is unclear in this

[25] See *Sotsialisticheskii Donbass*, 17 June 1938 (speech by A. S. Shcherbakov) and 6 August 1938 (article by N. Kasaurov).

[26] TsGANKh SSSR, f. 7566, op. 2, d. 114, ll. 14, 19 (signed by the Chief of the Cadre Department of Donbas Coal, Zaitsev).

case, too, how complete this list is, but almost all senior officials seem to have been dismissed, and the majority of them terrorized.

This onslaught on Donbas Coal was followed immediately by three show trials of coal-mining managers and engineers: the "Case of the Counterrevolutionary Rightist-Trotskyist Group at Mine Nos. 12–18 of the Budennovskii Coal Trust"; the "Case of the Counterrevolutionary Rightist-Trotskyist Wrecking Organization in the System of Donbas Coal"; and the "Case of the Counterrevolutionary Rightist-Trotskyist Group of Wreckers at Mine No. 18 of the Sovetsk Coal Trust." Of the sixteen defendants, twelve were sentenced to death and shot; the remainder were given from eighteen to twenty-five years imprisonment.[27] Undoubtedly, untold numbers of people were terrorized in connection with these trials. Nor did the conclusion of the trials bring about an end to the terror in the Donbas.

These senior officials in the party and the coal-mining industry composed but a small part of the overall victims of the Stalinist terror in the Donbas. Numerous lesser officials, activists, workers, scientists, and the like were directly affected. Other industries than coal-mining were also hard struck; so were the trade unions, cooperatives, collective and state farms, governmental, trade, and other organizations. A large number of people were executed and dumped into mass graves. One such grave, estimated to contain remains of "at least thousands of people," has recently been found in Rutchenkovo in the city of Donetsk.[28]

One can conclude from the data presented here that in 1936–8 the Stalinist terror was indeed extensive in the Donbas: It virtually decimated the party leadership and felled at least more than a quarter of senior mining officials. These findings, however, like the aforementioned KGB announcement, raise more questions than they answer. Following the nationwide pattern, the party officials in the Donbas were hit hardest by the terror: They were held responsible politically for all affairs in their domains.[29] Yet, was the extent of terror in the Donbas coal mines representative? Were the industrial managers more vulnerable to terror than, say, the writers, "the engineers of human soul"?[30] These questions begin to appear insignificant in light of the massive terror.

[27] *Sotsialisticheskii Donbass*, 30 July–2 August, 4–6 August, 21 September 1938.

[28] See, for example, *Vechernyi Donetsk*, 15 October 1989.

[29] Economic affairs seemed to have been of particular importance. According to a study of the Moscow party elite of 1917, "anyone whose occupation was connected with economics was a certain victim of the Great Purge." See J. Arch Getty and William Chase, "The Moscow Party Elite of 1917 in the Great Purges," *Russian History/Histoire Russe*, 5, part 1 (1978), p. 113.

[30] According to one account, by the end of 1937, of the 600 delegates to the First Congress of Soviet Writers, not less than one-third "had disappeared without trace." When Stalin died in 1953, more than 200 of the delegates had been "liquidated" and dozens were in

Whatever the case, this note makes two significant points. First, the open fonds in the Soviet archives provide some concrete data on the terror under Stalin. Although the data are incomplete, they provide a new perspective for research.[31] Second, local studies of the Stalin years now seem feasible, owing to the availability of historical sources. In a country as vast as the Soviet Union, center-periphery relations are a critically important issue. Yet because of the source problem, detailed examinations of it have been difficult.[32] With the availability of both the local press and archives to foreign scholars,[33] the traditional, Moscow-centered historical perspective of the Stalin years may soon be corrected.

prison. See Eduard Beltov, "Rastreliannaia literatura," *Vecherniaia Moskva*, 12 November 1988. According to another, during Stalin's reign, more than 1,300 writers perished, and approximately 600 more were imprisoned. See Grogorii Nekhoroshev, "Khotelos' by vsekh poimenno nazvat'. . . ," *Molodoi kommunist*, 1989, no. 12, p. 66. For an attempt to compile a list of "physicists, philosophers of science, biologists, and agricultural specialists who suffered repression," see David Joravsky, *The Lysenko Affair* (Cambridge, MA, 1970), Appendix A.

[31] Since the interview with Tsaplin was published, the archive of the State Planning Commission (Gosplan), which had been closed, was opened to public use. Note several recently published articles based on data from open Soviet archives such as Mark Tol'ts, "Repressirovannaia perepis'," *Rodina*, 1989, no. 11; S. G. Wheatcroft, "More Light on the Scale of Repression and Excess Mortality in the Soviet Union in the 1930s," *Soviet Studies*, 42: 2 (April 1990).

[32] Smolensk is an exception. Part of the Smolensk party archives was captured during World War II and was subsequently used extensively by Merle Fainsod, *Smolensk under Soviet Rule* (Cambridge, MA, 1958), Getty, *The Origins of the Great Purges*, Rittersporn, *Simplifications staliniennes et complications sovietiques*, and Nicolas Werth, *Etre communiste en URSS sous Staline* (Paris, 1981). There are also some studies of national republics and minorities based on a limited range of published sources. For example, Hryhory Kostiuk, *Stalinist Rule in the Ukraine. A Study in the Decade of Mass Terror (1929–1939)* (London, 1960).

[33] The open depositories of the GADO (see note 10) to which I was given access in the autumn of 1989 and the spring of 1990, provide substantial information on political, economic, and social life in the postrevolutionary Donbas.

Part IV: Impact and Incidence

11

Patterns of repression among the Soviet elite in the late 1930s: A biographical approach

J. Arch Getty and William Chase

Stalin's terror, in fact, begins to show a more rational pattern, if it is considered as a statistical matter, a mass phenomenon, rather than in terms of individuals.

Robert Conquest, The Great Terror

In the early years of the Gorbachev period, writers in the Soviet Union sought the origins of Stalinist terror in the person of the deranged dictator, the "administrative system" of the time, or the very nature of Leninism. As engaging as these hypotheses may be, they had little empirical evidence to support them. As more hard evidence has become available, attention and debate have shifted to the quantitative impact of the terror. In the former USSR, several new studies have sharply narrowed the range of estimates of aggregate numbers of victims and generally invalidated the highest Western guesses.[1] But the emphasis in the scholarly discourse on elaborating the overall dimensions of the terror has provided little new insight into the impact of the mass repression on particular groups.

Central to an understanding of the *Ezhovshchina* is an analysis of the

---

[1] For older Western estimates see S. Rosenfielde, "An Assessment of the Sources and Uses of Gulag Forced Labour, 1929–56," *Soviet Studies*, 1981, no. 1; S. G. Wheatcroft, "On Assessing the Size of Forced Concentration Camp Labour in the Soviet Union, 1929–56," *Soviet Studies*, 1981, no. 2; Robert Conquest, "Forced Labour Statistics: Some Comments," *Soviet Studies*, 1982, no. 3; S. G. Wheatcroft, "Towards a Thorough Analysis of Soviet Forced Labour Statistics," *Soviet Studies*, 1983, no. 2; S. Rosenfielde, "Excess Mortality in the Soviet Union: A Reconsideration of the Demographic Consequences of Forced Industrialization 1926–49," *Soviet Studies*, 1983, no. 3; Barbara Anderson and Brian Silver, "Demographic Analysis and Population Catastrophes in the USSR," *Slavic Review*, 1985, no. 3. Recent work from Russian archives includes V. N. Zemskov, "GULAG: istoriko-sotsiologicheskii aspekt," *Sotsiologicheskie issledovaniia*, nos. 6–7, 1990, "Spetsposelentsy," *Ibid.*, no. 11, 1990, "Zakliuchennye, spetsposelentsy, ssyl'poselentsy, ssyl'nye, i vyslannye: statistiko-geograficheskii aspekt," *Istoriia SSSR*, no. 5, 1991, as well as his interviews and articles in *Argumenty i fakty*, nos. 38, 39, 40, 45, 1989. See also A. N. Dugin, "Stalinizm: legendy i fakty," *Slovo*, no. 7, 1990; V. P. Popov, "Godudarstvennyi terror v sovetskoi Rossii, 1923–1953gg.: istochniki i ikh interpretatsiia," *Otechestvennye arkhivy*, no. 2, 1992; and Oleg Khlevniuk, "Prinuditel'nyi trud v ekonomike SSSR, 1929–1941", *Svobodnaia mysl'*, no. 13, 1992.

terror's victims: What types of people were repressed?[2] Although we have made great progress recently in positing aggregate totals, we have only begun to study the flip side of the quantitative coin: the statistical question of risk or vulnerability of various individuals to repression. Implicitly and explicitly, those who have studied the terror have argued that the political and social composition of the victims provides crucial insight into the reasons behind the repression. Yet most studies of the terror's victims have been impressionistic and not quantitative. Among studies of the *Ezhovshchina* that rely on victim selection to provide insight into the reasons for the terror, there is general consensus on the types of groups most likely to suffer repression.

Virtually all agree that the Old Bolsheviks were special targets of the terror. Robert Conquest writes of "the plan to destroy the Old Bolsheviks"; Isaac Deutscher claims that the terror "destroyed nearly the whole Old Guard of Bolshevism." John Armstrong states that the "Great Purge almost eliminated from the apparatus the Old Bolsheviks who entered the Party before the Revolution."[3] In support of the assertion, scholars have noted the sharp decrease in Old Bolshevik representation on the party Central Committee between 1934 and 1939, their prominence among defendants at the Moscow show trials, and the forcible disbanding of the Society of Old Bolsheviks.[4] No one has more forcefully conveyed the image of the Old Bolshevik as victim of the *Ezhovshchina* than Arthur Koestler in *Darkness at Noon*. Rubashov, the bespectacled Old Bolshevik *intelligent* of upper-class origins, is the prototypical victim of the Great Terror. The Rubashovs supposedly knew too much about Stalin's dubious and undistinguished past, recalled too much of the democratic Leninist tradition, and refused to worship or obey Stalin; therefore Stalin singled them out for destruction.

Former members of the defeated party oppositional groups are also believed to have been singled out as victims. Roy Medvedev writes that "almost all those who took an active part in the opposition movements of the twenties perished in the mass repression of the thirties."[5] Many defendants at the three major Moscow trials had belonged to an oppositional group and many arrested during the Great Purges were charged with belonging to an alleged oppositional conspiracy headed by Trotsky or some other former oppositionist.

---

[2] The terms *Ezhovshchina* and *Great Purges* will be used interchangeably to refer to the mass repression that began in 1936 and receded in 1939.

[3] Conquest, 151; Isaac Deutscher, *Stalin, A Political Biography*, New York, 1967, 345; John Armstrong, *The Politics of Totalitarianism: The Communist Party of the Soviet Union from 1934 to the Present*, New York, 1961, 108. See also Zbigniew Brzezinski, *The Permanent Purge: Politics in Soviet Totalitarianism*, Cambridge, MA, 1956, 102.

[4] For examples, Brzezinski, 102; Armstrong 108–109; Medvedev, 192–193, 200–202; Conquest, 123–133, 632.

[5] Medvedev, 31.

Also considered prominent among the victims were members of the Communist party. According to Brzezinski, the "major effort of the purge was directed at the Communist Party itself."[6] Those especially hard-hit among party members included Central Committee members (of 139 Central Committee members and candidate members elected in 1934, 98 perished), members of the Central Committees and apparat of republic-level party organizations, and leading officials in city, oblast, *okrug*, and raion party committees. There is general agreement with Armstrong's observation that "in general the impact of the purge seemed to vary in direct proportion to the importance of the Party posts involved. Nevertheless, the lower levels were heavily depleted." The most notable exception to this statement, Armstrong and others note, was the Politburo, which "appeared least altered by the purge."[7]

The military and its civilian oversight agencies are also considered to have been special targets of the Great Purge. Explanations differ sharply, but all who study the issue can agree with Borys Levytsky's assertion that "among the victims of Stalin's terror, the military establishment led by Marshall Tukhachevskii occupies a special place."[8]

Many in the secret police (the NKVD) were also destroyed. Medvedev notes the "physical destruction of thousands of officials in the punitive organs themselves."[9] Conquest writes that "3,000 of Iagoda's NKVD officers are reported executed in 1937," and that "Beria soon [in 1938] made almost a clean sweep of the old NKVD."[10] Whereas NKVD personnel do not appear to have constituted a significant proportion of the terror's victims, their role as victims is of particular interpretive value to historians such as Conquest and Medvedev for whom the repression of the agents of repression stands as evidence of Stalin's suspicious personality. For these historians, Stalin's personality remains one of the reasons for the terror.

The military and NKVD were not the only state agencies whose personnel were ravaged by the *Ezhovshchina*. Medvedev states that

Gosplan was devastated.... The Council of Peoples' Commissars had its share of victims.... Of course, the commissars were not arrested by themselves in 1937–38; the commissariats they headed were decimated. [After Ordzhonikidze's death] all the major departments [of the Commissariat of Heavy Industry] were ravaged.... The Commissariat of Foreign Affairs was savagely purged in 1937–38.[11]

"The Commissariats of Agriculture, Lumber, Industry, Internal Trade, and Defense Production were particularly affected" by the terror, and

---

[6] Brzezinski, 91.
[7] Armstrong, 108, 106.
[8] Borys Levytsky, comp., *The Stalinist Terror in the Thirties: Documentation from the Soviet Press*, Stanford, 1974, 22.
[9] Medvedev, 214.
[10] Conquest, 275, 623.
[11] Medvedev, 197–198.

there was a "thorough purge of Soviet diplomatic representatives abroad."[12]

No less affected by the Great Purge, according to most accounts, were factory directors, engineers, and technical personnel who administered industry. As Borys Levytsky put it,

Among the state functionaries and managers of the economy who were victims of the repressions, the Soviet "captains of industry" represent the strongest and most interesting group. ... It is estimated that 50 to 75 per cent of the middle and top management echelons fell victim to the repressions in the 1930s and that many subsequently perished.[13]

Armstrong concurs and argues that "the Old Bolshevik *Glavki* [Main Board] heads were almost eliminated, and the composition of the factory managerial force drastically altered."[14]

There is near unanimous agreement with Robert Conquest's claim that the terror struck the intelligentsia "with particular force." Certain groups within the intelligentsia are reputed to have suffered heavily. Conquest states that "the heaviest toll of all seems to have been among writers," although historians, scientists, linguists, philosophers, and professors also were repressed in large numbers.[15] Medvedev shares this opinion and adds that "In 1937 almost all major educationists were arrested. ... Education was engulfed in tragedy. Many outstanding educational administrators and theorists perished."[16]

Finally, most studies of the Great Terror present non-Russians as common victims. Sometimes members of specific ethnic groups are identified, as is the case in Conquest's assertion that Stalin's "former Georgian rivals and friends were mostly shot."[17] More often studies stress the "purge of nationality leaders," to borrow Brzezinski's phrase, or concur with Conquest's claim that there was a "general decision to destroy the old Parties in the national Republics."[18]

All agree that the Soviet elite suffered heavily. As this brief survey makes clear, many leaders of the Communist party, the various state bureaucracies, the military officer corps, and the intelligentsia are believed to have been particular victims of the terror. Without denying that many individual members of the Soviet elite were victims of the terror during the *Ezhovshchina*, the fact remains that to date no one has systematically studied the fate of the elite's members; our understanding of the impact on the elite remains imprecise and anecdotal. This study is based on the

---

[12] Brzezinski, 103.
[13] Levytsky, 19.
[14] Armstrong, 94.
[15] Conquest, 430, 437, 430–447.
[16] Medvedev, 199, 225.
[17] Conquest, 119.
[18] Brzezinski, 77; Conquest, 342.

premise that a statistical risk analysis of members of the Soviet elite on the eve of the terror might provide some insight into common characteristics or experiences that made groups within that elite more or less vulnerable to repression during the Great Purges. Such a method offers the possibility to test certain aspects of existing interpretations and perhaps to suggest directions for future research.

Studying the question of vulnerability to repression is not the same as studying the social composition of the victims. The progress of archival research suggests that we may soon have data on the characteristics of the GULAG inmates and other repressed populations. But to know the proportion of various social categories among the repressed is only part of the answer. If, for example, 90% of the GULAG population consisted of workers and peasants and 10% were from the intelligentsia, it would not be possible solely from this statistic to conclude that peasants and workers were more heavily repressed. One would have to know the proportions of peasants, workers, and intelligenty in the general population from which victims were selected; how many of what kinds of persons were "at risk" to be arrested? Vulnerability analysis, therefore, begins with a "global" population and then studies the reasons why members of it fall into subpopulations (those arrested or not arrested, for example).

We present the findings of a systematic statistical analysis of 898 members of the Soviet elite of the 1930s. Ideally, such an analysis would proceed from good data on the composition and characteristics of that elite on the eve of the terror. Unfortunately, such data on the overall party-state *nomenklatura* in the early 1930s are not currently available. Because we also have little information on the size and structure of the bureaucracy, traditional random or weighted sampling techniques are of little use; we can never be confident that a sample of a population is truly representative if we do not first know the global features of that population. Because of these source limitations, we have chosen to present an "availability sample," which can be defined as a group whose membership depends on the existence of sufficient source material. Although availability sampling is usually not as precise or robust as other techniques, it is valid in the absence of specified assumptions or suspicions that its members are some-how not representative. After analyzing the group at length, we cannot specify any such doubts and can be reasonably confident that our 898 subjects are a reflection of the preterror elite.

To have been included in the present study, the subjects had to meet several criteria. They had to have been born before 1915, their date and circumstances of death had to be known as did the nature of their work in 1936.[19] The most succinct way to communicate the group's composition is

---

[19] It is important to make clear that this analysis adopts a rather strict criterion for the *Ezhovshchina*'s victims. For this study's purposes, death in the custody of the NKVD

to identify the types of bureaucratic positions, occupations, and professions that the 898 group members held. The largest number were full-time party officials (143), among them Politburo and Central Committee members, and republic, oblast, and city party secretaries. The next two largest groups were members of the creative intelligentsia (147) and economic administrators (109). Among the creative intelligentsia were novelists, poets, artists, musicians, ballet dancers, scientists, and academicians. Among the economic administrators were commissars, deputy commissars, and collegium members of the Commissariats of Heavy Industry, Food Industry, Agriculture, Foreign Trade, and Light Industry as well as Gosplan officials and directors and deputy directors of trusts and main boards (*glavki*). Taken together, these three categories account for more than half of the group's members (360 of 671, or 54%) for whom occupations in 1936 were known. Slightly fewer than 10% of the group were military officials (64), including members of the General Staff and unit commanders and officials of the Commissariat of Defense.

None of the remaining eight categories accounted for more than 5% of the group. These categories included scientific research (i.e., heads and leading staff members of research institutes: 39); foreign affairs (officials as well as ambassadors: 32); police/judiciary/control organs (22); supra-ministerial policymaking bodies such as Sovnarkom (20); health and social welfare agencies (16); transportation organizations (i.e., Commissariats of Railroads, Water Transport, and Communications as well as directors of railroad lines: 15); and trade unions (12).

A society's elite is an amorphous, subjective, and ever-changing social group. Because of the tyranny of source constraints and the difficulty of deciding who comprised the elite, we cannot be sure that this slice is any more than a cross-section cut with an unavoidably dull knife. But given the variety of types of people in the group, it may not be far from representative of the elite. In any event, this is the most systematic biographical analysis of the fates of the largest number of members of the Soviet elite to date.[20]

Several biographical factors, or variables, might have had an effect on one's vulnerability as either a victim or survivor in the Great Purges. Some

defines a victim. This standard rather than arrest was selected because it is not uncommon for one source to list someone as arrested whereas another has the person holding a position after his supposed arrest. Given the confusion in the sources, arrest was an unreliable determinant of victimization. Biographies for this research were drawn from The Soviet Data Bank, a machine-readable data archive created by the authors. The biographical data and life histories of the 898 subjects were culled from a variety of published Soviet and Western sources and from the personal research files of contributing scholars, files that often contained data drawn from archives and other primary sources.

20 For other statistical analyses of purge victims, see: J. Arch Getty and William Chase, "The Moscow Party Elite of 1917 in the Great Purges," *Russian History/Histoire Russe*, 5, 1 (1978), 106–115; William Chase and J. Arch Getty, "The Soviet Bureaucracy in 1935: A Socio-Political Analysis," in John W. Strong, ed., *Essays on Revolutionary Culture and Stalinism*, Columbus, 1990, 192–223.

of these variables (age, social origins, and education, for example) fall into the category of general biography. Others, like length of party membership (*partstazh*), pre- and postrevolutionary political background, or oppositional membership, belong to political biography. In addition to such background attributes, a third type of variable relates to precise bureaucratic location and activity on the eve of the terror. Such variables provide a kind of snapshot or structural cross-section of the elite in 1936. Taken together, they should clarify whether background biographical factors or more immediate elements of the 1936 situation are more important in explaining the terror. The variables discussed in the rest of this chapter represent those that proved to be statistically significant by some measure.

In theoretical terms, the goal of this analysis is to define a hidden variable, *vulnerability*, which may – or may not – be a function of measurable biographical attributes. With a large group such as the one analyzed here, it is possible statistically to test the relationships between certain experiences and fates to reveal what made people with certain life characteristics more vulnerable. In so doing, it will be possible to test some of the operative assumptions about what types of people were likely targets of the terror.

Slightly fewer than half of this group's members were victims of the *Ezhovshchina*. Of 898 persons, 427 (47.6%) were victims of the 1936–9 terror. This proportion is close to that produced by studies of smaller subsets of the Soviet elite, and is lower than that cited by Khrushchev for Central Committee members (almost 70%).[21]

Before defining what criteria contributed to increasing one's vulnerability, it is worth examining those variables that, by a series of tests, proved significant and were therefore included in the model used to identify vulnerability.

Purges and biographical background

One of the most surprising results of this study concerns the age structure of those who were purged and those who survived. The mean age in 1936 of those purged was 47.6 years; the mean for survivors was 50.9 – a difference of more than 3 years. Although the difference is *statistically* significant, one should not jump to the conclusion that 3 years' difference between victims and survivors has vast *interpretive* significance. It would be rash to conclude that the purge was directed specifically against younger people.[22] Nor does this finding support the converse: that the terror was somehow aimed at older persons (Bolshevik or not).

[21] Getty and Chase, "The Moscow Party Elite of 1917" (50%). See also B. W. Wolfe, ed., *Khrushchev and Stalin's Ghost*, London, 1957, 124, 132 for Khrushchev's estimate in his "secret speech."
[22] The distribution of age for the entire group fell into an almost precisely normal distribution. The difference in mean age between those purged and those who survived was significant

Table 11.1. *Incidence of purges by birth environment*

Birthplace	Purged	Not purged
Village	85 (56.7%)	65 (43.3%)
Urban area	98 (41.7%)	137 (58.3%)
Total (for whom birthplace is known)	183 (47.5%)	202 (52.5%)

Note: tau $b = 0.146$, $\rho = 0.002$; $\gamma = 0.292$, $\rho = 0.001$.

Table 11.2. *Incidence of purges by social origins*

Social origin	Purged	Not purged
Peasants	77 (67.5%)	37 (32.5%)
Nonpeasants	131 (50.0%)	132 (50.0%)
Entire group	427 (47.6%)	471 (52.4%)

Note: tau $b = 0.152$, $\rho = 0.000$; $\gamma = 0.441$, $\rho = 0.001$.
This table is based on the following gross data, reorganized to isolate the chief differences from random:

Social origin	Purged	Not purged
Bourgeois	14 (73.7%)	5 (26.3%)
Artisans	15 (71.4%)	6 (28.6%)
Peasant	77 (67.5%)	37 (32.5%)
Noble	18 (47.2%)	20 (52.8%)
Professional	34 (48.6%)	36 (51.4%)
Workers	38 (43.7%)	49 (56.3%)
Employee	12 (42.9%)	16 (57.1%)
Total (for whom father's occupation is known)	208 (55.2%)	169 (44.8%)

Where one was born appears to have some relationship to one's subsequent fate. Of the 385 persons for whom place of birth is known, 150 were born in villages and 235 were born in cities or towns. Table 11.1 shows that those born in villages seem to have been more vulnerable than those born in urban areas.

When we turn to the related question of class origins (defined by the social category of the father), we find a similarly curious but significant picture. The virile class-conflict rhetoric of the period and the Bolshevik history of class persecution might suggest a terror directed against representatives of the "alien" classes: nobles, professionals, white-collar employees, and the like. On the contrary, and aside from the numerically few sons of bourgeois fathers, it was not the urban-born children of the upper classes who were the targets so much as the children of village-born peasants. It is sometimes asserted that most of the victims of the purges were of the intelligentsia or the prerevolutionary working class.[23] But the data indicate that such was not the case. In fact, the children of nobles and professionals as well as those of workers and employees were actually purged at rates below the mean.[24] Table 11.2 shows that the statistically significant division was between sons of peasants and sons of all others.

Given Stalin's well-known antipathy toward peasants, it is possible that those of peasant background were singled out for special repression. But as the following analysis will show, the distinction between peasants and nonpeasants has statistical importance only in relation to and in combination with other variables.

Purges and educational background

We are used to thinking that educational background divided the Soviet elite into two groups: those with prerevolutionary education and those educated in the Soviet period. It is often supposed that those with prerevolutionary educations might have been particular targets of a Stalinist purge because they were somehow less malleable, too intelligent, or otherwise unsuited for Stalin's new order; he may have wanted to purge those with tsarist-era educations in favor of more recently educated "new men."[25]

The data suggest, however, that this supposition has no statistical basis; the era of one's education had nothing to do with the selection of victims in this group. The difference in vulnerability between the two educational cohorts is not significant. (See Table 11.3.)

However, one aspect of this group's educational experience did significantly affect vulnerability. Regardless of when one was educated, the highest educational level attained affected vulnerability in a surprising way: The *less* educated suffered more. As Table 11.4 indicates, those with higher education were purged at a significantly lower rate than those without any higher education. This finding raises further doubts about the belief that the intelligentsia was singled out for repression.

---

at the 0.000 level (both for F score and T-test pooled variance probability). This 3-year difference loses interpretive importance, however, in light of standard deviations of 6.8 for the purged group and 11.2 for the survivors.
[23] Armstrong, 66.
[24] Based on father's occupation, for whom social origins are known, and as reported according to categories found in Soviet biographies.
[25] Sheila Fitzpatrick, "Stalin and the Making of a New Elite, 1928–1939," *Slavic Review*, 38, 3 (1979), 377–402.

Table 11.3. *Incidence of purges by educational era*

Period of education	Purged	Not purged
Prerevolutionary	150 (40.8%)	218 (59.2%)
Soviet	45 (37.2%)	76 (62.8%)
Entire group	427 (47.6%)	471 (52.4%)

Note: For those with known education. tau $b = 0.031$, $\rho = 0.24$; $\gamma = 0.074$, $\rho = 0.24$.

Table 11.4. *Incidence of purges by educational level*

Educational level completed	Purged	Not purged
Less than higher	37 (58.7%)	26 (41.3%)
Some higher or above	151 (36.7%)	260 (63.3%)
All educated (for whom educational era is known)	188 (39.7%)	286 (60.3%)
Entire group	427 (47.6%)	471 (52.4%)

Note: tau $b = -0.152$, $\rho = 0.001$; $\gamma = -0.420$; $\rho = 0.001$. Excluded are specialized "party courses" and workers' faculties (rabfaks).
This table is based on the following gross data:

Educational level completed	Purged	Not purged
Primary	11 (84.6%)	2 (15.4%)
Secondary	14 (48.3%)	15 (51.7%)
Vocational/technical	12 (57.1%)	9 (42.9%)
Some higher	63 (57.3%)	47 (42.4%)
Higher	76 (28.7%)	189 (71.3%)
Postgraduate	12 (33.3%)	24 (66.7%)
All educated	188 (39.7%)	286 (60.3%)
Entire group	427 (47.6%)	471 (52.4%)

The sharp break in the data, which explains the difference from random, comes between those with at least some higher education and those without, as Table 11.4 shows. One should make the following cautionary observation: As the data on educational level show (somewhat surprisingly), at least some higher education is nearly a ubiquitous condition for the group.

Purges and political background

Shifting the focus from social to political background, we find evidence to substantiate the traditional wisdom that party members suffered more heavily than the norm. Perhaps more noteworthy is the high survival rate among nonparty elite members: Almost 83% of them survived the terror. Even after accounting for the fact that nearly 80% of the group were party members, it is clear that this was first of all a party purge. (See Table 11.5.)

Table 11.5. *Incidence of purges and party membership*

Party membership	Purged	Not purged
Party members	394 (55.9%)	311 (44.1%)
Nonparty	33 (17.1%)	160 (82.9%)
Entire group	427 (47.6%)	471 (52.4%)

Note: tau $b = 0.319$, $\rho = 0.000$; $\gamma = 0.719$, $\rho = 0.000$. In this and other measures of relationships using cause of death as the dependent variable, 0.05 was the level of significance chosen.

Table 11.6. *Incidence of purges by partstazh*

Period joined party	Purged	Not purged
Before 1912	193 (55.6%)	154 (44.4%)
1912–20	186 (63.9%)	105 (36.1%)
Post-1920/never	48 (18.5%)	212 (81.5%)
Entire group	427 (47.6%)	471 (52.4%)

Note: tau $b = 0.257$, T-value $= 8.54$, $\rho = 0.000$. The 1912 and 1920 divisions in the table were produced by statistical groupings generated by the data.

Although the findings confirm Brzezinski's belief that the "major effort of the purge was directed against the Communist Party itself," they provide little support for Conquest's assertion that there was a "plan to destroy the Old Bolsheviks," or for Armstrong's claim that the "great Purge almost eliminated from the apparatus the Old Bolsheviks, who entered the Party before the Revolution." In fact, among party members, the connection between when one joined the party and one's subsequent fate in the purges is an interesting but nonlinear one: Those with the longest party membership (*partstazh*) were not necessarily the most vulnerable. Those who joined the party during the 1912–20 period, when party membership swelled, were purged more heavily than those who joined before 1912 or after 1920 (see Table 11.6).

Based on these findings, it would be risky to infer that victims were chosen based on the narrow historical period in which they joined the party. The differences in purge rates across the groups *before* 1921 are not very great, and it is more a matter of small increases or decreases in "risk" from period to period. Old Bolsheviks (those who joined the party before 1917) were indeed victims of the terror. Their rate of attrition (58.7%)

Table 11.7. *Incidence of purges on 1917 participants*

Revolutionary experience	Purged	Not purged
1917 participants	263 (62.2%)	160 (37.8%)
Nonparticipants	164 (34.5%)	311 (65.5%)
Entire group	427 (47.6%)	471 (52.4%)

Note: tau $b = 0.276$, $\rho = 0.000$; $\gamma = 0.514$, $\rho = 0.000$.

Table 11.8. *Incidence of purges on oppositionists*

Oppositional membership	Purged	Not purged
Oppositionists	143 (84.1%)	27 (15.9%)
Nonoppositionists	284 (39.0%)	444 (61.0%)
Entire group	427 (47.6%)	471 (52.4%)

Note: tau $b = -0.152$, $\rho = 0.000$; $\gamma = -0.420$, $\rho = 0.000$.

was higher than that for the entire group (47.6%), but roughly equivalent to that for party members in general (55.9%). In terms of statistical significance, however, there is no difference between Old Bolshevik vulnerability and that of the entire group, or that of party members generally.

Although their attrition rate was quite high, it represents neither the total annihilation of the Old Bolsheviks as a generation nor the complete destruction of the "Leninist guard." If we include in our consideration Old Bolsheviks *outside* the 1936 elite, some 70% seem to have survived, according to one calculation.[26] Old Bolsheviks did not suffer disproportionately in the Great Purges and there is little reason to believe that they were singled out as the targets of the *Ezhovshchina*. This evidence on Old Bolsheviks' vulnerability should not deflect attention from one of the more striking findings, namely that those who joined the party after the 1917 revolutions, and especially after the Civil War, were relatively "safe" from arrest in the *Ezhovshchina*. As we shall see, data on party membership are related to other "cohort" variables in the population as a whole.

Another cohort experience, participation in the 1917 revolutions, does suggest a significant relationship. As Table 11.7 shows, those who participated in the 1917 revolutions were purged at a significantly higher rate than those who did not.

[26] See Getty, *Origins of the Great Purges*, 176, for the Old Bolshevik calculation based on party membership figures in 1934 and 1939.

Oppositional membership also divided victims and survivors. As scholars and observers have rightly noted, former oppositionists were arrested en masse; relatively few survived.[27] The findings presented in Table 11.8 confirm this.

The data on party membership, *partstazh*, revolutionary experience, and oppositional membership seem puzzling at first glance. Statistically, being an Old Bolshevik was not related to one's vulnerability in the terror. Yet participants in the 1917 revolutions and former oppositionists (most of whom were Old Bolsheviks) were significant targets. The data seem contradictory. Part of the problem results from relationships among the three variables: Old Bolshevism, 1917 participation, and oppositional status overlap one another. All Old Bolsheviks were 1917 participants, but not all 1917 participants were Old Bolsheviks. Nearly all former oppositionists were Old Bolsheviks, but not vice-versa. Each of these three variables is affecting the other two while it affects purge vulnerability. Before we can understand the pristine effects of these three political variables, we must sort out the ways in which they overlap. Before doing so, however, we should look at the remaining personal and political factors.

Purges and bureaucratic position

Turning from one's biographical and political background to one's political and occupational position in 1936, we find important and significant relationships between bureaucratic rank on the one hand and fate in the purge on the other. As Figure 11.1 suggests, one's relative bureaucratic rank in 1936 was an important determinant of one's vulnerability.[28] The higher one ranked in the bureaucracy on the eve of the *Ezhovshchina*, the more likely one was to be its victim.

As discussed, there is widespread agreement that persons with certain bureaucratic or occupational specialties became victims because of their particular specialty. Our findings reveal that general proposition to be true, but there are some surprises when it comes to identifying which bureaucratic or occupational specializations most affected vulnerability. As

---

[27] That oppositionists were special targets has been confirmed by archival research in the former USSR. See *Izvestiia TsK KPSS*, no. 9, 1989, 35–39.

[28] Many members of the political elite held several positions simultaneously. For example, it was common for a party Central Committee member to hold a position in the state bureaucracy was well as serving as a deputy to some soviet body. Discerning bureaucratic ranks involved two steps. The first was to select the highest position held by an individual. The second was to calculate a value (from 1 to 20) corresponding to this bureaucratic rank. This value was a scalar assignment incorporating the formal rank (title) of a position (e.g., People's Commissar, department chief, etc.) and the administrative level (e.g., USSR, RSFSR, oblast, raion, etc.) at which that post was held. The resulting index was then collapsed into three categories to maintain roughly equal numbers in each category.

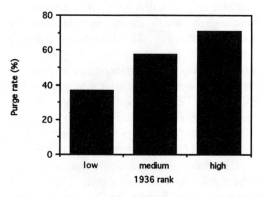

Figure 11.1. *Purge rate by bureaucratic rank (n = 496)*

Table 11.9. *Incidence of purges of bureaucratic specialty*

Bureaucratic specialty	Purged	Not purged
Military	44 (68.8%)	20 (31.3%)
Party	93 (65.0%)	50 (35.0%)
Economic	66 (60.6%)	43 (39.4%)
Intelligentsia	25 (17.0%)	122 (83.0%)
Other	107 (51.4%)	101 (48.6%)
Entire group	427 (47.6%)	471 (52.4%)

Note: For whom 1936 occupation is known, based on a
classification of the subject's principal bureaucratic post in 1936.
(tau b = 0.148; ρ = 0.000). Data in Table 11.9 is based on the
following raw data, refined to locate the principal differences
from random

Bureacratic post	Purged	Not purged
Central ministries	16 (80.0%)	4 (20.0%)
Military	44 (68.8%)	20 (31.3%)
Party	93 (65.0%)	50 (35.0%)
Economic administration	66 (60.6%)	43 (39.4%)
Transport	9 (60.0%)	6 (40.0%)
Police/judiciary/control	13 (59.1%)	9 (40.9%)
Unions	7 (58.3%)	5 (41.7%)
Health, social welfare	8 (50.0%)	8 (50.0%)
Journalism/publishing	10 (47.6%)	11 (52.4%)
Central government (TsIK)	33 (47.1%)	37 (52.9%)
Foreign affairs	11 (34.4%)	21 (65.6%)
Scientific research	12 (30.8%)	27 (69.2%)
Creative intelligentsia	13 (12.0%)	95 (88.0%)
Total (for whom 1936 occupation is known)	335 (49.9%)	336 (50.1%)

Table 11.9 shows, those who worked in the central party and state apparatus, the military, and economic administration were most vulnerable. But those who were members of the artistic and creative intelligentsia or who worked in scientific research were *relatively* safe.

That the party, economic, and military elites were devastated confirms the prevailing wisdom of the subject. Whereas the high attrition rate for these elites contributed to a substantial overall attrition rate for high ranking members of the state bureaucracy, there were some sections of the state bureaucracy where that rate was notably lower. Such was the case for those who worked in foreign affairs. It may be, as Medvedev claims, that "the Commissariat of Foreign Affairs was savagely purged in 1937–38," but in statistical terms those who worked there were *relatively* safe. The most surprising finding, however, is that members of the artistic, creative, and scientific elites were far less vulnerable. These findings offer no support to the assertion that the terror struck the intelligentsia "with particular force." Medvedev may be correct in asserting that "in excess of 600 writers . . . were arrested and destroyed in 1936–39," that the "repression struck at thousands of the technical intelligentsia," and that "Soviet science could not escape the tragic situation that took shape in the mid-thirties."[29] Statistically, though, it seems that the vast majority of the elite intelligentsia escaped repression.

Relationships and effects in the population as a whole

We have examined separately those variables that seem to have statistical and (potentially) interpretive significance in explaining or predicting one's vulnerability in the Great Purges. Members of certain groups seem to have been at greater risk: the village-born, those of peasant social origin, those with no higher education, party members, those with certain *partstazh*, opposition members, 1917 participants, those with higher 1936 positions, and those with certain 1936 bureaucratic specialties.

It is always tempting to combine such contingency tables into composites: Perhaps a village-born, less educated peasant party member who participated in the 1917 revolution, later joined the opposition, and then subsequently rose to high rank in a certain field would be the *most* vulnerable. Perhaps one might also want to posit a less vulnerable, apolitical, ancien régime type, with a particular social background or 1936 rank.

Although separate members of these discrete groups seemed relatively vulnerable or safe, it would be outrunning our data to draw a composite

---

[29] Conquest, 430; Medvedev, 231, 228, 223. The raw data for Table 11.9 also call into question Medvedev's suggestion that the "Commissariat of Foreign Affairs was savagely purged" (p. 103). Certainly all the purging was savage, but two-thirds of the foreign affairs personnel in this group survived.

"type." Each of the preceding tables makes a separate statement about differences between observed and predicted values. Without analyzing in detail the "background" relationships between these variables (some of which are obvious and some not), the results of separate contingency tables cannot automatically be synthesized with one another.

Populations behave differently than subpopulations under the effects of variables in combination with each other. So, three questions remain: First, what are the relationships among these variables? Second, what are the relative strengths of each in predicting purge vulnerability? Third, how much of the overall variation in vulnerability can these variables, in combination, predict? To answer these questions, we generated a model of purge vulnerability.

Fitting a model of purge vulnerability

There are several statistical approaches to building a model capable of explaining overall purge vulnerability. The following presentation uses logit modeling and multiple classification analysis (MCA) as the primary approaches, and presents a probabilistic model in Table 11.10.[30]

Only three of the original variables turned out to be important in explaining the overall process of purge vulnerability: *partstazh*, 1936 specialty, and oppositional membership. Why did the other variables drop out? Several of them were intercorrelated and overlapped one another: The variable *partstazh* thus "overwhelmed" the variables party membership and 1917 revolutionary participation – the effects of the latter two were being statistically reflected by *partstazh*.[31] Similarly, birth environment was "subsumed" by social origins.

Other variables "fell out" of the explanatory model because of either their ubiquity or rarity in the population. Thus educational level failed to enter the model because so many of the group's members had at least some

---

[30] Logit analysis, a specification of the log-linear model, is a method for modeling by predicting cell frequencies from multiple contingency (crosstabulation) tables. It works well with nominal and ordinal variables and does not depend on assumptions about the normal distribution of component variables. See David Knoke and Peter J. Burke, *Log-Linear Models*, Beverly Hills, 1980; and J. Morgan Kousser, Gary W. Cox, and David W. Galenson, "Log-linear Analysis of Contingency Tables: An Introduction for Historians," *Historical Methods*, 15, 4 (Fall, 1982), 152–169. Dummy-variable regression was rejected because the dangers of violating assumptions of normality and of excessive variation producing inflated r^2 values. Multiple classification analysis produced a more accurate r^2 that turned out to be quite comparable to the measures of association (entropy and concentration) generated by the logit approach. Age in 1936 was omitted from the model because of its lack of interpretive significance and its unusual variance compared to the others.

[31] Thus, all party members had a party stazh and all party members who joined before 1917 were 1917 participants.

Table 11.10. *Logit/MCA model of purge vulnerability*

Variable	Log odds	Beta score for main effects[a]
Purged	n/a	
When joined party (Partstazh)		0.29
Pre-1912	2.0	
1912–20	3.0	
1920s/never	1.0	
1936 specialty		0.23
Military	3.7	
Economic	2.7	
Party	2.6	
Other	1.4	
Intellectual	0.5	
Opposition membership		0.19
Yes	4.1	
No	0.8	

[a] Logit analysis compares the actual multiple contingency table with one predicted by the proposed model (which logit considers "random"). Thus, a good "fit" is signaled by a statistically *insignificant* difference ($\rho = 0.108$) in cell distribution between the two: between predicted and observed values. (Beta scores were derived from MCA. Reliable betas for interactions were not available because of missing cells.)
Notes: logit chi square = 15.7 with 10 DF; $\rho = 0.108$. logit entropy = 0.21; concentration = 0.26. MCA $r^2 = 0.25$.

higher education; changes in educational level could therefore produce little effect on purge vulnerability as a whole. Bureaucratic rank in 1936 could apply only to party/state/military officials and not to the intelligentsia and some other groups: Unlike other variables, less than half the population was "at risk" to have a measured rank. Although peasant background seemed an important variable in determining purge vulnerability, it is important to note that only one-eighth of the group were of peasant extraction. Therefore, the effects of being a peasant on the vulnerability of the total population were weaker than those for *partstazh*, 1936 specialty, or oppositional membership. In terms of explaining the process as a whole, therefore, such very common or very rare attributes were not helpful.

What, then, do we now know? *Partstazh*, 1936 specialty, and oppositional membership are clearly the strongest components of vulnerability.[32]

[32] These relative strengths are suggested by the beta scores for the three main variables in the far right-hand column of Table 11.10. Beta scores measure the relative strength of a variable in influencing the dependent effect (purge vulnerability). They are neither additive nor proportional but, compared with one another, assess the relative power of one

First of all, how strong is this model of purge vulnerability? Our analysis produced three separate measures of how well a model based on biographical factors "fits" the data: entropy and concentration (from logit) and r^2 (from MCA). As the notes to Table 11.10 show, these figures are close to one another and range from 0.21 to 0.26. Thus, these three variables can explain about one fourth of the phenomenon of purge vulnerability.[33] Assuming that our theoretical and measurement errors are minimized and that we have no serious specification problems in our variables, the ability to explain 25% of "purge outcomes" may suggest that much of the purging may have been unpredictable and chaotic: being arrested for alleged association with "enemies," being in the wrong place at the wrong time, or as one memoirist recalled the order for his arrest, "just local stuff."[34] Some studies producing "goodness of fit" numbers in this range have *emphasized* the residual, unexplained part and have concluded that chance cannot be discounted as an "explanatory" factor.[35] A view of the Great Purges as disorganized and based on factors other than the conscious selection of victims by individual volition or category is consistent with other evidence.

Yet Table 11.10 does provide some specific information on vulnerability. The column "log odds" gives probability information on the relative strength of individual values within the three variable components.[36] Thus, in the case of *partstazh*, those who joined the party during 1912–20 were, *in association with all other factors*, approximately three times as likely to be purged as those joining in the 1920s or later (log odds 3.0 vs. 1.0); and half again as likely to be purged as those joining before 1912 (log odds 3.0 vs. 2.0).

The analysis confirms the conventional wisdom that people with certain bureaucratic specialties in 1936 and those who had been oppositional members were very vulnerable.[37] Oppositionists were nearly five times as likely to be victims as nonoppositionists (log odds 4.1 vs. 0.8). But the most striking finding is that elite members of the intelligentsia working in intellectual/artistic/scientific activities in 1936 were safest from arrest. Party

variable against the others. Analyses of variance showed that these three variables were not significantly related. Thus *partstazh* was not a determinant of 1936 specialty.

[33] This is not the same thing as being able to explain the fates of one-fourth of the persons in the group. Model analysis seeks to explain *phenomena* (in this case, vulnerability) in relation to combined variables, not individual fates.

[34] Petro G. Grigorenko, *Memoirs*, New York, 1982, 85.

[35] See Christopher Jencks, et al., *Inequality: A Reassessment of the Effects of Family and Schooling in America*, New York, 1972. For criticism of Jencks, see the "Review Symposium on Christopher Jencks et al." in the *American Journal of Sociology*, 78 (1973), 1523–1544. One critic wondered why Jencks focused on the "hole" rather than the "doughnut."

[36] The log odds reflect the relative risk – within the variable and relative only to other values within it – of being purged.

[37] Note again that the log odds values for any one variable are not comparable to those in another. For example, the 3.7 value for military officials under "1936 specialty" is comparable to other scores within 1936 specialty, but has no relation to (or comparability with) any score under *partstazh* or another variable.

leaders were five times as likely to be arrested, and military officials were more than seven times as likely to perish as were *intelligenty*. The risk for the creative intelligentsia was even lower than that for all other miscellaneous groups. Although there is no doubt that members of the intelligentsia suffered during the repression, these findings make it clear that compared to members of the party, economic, and military elite – or even to all other groups – the intelligentsia was much less likely to have perished.

The model also allows us to refine our knowledge about the purge of Old Bolsheviks. As previously noted, about 31% of all Old Bolsheviks and 47.6% of those in this group perished. The difference is that Old Bolsheviks in the present group (by virtue of their inclusion in this group) were still in the elite in the 1930s and therefore more vulnerable than their inactive peers. Old Bolsheviks in the present group suffered not because they were Old Bolsheviks, but because they held prominent positions within the party, economic, and military elite, positions they held because they were Old Bolsheviks. When the party seized power in 1917, it placed its most trusted members into the bureaucracy's most important positions. Although the individuals may have changed, Old Bolsheviks as a group retained the most privileged and powerful positions. When the terror erupted in 1936–7, Old Bolsheviks were among the victims because of where they worked rather than because they were Old Bolsheviks. In short, specialty or "position" in 1936, rather than Old Bolshevik status, was the crucial determinant of purge vulnerability.

The effect of each variable in the model contributes or detracts from one's risk. Attributes that *reduced* risk include nonparty status, avoidance of political opposition, high education, an intellectual career, and, to a lesser extent, social class. So, someone having all these attributes – an apolitical urban-born intellectual from the middle or upper class who received a higher education before the revolution and who avoided political or economic administrative work – was far less vulnerable than others in the elite. Persons having some of these attributes had their risk reduced in proportion to the presence of those qualities, and raised in proportion to the presence of other factors. Those in the elite *outside* politics, for example, scientists, educational administrators, and artists, regardless of their "alien" class background, party status, age, or old regime education, were *relatively* safe from arrest. Personal attributes that *increased* risk or vulnerability in the elite were functions of political and administrative position. Statistically, it was a purge of politicians – oppositionist or otherwise.

So it was neither the Old(er) Bolsheviks nor the "new men," but rather those members of the party, economic, and military elite who belonged to what one might call the "class of 1912–20" who were most vulnerable.[38] Why? On the one hand, one could imagine that Stalin had grudges against

[38] This age group was also overrepresented in the GULAG camps in the 1930s, according to new material from GULAG archives: V. N. Zemskov, J. Arch Getty, and Gabor T.

this revolutionary generation, as he supposedly had against the Old Bolsheviks. Their populist and democratic formative experiences might seem ill-suited to Stalinist conformity, restoration of traditional values, and personal autocracy. They conceivably stood in the way of his alleged plan to elevate a new generation of ideological clones with no revolutionary baggage, and so it was necessary to obliterate them and therefore their values and experiences.

Aside from the problem of attributing common outlooks to an entire cohort, or such specific plans to one person, one can note that revolutionary background in itself (or similar early service) continued to be explicitly valued by the regime even after the terror. Old Bolsheviks continued to be recognized, honored, and applauded at party congresses, at meetings, and in the press for their distinguished service. Revolutionary credentials and Civil War experience continued to be publicly lauded and important credentials for promotion to high position. The older members of the Khrushchev-Brezhnev generation, after all, belonged to this cohort. It is therefore hard to use the findings presented here and what we know about the importance of Old Bolsheviks' credentials to support an interpretation that posits that Stalin planned the terror to destroy the revolutionaries *as such*.

But if we think of the "generation of 1912–20" rather as the "generation of 1936," as people with past political experiences who came to hold key administrative positions by 1936, we can make better sense of the data. If we consider revolutionary activity and party membership as components of 1936 position, we shift the focus from background biographical factors to elements that inhered in the *1936* political situation. If the case is weak for a volitional purge selection of 1917 revolutionaries, it is stronger for a selection based on 1936 position. This analysis lends considerable support to the hypothesis that the part of vulnerability that we can measure was related to variables operative on the very *eve* of the terror whose roots are to be found in the complex contemporary political situation of the mid-1930s and not in the long biographies of victims or the presumed generational hatreds of a tyrant.

Certain groups within the Soviet elite – high-ranking party, economic, and military officials, former oppositionists, and those who joined the Bolsheviks between 1912 and 1920 – were most vulnerable to repression. Other groups – most notably Old Bolsheviks and the intelligentsia – long believed to have been designated targets were not. By showing that Old Bolsheviks were not repressed *simply because* they were Old Bolsheviks, this study casts considerable doubt on the thesis that the terror's purpose was to destroy them as a category because they collectively represented a threat to Stalin. To know that the intelligentsia as a group was not a target will force us to rethink why some members of that group suffered in what was clearly a bloodletting among the political elite. Although it is not now possible to explain precisely why the *Ezhovshchina* happened, it is possible to identify those elements of the conventional explanatory models that have little or no empirical basis. To know that something is unfounded is the first step in learning what is true.

Quite apart from the matter of Stalin's unquestionable guilt, it seems that seeking to understand the causes of the terror solely in terms of "victim selection" on the basis of biographical categories will yield only partial results. Although we have demonstrated that the repression of the Soviet elite was not entirely random, the fact remains that the model cannot statistically explain three-quarters of the phenomenon. Such "negative findings" make an important point, because they demonstrate that much of the repression of the elite cannot be satisfactorily explained by biographical factors; the personal/political/biographical variables used here cannot statistically explain a large part of the phenomenon. This points to other possible ways to account for the "unexplained" portion of the process: chaos, unspecified variables, and/or chance. When the terror erupted in 1936–7, it quickly went out of control, chaotically reflecting personal hatreds and propelling itself with fear. Explanations of the terror based on personal and pathological selection of victims by simple category should be supplemented by approaches that account for lack of coordination, local confusion, and personal conflicts.[39]

In fact, this study's findings suggest that students seeking to understand the *Ezhovshchina* would do well to move away from the longtime obsession with finding any monocausal answer to why that maelstrom of repression and violence occurred, and entertain the obvious and logical notion that the period witnessed overlapping repressions, some of which emanated from the Kremlin or other centers of power, and others that emanated from other sources, be they agents of the state or citizens. An uncoordinated terror would produce results like these: a general movement against the elite plus considerable "spillover." On the other hand, a pattern like the one put forth might also easily result from a simple (if inefficient) massacre from the top. Given what we know about the political and social tensions that permeated Soviet society in the late 1930s, there seems little reason to

---

Rittersporn, "Victims of the Soviet Penal System in the Prewar Years: A First Approach on the Basis of Archival Evidence," forthcoming, *American Historical Review*.

[39] It is also possible that variables we do not recognize or cannot specify help to account for patterns of repression. These might include the political attitudes or orientations of individuals, personal "connections with enemies of the people," or simple proximity to a targeted individual. The existing anecdotal evidence provides many cases of people arrested for such reasons. But such possible attributes could not be included as explicit variables in this study since they would have been vague, subjective, and interpretative ones that could not be measured. The problem is how to specify such attributes: What constitutes proximity or connection? Simply working in the same office will not do. From a bureaucratic list of personnel it is not possible to determine which persons belonged to the personal circle or clique and which were "outsiders" or even police agents or spies in the office.

choose one interpretation over the other until we have conducted much more research.

Writing on the *Ezhovshchina* has sought to chronicle the fates of individuals, to deduce, project, or guess about the total number of victims, and to speculate about Stalin's role in the process. These approaches have been a function not only of the obvious historical importance of such questions, but also of the political needs of those seeking to define a usable past. But in their understandable haste to comprehend the scale and nature of that repression which so deeply scarred Soviet society, less attention has been paid to systematic investigation of relative vulnerability and to the actual risk faced by real people in their lives. The present study has been a contribution to this line of inquiry, and is based on the belief that before we can properly answer the haunting questions about "why," it seems important to know exactly about "what" we are talking. We need to build our understanding block by block, using the best available sources, and shaping the structure with the best tools available.

12

The impact of the Great Purges on Soviet elites: A case study from Moscow and Leningrad telephone directories of the 1930s

Sheila Fitzpatrick

Beginning in the late 1970s, a lengthy debate was carried on among Western scholars about the scale of the Stalinist terror of the late 1930s (the Great Purges). The discussion was stimulated by works like Solzhenitsyn's *The Gulag Archipelago* and Roy Medvedev's *Let History Judge* that were smuggled out to the West or circulated in *samizdat* in the Soviet Union. Drawing primarily on the testimony of individual survivors and their families, these works gave an exceptionally valuable qualitative picture but could not answer quantitative questions. Since little hard data was available, Western Sovietologists' estimates of the number of victims of the Great Purges of 1937–8 varied widely, ranging from hundreds of thousands of deaths to tens of millions.

Sovietologists like Robert Conquest – "cold warriors," as they were sometimes called by scholars of the younger generation – offered very high estimates of the number of Great Purge victims and regarded disagreement with their figures as prima facie evidence of pro-Soviet bias. "Revisionist" Sovietologists, for their part, thought the traditionalists' figures were exaggerated because of their *anti*-Soviet bias. In addition, some demographers and social scientists trained in quantitative methods argued that the highest figures were nonscientific and statistically implausible.[1]

It was in 1978, in the context of this debate, that I first thought of using Soviet telephone directories as a data source on the Great Purges. It seemed improbable at that time that the data on Stalinist repression locked in Soviet archives would become available in the foreseeable future, and

---

[1] A long-running debate on numbers began with Steven Rosefielde's article, "An Assessment of the Sources and Uses of Gulag Forced Labor 1929–1956," *Soviet Studies*, January 1981, which was severely criticized from a "revisionist" standpoint by Stephen Wheatcroft in "On Assessing the Size of Forced Concentration Camp Labor in the Soviet Union 1929–1956," *Soviet Studies*, April 1981. In their article "Demographic Analysis and Population Catastrophes in the USSR," *Slavic Review*, Fall 1985, Barbara Anderson and Brian Silver gave a valuable nonpartisan assessment of the statistical and demographic issues involved.

under these circumstances, any possible avenue seemed worth exploring. In connection with other research projects, I was already working on city directories of the 1930s such as *Vsia Moskva* and *Ves' Leningrad* and in-house institutional directories such as the 1937 *Spravochnik adresov i telefonov rukovodiashchego sostava Narodnogo Komissariata Tiazheloi Promyshlennosti*. It was only a short step from these sources to telephone directories. Once I discovered that successive editions of the Moscow telephone directory had appeared in 1937 and 1939, I set out to find them.

This turned out to be more difficult than I expected. Western libraries did not have all the directories, and even in Moscow only the Lenin Library appeared to have a complete run. The librarians, though uneasy about letting a foreign scholar use the 1937 and 1939 volumes, finally produced them. At this point, however, I ran into trouble at home. My preliminary report on the telephone study, delivered to the Russian Research Center at Harvard University in 1978, was very critically received,[2] probably mainly for political reasons (since Harvard at that time was an unfriendly environment for revisionist Sovietologists), but partly also for methodological ones. I took the methodological criticism seriously and decided to change my sampling technique, although this turned out to be easier said than done. It took me the best part of a decade to accomplish a new sampling because the Lenin Library, having brought me the 1937 and 1939 telephone books once, decided not to risk it a second time. For years, I routinely ordered these telephone directories whenever I went to Moscow, and the Lenin Library equally routinely refused my requests. It was not until 1985 that I got access to the full run of Moscow telephone directories for the 1930s and a partial run of Leningrad telephone directories.

In the extraordinary explosion of historical *glasnost'* of the past few years, Soviet scholars and publicists have begun to investigate the Great Purges, obtaining new data from Soviet archives that provide an infinitely better – though still incomplete – quantitative picture of the scope of Stalinist repression in the 1930s. From the recent researches of Zemskov and Dugin in the NKVD archives, it appears that the highest Western estimates on the size and mortality rate of GULAG's convict population were substantially exaggerated.[3] On the other hand, a range of new evidence,

---

[2] See Daniel Field's editorial comments on the occasion in *Russian Review*, October 1986, p. v, recalling that he was "surprised and bewildered by the fury the paper aroused in some members of the audience."

[3] Conquest's estimate of eight million political prisoners (not including common criminals) in labor camps at the end of 1938 is almost twenty times greater than the figure of under half a million "politicals" in GULAG cited by Dugin from NKVD archives, and four times as great as the *total* GULAG and prison population cited by Zemskov from the same source. According to Zemskov's figures, the entire convict population (including both "politicals" and "criminals") of GULAG's labor camps and labor colonies on January 1, 1939, numbered 1,672,438, with an additional 350,538 prisoners held in jails in mid-January of the same year – a total of a little over two million. Robert Conquest, *The Great Terror. Stalin's Purge of the Thirties* (London, 1971), pp. 708–9; N. Dugin, "GULAG:

including the discovery of mass graves at Kuropaty and elsewhere, suggests that many more "enemies of the people" may have been summarily executed in 1937–8 without ever entering the GULAG system than most scholars suspected.

This study, however, is not concerned with the total number of victims of the Great Purges. My aim is to differentiate the impact of the Great Purges on various elite groups in the first place, and to put the purges of 1937–8 in a broader chronological context of Stalinist repression in the second. Differentiation is important because the purges' dramatic and highly visible impact on the top political and bureaucratic elites may or may not have been reproduced at other levels of the society. The broader chronological context is important because Western scholars – regardless of whether their estimates of the number of Great Purge victims were high or low – may have come to exaggerate the discreteness and uniqueness of this historical episode and underestimate the continuities of the 1930s.

Subjects of investigation

This study attempts (1) to assess the impact of the Great Purges on different elite strata in the population of Moscow by comparing the dropout rate for two groups of individual telephone subscribers listed in the Moscow telephone directories of 1937 and 1939, and (2) to compare the impact of the Great Purges of 1937–8 on a random sample of individual telephone subscribers in Moscow with the impact of earlier waves of repression on similar random samples of individual telephone subscribers in Moscow and Leningrad.

The underlying premise of the study is that the impact of the Great Purges and other waves of repression affecting elites should have been reflected in increased dropout rates for telephone subscribers. It is assumed that when individuals fell victim to the Great Purges[4] or other waves of repression, they ceased to be listed as telephone subscribers.[5]

To assess the impact of the Great Purges on different elite strata, the study investigates two groups: (1) senior officials in the People's Com-

---

otkryvaia arkhivy," *Na boevom postu*, 27 December 1989, pp. 3–4; V. N. Zemskov, "Gulag (Istoriko-sotsiologicheskii aspekt)," *Sotsiologicheskie issledovaniia*, 1991 no. 6, p. 11.

[4] For the purposes of this essay, "falling victim to the Great Purges" means disappearing abruptly from public life as a result of being arrested as a counterrevolutionary or "enemy of the people." The data presented in this study refer only to the *fact* of an individual's disappearance from public life and civil society, not to the process or outcome (death, prison, GULAG, exile, etc.).

[5] Contemporary witnesses report that after such arrests in 1937–8, apartments were often closed up and sealed (*opechatany*). Even if family members remained in the apartment and kept the telephone, they would not have been listed under the name of an arrested enemy of the people.

missariat of Heavy Industry (henceforth, NKTP) who are listed both in
NKTP's in-house *Spravochnik* for 1937 and in the *1937 Moscow Telephone
Directory*, and (2) a control group – a random sample of individual
subscribers listed in the *1937 Moscow Telephone Directory*.

For the purposes of this enquiry, both the NKTP officials and the
individual Moscow telephone subscribers are treated as members of Soviet
elites, the former by virtue of holding high government office and the latter
by virtue of possessing individual telephone subscriptions in Moscow at a
time when only a small minority of the city's population enjoyed that
privilege.[6] The NKTP officials, however, are taken to occupy *a higher
position in the elites* than the average individual Moscow telephone subscriber, since they were members of the nomenklatura (*rukovodiashchie
kadry* or *otvetrabotniki*, in the terminology of the time).

To access the comparative impact of the Great Purges and earlier waves
of repression on Soviet elites, the dropout rate of the control group of
individual subscribers listed in the *1937 Moscow Telephone Directory* is
compared to that of similar random samples of individual subscribers
listed in the Moscow telephone directories of 1928, 1930, 1932, and 1935,
and the *1934 Leningrad Telephone Directory*. This offers the possibility of
comparing the drop-out rate associated with the Great Purges (1937–8)
with rates associated with Cultural Revolution (1928–31), passportization
(1933), and the mass repression in Leningrad that followed Kirov's assassination (1935).

Data sources

The data sources used in this study are as follows:

1. The 1937 internal directory (*Spravochnik*) for the Commissariat of
Heavy Industry of the USSR,[7] which lists the 255 top officials of
NKTP as of January 1937. The entries include full names and patrony-
mics, home addresses, and home telephone numbers.
2. The Moscow telephone directories for 1928,[8] 1930,[9] 1932,[10] 1935,[11]

[6] The *1937 Moscow Telephone Directory* lists about 58,000 individual subscribers, and the
1939 directory about 74,000. In 1939, the total population of the city of Moscow was
4,132,000 persons (*Itogi vsesoiuznoi perepisi naseleniia 1959 goda. SSSR (Svodnyi tom)*
(Moscow, 1962), p. 30). Since the size of an average urban family in the RSFSR at the end
of the 1930s was 3.5 persons (q.v. *Itogi vsesoiuznoi perepisi naseleniia 1959 goda*, pp.
242–3), this meant that fewer than one in every sixteen families had individual telephone
subscriptions.
[7] *Spravochnik adresov i telefonov rukovodiashchego sostava NKTP* (Moscow: Narodnyi
komissariat tiazheloi promyshlennosti SSSR, 1937). The volume went to press on 27
January 1937.
[8] *Spisok abonentov Moskovskoi gorodskoi telefonnoi seti 1928* (Moscow, 1928). The directory, which gave no date for going to press, has a preface dated March 1928 and claims to
be current as of 1 January.

1937,[12] and 1939.[13] The approximate number of individual subscribers in each directory is 28,000 (1928), 33,000 (1930), 37,000
(1932), 47,000 (1935), 58,000 (1937), and 74,000 (1939).
3. The Leningrad telephone directories for 1934[14] and 1936.[15] They
   contain about 44,000 and 50,000 individual subscriber listings
   respectively.[16]

Explanation of tables

Table 12.1 presents data on two elite groups: senior NKTP officials[17] in
1937 and a control group of randomly selected individual Moscow telephone
subscribers in 1937. The two sources of these data, the NKTP *Spravochnik*
and the *1937 Moscow Telephone Directory*, were published almost simultaneously,[18] which allows direct comparison. The two groups consist of
(1) 163 senior NKTP officials listed both in the *Spravochnik* and the *1937
Moscow Telephone Directory*,[19] and (2) a random sample of 721 individual

9 *Spisok abonentov Moskovskoi gorodskoi telefonnoi seti 1930 g.* (Moscow, 1930). The
directory, which gave no date for going to press, has a preface dated May 1930 and claims
to be current as of 1 January.
10 *Spisok abonentov Moskovskoi radio-telefonnoi seti* (Moscow, 1932). The directory went
to press in February 1932.
11 *Spisok abonentov Moskovskoi gorodskoi telefonnoi seti 1935 g.* (Moscow, 1935). The
directory went to press in October 1934.
12 *Spisok abonentov Moskovskoi gorodskoi telefonnoi seti 1937 g.* (Moscow, 1937). The
directory went to press in October 1936 but includes appendices for late entries and
cancellations up to 1 January 1937.
13 *Spisok abonentov Moskovskoi gorodskoi telefonnoi seti 1939 g.* (Moscow, 1939). The
directory went to press in December 1938 and includes new entries and withdrawals up to
1 November 1938.
14 *Spisok abonentov Leningradskikh telefonnykh stantsii. Iul' 1934* (Leningrad, 1934). The
directory went to press in February 1934.
15 *Spisok abonentov Leningradskikh telefonnykh stantsii 1937* (Leningrad, 1937). The directory went to press in January 1936 but was not cleared for publication (*podpisan k
pechati*) until May 1937.
16 In the prewar period, Moscow telephone directories were normally published every other
year. In contrast to later Soviet practice, the prewar telephone books were primarily
directories of individual subscribers, listed by last name, and giving the subscribers' initials
and addresses, and, in some cases, occupations. They also listed the numbers of telephones
in communal apartments directories (by street address, without indicating the names of
communal subscribers), but these listings have not been used in the present study.
17 "Senior officials" are all members of the collegium of NKTP, heads of *glavki* and their
deputies and assistants (*pomoshchniki*), and heads of administrations, sectors, and departments of NKTP and their deputies, together with all the listed directors and chief
engineers of major Moscow factories and heads and deputies of major Moscow trusts.
The group does *not* include the service personnel (maintenance, garage, etc.) or the Supply
Department officers who are also listed in the *Spravochnik*.
18 *Spravochnik adresov i telefonov rukovodiashchego sostava NKTP* went to press on 27
January 1937; *Spisok abonentov Moskovskoi gorodskoi telefonnoi seti 1937 g.* went to
press in October 1936 but includes late entries up to 1 January 1937.
19 This group constitutes 64% of the total of 255 senior officials listed in the *Spravochnik*.

Table 12.1. *Telephone listings of senior officials of NKTP and control group, 1937 and 1939*

1	2	3	4	5
Group	Number in 1937 directory	Number in 1939 directory	Dropout rate (%)	Standard deviation (%)
Senior NKTP officials (from *Spravochnik*)	163	65	60	±6[a]
Control group[b]	721	606	16	±2

[a] Standard deviation computed as for a normal distribution.
[b] Random sample of individual subscribers to *1937 Moscow Telephone Directory*, obtained as described in note 11, above.
Sources: *Spravochnik adresov i telefonov rukovodia-shchego sostava NKTP* (Moscow, 1937); *Spisok abonentov Moskovskoi gorodskoi telefonnoi seti 1937 g.* (Moscow, 1937); *Spisok abonentov Moskovskoi gorodskoi telefonnoi seti 1939 g.* (Moscow, 1939).

subscribers to the *1937 Moscow Telephone Directory*. The *1939 Moscow Telephone Directory* was used to obtain a dropout rate for each group over the period beginning in January 1937 and ending late in 1938 – that is, over the period referred to in Western historiography as the Great Purges.

Table 12.2 focuses on the dropout rate of a random sample of persons identified by profession in the 1937 telephone directory ($N = 239$). It should be noted that this is a random sample not of all professionals who were individual telephone subscribers, but only of those who chose to identify themselves as professionals in the telephone book.[20] The samples are small for most of the professions listed, and some results (e.g., the dropout rate for lawyers) should be treated with great caution

There are no obvious differences (e.g., weighting of the subset for or against higher ranks) in the composition of the main set and the subset. Even very prominent political figures and government leaders might be listed in the telephone directories of the 1930s, although those who lived in the Kremlin and the *Dom pravitel'stva* had unlisted numbers. Of the five top officials in NKTP (Mezhlauk, the Commissar of Heavy Industry, and his deputies Zaveniagin, Bruskin, Serebrovskii, and Osipov-Shmidt), three were listed in the *1937 Moscow Telephone Directory* and two were not. A number of lower-ranking NKTP officials were not in the telephone directory because they lived in communal apartments and hostels or were temporarily resident in hotels.

[20] Comparing the entries in the Moscow telephone directories of the 1930s with those of the Moscow city directories (*Vsia Moskva: adresno-spravochnaia kniga* for 1930, 1931, and 1936), it looks as if members of the medical profession routinely identified themselves as such in the telephone directory, but members of other professions did not do so consistently.

Table 12.2. *Rate of dropout of random sample of individual telephone subscribers identified as professionals, 1937–1939*

1 Professional subscribers[a]	2 Number in 1937 directory	3 Number in 1939 directory	4 Dropout rate (%)	5 Standard deviation (%)
Engineers	89	78	12	±4
Doctors[b]	63	61	3	±2
Artists[c]	29	24	17	±8
Lawyers	10	7	30	±17
Teachers[d]	25	21	16	±8
Other	23	19	17	±8
Total	239	210	12	±2

[a] Sample obtained by taking the last listing on each page of *Spisok abonentov Moskovskoi gorodskoi telefonnoi seti 1937 g.*, pp. 1–240, of a subscriber identified by profession (physician, professor, engineer, etc.)
[b] Including dentists and veterinary surgeons.
[c] Including writers, journalists, actors, composers, cinematographers.
[d] Including professors.
Sources: *Spisok abonentov Moskovskoi gorodskoi telefonnoi seti 1935 g.* (Moscow, 1935); *Spisok abonentov Moskovskoi gorodskoi telefonnoi seti 1937 g.* (Moscow, 1937); *Spisok abonentov Moskovskoi gorodskoi telefonnoi seti 1939 g.* (Moscow, 1939).

because of the size of the standard deviation. For the purposes of this study, engineers are a particularly relevant group because their profession was shared by a large proportion of the senior NKTP officials analyzed in Table 12.1 (though few of the officials chose to identify themselves by profession).

Table 12.3 compares the 1937–9 dropout rate individual telephone subscribers obtained in Table 12.1 with earlier dropout rates in Moscow and Leningrad. The dropout rate for the random sample of 1928 subscribers is calculated from the 1928 and 1930 Moscow telephone directories, the rate for 1930 subscribers from the 1930 and 1932 telephone books, and so on. In the Leningrad case, the rate of dropout for 1934 subscribers is calculated from the 1934 and 1937 Leningrad telephone directories. Column 5 of Table 12.3 removes "normal" attrition (through death, discontinuance of service, etc.), arbitrarily estimated at 4% per annum, in order to give a clearer picture of the pattern of "excess" dropout associated with mass arrests and enforced departure from the city. Column 6 sets out the absolute numbers obtained by calculating the adjusted dropout (given in percentage terms in col. 5) for *all* individual telephone subscribers listed in the biannual telephone directories.

Table 12.3. *Comparison of dropout rate of random samples of individual subscribers listed in Moscow and Leningrad telephone directories, 1928–1937*

1 Samples[a]	2 No. in sample	3 No. still listed in next directory	4 2-year dropout rate (%)	5 Adjusted dropout rate (%)[b]	6 Adjusted dropout (abs. no.)[c]	7 Standard deviation (%)
Moscow						
1928	420	344	18	10	3,000	±2
1930	589	439	25	17	6,000	±2
1932	455	362	19[d]	11	4,000	±2
1935	590	511	13	5	2,000	±2
1937	721	606	16	8	5,000	±2
Leningrad						
1934	528	359	32	24	11,000	±4

[a] The samples were obtained by taking the top name in each column of individual subscriber listings.

[b] The adjusted dropout rate excludes an estimated 4% "normal" attrition of subscribers per annum.

[c] This figure, rounded to the nearest thousand, is obtained by applying the adjusted dropout rate to the total number of individual subscriber listings in each directory.

[d] Since there was an unusually long interval (32 months) between this directory and its successor, the dropout rate has been prorated.

Sources: Spisok abonentov Moskovskoi gorodskoi telefonnoi seti 1928 (Moscow, 1928); *Spisok abonentov Moskovoskoi gorodskoi telefonnoi seti 1930 g.* (Moscow, 1930); *Spisok abonentov Moskovskoi radio-telefonnoi seti* (Moscow, 1932); *Spisok abonentov Moskovskoi gorodskoi telefonnoi seti 1935 g.* (Moscow, 1935); *Spisok abonentov Moskovskoi gorodskoi telefonnoi seti 1937 g.* (Moscow, 1937); *Spisok abonentov Moskovskoi gorodskoi telefonnoi seti 1939 g.* (Moscow, 1939); *Spisok abonentov Leningradskikh telefonrykh stantsii. Iul' 1934* (Leningrad, 1934); *Spisok abonentov Leningradskikh telefonrykh stantsii 1937* (Leningrad, 1937).

Conclusions

The major findings of this study are as follows:

1. Sixty percent of the senior officials of NKTP listed in the *1937 Moscow Telephone Directory* were missing from the directory in 1939. The comparable rate for a random sample of Moscow telephone subscribers was 16% (± 2%), that is, about a quarter that of the senior NKTP officials.

2. The "professional" group of telephone subscribers, taken as a whole and allowing the appropriate margin for statistical error, fared no differently from the general group of telephone subscribers. This was also true of the subset of engineers, whose dropout rate was only about a fifth of that of senior NKTP officials. Doctors were distinguished by an exceptionally low dropout rate of 3% (± 2%). Lawyers, by contrast, may have had an unusually high dropout rate (30%, with a standard deviation of ±17%).

3. The dropout rate for individual telephone subscribers in 1937–8, the Great Purge period, was not high compared to dropout rates in earlier periods, notably Moscow in 1930–1 and – most strikingly – Leningrad in 1934–5. Indeed, it was the second lowest rate in the whole set (fifth out of six), the lowest of all being 1935–6. These rates, however, apply to groups of very different size. In 1937, for example, there were twice as many individual telephone subscribers in Moscow as there had been in 1928, meaning that the 1928 subscribers constituted a more elite segment of the population. If we exclude "normal" attrition from the rates and use the adjusted percentages to calculate an absolute number of "excess" dropouts for each time period, 1937–8 moves into third place, higher than any earlier Moscow dropout except that of 1930–1 (and substantially above the immediately preceding years, 1935–6), but less than half the Leningrad dropout in 1934–5.

The significance of these findings depends on the theoretical soundness of the original premises and methodology and the technical soundness of the data. If, as a result of some factor I have overlooked, dropout rates for individual telephone subscribers cannot be correlated with the Great Purges or other waves of Stalinist repression, even the most statistically significant findings, such as the strikingly large difference between the dropout rates for senior NKTP officials and the control group of 1937 Moscow telephone subscribers, might have to be discounted. I cannot imagine what kind of factor this might be, but the possibility ought to be mentioned. If the data are technically flawed, for example, by an unacceptably high rate of typographical error in the printing of the telephone directories, this could disqualify findings that are relatively near the borderline of statistical significance, while leaving the major findings intact.

Assuming that the findings are valid, how are they to be interpreted?

The major conclusion to be drawn from the 1937–9 data is that *senior NKTP officials were a highly vulnerable group* in the Great Purges. Their dropout rate was strikingly higher than any other encountered in this investigation, and four to five times as great as that of the average engineer who was an individual telephone subscriber (even though many senior NKTP officials were engineers by profession). It appears, therefore, that *holding high office, rather than profession or area of employment, was a key variable* in determining vulnerability.

The special vulnerability of senior party and government officials, and of industrial leaders in particular, is well attested from other sources. Soviet industrialists were specific targets of attack in the Piatakov Trial (January 1937) and at the February–March (1937) Plenum of the party Central Committee, and the contemporary press gives many examples of the unmasking of enemies of the people in this milieu. Further evidence is provided in memoir- and interview-based accounts such as those of Roy Medvedev and the industrial journalist, later historian of industry, A. F. Khavin.[21]

It is possible to find some independent evidence confirming that individual senior NKTP officials in our sample fell victim to the Great Purges. Of 163 senior NKTP officials who are listed in the 1937 telephone directory, 98 are missing from the 1939 directory. Nineteen of the dropouts (19%) can be individually identified as Great Purge victims.[22] Of the remaining 78

---

[21] See, for example, Roy A. Medvedev, *Let History Judge. The Origins and Consequences of Stalinism*, 2nd ed. (New York, 1989), pp. 444–5; A. F. Khavin, "Razvitie tiazheloi promyshlennosti v tret'ei piatletke (1938–iiun' 1941 gg.)," *Voprosy istorii*, 1959 no. 1; idem., "Ot VSNKh k sovnarkhozakh nashikh dnei," *Istoriia SSSR*, 1960 no. 4; idem., "Kapitany sovetskoi industrii 1926–1940 gg.," *Voprosy istorii*, 1966 no. 5.

[22] The nineteen are A. P. Serebrovskii, O. P. Osipov-Shmidt, A. I. Zykov, E. L. Brodov, G. I. Kanner, E. M. Alperovich, G. N. Grozdev-Tokarenko, S. G. Zhuravlev, D. E. Perkin, I. A. Pogosian, A. D. Pudalov, L. A. Raskin, I. I. Melamed, B. N. Iashchechkin, S. N. Batulin, S. K. Agamirov, K. M. Begge, P. S. Borisov, and M. I. Frumkin. Only one NKTP official listed in both the 1937 and 1939 telephone directories is known to have been a Great Purge victim (Aleksandr Armand, son of Inessa). Presumably he was arrested after 1 November 1938. Data on individual members of the NKTP group have been taken from the files of the Soviet Data Bank in the United States (a project for computerization of office-holding data on party and state officials in the 1920s and 1930s, directed by Profs. J. Arch Getty of the University of California at Riverside and William Chase of the University of Pittsburgh); the computerized biographical data bases created under the leadership of V. Z. Drobizhev and A. K. Sokolov at the Laboratoriia po primeneniiu matematicheskikh metodov i EVM v istoricheskikh issledovaniiakh at the Moscow State Historical-Archival Institute; U.S. Embassy reports from Moscow in the U.S. National Archives; and my own biographical files, based on a variety of sources including *Za industrializatsiiu* and other contemporary Soviet newspapers. My thanks are due to J. Arch Getty, Anne Todd Baum, and V. Z. Drobizhev for searching the data bases.

members of the NKTP group, 67 have biographical files in the computerized Soviet Data Bank, but none of these files shows an employment history after 1938.[23]

According to our data, between January 1937 and November 1938, *senior NKTP officials were three to four times as likely to "disappear" from the telephone book as the average Moscow subscriber.* This is one of the more surprising findings of the study, not only because the difference in vulnerability is very large but also because the dropout rate for the control group is comparatively low. It has often been assumed that whereas the top political and bureaucratic elites took the main blow in the Great Purges, the impact spread downwards and outwards in a ripple effect. If this were so, the impact on an elite group like Moscow telephone subscribers ought to be considerable. Our data, however, suggest a fairly limited impact. This would be more compatible with either of two alternative hypotheses. The first hypothesis is that the impact of the Great Purges was strongly localized on the top elites and did not significantly affect other social groups. The second – in my opinion, the more plausible – is that the specific point (or points) of direct impact was localized, but the whole society, or large parts of it, experienced a secondary impact in the form of heightened political tension and increased arrests.

The dropout rate for individual Moscow telephone subscribers in 1937–8 was 3% higher than the figure for 1935–6. But this difference is on the borderline of statistical significance. More important is the fact that the statistics put an upper limit[24] on the possible rise in the dropout rate of Moscow telephone subscribers between 1935–6 and 1937–8: If these data are accurate, *no more than 7% of the group* could have fallen victim to the Great Purges.

It must be remembered, however, that in a large group even a small percentage may be quite significant in terms of absolute numbers. Even given a dropout rate for senior NKTP officials three to four times higher than that of the control group of individual telephone subscribers, there might well be more victims in the latter group than the former. In a group of 58,000 persons (the number of individual telephone subscribers in Moscow in 1937), for example, a purge-associated "excess" attrition of as little as 5% would produce almost 3,000 victims. If we postulate for the purpose of argument that the senior NKTP officials of our study were part of a top bureaucratic elite stratum of 5,800 persons, even a 50% purge rate in this group would produce only the same absolute number of victims as the 5% rate postulated for the much larger group of telephone subscribers.

---

[23] It should be noted, however, that the sources of biographical and employment information on which the Soviet Data Bank (see above, note 22) drew are much poorer for the post-1938 period than they are for pre-1938.

[24] See Table 12.3, cols. 4 and 6. With a standard deviation of ±2 for the two figures (13% and 16%), the lower limit for the "excess" dropout rate is zero.

The corollary of the comparatively low dropout rate for Moscow telephone subscribers in 1937–8 was the comparatively high dropout rate for subscribers at other times – notably 1930–1 in Moscow and 1934–5 in Leningrad.[25] If there is a correlation between high dropout and repression, there must have been *earlier episodes of repression that affected telephone subscribers even more severely than the Great Purges.*

For the period 1928–31, the episodes likely to have produced "excess" attrition are Cultural Revolution[26] and the liquidation of the New Economic Policy (NEP). The two groups of telephone subscribers that were particularly at risk of arrest in these episodes were "bourgeois specialists" in the first case, and Nepmen in the second.[27] Using the Moscow city directory,[28] it is possible to discover the occupation or place of employment of almost half the individuals who dropped out of the Moscow telephone directory between 1930 and 1932. Of these, 41% were professionals ("bourgeois specialists")[29] and 30% were "Nepmen"[30] – a total of 71% of the group whose occupation can be identified.

In the period between the completion of the 1932 and 1935 Moscow directories, "excess" attrition was presumably linked with passportization, that is, the introduction of internal passports and city residence permits in Moscow at the beginning of 1933. This measure, carried out by the OGPU, was accompanied by the expulsion of "social aliens" (including *byvshie*, members of the prerevolutionary privileged classes) from the city.[31] According to a usually well-informed emigré journal, the target figure for expulsions from Moscow was 500,000.[32]

---

[25] Note that the two Leningrad telephone directories used here, those published in 1934 and 1937, were the only ones available for this investigation.

[26] That is, the class-war Cultural Revolution of the First Five-year Plan period, epitomized by the 1928 Shakhty Trial and the 1930 Industrial Party Trial of "wreckers" from the old intelligentsia: q.v. Sheila Fitzpatrick, ed., *Cultural Revolution in Russia, 1928–1931* (Bloomington, IN, 1978).

[27] One might expect the Nepmen to have dropped out in 1928–9 rather than in 1930–1, but this is not borne out by the evidence of the city directories. Form the occupational and business identifications of city residents listed in *Vsia Moskva* and *Ves'Leningrad*, it can be seen that the Nepmen often hung on (though not always with their former business association) until 1930 or 1931.

[28] *Vsia Moskva. Adresnaia i spravochnaia kniga na 1930 g.* (Moscow, 1930).

[29] N = 27 persons (5 doctors and dentists, 9 teachers and professors, 2 engineers, and 11 writers, journalists, artists, and other cultural professionals). This count is bound to have missed a number of "bourgeois specialists" who gave a job identification rather than a professional one. In addition to those who identified themselves as engineers, for example, another seven who identified themselves by an industrial place of employment are likely to have been engineers.

[30] N = 20 persons. Note that the "Nepmen" category is broadly defined to include all merchants, manufacturers, stockbrokers and others in the private sector, independent artisans, and also artisans in cooperatives.

[31] See the law of 27 December 1932: "Ob ustanovlenii edinoi pasportnoi sistemy po Soiuzu SSR i obiazatel'noi propiske pasportov," *Sobranie zakonov i rasporiazhenii raboche-krest'ianskogo pravitel'stva SSSR*, 1932 no. 84, art. 516. Those expelled from the city were allowed to resettle in any nonpassportized region, i.e., in the countryside or in a city

The external event that must be associated with Leningrad telephone subscribers' exceptionally high attrition in 1934–5 was the wave of arrests and deportations of Leningrad residents following Kirov's murder in December 1934. According to our data, this was by far the most damaging episode of the 1930s for the elite segment of the population with individual telephones group (though its impact on this comparatively large group was only half as strong as that of the Great Purges on the small group of senior NKTP officials). Adjusting for "normal" attrition (see Table 12.3), we can calculate an "excess" attrition of 11,000 subscribers in Leningrad in 1934–5, compared with 6,000 in Moscow in 1930–1 and 5,000 in 1937–8.

Among those who "disappeared" from Leningrad at this period, some were no doubt party and government officials being reassigned to new posts in other parts of the country in the mass transfers that followed the Kirov murder. Others were probably bureaucrats and specialists moving to Moscow along with their institutions (e.g., the Academy of Sciences) in 1934 and 1935. But arrests and deportations – particularly the latter – were surely the major factor. The eccentric feature of the mass repressions in Leningrad after the Kirov murder was that former aristocrats and other members of the prerevolutionary privileged classes were a prime target,[33] despite the lack of any logical connection between this group and the murder. Many of the 1935 Leningrad dropouts were in this category.[34]

To sum up, this study provides additional confirmation for the thesis that high officeholders as a group were extremely vulnerable during the Great Purges. It also shows that the officeholders' risk was three to four times as great as that of ordinary Moscow telephone subscribers. The telephone subscribers' risk of "disappearance" during the Great Purges was actually smaller than it had been (albeit for a smaller group of subscribers) earlier in the decade, notably in 1930–1 in Moscow and in 1934–6 in Leningrad. This suggests that whereas the years 1937–8 con-

---

or town where passports and residence permits had not yet been introduced. But they lost their ration cards, and were only allowed to take a limited amount of personal and household possessions with them.

[32] *Sotsialisticheskii vestnik*, 1933 no. 8, p. 16. The figure was subsequently lowered to 300,000, according to this source, because of the high volume of protests and interventions on behalf of "socially alien" but well-connected Muscovites. But an earlier issue of the same journal (1933 no. 3, p. 16) noted that many residents who were at risk under the new law left the city voluntarily before passportization to avoid being stigmatized by expulsion.

[33] See the NKVD announcement of the Leningrad arrests and deportations – ostensibly linked with "violation of the rules of residence and the law on the passport system" – in *Za industrializatsiiu*, 20 Mar. 1935, p. 2.

[34] In this connection, it should be noted that our data base – telephone directories – may overrepresent prerevolutionary elite members (*byvshie*). It was very hard to acquire new apartments and telephones, particularly noncommunal ones, in the 1920s and the 1930s. It was presumably easier (barring arrest or deportation) to retain an individual telephone subscription that had been established before the Revolution.

260   *Sheila Fitzpatrick*

stituted an unparalleled episode of terror as far as the top political and bureaucratic elite was concerned, this was not so for a more broadly defined social elite (or, it might be inferred, for the urban population as a whole). It may be that Solzhenitsyn's image[35] of successive waves of repression, each striking some specific (social, occupational, ethnic) populations as well as having a random impact on the population as a whole, is a more useful starting point for social historians than an exclusive focus on the Great Purges.

[35] See Aleksandr I. Solzhenitsyn, *The Gulag Archipelago, 1918–1956. An Experiment in Literary Investigation*, vols. 1–2, trans. Thomas P. Whitney (New York, 1973), pp. 24–6.

13

Victims of Stalinism: How many?

Alec Nove

Glasnost', the opening to scholars of hitherto secret archival material, has made possible a marked reduction of our area of ignorance. Combined with new demographic data, especially that relating to the suppressed census of 1937, it enables us to make with fair confidence an estimate of the likely number of abnormal deaths in the thirties and of the numbers in prisons and camps at various dates through 1950. Two articles of mine published in *Soviet Studies* (April and October 1990) presented some of the data. New information enabled me to modify some of the conclusions of the first article, and since then still more archival material has seen the light of day. So this would seem to justify a new and more comprehensive (and comprehensible) paper.

Before plunging into detail, several warnings are in order. Firstly, the archives themselves for the years of the terror, even those intended to be secret, by no means always provide a reliable source of information. A good example of this is an official letter about the 1937 census from Kurman, a census official, written shortly before his own arrest; in this letter he did not dare mention the word *famine* as having affected the population in 1933 (though, as we shall see, he used suggestive circumlocution) and, in referring to Kazakhstan, he plainly exaggerated the number of Kazakhs who fled from the USSR to conceal the number who died (or he himself was the victim of false reporting from Kazakhstan).[1] A second example: It is becoming clear that the population figure published for 1939 was overstated, but this has to be deduced from indirect evidence. Nothing has yet come to light in the archives that actually says so. Doubtless it was silently understood that anyone querying the figure of 170 million would quite probably soon join the authors of the 1937 census in the next world.

---

[1] Quoted by V. Tsaplin, "Statistika zherty naseleniya v 30e gody," *Voprosy istorii* no. 4, 1989, p. 177.

Additionally, the figures on famine-related deaths cannot be precise, for "definitional" reasons. Some whose health was undermined by hunger died in subsequent years of disease; the Kazakh demographic catastrophe involved a typhus epidemic. Ukrainian statistics show a very large decline in births in 1933–4, which could be ascribed to a sharp rise in abortions and also to the nonreporting of births of those who died in infancy.

Figures purporting to represent the numbers of victims of "Stalinist repression" are also subject to definitional ambiguity. This particularly affects *exiles*. These range from those who were given a *minus* (i.e., could live anywhere "minus" a list of forbidden cities) through to those exiled to remote areas often under harsh conditions, but not kept behind wire. Two examples, one fictional and one real, of this latter category: Sasha Pankratov, the hero of Rybakov's *Deti Arbata*, and Ariadna Efron, daughter of Marina Tsvetayeva, whose sufferings are described in her letters to Pasternak.[2] For purposes of demographic statistics, most exiles were just part of the civilian population, but clearly they were also victims of "repression," and their numbers are not yet known. There is also an unclear category, *spetspereselentsy* (special resettlers), that may or may not be identical with those detained in *spetsposeleniya* (special settlements), where conditions may have approximated those of the labor camps. There were also so-called *kolonii*, under the NKVD. It was a surprise for me to learn that the Gulag in its strict sense contained a minority of detainees in 1939; as we shall see, the evidence points that way.

The data on *political* prisoners and on executions also suffer from unclarities. Thus some figures speak of those who committed counter-revolutionary crimes, which I take to cover anyone charged under article 58. But many who could be regarded as political prisoners were charged under other articles. In any case, the *osobye soveshchaniya* (special councils) could imprison and exile persons on mere suspicion of being "socially dangerous elements."

Also, the evidence on mass shootings at Kuropaty and similar places suggests that many were shot without any formal charges at all. This would certainly apply also to the Polish officers killed at Katyn and elsewhere. Nor can one have confidence about the reporting of deaths in detention, and we shall see that Tsaplin shares this view. So such figures as we have must be cross-checked against demographic data.

Let us begin with the basic demographic data on the 1930s. Central to the analysis is the 1937 census. Stalin had told the Seventeenth Party Congress that the population as of January 1934 exceeded 168 million. For January 1, 1933, the official figure published at the time was 165.7 million. All commentators, from Lorimer to Danilov, agree that this number is too high. Many calculations, including my own in early editions of my

[2] See *Novyi mir*, no. 11, 1988.

Economic History,[3] used the contrast between such figures and the total of "only" 170 million in the 1939 census as a basis for calculating demographic losses. But we were wrong.

The key to understanding is the publication of data taken from the suppressed 1937 census. The total population in 1937 came to 162 million, and clearly the contrast between this and the (false) figure cited by Stalin (168 million in 1934) cost the lives of the census organizers, the chief of whom was the distinguished Sorbonne-educated statistician, O. Kvitkin. Anyway, the figure 162 million must replace the 1937 population cited in the *Narodnoye khozyaistvo* annual for 1962: 163.8 million, which many, including myself, wrongly surmised to have been the 1937 census figure. The figures on the 1937 census come from several sources, the first of which is the article by V. V. Tsaplin,[4] the Director of the Central State Archive of the National Economy (TsGANKh SSSR) in Moscow, who used the material in the Statistical Offices archives (the office was known by the acronym of TsUNKhU in the thirties). Secondly, the historian Yu. Polyakov and his associates were given access to the actual materials of the census in the Central State Archive of the National Economy (TsGANKh), and they reproduced many figures and the accompanying correspondence.[5] (I did not have this material when I wrote my articles in *Soviet Studies*.) Thirdly, the research of Wheatcroft and Maksudov,[6] who (separately) were also given access to archives, provided important "indicators" as to the meaning of the figures. Polyakov and his colleagues also found vital material to enable us to interpret the 1939 census.

How is it that Stalin, and before him TsUNKhU, got the figures for 1934 so wrong? Stalin seems to have believed (?) the official claim that the population had increased by 2.3 million in 1933 (165.7 + 2.3 = 168). But 165.7 was also wrong. Tsaplin points out that TsUNKhU kept two sets of books, "one for the press, one for official use," and that the unpublished estimate for 1934 was 160.5 million, and that the population *fell* in 1933 (according to the TsUNKhU archives) by "almost 1.6 million." Tsaplin cites Kraval' (one of Kvitkin's assistants in organizing the 1937 census) to the effect that the population increase in 1935 and 1936 averaged 1.4–1.5% per annum, which, if the total for 1937 was 162.0 million, suggests a January 1934 total of about 158 million. This could be consistent with 160.5 million if one allows for unrecorded deaths, which, as we shall see, were of particular importance in 1933.

[3] A. Nove, *The Economic History of the USSR* (1969).
[4] Tsaplin in *Voprosy istorii* no. 4, 1989.
[5] Yu. Polyakov, V. Zhiromskaya, I. Kiselev, "Polveka molchaniya," *Sotsiologicheskie issledovaniya* nos. 6, 7, 8 of 1989 (cited henceforth as Polyakov).
[6] Personal communication to author from Maksudov, and S. G. Wheatcroft, "More Light on the Scale of Repression and Excess Mortality in the Soviet Union in the 1930s," *Soviet Studies*, vol. 42, no. 2, April 1990, 355–67 (reprinted as Chapter 14 in this volume).

The census takers in 1937 were aware that their total would look too low. The first figure they arrived at was 156 million, excluding the military, prisoners, and individuals on journeys. It is this figure that an imprisoned statistician conveyed to Antonov-Ovseyenko and that he quoted on his release. His (and the statistician's) memory was good, but the figure was incomplete. The military had to be added and the NKVD itself and those "specially counted" (*perepisany v osobon poryadke*), that is, prisoners of various categories; these were given as 2,653,035, and the military including NKVD troops and guards, Kraval estimates as 2 million.[7] Allowing for a few other omissions one can arrive at 162.0 million. But this figure was well below the numbers implied by the registration of births and deaths; this showed an increase over the 1926 census figure of 21.3 million, that is, the total should have been not 162 but 147 + 21.3 = 168.3 million. M. Kurman, one of the men in charge of the 1937 census, attempts to explain, no doubt anticipating strong official disapproval.

Apart from minor errors and omissions, he advances two reasons to account for the discrepancy: the alleged flight of two million Kazakhs and other Central Asians, and "the under-recording of deaths in the previous decade." Kurman's letters were cited briefly by Tsaplin and at much greater length in a supplement to Polyakov's article.[8] Tsaplin's two citations from Kurman read as follows:

Special investigations on the spot showed that in the Ukraine, the Azov Black Sea, Saratov, and Stalingrad krais and the Kursk and Voronezh oblasts there were significant numbers of unregistered deaths. On the basis of available materials, it may be said that in 1933 one million deaths were not recorded. According to the department of population the number of deaths in 1933 came to 5.7 million, and with the addition of those not recorded it was 6.7 million.

It may be estimated that of the total number of unrecorded deaths [in 1929–37] at least 1.0–1.5 million relate to deaths whose registration was not included in the general citizens' records: *spetspereselentsy*, those imprisoned in concentration camps and others. These data must evidently be with the Gulag and the NKVD.[9]

Kurman divided the USSR into five demographic categories, group five being

basically agricultural areas with unfavorable population movement and a larger than average number of deported kulak elements. . . . In this category are the agricultural areas of the Ukraine (except the Donbas), Kazakhstan, Kursk *oblast'*, Saratov *oblast'*, the Volga-German ASSR, Kuibyshev *oblast'*, the Azov-Black Sea *krai*, the Russian areas of the North Caucasus, parts of the Voronezh and Stalingrad *oblasti*. It is noteworthy that in this category are the areas where the resistance of the kulaks to collectivization was particularly bitter and sharp, which affected the size of the population.[10]

[7] Tsaplin, p. 176.
[8] Polyakov (no. 6) pp. 8–12.
[9] Tsaplin, pp. 177–8.
[10] Polyakov (no. 6) p. 11.

He went on to give as an example the Dnepropetrovsk oblast (Ukraine), where the population increased between 1926 and 1937 by 6.8%, but the *rural* population fell by 26.3% (the urban population rose by 177%). Kurman could not in 1937 utter the word *famine*, but he clearly pointed to the areas most affected by it.

Archive director Tsaplin noted in his 1989 article that in 1927–31 the average number of deaths was 2.6 million. The number of registered deaths in 1932 and 1933 totalled 8 million. He cited a document in the archives that states that "just in the Ukraine the number who died (in 1933) was 2.9 million, i.e., over half of the total deaths in the USSR, although the Ukraine's population is only a fifth of the USSR." This implies a total *registered* death toll in that year of close to 5.8 million. If one adds a million to the total, the "abnormal" deaths in 1933 would amount to 4.2 million (6.8 – 2.6).

Tsaplin's conclusion: Up to the census date (January 1937), 3.8 million died from the famine, from starvation or disease; 1.5 million perished "in places of detention," and a further 1.3 million "could be considered as dead from hunger or in places of detention," and 2 million "fled abroad."[11]

All of this final 2 million did not "flee abroad." Estimates of the numbers who did range up to 200,000. A remarkable article by three Kazakh historians[12] asserts that 42% of the entire Kazakh population, 1,750,000 persons, perished in 1931–3. Maksudov has expressed the view that the real figure was at most 1.5 million, because the flight of Kazakhs to adjoining Central Asian republics was underestimated by the authors. But such a figure is horrible enough. The pastoral seminomadic way of life was destroyed, typhus killed many in the settlements into which they were herded, and nearly all their sheep perished too.

If these figures are added to Tsaplin's calculation, then, up to January 1937 the number of abnormal deaths would amount to 3.8 + 1.5 + 1.3 + 1.5 = 8.1 million. The "deaths in detention" figure of Tsaplin's would include so-called kulaks, many of whom were deported under appalling conditions.

It is also noteworthy that the British-Australian scholar Wheatcroft was able to obtain the details of death rates by *oblasti* and by months for the years of famine, both for the Ukraine and much of the RSFSR that distinguished between urban and rural death rates. These figures show conclusively that, though the situation was appalling in the Ukraine, deaths were also massive in the North Caucasus and Lower Volga regions.[13]

Tsaplin's estimates for famine deaths was, as we have seen, 3.8 million plus some part of the 1.3 million he attributes to famine or to deaths in

[11] Tsaplin, p. 178.
[12] Zh. Abylkhozhin, M. Kozybaev, M. Tatinov, "Kazakhstanskaya tragediya," *Voprosy istorii* no. 7, 1989.
[13] S. Wheatcroft, especially pp. 361–2.

detention – let us say 4.5 million. To these must be added victims of the Kazakh disaster, which would bring famine deaths to 6 million. The Boston-based scholar Maksudov would add firstly, some additional hundreds of thousands to reflect the high probability that the very low reported births in the Ukraine in 1933 must have been due in part to concealment of births of infants who soon died (there was also a sharp rise in abortions). His view finds support in figures quoted by Polyakov from a Leningrad demographic report found in the archives: 782,000 births in 1932, 358,000 births in 1933, in the Ukraine.[14] Maksudov also points to the death rates in 1932 and 1934 as being above normal – though of course nowhere near the catastrophic figures of 1933. He argues that death from famine and famine-related disease might well have reached 7 million, inclusive of Kazakhstan, with the Ukraine alone at least 4.5 million, possibly 5 million.[15]

A similar conclusion is reached by Michael Ellman in his note published in *Soviet Studies* (no. 2, 1991), but by another route. He bases his arguments on an article by three Soviet statisticians, E. Andreyev, L. Darskii, and T. Kharkova, published in *Vestnik statistiki* in 1990.[16] These authors state that the population declined by 5.9 million in the single year 1933. The source for this they leave unclear. As already mentioned above, Archive Director Tsaplin found in the archives a figure of minus 1.6 million for that year, to which must be added unrecorded deaths, which census official Kurman had estimated at 1 million. Since Kurman had plainly underestimated deaths among Kazakhs (many of which are very likely to have been unrecorded), the million might perhaps be doubled. But it is hard, without some further proof, to accept a figure of minus 5.9 million for that one year, and, for reasons already advanced, one can reach 7 million victims of hunger without having to do so. In the same article by the three Soviet statisticians, the authors cite without critical comment a Soviet source that claims that 7 million were shot in the years 1935–41, although this would be quite inconsistent with their own year-by-year population series published in the same article.[17]

Polyakov and his colleagues reproduce a table containing the 1937 census results broken down by oblasti and republics, but unfortunately with no breakdown between urban and rural areas. The Ukraine showed a decline of 1.9% in population between 1926 and 1937. Not only such predominantly rural *oblasti* as Vinnitsa and Chernigov, but even more urbanized areas like Kiev and Kharkov, showed declines of over 10%. To see why, one only has to look at the appalling death rates cited by Wheatcroft. There were also big declines in Saratov (−23%!) and Voronezh (−15%). The decline in Kazakhstan was "only" 16%, but Polyakov cites

---

[14] Cited by Polyakov (no. 6) p. 21.
[15] Research data transmitted to the author by Maksudov and used here with his permission.
[16] E. Andreyev, L. Darskii, and T. Kharkova, "Opyt otsenki chislennosti naseleniya, 1926–41," *Vestnik statistiki* no. 7, 1990.
[17] Ibid., 40.

year-by-year population data for that republic that confirms the scale of
the disaster there:

1930	5873.0 thousands
1931	5114.0 thousands
1932	3293.5 thousands
1933	2493.5 thousands
1934	2681.8 thousands[18]

As already mentioned, many Kazakhs fled to adjoining Soviet republics,
and some across the frontier to China and Iran.

According to the journalist M. Tol'ts,[19] a commission was set up,
headed by Ia. Iakovlev, the Head of the Communist Party Central Committee Agricultural Department (and former Commissar of Agriculture), to
look into the alleged errors of the 1937 census. The commission recommended adding 3% to 4% to the total, but on September 25, 1937, the
Sovnarkom decided to declare the entire census to be "defective" and to
suppress it.

Let us go on now to the 1939 census. If the 1937 total was 162.0
million, then a figure in excess of 170 million is inherently implausible,
and both Tsaplin and Polyakov, and also Tol'ts and Andreyev et al. reject
it. Tsaplin considers the implied rate of natural increase (despite the ban
on abortion) to be far too high. He cannot accept anything higher than
168.8 million and considers it likely that there were some 1.3 million
"unregistered deaths in detention." Tsaplin and Tol'ts both cite a preliminary report on the 1939 census, which gives the civilian population as
161.5 million, plus 5.8 million military personnel and prisoners, which
adds up to 167.3 million. Allowing for some undercounting, Tol'ts is
willing to accept a figure of 168 million, but regards the official 170.5 as a
falsification.[20] Andreyev et al. cite 168.8 million as the highest acceptable
figure.[21]

Tsaplin's total for the entire decade was 7.9 million dead plus 2 million
who "fled," a total population loss of 9.9 million.[22] As we have seen, most
of those who "fled" in fact died, so his total of abnormal deaths would be
closer to 9.5 million. These would be surplus *deaths*.

Maksudov in his book[23] calculated abnormal deaths in the 1930s by
careful analysis of the age and sex compositions in the 1926 and 1937
censuses. Subject to margins of error, he estimated such deaths to be 9.8
million. However, if the 1939 census was tampered with, the figure could
well be higher. How much higher depends on the nature of the tampering;
Maksudov told me privately that a total of (say) 11 million is not excluded.
But one must bear in mind that the appearance in the census of "dead

[18] Polyakov (no. 6) p. 21.
[19] M. Tol'ts, "Repressirovannaya perepis," *Rodina* no. 11, 1989, p. 59.
[20] Tol'ts, p. 60.
[21] Andreyev et al., p. 36.
[22] Tsaplin, p. 134.
[23] S. Maksudov, *Poteri naseleniya SSSR*, Chalidze publications, Benson, VT, 1989.

souls" that had never been born at all does not justify their inclusion on our list of Stalin's victims.

"Tampering" of another kind has been documented. The Soviet scholar Polyakov cites a document (from the "supersecret" part of the census) to the effect that a disproportionate number of prisoners in some areas had to be concealed by the census takers by transferring them *"ravnomerno, melkimi pachkami"* (evenly, in small batches) to other areas. Thus 306,000 were to be "moved" (statistically) away from the Far East. The source quotes letters from puzzled local statisticians ordered to do this, who wanted to know into what categories (urban-rural, age, etc.) to record such additional persons.[24]

It is important to stress that all these figures relate to the period up to January 1939. Victims who died in subsequent years are not included; neither are many exiles who were not kept behind wire.

Do these figures "fit" into more general demographic data? In his book, Maksudov cites contemporary population estimates for the end of 1930 (160.6 million) and for the middle of 1931 (162.1 million) and considers them to be likely reliable.[25] The actual increase of population for 1926 to 1931 averaged close to 3 million per annum, with a tendency for the rate of increase to fall slowly. Suppose that the population would have risen in the decade of the thirties by some 2.7 million per annum under normal conditions. Then, if the figure for January 1931 was about 161 million, there should have been an increase to January 1937 of about 16 million, and not 1 million. A "demographic gap" of 15 million is suggested by such figures. But this gap does not represent surplus deaths, because it includes those not born. Also, there is some evidence (*pace* Maksudov) that the 1930–1 estimates were somewhat too high, as has been argued by Danilov,[26] among others; and Andreyev and his associates cite a figure of 159.8 million for January 1931.[27] They also allow for a small undercount in 1937 census, which would make the increase in 1931–7 not 1 million but 3 million, so then the gap becomes 13 million. As for the period 1937–9, there is no demographic gap. Even the lower estimate of 168 million (as against the official 170.5 million) represents increases of almost 3 million a year over the 1937 figure. The outlawing of abortions could have been responsible for higher-than-average births, but clearly the abnormal deaths in those years do not show up as a major demographic "blip" – which in no way disproves the proposition that many hundreds of thousands were shot in 1937–8 (but not 7 million!). The evidence seems consistent with the view that 10–11 million perished in the thirties, with the peasants numerically the main victims.

[24] Polyakov (no. 8) p. 44.
[25] Maksudov, p. 128.
[26] V. Danilov in *Arkheograficheskii ezhegodnik*, 1968, pp. 248–9.
[27] Andreyev et al., p. 7.

Now on to the numbers in the "care" of the NKVD. For January 1937, Polyakov publishes a breakdown by area of detainees numbering a total of 2,389,570 (of which 571,932 were women).[28] In 1937, the average number detained in the Gulag was given by the Soviet historian Zemskov in *Argumenty i fakty* as 994,000, the total rising to a maximum of 1,360,000 in 1939.[29] It follows that the larger part of the detainees were not "technically" in the Gulag, but rather in prison, "colonies," and *spetsposeleniya*. The same conclusion is suggested by the evidence for 1939 (unless we suppose all the evidence to be faked in the archives).

I am able (with the author's permission) to quote from a yet unpublished study by Maksudov, who examined the archives, which is largely confirmed by Polyakov and his collaborators. According to this data, 5,839,000 persons were "specially counted" in the 1939 census. Of these, the military accounted for 1,903,000 and NKVD personnel for 366,000. The total number of detainees in NKVD-run establishments was 3,593,000, of whom "only" 1,360,000 were in the Gulag *camps*. To be sure, Zemskov's published data indicate the incompleteness of his statistics, for his interview in *Argumenty i fakty* mentions that very large numbers of prisoners in most years were transferred to (and from) "other places of detention," and many were described as "released."

Zemskov's figures for the years 1937–9 are given in Table 13.1. These data related only to the "camp population of the Gulag," *not* to all detainees and prisoners.

A valuable cross-check or correction for these figures comes from the work of lawyer-historian A. Dugin.[30] He cites figures that cover "camps" (*lageri*), *kolonii* and, in some years, include prisons. But his data specifically exclude what are called "exiled settlers" (*ssylnye poselentsy*). Table 13.2 contains Dugin's figures for some of the years that interest us, which he obtained from the Central State Archive of the October Revolution (TsGAOR) and the higher state organs. It can be seen that the figures of the *lageri* for 1937–9 are identical to those cited by Zemskov.

The death rate is astonishingly low in the prewar years, though it then rises steeply, reaching (for the Gulag only) 248,777 in 1942.[31] One wonders how the statistics handled the mass shootings that are known to have occurred. Were the victims recorded as "released" or "transferred" (to the next world)? Were these the "unrecorded deaths in detention" mentioned in Tsaplin's study?

How many were shot? The figures are certainly incomplete. V. Kumanov, writing in *Pravda*, quoted figures for those shot by order of the "troikas,"

---

[28] Polyakov (no. 8) p. 35. Tsaplin, p. 176, cites a figure of 2,653,036 in "special contingents," but his figure may include guards.

[29] Interview with Zemskov. *Argumenty i fakty* no. 45, 1989, pp. 6–7.

[30] A. Dugin, "Stalinizm: legendy i fakty," *Slovo* no. 7, 1990, pp. 35–43.

[31] Zemskov, p. 7.

Table 13.1. *Inmates in the Gulag, 1937–1939*

Inmates	1937	1938	1939
Total, January 1	820,881	996,367	1,317,195
Total arrived:	884,811	1,036,165	749,647
from NKVD camps	(211,486)	(202,721)	(348,417)
from other detention	(636,749)	(803,007)	(389,994)
from having escaped	(35,460)	(22,679)	(9,838)
other	(1,116)	(7,758)	(7,398)
Total departed:	709,325	715,337	722,434
to NKVD camps	(214,807)	(240,466)	(347,444)
to other detention	(43,916)	(55,790)	(74,882)
Released	(364,937)	(279,966)	(223,622)
Died	(25,376)	(90,546)	(50,502)
Escaped	(58,264)	(32,033)	(12,333)
Other	(2,725)	(11,536)	(13,651)
Total, December 31	996,367	1,317,195	1,344,408

Source: *Argumenty i fakty* no. 45, 1989, p. 7.

Table 13.2. *Number of persons (in thousands) in camps and colonies for selected years*

Location	1937	1938	1939	1950
Lageri	820.9	996.3	1317.2	1416.3
Kolonii	375.5	885.2[a]	335.2[b]	1145.0

[a] Including prisons
[b] Excluding prisons

special councils, and special tribunals, as 1,118 in 1936 and 353,074 in 1937. He added that in his opinion others were doubtlessly shot by order of other official bodies.[32] Then *Moskovskie novosti* on March 4, 1990, published the total number arrested "for counterrevolutionary and state crimes" in the entire period 1931–53 as 3,778,234, of which 786,098 were shot. Of the latter, 1,422 were foreign Communists. These arrests and executions presumably occurred under article 58 of the Soviet penal code.

In 1992, V. Popov in *Otechestvennye arkhivy* cited figures for those politically "repressed" for every year from 1921 to 1953. The figure cited here for executions in 1937 is there repeated, and the total shot in 1938 is given as 328,618. The number executed in these two years very far exceeds the total for all the other years put together. Already in 1939, after the removal of Ezhov, they shot a "mere" 2,552. Interestingly, whereas the

---

[32] G. Kurman in *Pravda* June 22, 1989.

numbers in prisons, camps, and exile reached its highest point after the war, the level of executions remained low, and indeed in some years fell to zero. (The death penalty was formally abolished in 1947 and restored in 1950.)[33]

Dugin in his article in *Slovo* reproduced a letter to Khrushchev that the total arrested for counterrevolutionary crimes from 1921 to 1953 was 3,777,380, of which 642,980 were shot. These figures differ somewhat from those given in *Moskovskie novosti*. Also the NKVD/MVD reported in 1955 that they had files on a total of 9.5 million *zasklyuchennykh* (detainees), that is, those who had at any time been incarcerated, the majority being criminals. Dugin has studied tables showing numbers "in" and "out" of detention for the period 1930–53, and comes to the conclusion that the probable total number passing through camps, colonies, and priosons in the whole period came to 11.8 million or 8,803,000 for the period 1937–1950. He also reproduces a table showing numbers in *lageri i kolonii* on July 1, 1946, to be 1,371,986, of which 516,592 were condemned for counterrevolutionary activities (203,607 for "treason to the Motherland," 15,499 for "spying," etc.).[34] These figures naturally exclude exiles and possibly also the prison population. He criticizes those (including Roy Medvedev and Solzhenitsyn, as well as Conquest) who persist in citing much higher figures that cannot be supported by evidence. It must be supposed that many others who were "political" were arrested (and shot), charged under other articles of the law code, or not charged at all. This would surely relate to many if not all of those buried in mass graves in such places as Kuropaty and the Polish officers who died in Katyn and elsewhere. Dugin treats as "political" only those who were arrested and charged under article 58, implying that the rest – the large majority – could be seen as criminals. Surely this is too narrow a definition, though we have no means of even roughly estimating how many persons were involved.

Another source gives the following figures: A. Emelin, a military historian, writing in *Voenno-istoricheskii zhurnal*, states that in June 1941 there were 2.3 million *zaklyuchennye* (detainees), which may be the total for the Gulag, colonies, and prisons, excluding *spetsposeleniya* (see above). By the end of 1941, 420,000 of these detainees were serving in the Red Army. In 1941–3 a million "previously sentenced" persons were serving.[35]

For the postwar years we have more data from the historian Zemskov.

---

[33] V. Popov in *Otechestvennye arkhivy*, 1992, no. 2. According to J. Arch Getty, Popov's figures came from the hitherto "special," i.e., *closed* section of the GARF (*Gosudarstvennyi Arkhiv Rossiiskoi Federatsii*) that now unites several collections, including the holdings of the former TsGAOR or *Tsentral'nyi Gosudarstvennyi Arkhiv Oktiabr'skoi Revolutsii i Sotsialisticheskogo Stroitel'stva SSSR*. GARF (TsGAOR) fond 9401, op. 1, delo 4157, p. 202. Popov at the time his article was published was not permitted to cite the sources for his figures.

[34] Dugin, p. 44.

[35] A. Emelin, in a round-table discussion, "Chelovek i voina," *Voenno-istoricheskii zhurnal* no. 9, 1990, p. 9.

On January 1, 1950, the Gulag contained 2,561,351 persons (1,416,300 in *lageri* and 1,145,051 in *kolonii*, as Dugin also states). Of this total, 578,912 had been sentenced under article 58, that is, for "counter-revolutionary offenses." In December 1948 there were 230,614 inmates in prisons (*tiurmy*). In addition there were 2,660,040 persons in *spetsposeleniya* and in various forms of exile (*ssylka i vysylka*). These would include many of the so-called punished peoples (Kalmucks, Chechens, Crimean Tartars, etc.),[36] those deported from the Baltic republics, Vlasovites, collaborators, some former prisoners of war, and so on (some in these categories could also be found in the Gulag). The resultant total, 5.5 million, is not comparable with the lower figures cited for the prewar years. The reason for the discrepancy is that the 5.5 million specifically include all forms of exile, whereas those figures cited for 1937 and 1939 include only persons kept behind wire. Many were not, as two examples from literature illustrate. In Solzhenitsyn's *Cancer Ward* a woman, one of thousands expelled from Leningrad because of their gentry origin, is washing the floor of a hospital ward. She would have appeared in the statistics as a "free" laborer. And a harrowing story (autobiographical) by Tendryakov[37] refers to exiled "kulaks" left free without ration cards or resources to die in the street of starvation, though no doubt others managed to get work of some kind. (I have not seen any prewar figures for exiles of these various categories.)

Moskovskii novosti no. 41 (October) 1990 reprints a report made at the time by the NKVD/MVD as to the number of persons in *spetsposeleniya* as of October 1946. They numbered 2,463,940, of which 655,674 were men, 829,084 were women, and 979,182 were children under sixteen years of age. The large number of women and children is explicable by the fact that the bulk of the "settlers" consisted of deported nationalities, that is, the "punished people," to use Alexander Nekrich's phrase. The document gives the various categories of persons as follows:

Chechens and Ingushes	400,478
Karachai	60,139
Balkars	42,817
Kalmuks	81,673
Crimean Tartars, Greeks, Bulgars	193,959
Germans	774,178
"Mobilized Germans"	121,459
Former kulaks	577,121
Turks, Kurds, Khemishi	84,402
"OUN" (Ukrainian nationalists)	29,351
"Volksdeutsch"	2,681
Helpers of Germans	3,185

---

[36] The term "punished people" was coined by A. Nekrich in his book bearing the same name.

[37] V. Tendryakov, "Khleb dlia sobaki," *Novyi mir* no. 3, 1988.

"Istinna" Christian sect	1,212
Deported from Lithuania	5,426
Vlasov soldiers	95,386

By what must be a printer's error, this report is dated March 18, 1944, even though its title refers to 1946. (It must be 1946. The men of the Vlasov army had not been captured yet and the expulsions not yet begun.)

Although they add up to close to 2.5 million, the preceding figures look suspiciously low, if they are taken to represent all forms of exile. It is known that all the Crimean Tartars were ordered out of the Crimea, and the total cited here is only a fraction of those affected. Deportations from Lithuania and from the other Baltic republics were surely also much higher, though some occurred after 1946. The total deported in 1944–5 was estimated by Roy Medvedev as 5 million. Although there was a high death rate, it seems clear that a large number of exiles in the stated categories must have been living outside the special settlements. All of which suggests that the figure for prisoners plus exiles of all types quoted previously for the year 1950 may be incomplete. Finally, many scholars maintain that collectivized peasants were in effect tied to their villages, in a real sense enserfed. They naturally apppear in statistics as just ordinary rural citizens. But were they free? Indeed, there were periods in which urban workers too were tied to their jobs, and the *propiska* system inhibited (and still to a milder degree inhibits) free movement. But it would be surely going too far to include all these rural and urban workers among "Stalin's victims," unless one wishes to say that the victims include the bulk of the peoples of the Soviet Union.

Finally, let us return to the question of the total number of victims in the entire Stalin period. We have seen that the figures for the thirties do provide a basis for calculations and permit what can be called a demographic cross-check (in fact, two cross-checks: demographic extrapolation, plus Maksudov's analysis of age and sex composition found in the census data). No doubt there were victims of repression in the war years, but they are not separately identifiable from the huge losses due to other causes in the years 1941–5 (except that we do have official figures for the deaths in the Gulag camps, amounting to 900,000 between 1930 and 1953). In 1946 there was a famine in some areas caused by wartime devastation, and this cannot be treated analogous to the man-made famine of 1933. In the years 1947–53, there was a normal rate of natural increase of population in the USSR, after the wartime catastrophe had led to a population decline reliably estimated as around 27 million (this includes the excess of "normal" deaths over the very low wartime births, emigration, and war losses of every kind). Andreyev and his colleagues, in another article, reach a total of 26.6 million.[38] It therefore follows that there is no indirect, demographic

---

[38] *Vestniki statistiki* no. 10, 1990.

way of determining abnormal deaths in Stalin's last years. Besides, the several hundreds who were shot in the "Leningrad Affair" or the members of the Jewish Anti-Fascist Committee, also shot in these years, could have only imperceptible effects on aggregate death-rate statistics.

The total number of victims cited in this paper are well below the figures calculated by Dallin and Nikolaevsky, Conquest, and some authors (e.g., Antonov-Ovseyenko) in the Soviet Union itself. Some of the highest figures are indeed incredible. Maksudov has pointed out that if Conquest were right, and 12 million political and 3 million criminals were in detention in 1937–8, and if (as Conquest himself states) most were men between the ages of thirty and sixty, this would mean that half or more of the men of that age group were behind bars, because there were only 24 million men between thirty and sixty in the whole Soviet Union at this time![39] The much lower figures that are now being cited from the archives are bad enough, probably a world record in the proportion "repressed," that is, imprisoned, exiled, and executed. Of course, the percentage of intellectuals, party officials, and army officers among those repressed was very much higher than average, though in sheer numbers it is clear that the largest number of victims were peasants. Deaths attributable to famine and its consequences seem to have been close to Conquest's estimate (he seems somewhat too high for the Ukraine, but somewhat too low for Kazakhstan). But he does seem altogether too high in his estimates of the number of dead *kulaks* and of those shot and incarcerated in the Great Purge.[40]

It is my view that when the dust settles, the number of Stalin's victims, dead and repressed, will not be much different from the figures cited in this chapter. However, we need to have more data on the exiles of various categories and more data from the postwar period and the period before 1930.

[39] Maksudov, p. 124,
[40] Conquest's error, in his otherwise admirable *Harvest of Sorrow*, lies, in my view, in citing too high a figure for the number of so-called kulaks and their families who were deported, and then assuming that nearly all these perished in the Gulag. This is not to deny that many perished in the harsh conditions of deportation.

14

More light on the scale of repression and excess mortality in the Soviet Union in the 1930s

Stephen G. Wheatcroft

The academic debate concerning the scale of repression and excess mortality in the USSR during the 1930s has been raging inconclusively for decades. The spread of *glasnost'* in the USSR has so far done little to dampen the attitudes of the rival contenders in this debate in the West. Both Robert Conquest and myself have repeatedly claimed that the new evidence appearing in the Soviet Union has supported our conflicting claims. Conquest is clearly impressed with the bulk of literary evidence, which does indeed tend to agree with his conclusions; much in fact is based upon his own work. My attitude has always been to try to evaluate the nature of the available evidence, to check its origins and the method of argumentation; in these terms the evidence that has been appearing in the Soviet press has been very mixed.[1]

Although there is a role for literary and propagandist works to force a process of rethinking upon closed minds, there is also a need for serious historical work to produce an unemotional and accurate portrayal of reality. So far we have seen relatively few serious historical works on this subject. Such work will require more than literary creativity; it will need a professional, objective evaluation of evidence which until recently has not been available for examination.

In recent months especially there have been tremendous breakthroughs in the availability of archival material in the Soviet Union, and this new

I am grateful to the Australian Research Council for funding my research on Soviet History, and to Melbourne University for providing me with study leave. Professor R. W. Davies as always gave me great support in this work. I am particularly pleased to be able to report the assistance that I was given in the USSR by Professor V. P. Danilov, Dr. Mark Tolts, and Dr. V. Zemskov. I am also particularly grateful to Dr. Tsaplin and the archivists at TsGANKh SSSR and also to GAU SSSR.

[1] Until recently the most substantial new evidence to emerge from the Soviet Union has been the discovery of a series of mass graves in Kuropaty and elsewhere. But despite very large claims for the scale of these massacres, there is as yet little convincing evidence that they are on the scale claimed. There is a commission investigating these discoveries and it is to be hoped that their findings will soon be published.

276   *Stephen G. Wheatcroft*

material casts considerably more light on several important aspects of Soviet demography in this period.

New evidence on the 1937 census and intercensal population movements

The demographer Mark Tolts revealed in late 1987 that results of the 1937 census had indicated a population of 162 million.[2] This flatly contradicted the claims of Rosefielde and Yuri Antonov-Ovseenko that the 1937 census had indicated that the population in the USSR was only 156 million[3] and that an additional 6 million deaths needed to be added to estimates of excess mortality. Subsequently Vsevolod Vasilievich Tsaplin, the Director of the Central State Archive of the National Economy of the USSR (TsGANKh SSSR), has revealed more information about the 1937 census, intercensal population movements, and contemporary evaluations of them.[4] Tsaplin reported that the NKVD contingent[5] listed in the 1937 census was 2,653,036,[6] that 5.7 million deaths were recorded in the famine year of 1933 instead of the average number of 2.6 million per year for 1927–31,[7] and that Kurman, the Deputy head of the Department of Population and Health Statistics in the Central Statistical Department (TsUNKhU), had sent a formal statement (*dokladnaya zapiska*) to Kraval, the Director of TsUNKhU, on 14 March 1937 arguing, amongst other things, that the mortality recorded in 1933 underestimated reality by 1 million.[8] The content and importance of Tsaplin's article is covered in more detail by Alec Nove in the previous chapter.

New evidence on the scale of the labour camps and exiles

Even more recently the historian V. Zemskov has published several series of figures on population movements in the Gulag from 1934 to 1947,[9] the

[2] M. Tolts "Skol'ko zhe nas togda byli?," *Ogonek*, 1987, no. 51. See also Tolts, "Nedostupnoe izmerenie," in: *V chelovecheskom izmerenii* (Moscow: Progress, 1989).
[3] Steven Rosefielde, "Excess Mortality in the Soviet Union: A Reconsideration of the Demographic Consequences of Forced Industrialisation, 1929–49," *Soviet Studies*, 35, no. 3 (July 1983), pp. 385–405; A. Antonov-Ovseenko, *The Time of Stalin: A Portrait of Tyranny* (New York: 1983), p. 207.
[4] V. V. Tsaplin, "Statistika zhertv Stalinizma v 30-e gody," *Voprosy Istorii*, 1989, no. 4, pp. 175–81.
[5] I.e., labour camp inmates, labour colony inmates, exiles, special migrants, labour camp guards, etc.
[6] Tsaplin, p. 176.
[7] Ibid. pp. 177–8.
[8] Ibid. pp. 176–7.
[9] "'Arkhipelag GULAG': glazami pisatelya i statistika," *Argumenty i fakty*, 1989, no. 45 (11–17 November), pp. 6–7.

scale of special exiles (*spetsposelentsy*) on 1 January 1953,[10] the scale of the different categories of exiles on 1 January 1953, together with a listing of the charges for which they were sentenced,[11] and the scale of the special NKVD camps for former military prisoners.[12] These materials indicate that the maximum number of prisoners in Soviet labour camps between 1930 and 1947 was 1.5 million in 1941; this figure excludes prisoners in "corrective labour colonies," prisoners in jail, and exiles. There were 352,000 prisoners in corrective labour colonies on 1 March 1940. During this period prisoners in labour camps suffered a peak level of mortality of 230 per thousand in 1942–43 and an average of 70 per thousand for 1934–47.[13] Concerning other categories of repression Zemskov's data refer primarily to their size on 1 January 1953. There were over 2.75 million *spetsposelentsy* recorded on 1 January 1953, of whom 1.2 million were Germans, just under half a million North Caucasian tribesmen, over 200,000 with Crimean nationalities, almost 140,000 Balts, and just 24,686 former kulaks.[14] The number of exiles recorded for 1 January 1953 was apparently 65,332, of whom 52,549 were male and 12,783 female.[15]

Another recent article, by military historian Major General V. Nekrasov, has reported, from what appears to be a similar official MVD source, that there were 2.3 million prisoners at the beginning of the war, that during 1941–44 another 2.55 million people were made prisoners, that 3.4 million prisoners left, and that 1.45 million remained as prisoners on 21 December 1944.[16] These figures are much larger than those given by Zemskov and appear to include prisoners in jail and in labour colonies, as well as in the labour camps.

Nekrasov also reported that there were 2,526,402 prisoners in March 1953, before 1,181,264 were amnestied by Beria following Stalin's death.[17] From the text it is unclear exactly what categories of prisoners are being referred to, but it appears to refer to all categories, i.e., prisoners in the labour camps, in the corrective labour colonies, and in jail.

Combining the figure of 2.53 million prisoners which we presume refers

[10] *Argumenty i fakty*, 1989, no. 39 (30 September–6 October).
[11] *Argumenty i fakty*, 1989, no. 40 (7–13 October).
[12] *Argumenty i fakty*, 1989, no. 38 (23–29 September).
[13] These figures have been calculated from the reported numbers of deaths in the camps and the average number of inmates given by Zemskov in *Argumenty i fakty*, 1989, no. 4–5.
[14] Over 5 million kulaks (including members of families) had been exiled in 1930–32. Zemskov further cites a figure originally given by Ivnitsky indicating that 990,470 of these original kulaks (including families) were still located in their place of exile in 1989. Many of these former kulaks would have been unlisted victims in the famine of 1932/33, the war-time difficulties of 1942 and 1943, and also the famine of 1947/48.
[15] V. Zemskov, *Argumenty i fakty*, 1989, no. 40. 51,848 were classified as *ssylno-poselentsy* (resettled exiles), 7,605 as *ssylnye* (exiles), and 5,869 as *vyslannye* (banished).
[16] The discrepancy of 0.4 million presumably indicates the number of prisoners released or escaped during this period.
[17] V. F. Nekrasov, "Desyat' 'Zheleznykh Narkomov,'" *Komsomol'skaya Pravda*, 29 September 1989.

to the camps, colonies, and jail, with the 2.75 million *spetsposelentsy* and
the 65,332 people in different forms of exile or banishment, the total in
these categories is 5.35 million. These figures are, of course, considerably
smaller than those cited by Conquest and Rosefielde for the Gulag population
alone.[18]

New evidence on the scale and nature of famine mortality

On my recent visit to the Soviet Union in October 1989 I was given access
to the TsUNKhU files on the natural movement of population in the 1930s
and to the 1939 census in the Central State Archive of the National
Economy of the USSR. The following notes, tables, and graphs report on
the remarkable material that I was able to find, which casts considerably
more light on the nature, scale, and effect of the 1932/33 famine.

1. The scale of the demographic crisis of 1932/33 in relation to natural population movements 1926–40

(a) Indications from the registration data

The archives contain a series of documents summarising overall natural
population movements for several series of years. These indicators of birth
and death rates were calculated from the data collected by the civil registration office (ZAGS). They enable a continuous series of birth and death
rates to be constructed for the whole intercensal period. Despite the great
interest in this topic, these official figures for birth and death rates between
1928 and 1937 have never been published (See Table 14.1).

Although there is some slight inconsistency between parts of these data,
the overall pattern is clear and indicates an almost doubling of mortality in
1933 and a very severe decline in natality in 1933 and 1934. The rise in
mortality at the same time as a decline in natality indicates a particularly
serious situation. Since infant mortality is always higher than adult mortality,
the normal level of mortality would generally fall with a decline in natality.
If the data were adjusted for the age structure of the population the force
of mortality would appear to be even greater.

Estimates of surplus mortality depend upon the level of mortality that is

---

[18] In the recent debates on this subject Rosefielde had proposed a figure of over 10 million in
the Gulag system in the late 1930s (S. Rosefielde, *Soviet Studies*, 33, no. 1 (January 1981),
pp. 51–87) and Conquest had proposed a figure of 8 million in the camps in 1938 (R.
Conquest, *The Great Terror*, (Harmondsworth: 1971) Appendix A, p. 709). I have
repeatedly argued that I could see no convincing evidence that the scale of labor camp
prisoners (excluding exiles) could have been more than 4 to 5 million. (S. G. Wheatcroft,
Soviet Studies, 33, no. 2 (April 1981), *Soviet Studies*, 35, no. 2 (April 1983).

Table 14.1. *TsUNKhU data on the natural movement of the population of the USSR 1926–1940*

| | | Crude birth rates (births per 1000 population) | | | | Crude death rates (deaths per 1000 population) | | |
	1	2	3	4	5	6	7	8
1913	45.6		47.0	47.0	28.9		30.2	30.2
1925		44.2*		44.5		22.9*		23.2
1926	43.7	43.5*	44.0	44.0	20.0	19.9*	20.3	20.3
1927	43.3			43.6	21.0			21.3
1928	42.2		44.3	42.5 44.3	18.2		23.3	18.5 23.3
1929	39.8			40.1	20.3			20.6
1930	37.1	37.9		37.9	19.6	19.7		19.7
1931	34.6	35.4		35.4	19.2	19.6		19.6
1932	31.0	31.9		31.9	19.8	20.5		20.5
1933	23.9	25.3		25.3	37.8	37.7		37.7
1934	24.9			25.6/26.4	19.7			19.8
1935	32.1			33.0/34.0	17.5			17.6
1936		32.6		32.6			18.2	18.2
1937		38.8	38.7	38.7			18.9	17.9/18.9
1938			37.5	37.5			17.5	17.5
1939			36.5	36.5			17.3	17.3
1940			31.2	31.2			18.0	18.0

Notes: A great degree of uncertainty relates to the currently published mortality figure for 1928, which is over 28% higher than the archival figure for European Russia only. For 1926 the currently published USSR figure was only 1.5% larger. The currently published figures show a significant growth in mortality between 1926 and 1928, while the archival source shows a fall. For reasons which will be explained below I am inclined to accept that the archival data in 1928 are somewhat more distorted than in the early 1930s.

Sources: Previously unpublished:
European part of USSR,
Columns 1, 5; 1913, 1926–35: TsGANKh (SSSR), f. 1562, op. 20, d. 42, l. 85
USSR (pre-1939 boundaries)
Columns 2, 6; 1930–33: TsGANKh (SSSR), f. 1562, op. 20, d. 42, l. 76
Columns 2, 6; 1936–37: TsGANKh (SSSR), f. 1562, op. 20, d. 108, l. 40
Previously published:
European part of USSR,
Columns 3, 7; *1925, 1926: *Estestvennoe dvizhenie naseleniya SSSR, 1926* (Moscow: 1929), p. 10
USSR (pre-1939 boundaries)
Columns 3, 5; 1913, 1926, 1928, 1937–1940: *Narodnoe Khozyaistvo SSSR, 1922–1972* (Moscow: 1972), p. 40
Calculated from other columns: Column 4, 8.

assumed to be normal.[19] Assuming that the 1932 rate of mortality (20.5 per thousand) is accepted as normal, the rise in mortality to a rate of 37.7 per thousand in 1933 would imply a level of 2.75 million excess deaths.[20]

[19] See Barbara A. Anderson and Brian D. Silver, "Demographic Analysis and Population Catastrophes in the USSR," *Slavic Review*, (Fall 1985), pp. 517–36 for a thorough discussion of this truth.
[20] $160 \times (0.0377 - 0.0205) = 2.75$ million.

If we were to accept a normal level of mortality as 19.7 per thousand, the elevation in mortality in 1933 would be equivalent to 2.9 million, and additional losses could be added for the higher than normal mortality in 1932 which would total another 0.1 million, i.e., 3 million excess deaths in all.

Accepting the 1932 level of natality of 31.9 per thousand as normal, the decline in natality to about 25 per thousand in 1933 and 1934 would indicate an extra decline in natality of 1.1 million for each of these years, i.e., 2.2 million in all. However, this level of loss could easily be doubled by accepting a level of 35 per thousand as normal natality and assuming that the decline in natality was also present in 1932, 1934, and 1935.

The population loss indicated by these figures varies between 5 and 7 million depending upon assumptions as to the normal levels of births and deaths. In each case about half of this loss is attributable to excess mortality and half to excess fertility decline.

Even if we accept that these figures are incomplete, and that the scale of mortality in the omitted categories was much higher than the mortality in the part of the country covered by these registration figures, it seems unlikely to me that we would be able to find more than 1 or at most 2 million extra deaths to add to 2.75 to 3 million calculated above.[21]

Previously I had always argued that the demographic evidence did not incline me to believe that the scale of mortality from the 1932/33 famine was comparable with that from the 1921/22 famine and that it was unlikely to have been more than 3 to 4 million. The evidence of these registration figures inclines me to revise my position and to suggest that the scale of mortality from the 1932/33 famine may have been somewhat larger than I had earlier suggested and might be as high as 4 to 5 million.

These figures are much lower than many of the excess mortality and population loss figures that are cited in the West. Mace believes that 5–7 million for the Ukraine alone is a "conservative figure,"[22] Conquest claims 5 million Ukrainian famine deaths, and 8 million overall including the North Caucasus and Kazakhstan; but on top of this he wishes to add another 6.5 million deaths "as a result of dekulakization."[23] The figures given by Mace and Conquest are impossible to accept.

[21] According to Tsaplin, Kurman, the deputy head of the Department of Population and Health Statistics in TsUNKhU, believed that the scale of under-reporting of mortality was 1 million among the civil population, and that deaths in the non-civil population, 1926–37, would reach 1.5 million. See note 8.
[22] James E. Mace, "The Famine of 1933: A Survey of Sources", in: R. Serbyn & B. Krawchenko, eds., *Famine in Ukraine 1932–1933*, (Edmonton: Canadian Institute of Ukrainian Studies, University of Alberta, 1986), p. 50.
[23] R. Conquest, *The Harvest of Sorrow: Soviet Collectivisation and the terror famine* (London: Hutchinson, 1986), p. 306.

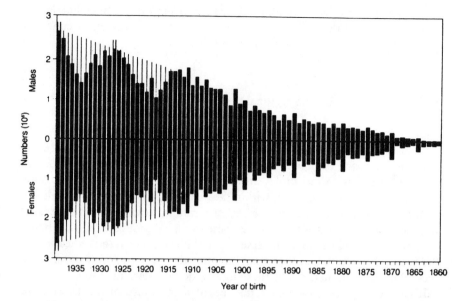

Figure 14.1. *Male and female population in the USSR (in 1939, by age, in millions)*

(b) Indications of the population loss in the 1932/33 famine from the age structure in the 1939 census

Because the detailed age structures of the censuses of 1937 and 1939 would have provided a graphic detailed indication of the birth and infant losses during the famine period, they were never published. Although the 1937 census materials have now been located, they were not available to me on my last visit to the Soviet Union. The following graph is based on the results of the 1939 census and provides an indication of the losses for the population of the USSR as a whole (see Figure 14.1).

In order to assist the conceptualisation of the extent of birth and infant losses in the 1930s and to compare it with the 1914–22 losses I have somewhat arbitrarily indicated on the graph the smooth progression from the size of the 1914 born cohorts to those born in the last two years before the census. The two gaps that emerge span the years 1914–25 and 1928–38. It can readily be calculated that the 10-year gap 1928–38 implies the loss of 11.6 million people born in these years, or 27.5% of the survivors of these cohorts. By contrast, the 11-year gap 1914–25 implies the loss of only 9.9 million of the cohort born in these years, or 26.9% of the survivors.

This very rough calculation indicates that the effect of the demographic crisis of the 1930s was comparable with and probably somewhat larger than the effect of the crisis of the war, civil war, and famine, as concerns the survival of the cohorts born in these disturbed times.

2. The regional spread of the famine

Table 14.2 lists the regional mortality registration data for 1930–33. The data have been regrouped into the five major areas that I tend to use for most of my work on agricultural and demographic developments. These data are undoubtedly incomplete in several respects: Some important regions like Kazakhstan are excluded; within the given regions the data are unlikely to include deaths of prisoners in labour camps, colonies, and places of special exile. The mortality amongst these excluded groups would probably have been particularly high in these years.[24] Nevertheless, the indication of the scale of the demographic crisis for the civilian population covered by these data is so immense that these figures deserve careful study.

It can readily be shown that the recorded mortality in the Ukraine in 1933 was enormous and well over triple the 1930 and 1931 levels. Within the Ukraine, Kharkov and Kiev oblasts were by far the worst affected, with levels of annual mortality in 1933 more than three and a half times higher than in 1932. The levels of mortality in Vynnitsa, Odessa, and Dnepropetrovsk oblasts were all between two and a half and three times the 1932 level. The only non-Ukrainian region to exceed those levels of elevation in mortality was the Lower Volga krai, where mortality rose to over three times the 1932 level. The level of mortality increase in the North Caucasus, at over two and a half times the 1932 level, was comparable with some of the Ukrainian oblasts. The level of mortality increase in the Central Chernozem, 86% above the 1932 level, was only just above the national average. By comparison, mortality increases in the Northern Industrial Consumer Region and especially in Moscow and Leningrad oblasts were far less marked.

The archival data also provide us with an urban/rural breakdown of mortality in the famine year 1933 which is presented in Table 14.3.

These figures indicate that in Moscow and Leningrad oblasts the level of urban mortality was very low (at roughly normal levels) and that rural mortality was only slightly raised. In the more northern and western parts of this region mortality was generally much higher, especially in the urban

---

[24] Although the Zemskov data mentioned above allow us to assess the scale of population in the labour camps in these years as rising from 268,700 in January 1932 to 510,307 in January 1934, the figures for mortality in the camps are only given from 1934. Deaths from starvation may be assumed to have been particularly high in the places of kulak exile, where some 5 million people were exiled.

Table 14.2. *Regional mortality data per thousand population calculated by TsUNKhU statisticians from the available registration data*

	1930	1931	1932	1933	Elevation 1933/1932
USSR	19.7	19.6	20.5	37.7	+83.9%
RSFSR	20.9	21.1	20.7	31.4	+51.7%
UkSSR	17.3	16.4	21.0	60.8	+189.5%
BSSR	14.6	13.3	12.3	15.2	+23.6%
(1) Northern Consumer Region					
Northern Krai	28.6	28.2	25.1	35.6	+41.8%
Karelia ASSR	27.3	26.2	29.0	27.1	−6.6%
Leningrad Oblast	18.4	18.7	19.1	19.6	+2.6%
Western Oblast	17.8	17.5	18.2	18.0	−1.1%
BSSR	14.6	13.3	12.3	15.2	+23.6%
Moscow Oblast	16.8	16.7	16.1	20.0	+24.2%
Ivanovo Oblast	20.4	22.0	20.8	23.5	+13.0%
Gorky Oblast	28.3	27.8	23.9	30.9	+29.3%
(2) Southern Consumer Region					
(a) ZSFSR					
Azerbaidzhan	21.3	27.0	34.0	23.6	−30.6%
Georgia	14.7	15.0	16.1	16.6	+3.1%
Armenia	17.3	15.3	13.5	n.d.	n.d.
(b) Central Asia					
Uzbekistan	23.4	20.2	26.8	22.8	−14.9%
Turkmenia	24.9	22.6	27.3	27.6	+1.1%
(3) Southern Producer Region					
(a) Ukraine					
Kiev Oblast		16.2	26.3	96.9	+268.4%
Cherigov Oblast		18.4	19.9	42.1	+111.6%
Vynnitsa Oblast		16.5	20.2	58.7	+190.6%
Kharkov Oblast		16.6	20.8	79.3	+281.3%
Dnepropetrovsk Oblast		14.4	17.5	46.8	+167.4%
Odessa Oblast		13.9	17.0	49.1	+188.8%
Donetsk Oblast		18.5	21.5	30.4	+41.4%
(b) Other					
North Caucasus Krai	20.8	19.5	20.8	55.0	+164.4%
Moldavian ASSR		17.7	25.1	59.6	+137.5%
Crimean ASSR	14.9	14.3	16.4	25.2	+53.7%
(4) Central Producer Region					
(a) Central Chernozem	19.8	16.8	16.8	31.3	+86.3%

Table 14.2. *Continued*

	1930	1931	1932	1933	Elevation 1933/1932
(b) Volga					
Lower Volga Krai	18.6	16.8	19.0	59.4	+212.6%
Tatar ASSR	22.4	20.4	17.5	29.3	+67.4%
Bashkir ASSR	15.3	20.8	15.0	24.3	+62.0%
(5) Eastern Producer Region					
(a) Urals	27.4	31.1	28.4	37.9	+33.5%
(b) Siberia					
Western Siberia	22.4	26.3	32.4	29.2	−9.9%
Eastern Siberia	19.4	18.2	21.0	31.3	+49.0%
Far Eastern Region	14.2	12.2	12.8	n.d.	n.d.
(c) Kazakhstan	no data				

Source: TsGANKh (SSSR), f. 1562, op. 20, d. 42, l. 76.

areas. Belorussia was reported to have had a relatively high level of urban mortality and relatively low level of rural mortality.

In the Ukraine in 1933 the level of urban mortality was reported to be about 50% above the 1932 level and about the same level as for RSFSR towns in general. However, the level of rural mortality appears to have been more than twice as large as for the RSFSR and almost three times the Ukrainian level for 1932. The Crimea seems to have been exceptional in having very low levels of rural mortality.

In the Central Producer Region there were reported to be generally very high levels of urban as well as rural mortality. Urban mortality is reported to have been much higher in this region than in the Ukraine. And although rural mortality was very high in Saratov and the Lower Volga, it appears to have been surprisingly low in the Central Volga krai, given the high level of urban mortality in this district. This could indicate that the urban mortality in the Volga was more the result of epidemic illness than of pure famine, or it could indicate a difference in policy as regards keeping the rural population out of the towns.

It is quite clear from these figures that the spread of the famine was very widespread and complex, and does not fit easily with some of the claims that have been made about particular nationalities.

3. The chronology of the famine in the RSFSR and the UkSSR

Perhaps the most revealing tables in the archive are those on the chronology of the famine. Tables 14.4 and 14.5 provide an indication of the monthly

Table 14.3. *Regional mortality in the famine with a rural/urban breakdown*

	Urban	1932 Rural	Urban/rural	Urban	1933 Rural	Urban/rural
RSFSR	22.6	18.9	119.6%	32.1	33.3	96.4%
UkSSR	20.0	21.3	93.9%	32.2	67.8	47.5%
BSSR	13.0	9.8	132.7%	23.6	12.5	188.8%
(1) Northern Consumer Region						
Northern Krai				35.5	33.2	106.9%
Karelia				28.5	26.1	109.2%
Western				28.5	22.4	127.2%
Ivanovo				24.7	23.3	106.0%
Gorky				28.1	31.7	88.6%
Moscow				18.5	21.4	86.4%
Leningrad				18.1	22.0	82.3%
BSSR				23.6	12.5	188.8%
(2) Southern Consumer Region						
(a) ZSFSR			no data available			
(b) C. Asia			no data available			
(3) SPR						
(a) UkSSR						
Kiev				40.3	96.3	41.8%
Kharkov				34.8	87.5	39.8%
Odessa				38.6	52.5	73.5%
Vinnitsa				31.8	59.9	53.1%
Dnepropetrovsk				29.0	52.5	55.2%
Donbass				24.9	38.9	64.0%
Chernigov				40.9	41.6	98.3%

Table 14.3. *Continued*

	Urban	1932 Rural	Urban/rural	Urban	1933 Rural	Urban/rural
(b) Other						
N. Caucasus				47.1	57.3	82.2%
Moldavian ASSR				30.3	61.9	48.9%
Crimean ASSR				35.9	12.1	296.7%
(4) Central Producer Region						
(a) Central Black Earth				39.1	34.1	114.7%
(b) Volga						
Lower Volga				56.0	62.4	89.7%
Stalingrad				45.8	38.1	120.2%
Saratov				67.8	81.3	83.4%
Central Volga				79.7	33.9	235.1%
Tatar ASSR				44.1	24.0	183.8%
Bashkir ASSR				35.9	23.0	156.1%
(5) Eastern Producer Region						
(a) Urals				37.7	39.4	95.7%
Urals Sverdlovsk				35.1	42.6	82.4%
(b) Siberia				41.8	36.6	114.2%
Chelyabinsk				47.4	33.6	141.1%
Obsk-Irtysh			no data available			
Eastern Siberia			no data available			
(c) Kazakhstan			no data available			
(d) Far Eastern Region						

Source: TsGANKh (SSSR), f. 1562, op. 20, d. 41, ll. 15–46.

Table 14.4. *Monthly population movements in the RSFSR, 1932–1934*

Date	Urban population			Rural population		
	CBR	CDR	Growth	CBR	CDR	Growth
1932						
January	31.6	20.7	+10.9	47.9	17.9	+30.0
February	32.1	23.6	+8.5	44.2	20.6	+23.6
March	30.4	26.7	+3.7	38.1	20.4	+17.7
April	27.0	25.4	+1.6	31.6	20.0	+11.6
May	26.5	23.7	+2.8	29.9	17.0	+12.9
June	27.2	24.2	+3.0	31.5	15.7	+15.8
July	28.9	25.2	+3.7	34.9	19.1	+15.8
August	28.7	23.3	+5.4	34.2	25.1	+9.1
September	29.0	20.6	+8.4	32.9	20.2	+12.7
October	28.7	18.7	+10.0	32.3	17.1	+15.2
November	26.3	19.3	+7.0	31.3	16.7	+14.6
December	25.0	19.6	+5.4	28.2	16.5	+11.7
1933						
January	24.7	23.7	+1.0	38.7	22.6	+16.1
February	25.4	30.3	−4.9	39.0	30.9	+8.1
March	23.7	35.6	−11.9	35.9	35.6	+0.3
April	22.1	36.5	−14.4	30.2	35.6	−5.4
May	20.6	37.0	−16.4	28.4	38.5	−10.1
June	21.4	38.8	−17.4	30.7	44.3	−13.6
July	22.3	40.0	−17.7	32.4	47.5	−15.1
August	22.1	39.7	−17.6	33.4	43.6	−10.2
September	20.4	30.0	−9.6	30.3	32.1	−1.8
October	19.6	26.7	−7.1	29.1	25.0	+4.1
November	16.8	22.8	−6.0	27.5	21.3	+6.2
December	17.7	24.2	−6.0	25.0	22.5	+2.5
1934						
January	16.7	20.7	−4.0	30.6	20.9	+9.7
February	16.8	20.9	−4.1	27.9	21.5	+6.4
March	16.5	22.7	−6.2	23.4	21.7	+1.7
April	15.7	21.6	−5.9	19.8	21.2	−1.4
May	16.2	19.7	−3.5	19.5	18.3	+1.2
June	18.5	19.6	−1.1	24.9	18.7	+6.2
July	21.7	20.7	+1.0	31.8	24.3	+7.5
August	24.3	21.1	+3.2	35.2	29.2	+6.0
September	24.1	19.1	+5.0	34.6	27.0	+7.6
October	25.4	16.5	+8.9	35.2	20.5	+14.7
November	23.7	15.8	+7.9	35.3	18.4	+16.9
December	23.1	17.6	+5.5	31.2	20.5	+10.7

Source: TsGANKh (SSSR), f. 1562, op. 20, ed. 41, l. 15.

288 *Stephen G. Wheatcroft*

Table 14.5. *Monthly population movements in the UkSSR, 1932–1934*

Date	Urban population			Rural population		
	CBR	CDR	Growth	CBR	CDR	Growth
1932						
January	23.9	13.1	+10.8	35.3	15.1	+20.2
February	24.4	15.1	+9.3	32.1	18.0	+14.1
March	24.5	18.2	+6.3	28.8	20.6	+8.2
April	24.0	20.2	+3.8	26.3	23.0	+3.3
May	24.3	18.2	+6.1	24.6	24.1	+0.5
June	24.5	23.3	+1.2	23.1	27.3	−4.2
July	25.4	28.8	−3.4	26.4	25.2	+1.2
August	26.7	24.8	+1.9	24.6	22.9	+1.7
September	24.6	20.6	+4.0	22.8	21.4	+1.4
October	23.0	20.5	+2.5	21.8	22.4	−0.6
November	20.3	19.2	+1.1	18.5	19.1	−0.6
December	18.5	17.8	+0.7	14.5	16.6	−2.1
1933						
January	18.4	22.4	−4.0	19.1	22.6	−3.5
February	18.1	26.6	−8.5	14.6	35.5	−20.9
March	17.4	42.0	−24.6	11.8	72.5	−60.7
April	15.9	40.6	−24.7	11.3	103.4	−92.1
May	15.7	41.3	−25.6	12.2	145.4	−133.2
June	15.8	47.7	−31.9	12.8	196.3	−183.5
July	17.1	49.2	−32.1	14.1	133.0	−118.9
August	19.2	38.4	−19.2	17.0	43.7	−26.7
September	16.9	26.3	−9.4	15.6	23.2	−7.6
October	14.1	19.8	−5.7	15.0	13.1	+1.9
November	11.9	16.4	−4.6	11.7	11.6	+0.1
December	10.8	15.8	−5.0	7.8	12.5	−4.7
1934						
January	12.2	16.2	−4.0	15.6	17.4	−1.8
February	12.4	14.5	−2.1	10.3	15.3	−5.8
March	12.4	15.7	−3.3	8.1	18.6	−10.5
April	12.3	14.5	−2.2	6.8	15.5	−8.7
May	14.5	14.4	+0.1	10.1	13.7	−3.6
June	18.5	18.9	−0.4	15.0	15.0	0
July	22.9	21.7	+1.2	23.3	15.7	+7.6
August	25.0	22.4	+2.6	32.5	21.8	+10.7
September	25.7	22.1	+3.6	35.3	24.9	+10.4
October	27.1	21.2	+5.9	37.6	23.1	+14.5
November	24.3	15.6	+8.7	35.4	14.6	+20.8
December	23.9	16.2	+7.7	27.6	15.5	+18.1

Source: TsGANKh (SSSR), f. 1562, op. 20, ed. 41, l. 16.

mortality and natality registered for the urban and rural populations of the RSFSR and Ukraine SSR in 1932–34.[25]

It will be noted that the sharpest decline in birth rates was reported in April 1934 for both towns and countryside in the RSFSR and for the rural areas in the Ukraine. This was nine months after the peak mortality that was registered in July 1933. For the Ukrainian towns the sharpest decline in birth rates came in December 1933, which was nine months after the first sharp rise in mortality from 26.6 to 40 per thousand between February and March 1933. It may be assumed therefore that this low point in the dynamic of birth rates is reflecting a decline in conceptions rather than difficulties at the time of birth. Checking the birth rates against the death rates, there appear to be no obvious discontinuities in these series.[26]

These tables indicate that crisis mortality mounted sharply from early 1933 to reach a peak in the rural areas of the Ukraine in June 1933, and in most other areas in July 1933. This was right at the end of the 1932/33 crop season and just before the 1933 harvest. The level of crisis mortality recorded in all districts fell very sharply in August and September 1933, but for reasons explained above the low point in birth rates came later.

4. A few comments on the reliability of these demographic data

There are, of course, problems concerning the reliability and the comprehensiveness of these data. No statistical data are ever absolutely accurate, and we are dealing here with a society with enormous political, economic, and social problems. Most statistical systems break down when it comes to recording mortality during a famine, and the system may well have broken down in Kazakhstan and in certain parts of the Ukraine. Nevertheless, the statistical system did produce a series of results which are a reflection of the demographic crisis the society was undergoing, and were certainly not the kind of results that the political authorities wanted.

I have argued elsewhere that although the central Soviet statistical system was greatly compromised by its merger into Gosplan in 1930, there was a partial renaissance of statistics when Osinsky took charge of the newly established Central Administration of National Economic Accounts (TsUNKhU) in early 1932.[27] And while it is true that Osinsky's position

---

[25] Monthly data are also available for most of the separate regions and the major cities for this period. These more detailed data will be analysed elsewhere.

[26] Conquest has claimed that the registration system for births and deaths was disbanded after October 1932 (Conquest, *The Harvest of Sorrow*), but he offers no convincing evidence for this, and there are surprisingly few indications of disruption in the available series of data. Considering the enormity of the crisis, it is indeed remarkable that the system was able to collect these data.

[27] S. G. Wheatcroft, "Statistical Sources for the Study of the Social History of the USSR", in: S. Fitzpatrick and L. Viola eds., *Sources for the Study of the Social History of the USSR*,

was soon to be weakened by the appointment of Kraval as his deputy, and that a hysterical Party/State decree of September 1935 was to put increasing pressure on the officials responsible for registering population movements,[28] there are grounds to believe that these demographic data for the 1932–34 period were relatively uninfected by Kraval and Stalin.

Conclusions

The new material on labour camps and other repressed groups has tended to confirm my arguments that the level of population in the Gulag system in the late 1930s was below 4 to 5 million. Zemskov's figures indicate that the Gulag population (excluding colonies) reached an early peak of 1.5 million in January 1941, and this can be reconciled with Nekrasov's figures of 2.3 million at the beginning of the war, if we include prisoners in labour colonies and jail. There were also at this time a large number of *spetsposelentsy*: By 1939, according to both Ivnitsky and Zemskov, there were only 0.9 million of the original 5 or so million former kulaks in their place of exile. Even if we allow another 1.5 million for Baltic and other mass groups in *spetsposelentsy*, there would still be in the order of about 4 million. Although this represents to my mind a sufficiently large and disgraceful scale of inhumanity, these are very much smaller figures than have been proposed by Conquest and Rosefielde in the West and by Roy Medvedev and Antonov-Ovseenko in the USSR.

Concerning the scale of the famine in 1932/33, we now have much better information on its chronology and regional coverage amongst the civilian registered population. The level of excess mortality registered by the civilian population was in the order of 3 to 4 million. If we correct this for the non-civilian and non-registered population, the scale of excess mortality might well reach 4 to 5 million, which is somewhat larger than I had earlier supposed, but which is still much lower than the figures claimed by Conquest and Rosefielde and by Roy Medvedev.

Much more serious work is needed before we approach a definitive answer to the problem of the scale of repression and excess mortality, but I hope that we will finally be done with some of the unrealistic figures that have so often haunted this subject.

published as a special issue of *Russian History/Histoire Russe*, 12, nos. 2–4, 1985, pp. 217–46.

[28] This is the notorious decree accusing the registration officials with double-recording deaths and under-recording births. See "O postanovke ucheta estestvennogo dvizheniya naseleniya", *Sobranie zakonov*, 1935, no. 54, article 432, dated 21 Sept. 1935.

Index

Agabekov, G., 22
Agranov, Ia., 23, 24, 25, 27
agriculture, 67, 75, 116–23, 173, 187, 194, 197
Andreev, A., 36, 37
Azov-Black Sea krai, 264

Beloborodov, A., 28, 29
Beria, L., 5, 38, 39, 52, 141, 227, 277
Budennyi, S., 58
Bukharin, N., 23, 28, 48 n29, 55, 56, 58, 59, 109, 110
  trial of, 35, 49, 57
Busygin, A., 145, 146 n18
byvshie liudi, 66, 70–81, 89, 90 n130, 95, 97, 258, 259 n34

censuses
  1926, 267
  1937, 11, 12, 261, 262–3, 264, 267, 268, 276, 281
  1939, 11, 12, 267, 269, 281
center-periphery conflicts, 5, 16
Central Committee (*Tsentral'nyi Komitet/* TsK), 22, 38, 108, 110, 111, 140, 169, 226, 227, 230, 231, 237 n28
  January 1933 Plenum, 22
  December 1936 Plenum, 57
  June 1936 Plenum, 50–1, 53
  February–March 1937 Plenum, 15, 16, 30, 51, 55, 56, 57, 58, 175, 184, 185, 196 n114, 256
  June 1937 Plenum, 36, 187, 188 n87
  January 1938 Plenum, 169, 171
Central Control Commission/Party Control Commission (*Tsentral'naia Kontrol'naia Komissiia/*TsKK), 23
  Ezhov and, 24
Central Black Earth Region, 68, 73, 82, 85, 88, 93

Central Industrial Region, 284
Central Volga krai, 68, 85, 284
Chechens, 272
Cheliabinsk Tractor Factory, 148
Chernigov Oblast, 266
chistki
  in the Red Army, 199, 201, 202–5, 206–7, 209, 211
  1935 party purges, 49, 60 n85
Chubar', V., 110
collective and state farms, 6, 72, 73, 75, 76, 77, 78, 79, 84, 87, 88, 90, 92, 94, 97, 114, 120, 122, 129, 138, 160 n91, 191, 195, 196 n117, 217 n10
  expulsions from, 79, 87, 194 n107
collectivization of agriculture, 66, 67, 68, 71, 75, 81, 85, 86, 89, 97, 98, 100, 102, 104, 109, 121, 192, 217, 264, 273
Comintern, Seventh Congress of the (1935), 24
Commissariat of Heavy Industry, *see* NKTP
Communist Party
  Eighteenth Party Congress (1939), 141
  expulsions from, 9, 16, 53, 117 n5, 169 n8, 170–1, 176t, 177–81, 182t, 186, 189t, 190, 193, 195, 217, 221
  Orgbureau, 30
  Politburo, 23, 24, 26, 37, 38, 42, 43, 44, 50, 53, 191, 192, 193, 227, 230
  ppo (primary party organizations), 9, 14, 170, 174, 186, 190 n93, 211, 212
  repressions within the, 227, 228, 234–7, 239–44, 270, 274
  Seventeenth Party Congress (1934), 23, 43, 45, 46, 107, 109, 262
  see also Central Committee, Central Control Commission
Constitution of 1936, 15, 28, 51, 184, 185
Crimean Tartars, 272, 273

291